CHANNEL ISLANDS AVIATION HISTORY

From the Dawn of Flight
to the Second World War

ROGER E. HARRIS

The first aircraft to land at Jersey Airport were two Jersey Airways D.H. 86 Express machines from Heston led by Captain Bill Caldwell in G-ACZO, *The Quaine Bay* (right) closely followed by G-ACZR, *La Saline Bay* (left) with Caldwell taking the title of being the first pilot to officially land at the airport. The passengers in the two craft included mainland guests and visiting pressmen. The Piers and Harbours Committee entertained the principal guests with lunch at the St. Brelade's Bay Hotel while the Press were given lunch at The Grand.

Stenlake Publishing Ltd

© 2022 Roger E. Harris
First Published in the United Kingdom, 2022
Stenlake Publishing Limited.
54-58 Mill Square, Catrine, KA5 6RD.
www.stenlake.co.uk.

ISBN 978-1-84033-932-1

Printed by
Blissetts,
Unit E1-E8 Shield Drive,
West Cross Ind Pk,
Brentford, TW8 9EX

Acknowledgements

I owe a huge debt of gratitude to many people who have made every effort to assist me in my research over the years or contribute in various ways to the completion of my books. It is impossible to name them all, but I would like to acknowledge the special assistance of some.

You will read in the introduction that follows, that this book has taken forty years to come to fruition and unfortunately in that time some people who helped me have sadly died. I only know of some who have passed away, but I do not know the health of others. It is very difficult to ask somebody if they are still alive, it is even more disturbing to ask their relatives. As I would rather record people as they were when they helped me, and to save embarrassment and hurt I have not indicated in the following list if a person has passed away. I hope this does not offend anyone. My grateful thanks go to:

Ray Bellows.
David Burke.
Geoff G. Cory, for his encouragement and motivation.
Graham Cowell.
Neville Doyle, author of *From Sea-Eagle to Flamingo* who inspired me and generously scoured his own archives to answer my many queries.
Scott T. Hards for locating and communicating with the reclusive artist Koike Shigeo on my behalf.
Moira and David Edwards who supplied scans of some elusive postcards in their Guernsey collection.
Eileen Finch.
Linda Harris, my wife, who valiantly proofread and corrected my erratic grammar and dyslexic spelling in the first manuscripts.
Lucy Harris, my daughter, who translated all the French research documents and with whom I spent some special happy hours researching together in the final year of Colindale Newspaper Library.
Warwick Jacobs for access to his Saro Photos.
P. Law, for his photograph collection.
Richard Mayne, for his private archives.
O.W. "Bill" Newport, for our long conversations and for helping me acquire many important items from his own collection.
Roger Pring, for his eccentric advice and encouragement in producing books with Adobe InDesign.
Andrew Rundle.

Terry Scott for access to his Saro Photos.
Koike Shigeo for his kind permission to reproduce his stunningly beautiful painting of the Imperial Airways Sea Eagle in flight to Guernsey.
John Simpson for his unpublished research.
Don Somerville for scans of his collection of the French Seaplane base in Guernsey.
Tony Watts.
Malcolm Webber, my old Grammar School friend now living as a translator in Sweden who forensically proofread each chapter of the final manuscript as it was produced.

Members of the Channel Islands Specialist's Society.
The Readers at the Public Record Office, Kew.
The Librarians of the, now closed, Newspaper Library, Colindale.
The Librarians of the News Room at the British Library, St. Pancras.
Ricky Allen and Rebecca Nel. Library Assistants, of the Priaulx Library, Guernsey.
Susan Armstrong, Senior Library Assistant, Jersey Library.
Dave Robinson of Aviation Ancestry.

I would also like to thank and recommend the following dealers who have always gone out of their way to assist me in my research:
Paul Balshaw, Antiques, Jersey.
Phil G. Brehaut, Guernsey.
Agyll Etkin U.K.
Graham Gleeson, France.
Tom Green, U.K.
Tom Harris, U.K.
H. R. Harmer, U.S.A.
Andy Makin, Darrowby Antiques, Jersey.
Madame Patricia Odjakdjian, Paris.
George Robbé.
Thomas Stanley, U.K.
Derek Tomlin, Guernsey.
Norman Wilkinson, Channel Islands Auctions, Guernsey

Front cover: The Guernsey Airways Ltd. Windhover G-ABJP in St. Peter Port Harbour, passing the GWR Royal Mail ship *St. Helier* (no longer a rival). The Windhover is exiting the harbour with castle Cornet in the background.

Back cover: Jersey Airways operated six Dragons during Easter week 1934 and from Easter Thursday they ran two services a day. Over the weekend they flew numerous extra services with some of the craft making three return trips in a day. The longer service from Heston flew 39 flights over the weekend and carried 130 return passengers.

CONTENTS

Introduction	4
The Dawn of Aviation	6
The First Aircraft to Reach the Channel Islands	8
1914 – 1918 The First World War in the Channel Islands	18
1918 The First Flights from England to Jersey Accidental and Intended	25
The "Seaplane Special" Newspapers Delivered by two Avro Seaplanes the First Inter-Island Passenger	30
Visit of the R-36 Airship to Jersey	33
Visit of an RAF Felixstowe F5 Flying Boat to Jersey	36
Two RAF Flying Boats Visit Jersey and Guernsey	37
The First Scheduled Air Passenger Service	38
A French Naval Seaplane Emergency Landing in Jersey	43
Imperial Airways Flying to the Channel Islands	45
The First Regular Passenger Service from Jersey	58
The First Landplane to Land on Jersey	60
An RAF Seaplane Mishap off Guernsey	61
The First Terra Firma Landing on Guernsey	63
Visiting Flights of RAF Supermarine Southamptons	64
The Tour and Travel Association 'Seagull' over Jersey	64
A Busy Day in Jersey	67
A New Airline – Kirsten and Mace Ltd the Saro Cutty Sark Becomes a Silver Bat	67
The Airship R100 Visits Guernsey	70
Visit of the Prototype Saro Cloud to Jersey	73
The Second Landplane to Land on Jersey	75
The First German Visitor	77
Only Three Other Fleeting Visitors to Jersey In 1931	78
A Second Saro Cloud Visits Jersey	80
The Monocoupé 70 – Second Landplane to Land on Guernsey	81
Imperial Airways Air-Taxi Flights to Jersey	82
Aviation in Sark – a Spy Comes to Lunch	83
Flying Officer Donald Ivins, Jersey's Most Frequent Visitor	87
The Portsmouth Connection	88
Numerous Flights to Jersey but None to Guernsey	90
John Grierson Visits Jersey in the Rouge et Noir	97
The First Landing of a Landplane on Alderney	98
Aerial Reconnoitres of the Proposed Site for Jersey Airport	100
The Blue Fox – The First Air Accident in Jersey	103
The First Jersey Aerial Pageant	106
The First Aircraft Built in Guernsey	111
The Birth of Jersey Airways Ltd	114
The Rapid Expansion of Jersey Airways	116
Guernsey Visitors, Crashes and More	130
The Gliding Clubs of Guernsey and Jersey	140
Jersey Airways Ltd goes from Strength to Strength	145
Spectacular RAF Landings in St Peter Port Harbour	153
Guernsey Airways Ltd	154
Cobham Air Routes Ltd	158
The First Plymouth to Jersey "Airmail Service" Flight	165
The Visit of HRH Edward Prince of Wales to Guernsey	166
The Guernsey Pou Du Ciel	169
Guernsey's L'Erée Aerodrome	171
The Hindenburg over Alderney	177
Jersey Airways Ltd opens Alderney Airport	179
Demise of Guernsey Airways Ltd	181
The Opening of The States of Jersey Airport	187
Jersey Airways Ltd – Consolidation not Innovation	193
Birth of the De Havilland D.H.95 Flamingo	202
The Opening of the States of Guernsey Airport	203
The Flight Towards Occupation	213
Selected Bibliography and Sources	215

INTRODUCTION

This book has had a long gestation and is the prodigy of a much larger two volumed book entitled *Pioneer Aviation in the Channel Islands* published by the Channel Islands Specialists' Society. (www.ciss.uk).

In 1969 I joined the Channel Islands Specialists' Society, a Society founded in 1950 to study the stamps and postal history of the Channel Islands, but by 1969 the remit had widened to included postcards, ephemera, and travel and social history with detailed research into various aspects of the history of the islands where it pertained to the mail. A theme of special interest to most of the members is the German occupation of the Channel Islands during the Second World War and of special interest to me was mail of English deportees taken from the islands and interned in Germany in 1942. Nothing was known of this subject and the CISS committee asked me to write a book about my collection. As I started to write, I soon realised that I could not restrict my research solely to the mail of the internees, but that I also needed to tell the history of their deportations, and so a two volumed book was published in 1979 and 1980; *Islanders Deported Part 1 the history*, and *Islanders Deported Part 2 the postal history*.

My interests were not confined to the deportees as I was also compiling collections on various other Channel Islands subjects, one of these being the history of airmails to and from the islands. *Islanders Deported* proved to be a great success and based on this success, the committee of the CISS asked me to write another book on my airmail collection. Once again when I started research, I realised that I could not write about the airmail letters without explaining the whole history of pioneer flight to the islands. The earliest airmail letters addressed to the islands had been flown by balloon out of the siege of Paris in 1870, and Channel Islands pioneer flight would continue to develop throughout the whole of a century following.

There was very little written about pioneer aviation in the Channel Islands. In 1965 and 1966 J. Edouard Slade, a Companion of the Royal Aeronautical Society, privately published two small volumes of a book entitled *The Pioneer Days of Aviation in Jersey*. Despite a large bibliography in his book, his research relied heavily on reports in the Jersey newspapers and as the title indicated, was purely centred on Jersey and included no illustrations. Slade's account comes to an abrupt end in December 1933 with the birth of Jersey Airways Ltd. which he considered marked the end of the pioneer era.

A more erudite work with extensive research was self-published in 1991 by Neville Doyle, an Associate of the Royal Aeronautical Society, entitled *From Sea-Eagle to Flamingo – Channel Island Airlines 1923-1939*. Doyle's work has been a great inspiration to me, and I am very grateful to Neville for his generous help and guidance with my own research. Although Doyle wrote about all the islands, you can see from his title that he confined his research to the commercial airlines during a limited timeframe that culminated with the outbreak of the Second World War. There is no mention of private or military flights in his book or any reference to local flights within the islands, but he did manage to obtain a few interesting photographs and illustrations to enhance his manuscript.

I decided that my aviation book would be a totally new concept that encapsulated every aspect of Channel Islands aviation history and collecting. As well as being a complete history of pioneer aviation in the Channel Islands, it would also cater for the airmail collector, the collector of aviation postcards and photographs and the collectors of airline timetables and ephemera. As part of its unique concept, it would also catalogue the value of every item illustrated. The Channel Islands were inimical to aircraft flight and so I, somewhat naively, decided that I would set out to record every attempt made by any aircraft to fly to the islands from the dawn of aviation up to nationalisation of the airlines after the Second World War. My intention was to describe each machine and detail its history, name the pilot and any passengers who flew, while researching their biographical histories to record the more interesting stories. I had an extensive collection of photographic postcards and photos of aircraft in the islands and my final somewhat foolish intention was to illustrate every flight that took place with a photograph of the aircraft, preferably in the islands.

1980 was when I had been asked to write the book, but it was also when the first major hiccup to my research and writing occurred; I changed careers! For fifteen years I had been a teacher working in London and abroad before returning to London to finally become the deputy head of the 6th form of a comprehensive school where I taught art and design. While teaching, I studied set design for television at evening classes at Chelsea Art College and in 1980 I gained a post in the design department of BBC TV at Television Centre in London. The work was exciting and interesting, but the days were long, and filming would often require me to be away from home for six weeks at a time. Research and writing were impossible although I did manage to continue collecting research material for later investigation. When I retired from film and television in 2010, I was finally free to devote more time to my research and writing.

I spent many hours in the Newspaper Library at Colindale pouring over every Channel Islands newspaper published from 1910 to 1947. When we knew that the Library was closing in 2013, I was joined in my research by my daughter Lucy who is a "real" historian (she once joyously found a copy of my *Islanders Deported* in her staff library when she worked at the Imperial War Museum.) Together we spent many days on the final research, only breaking for our picnic lunches, and working right up to the last nostalgic day when the librarian rung the "closing time" bell for the final time. A year later I was once again able to reference certain newspapers through the British Library Newsroom at St. Pancras; the resources were the same, but it never had the romantic wood and leather atmosphere of Colindale.

The internet is undoubtedly the ultimate antithesis to the charming old Colindale Library. Over the years online resources have blossomed, many of these are very useful and some I have returned to time and again to clarify dates and records, but as with all online resources the researcher has to be very wary of the "facts" portrayed. The Channel Islands has its own Wikipedia website called "IslandWiki". It is a very interesting site, but bizarrely only references aviation in Jersey, not Guernsey or Alderney. The Jersey aviation site has some wonderful photographs and new ones are uploaded frequently, but many of the attributions are very doubtful with some post-war aircraft listed as being in the 1930s while a few locations are obviously not in the Channel Islands. Ebay has also been a superb source for original material; I came to it probably a few years late, but even so have managed to acquire some notable items from wonderful old collections.

During my research I was repeatedly made aware of the need to return to source material and early records as I found historical inaccuracies repeated time and again. For years I came across references to a Jersey Airways Ltd. aircraft named *Bonne Nuit Bay*, but could never find a photograph of this aircraft or any official record of it. Even the very authoritative Neville Doyle referred to it in his book and it was only when I saw a reference to its registration G-ACNP that I realised that the craft was actually *Plemont Bay*, an aircraft that nobody recorded. There never was an aircraft named *Bonne Nuit Bay* despite every book and online source referencing it. Similarly, most reports of the French seaplane base in Guernsey during the First World War repeat the statement that the French seaplanes flew mail back to their base in Cherbourg despite the fact that there is no record of this actually happening. Monsier L.V. Lambert, the French Consular Agent in Guernsey in 1964, who had been one of the pilots, stated in correspondence to Bill Newport (CISS President) that this never happened but still collectors like to think that it did. The internet is a prime source for these inaccuracies especially blogs that love to repeat urban myths. Ruth Ozanne repeated a wartime rumour in her book *The Diaries of Ruth Ozanne 1940 - 1945*, that stated Cecil Noels' miniature aircraft the *Wee Mite* had been discovered by the Germans in March 1941 in the loft above St. Peter Port Garage and had been shipped back to Germany. The truth of the rumour was that the damaged Avro Avian belonging to the Guernsey Aero Club had been discovered in Motor House Garage and taken by the Germans. The *Wee Mite* crashed in January 1935 and was officially recorded "broken up" in March 1936, but still reports regularly appear on the internet or even in Channel Islands newspapers stating that Cecil Noel's *Wee Mite* was found by the Germans.

With a huge manuscript of 560 pages and over 1,100 photographs and illustrations to fit into the pages I knew that I would never be able to brief a typesetter to set my pages. I discussed my problem with a friend who for many years had been an author and publisher. His advice was that I would have to format the book myself and to do this I needed to learn the Adobe programmes that many professional publishers use to compile books. At the ripe age of 70, I was going to have to return to art college yet again! In 2016 I set off to Richmond College of Art and then Putney Art School for a year of daytime courses to learn the computer programmes Adobe Photoshop, Illustrator and the all-important InDesign. A year later, armed with my newly learnt skills, I was finally able to start compiling the book.

In 2020, forty years after first being asked to write the book, I finally achieved the task although it ended being much larger than anybody, including me, anticipated, and at 560 full colour A4 size pages it was no longer commercially viable, as such a tome would require hard back covers. My publisher, Richard Stenlake offered some sage advice; the book in that form would have a specialist and limited market that would be more economical to sell in two paperback volumes, while he would be interested in publishing a smaller black and white book (all the old photographs were in black and white anyway) that concentrated solely on the history of aviation and omitted all the collectors' interests of airmails, timetables, posters and ephemera that required coloured images.

The Channel Islands Specialists' Society were happy to publish a full colour limited edition book in two volumes entitled *Pioneer Aviation in the Channel Islands* and Richard Stenlake would publish the edited black and white book – *Channel Islands Aviation History*.

THE DAWN OF AVIATION

Mission Impossible

It is unsurprising that aviation in the Channel Islands started late and developed slowly as the Channel Islands, although very beautiful, have the least conducive terrain possible for powered flight. The main islands of Guernsey and Jersey with the smaller island of Alderney to the north and the even smaller islands of Sark and Herm off the coast of Guernsey all consist of a high ground consisting of undulating hills divided into small fields, boarded by coastlines of steep rugged cliffs and surrounded by a hostile sea with hidden rocky outcrops. The only long firm flat surfaces where an aircraft might safely land are the sandy beaches of Jersey and possibly a few on Guernsey that are less firm, but even the beaches are covered by the sea for the greater part of each day.

The first aircraft to visit the islands arrived via the sea, but this was a very dangerous undertaking and even when an aircraft managed to conquer the terrain the pilot still had to cope with the extremes of the Channel Islands' weather and the curse of fog! Despite these hazards, determined pilots, many brave and some foolish, attempted flight in the Channel Islands. There was never a cohesive Channel Islands air service, indeed there was seldom a service that linked the islands as most of the attempted flights were between the mainland and one of the islands. An integrated Channel Islands air service would only be achieved when the three main Islands built their own airports.

The Channel Islands in relation to England and France.

First Flight in Jersey

It is thought that kite flying, and even manned kite flying originated in China several hundred years BC but documented manned flight in the Western World did not start until 1783 in France. In that year the Montgolfier brothers, Joseph-Michel and Jacques-Étienne, were experimenting with hot air balloon construction while the Robert brothers, Jacques-Charles and Nicolas-Louis, were using the newly discovered hydrogen gas to lift balloons. On 4th June 1783 the Montgolfier brothers launched the world's first unmanned hot air balloon, and on 27th August the Robert brothers launched the world's first unmanned, hydrogen filled balloon from the Champ de Mars in Paris; manned balloons quickly followed.

It was from the school grounds of the ancient free Grammar School of St. Mannelier in Jersey in 1790, that a French Master, Mr Granger, aided by his pupils, was experimenting with balloon flight. The weekly, first ever Jersey newspaper (printed in Jersey French), the Gazette de l'île de Jersey, reported on Saturday 5th June 1790 that Mr Granger had announced that he would send up a balloon from the school grounds on 12th June, subject to fine weather. The newspaper stated that the circumference of the balloon was 90 feet. However, this was measured using the ancient Jersey foot (consisting of 12 Jersey inches) which is equal to 11 imperial inches, and equates to an imperial measurement of 82.6 feet with a diameter of 26.29 feet. The edition for the following Saturday 12th June, announced that the flight would take place that day at six o'clock from the courtyard of the school. The balloon was now described as being 36 feet high, with a circumference of 104 feet. It has to be assumed that the balloon was a success for on the following Saturday, 19th June, the Gazette de l'île de Jersey announced that Mr Granger would send up a "very large balloon" from Mont de la Ville, a recently created parade ground near Fort Regent near the sea. The balloon remained airborne for 45 minutes but its flight culminated by dropping into the water. Balloon flight would always be dangerous on an island where the sea was never more than 2.5 miles away and sensibly Mr Granger never attempted manned flight.

Powered Flight

Wright Flyer at Kitty Hawk

On 17th December 1903 at Kill Devil Hill near Kitty Hawk in North Carolina, USA, the brothers, Wilbur and Orville Wright, executed the world's first powered manned flight of under a minute over some 300 yards in a primitive "pusher" powered biplane the *Wright Flyer* piloted by Orville Wright. Wilbur and Orville Wright received little encouragement from the American authorities, and disenchanted, the Wright brothers accepted an invitation by the *Compagnie Générale de Navigation Aérienne* to fly their craft in France to dispel European doubts that they had indeed conquered heavier-than-air flight. In 1907 the brothers shipped one of their biplanes across the Atlantic to Le Havre, and in August 1908 Wilbur Wright flew the craft at Le Mans where the flight was filmed. The silent grainy film had scenes of the craft being prepared for take-off and in flight as well as close-up shots of the pioneer aviator, and the resulting film inspired a wave of experimentation in Europe. On 11th January 1909 the film was even shown in Jersey in the new *Cinemata-Vaudeville* that had only opened the previous month in St. Thomas' Hall, later known as the Playhouse Theatre.

Development and experimentation by French aviators in 1908 and 1909 spawned the Aviation Fête, where different types of aircraft were exhibited. The world's first Aviation Meeting was in July 1909 at Douai on the aerodrome of Brayelle where two men became famous flying celebrities. Aviator Louis Paulhan on 15th July flew for an hour setting a new endurance record while Louis Blériot established a record circling the aerodrome in his monoplane. Ten days later on 25th July 1909 he would become world famous by making the first airplane flight across the English Channel to win a prize of £1,000 offered by the *Daily Mail* newspaper.

On the morning after his flight from Calais to Dover, Louis Blériot's aeroplane was put on display in 'Selfridge's' department store on Oxford Street in London.

Despite the developments in France, flight remained non-existent in the Channel Islands with most Islanders completely unaware of what a flying machine even looked like. Few images of aircraft reached the islands but there exists this attractive and realistic postcard printed with the legend *Jersey in an Airship* showing a good graphic of an early biplane of correct aerodynamic structure not unlike a *Wright Flyer*. A concertina strip of photographs of Jersey is attached to the inside of the card, but such a craft would never fly in the islands.

THE FIRST AIRCRAFT TO REACH THE CHANNEL ISLANDS

The St. Malo to Jersey Hydro-Aéroplane Race

26th August 1912 was not only a momentous day in the history of aviation for the Channel Islands, it was also a highly significant date in the development of world aviation. The announcement of a hydro-aéroplane race from St. Malo in France to the beaches of St. Helier in the summer of 1912 caused frenetic excitement in the Jersey populace, the majority of whom had never seen an aircraft. The historical significance of the event was hardly acknowledged at the time and is only truly recognised by aviation historians today. Louis Blériot was the first person to fly the English Channel in a powered aircraft on 25th July 1909, but his flight did not require the skill and endurance of the pilots who flew to Jersey. The distance flown by Blériot was 22 miles; the Jersey race was a total of 92 miles.

The aviators who flew to Jersey, bizarrely, never visited the island beforehand and so had no idea where to land, all they had was a map of the route with dangerous areas marked in red. These were areas that they should avoid because of hidden rocks and in which their escort vessels would be unable to effect a rescue; unfortunately the sea is not delineated with corresponding red areas. The pilots had to fly north-east to the Chausey Islands and then north-west to Jersey, but if they missed the relatively small island of Jersey there was only the open Atlantic before them. Their flights required accurate navigation that none of them managed perfectly. At the end of the flight, they had to put down in a rough sea, refuel and then take-off again in the same turbulent waves and find their way back to St. Malo in diminishing daylight.

The Development of Marine Aviation

Marine aviation in 1912 was in its infancy and a boat that could fly or a 'seaplane' where the hull of the craft sat in the water and lifted out on take-off was still some way off. A marine aeroplane had to sit on or in the water and there was no technology invented that could propel the craft fast enough through the water to make it lift up and out of the water and into the sky. The hydrodynamics had to be overcome before the aerodynamics could come into force. A solution to the problem was to start with the craft already out of the water balancing on floats that would allow it to skim across the surface thereby achieving the required air speed to lift it off the water, but even designing such floats was an uncharted technology.

The breakthrough in float design and float configuration came from a very unlikely source. In 1909, Henri Fabre was a newly qualified engineer who had never flown in an aircraft either as a pilot or even as a passenger. His father, Augustin Fabre was a rich ship owner and he gave his 27-year-old son 100,000 francs to design and build a seaplane. The young Fabre set about carrying out aerodynamic flight tests, some from kites flying at 1,000 feet, as well as hydrodynamic tests on catamarans. From these tests he designed a new type of float with a flat flexible underside made from a sheet of plywood that acted like a drum skin with a rigid cylindrical top. At the same time, his aerodynamic experiments produced the Fabre propeller with a variable pitch; this was an extremely complicated technical development new to aviation. On 8th July 1909 Fabre tested his first seaplane, but the engines were too heavy, and the floats were aligned at the wrong angle and

On 28th March 1910 on the Étang de Berre, a calm lagoon on the Mediterranean coast near Marseille, Henri Fabre carried out incremental tests on his new craft starting with small taxi runs. The conditions on the water were perfect with an almost mirror like surface. The floats worked perfectly, and Fabre's *Canard* with the lightweight engine took to the air with a pilot who had never flown an aircraft before. Although the *Canard* was unwieldy, Fabre continued testing the craft until the wind increased and the lagoon developed waves. He then moved into the shelter of the harbour of La Méde where he carried out more flights before a group of official witnesses to be officially recorded as the first man to take-off from and touch down on water in a powered aircraft. With the invention of Fabre's *Canard* and his floats, a viable hydro-aéroplane had at long last arrived even if it did look as if it was flying backwards. The concept of an airframe held out of the water on three floats was quickly developed by other aviators who developed different types of floats and configurations. These hydro-aéroplanes were very much the playthings of rich men as the air transport industry failed to see the advantages of water landings and both the British and French Admiralty remained aloof although this would change with the threat of war.

dug into the water preventing take-off. Although the seaplane had failed, the value of Fabre's basic configuration of three floats, two at the front and one behind was firmly established and would be adopted by other designers in the coming years. Fabre then went on to design a new hydro-aéroplane based on the canard (duck) configuration of a stabilizer at the front and wings to the rear with his floats in the same configuration. Although the craft appeared incredibly fragile it actually proved to be relatively stable and he equipped her with a newly designed seven-cylinder rotary Gnome engine capable of producing 50 hp, but weighing less than 150 lbs.

The Hydro-Aéroplane 'Concours'

In 1912, in order to convince naval doubters and stimulate research, a series of meetings for marine aeroplanes was organised. In Monaco where annual speed-boat races were held to coincide with the Carnival, Georges Prade of the Monaco Committee suggested setting up the Monaco Hydro-aéroplane Competition with various 'trials' running from 24th until 31st March 1912. Eight pilots entered the Monaco competition with six different types of machine. The competition proved a great success even though two of the craft crashed and a third sank after hitting an underwater obstruction. The hydro-aéroplane 'Concours' was now established and a circus of meetings and displays around the coasts and on the lakes of Europe was planned for 1912 with the same core group of pilots and hydro-aéroplanes. The next Concours was to be held at St. Malo, the ancient Breton port, from the 24th to 26th August, but this meeting was to be infinitely more challenging to man and machine as it was to culminate in a race across the open sea to the island of Jersey and back to the harbour in St. Malo.

The poster advertising the St. Malo Concours d'Hydro-Aéroplanes organised by L'Automobile-Club de France at St. Malo, Dinard and Jersey. 24th, 25th & 26th August 1912. When the St. Malo hydro-aéroplane 'Concours' was proposed, the technology of marine aviation had no governing body to nurture its development and the organisation of the meeting was adopted rather incongruously by 'L'Automobile-Club de France'. The Club's President, Mousier Edouard Surcouf, approached Mousier Jouve, the Vice-Consul of France in Jersey for assistance with the Jersey stage of the race from St. Malo, and Mousier Jouve in turn contacted the Jersey equivalent of the French Automobile Club, the 'Jersey Motor Association'.

The St Malo Concours and Race to Jersey

The Jersey Motor Association bore little resemblance to its mighty French counterpart. The first automobile arrived in Jersey in 1899 and received a very hostile reception from some local country inhabitants who stoned it on its first excursion. In 1908 the newly inaugurated Jersey Motor Association held the first of what was to become an annual motorcar parade on the island, and the cavalcade of 1911 managed to muster twelve automobiles, probably the total number of resident Jersey vehicles. The Secretary of the club Mr R. R. Lempriere was also Viscount of Jersey, while another member was His Excellency the Lieutenant Governor of Jersey, Major General Sir Alexander Nelson Rochfort, K.C.B., C.M.G. These notable gentlemen formed the Jersey Organising Committee for the St. Malo race and invited the Constable of St. Helier, Mr Pinel as well as the Vice-Consul of France, Monsier Jouve, to join them. The Island Police and the Jersey Militia were placed at their disposal, but despite the committee's influence, the British Admiralty remained aloof and refused to offer any support in the form of escort boats for the flyers. By contrast the French Navy supplied four warships, the armoured cruiser *Gloire*, flagship of Rear-Admiral Favereau, and three destroyers, *Catapulte*, *Belier* and *Arquebuse* as well as twelve fast torpedo boats as escorts for the twelve hydro-aéroplanes in the race.

The St. Malo hydro-aéroplane Concours was set to run over an extended weekend of three days; each day the race would be longer and more difficult until it culminated on the Monday with the race to Jersey and back. Twelve hydro-aéroplanes entered for the Concours, but only nine managed to fly on the first day. Penalty points were awarded for each race so that the fastest aircraft to finish a race would be awarded only one point while a craft that failed to complete the course could receive twelve penalty points with even more penalty points awarded if a craft failed to enter one of the three races. The actual timings of the aircraft were adjusted by a complicated handicap system that favoured the slower, heavier machines that had their times reduced incrementally dependent on the number of passengers (or equivalent weighted ballast) that they carried. This handicap favoured the heavy biplanes over the lighter and faster monoplanes and in the case of the Jersey race it gave them an unintended advantage as the passengers acted as navigators and engineers, while the solo pilot had to be his own observer and navigator. Six cash prizes would be awarded to the flyers who received the least penalty points in the three races overall and an additional cash prize known as the 'Prix de Jersey' would be awarded to the outright winner of the Jersey race.

The Jersey Motor Association's role in the race, to refuel twelve hydro-aéroplanes on the water, required the acquisition of twelve steam or motor boats fitted out to carry the cans of petrol for each of the aircraft. The concept of a petrol station was yet to reach the Channel Islands, and an 'Agent' in Jersey imported petrol for the few automobile owners on the island, but he held no spare stocks from which supplies could be drawn. Instructions were unforthcoming from France regarding the quantities of petrol required by the hydro-aéroplanes until two days before the race when the committee was informed that the aeroplanes also required aviation lubricating castor oil, a product unknown on the island.

The proposed arrival line for the hydro-aéroplanes in St. Aubin's Bay was from the harbour light on the pier head of St. Helier Harbour to the castle at St. Aubin, but this was redefined when it was realised that the seabed was shallow and rocky between Elizabeth Castle and the harbour and would be hazardous for the torpedo and fuel boats and the hydro-aéroplanes. It was decided to reduce the arrival line further to concentrate the spectacle for the onlookers and make it more convenient for the fuel boats to reach their air-machines as nobody could predict exactly where they would set down. A new arrival line was plotted between the castle keep of Elizabeth Castle, which would fly a 24 ft long black and white pennant, and a marker boat in St. Aubin's Bay flying a large red flag. Stewards from France were to be stationed in the castle keep and the Jersey Militia and the Postmaster of Jersey worked together to lay a direct telephone line from the Castle to the Post Office in Broad Street from which telegrams could be immediately sent to St. Malo giving the times of arrival and departure of each of the machines.

No provision was made for guarding the hydro-aéroplanes from the populace as the race was planned to take place in the afternoon when the tide was high with the machines floating on the water and refuelled at sea from the fuel boats. The pilots objected to the afternoon start time as it meant that they would be returning to St. Malo in failing daylight and they insisted that the race should be run early in the morning. This change was met with incredulity in Jersey. The hydro-aéroplanes would now arrive on a rapidly ebbing tide which would leave them high and dry on the sands of St. Aubin's Bay. The fuel would have to be carried up the beach from the boats for the refuelling on the sands, and the hydro-aéroplanes would require turning and manhandling across the sands to the receding water line before they could take-off. Only two constables had been assigned to patrol the beach above high water and incredibly, and almost fatally, nobody thought to increase their numbers.

Hydro-aéroplane Entries for the St. Malo Concours 24-26 August 1912

No	Pilot	Hydro-aéroplane	Engine	Hull
1	François Molla	R.E.P. monoplane	Gnome 80 hp	R.E.P. floats
2	Émile Train	Astra-Train monoplane	Gnome 80 hp	Train floats
3	Charles Weymann	Nieuport monoplane	Gnome 80 hp	Nieuport floats
4	Jean Benôit	Sanchez-Besa biplane	Renault 100 hp	Tellier floats
5	Paul Rugère	Sanchez-Besa biplane	Renault 70 hp	Tellier floats
6	Marcel Chambenais	Borel monoplane	Gnome 80 hp	Borel floats
7	André Beaumont	Dannet-Lévêque biplane type C	Gnome 80 hp	Denhault hull
8	Guillaume Busson	Deperdussin monoplane	Gnome 80 hp	Tellier floats
9	Eugène Renaux	Maurice-Farman biplane	Renault 70 hp	Fabre floats
10	René Labouret	Astra C.M. biplane	Renault 100 hp	Tellier floats
11	René Mesguisch	Paulhan-Curtiss biplane	Paulhan-Curtiss 75 hp	Curtiss floats
12	Frank Barra	Paulhan-Curtiss biplane	Paulhan-Curtiss 75 hp	Curtiss floats

On the weekend of the Concours the weather conditions were abominable with a rough sea, cold rain and gusting winds, but it was already decided that the race would take place regardless of the weather because this was the only way to demonstrate the true worth and capabilities of the hydro-aéroplane. Each of the twelve entries was given a race number which was emblazoned on their wings, tail and fuselage. On the first race day, Saturday 24th August, twelve craft entered the race but four crashed before the Concours began and only five pilots received position points for completing the race while the three others qualified to take part in the two succeeding trials. On Sunday 25th August, the weather was more favourable, but the race was still marred by two accidents. René Mesguisch who had engine failure in his Paulhan-Curtiss biplane was forced to come down on land and was seriously injured when his aircraft was reduced to a wreck. Of the twelve hydro-aéroplanes that originally entered the Concours, only five now remained to take part in the race to Jersey on the Monday.

The Race to Jersey

On Monday 26th August 1912, despite strong winds and rain squalls, the first ever international race by hydro-aéroplanes across an open sea took place between St. Malo and St. Aubin's Bay via a detour around the Chausey Islands lighthouse; a round trip of 90.5 miles. Of the five hydro-aéroplanes that entered the race, three were large biplanes, including the all-steel Sanchez-Besa biplane (race number 4) with a wingspan of 55 ft 9 ins. supported on Tellier floats, with a Renault 100hp engine and piloted by Jean Benoit; the Astra C.M. biplane (race number 10) with a wingspan of 40 ft, a length of 36 ft and a height of 11 ft, also on Tellier floats, powered by a similar Renault 100 hp engine and piloted by René Labouret and, largest of all, the Maurice-Farman biplane (race number 9) with a wingspan of 66 ft and a length of 42 ft on Fabre floats, but with a smaller Renault 70 hp engine, and piloted by Eugène Renaux. The two monoplanes in the race were the diminutive single-seater all steel Esnault-Pelterie, R.E.P. monoplane (race number 1) with a wingspan of a mere 37 ft, a length of 24 ft 6 ins. and a height of 9 ft, supported on her own design R.E.P. float,

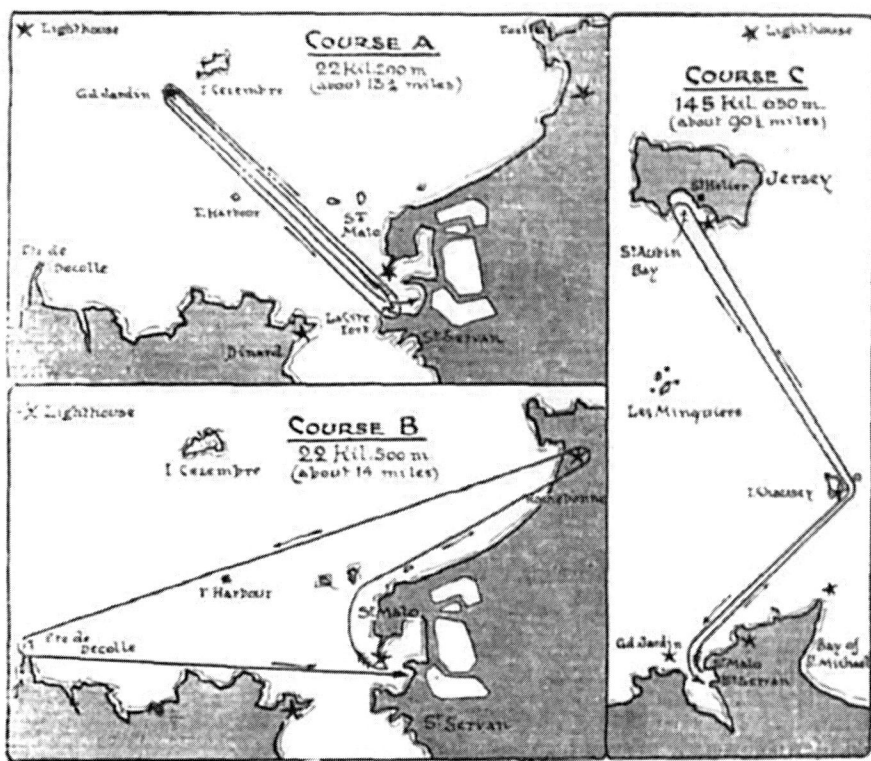

Sketch maps of the three racecourses as they appeared in *Flight* magazine.

powered by a Gnome 80 hp engine and piloted by François Molla, and the slightly larger two-seater Nieuport IV H monoplane (race number 3) with a wing span of 39 ft 8 ins., a length of 26 ft 11 ins. also supported on her own design Nieuport floats and also powered by a Gnome 80 hp engine and piloted by the American, Charles Weymann.

The race would commence at 08.00 hours with the sound of a signal cannon and as the trial was a timed race, the pilots were permitted a one-hour 'window' in which to take-off.

Unexpectedly, at 09.45 hours, Renaux returned to St. Malo in his Maurice-Farman. Whether he had mechanical problems, or he never intended to fly the whole course and his entry was purely tactical to gain him larger prize money is unknown; whatever his reason, there were now only four hydro-aéroplanes left in the race to Jersey.

The inhabitants of Jersey only learnt of the intended early morning start to the race from Saturday's *Evening Post*. Nevertheless, from before dawn

The all-steel Sanchez-Besa biplane (race number 4), piloted by Jean Benoit was first to be launched. It was the only entrant with a "pusher" propeller, and it was first to cross the start line with two passengers on board at 08 hrs. 09 mins. 05 secs.

Left: Four minutes later, the red single-seater Esnault-Pelterie, R.E.P. monoplane (race number 1), piloted by François Molla, was the second to depart.

Below: The R.E.P. monoplane crossed the start line at the entrance of St. Malo Harbour at 08 hrs. 13 mins. 17 secs., while almost twelve minutes later, Eugène Renaux took to the air with one passenger on board his huge Maurice-Farman biplane at 08 hrs. 24 mins. 52 secs.

Below: The Astra C. M. biplane (race number 10), piloted by René Labouret took to the water carrying only one passenger.

Above: The Astra C. M. riding high on her floats crossed the start line at 08 hrs. 26 mins. 12 secs.

Below: The two-seater Nieuport IV H monoplane (race number 3) piloted by the American, Charles Weymann, had one passenger, Lieutenant de Montjoi.

Above: Over 30 minutes after the Astra left, Weymann was last to leave in the Nieuport, narrowly making the departure 'window' with 3 minutes to spare by crossing the line at 08 hrs. 56 mins. 26 secs.

people from all the Parishes made their way to St. Helier in every type of vehicle, on foot, or in packed trains. Even before 06.00 hours sailing boats and motor launches were boarding passengers eager to get a closer view from out in the bay, while a motor yacht and launch towed two lines of luggers containing petrol cans out to the finishing line where they anchored to await the arrival of the flyers. The weather was deteriorating, a heavy sea was running in the bay and some of the smaller boats decided it was safer not to leave the protection of the breakwater. At 07.30 hours Elizabeth Castle received a message from the Coastguard Station that the French destroyer *Belier* could be observed approaching the island. The destroyer put down anchor in the Inner Roadstead close to Elizabeth Castle and four official timekeepers from the Automobile Club of France were rowed across to the castle keep. The anchoring of the *Belier* in the Small Roads near the area that was closed to the hydro-aéroplanes would later result in near catastrophe as the flyers were attracted to her and assumed that she marked the finishing line.

By 08.00 hours thousands of people thronged the seafront from Albert Pier to First Tower, while along Victoria Avenue as far as Millbrook the road was blocked by vehicles. People gathered wherever they thought was the best vantage point. Beaumont attracted a large crowd, as did Millbrook where a little French band was playing; even St. Aubin beyond the far end of the finish line had a large group. On the ramparts of Fort Regent hundreds of soldiers were silhouetted, while hundreds more civilians had climbed to the top of Westmount in order to obtain the first sighting. By far the biggest throng was at the base of Westmount around the West Park slipway where a reporter from the *Morning News* recorded it being "black with people who, as it turned out, were in the best position of all." The winds increased and the seas became rougher until the whole bay was white crested waves. Both the Harbour Committee's tug *Duke of Normandy* and the Viscount's motor yacht, each carrying dignitaries, had been cruising the finish line for almost an hour but chose to return to the shelter of the harbour. Sections of the crowd became despondent as rumours spread that the race would have to be abandoned, but shortly before 08.30 hours the Coastguard Station relayed a message to Elizabeth Castle that four French torpedo boats could be observed approaching the island very fast from the south-east. These heralded the approach of the hydro-aéroplanes and when the pre-arranged pennant was hoisted on the castle keep announcing their sighting, a great roar erupted from the soldiers on the Fort Regent ramparts. Soon after 08.45 hours keener sighted observers and those with binoculars or telescopes pointed out a black speck on the horizon that might have been a gull if it were not for its steady flight and rapidly increasing size. Soon the general cry went up "it's a biplane" as the Sanchez-Besa could be discerned far away over Icho Tower, bearing down towards St. Helier and the bay. (The Icho Tower is a Martello Tower built in 1811 on a rock, one and a quarter miles off the Jersey shore.).

If the waiting hordes on the Jersey seafront were disappointed that only four of the promised twelve flying machines made it to Jersey, it did not diminish their enthusiastic welcome. It was probably fortuitous that only four machines landed over an extended finish line of several miles as the compact arrival of twelve machines might have been fatal. Benoit in his Sanchez-Besa landed by the most densely populated part of the seafront and when the R.E.P. came down within a few hundred feet the excited crowds took advantage of the receding tide and rapidly engulfed the two machines. Men and women ran into the water to reach the aviators and within a few moments the pilots were overwhelmed with requests for their autographs on any available piece of paper, or lacking paper on

Crowds saw the 'First Plane to Land in Jersey', the Sanchez-Besa hydro-aéroplane cross the finishing line at 09.04 hours on 26th August 1912.

Upper left: Benoit was first to make landfall on Jersey in the Sanchez-Besa hydro-aéroplane, but he would soon regret it as he became stranded on the sands at West Park by the receding tide. The position of the French destroyer *Belier* had misled Benoit, in the Sanchez-Besa, and instead of passing over the correct finish line, he turned away to starboard and flew between the Castle and St. Helier Harbour, gradually dropping from his altitude of 300 feet to glide down with a perfect landing on the water close to the St. Helier side of the Castle bridge at 09 hrs. 04 mins. 37 secs. Realising that he was in rapidly shallowing water over a dangerously rocky seabed, he restarted his engine to skim the biplane over the sea until he could run up safely onto sand on the First Tower side of the Sea Bathing Pool close to the West Park slipway, much to the excitement of the massive crowd of spectators gathered there. Even before he had completed this taxi manoeuvre the awaiting throng sighted two more hydro-aéroplanes travelling towards them at great speed.

Lower left: The little R.E.P. monoplane piloted by Molla was the second craft to arrive. He had also been distracted by the *Belier* and took the incorrect course following a similar line to the Sanchez-Besa and came to rest within 100 yards of Benoit's machine at 09 hrs. 11 mins. 49 secs. Molla, who was flying solo had already experienced navigational problems round the Chausey Islands and was concentrating on following the Sanchez-Besa rather than identifying the official finish line.

Three and a half minutes later, Labouret's Astra with the benefit of a navigating passenger, was the third machine to reach the island, but the first to cross the official finish line at 09 hrs. 15 mins. 35 secs. Labouret maintained a good altitude until he had almost reached the shore when he turned to the left and flying parallel with the beach, planed down onto the surface of the water some 50 yards from the shore abreast of Beaumont. He remained floating in the shallows, a strategy that would benefit him greatly.

Almost 30 minutes elapsed before the final machine came into view, but the greater speed of the Nieuport monoplane piloted by Weymann was very evident. Even though Weymann had a passenger assisting, they failed to locate the official finish line and the Nieuport darted steeply down to alight in the Inner Roadstead near the French destroyer *Belier*. A photograph, taken from the deck of the French Destroyer *Belier* and published in *Le Monde Illustré* is the only known image of Weymann's Nieuport in Jersey waters. Realising his mistake, it took several false starts before Weymann could get the Nieuport airborne again, but after a near disastrous take-off when he almost crashed into the Albert Pier, he made a wide sweep round the breakwater, flew round the Bay and crossed the official finish line at 09 hrs. 44 mins. 23 secs. before performing a very neat landing close to the Astra.

gentlemen's starched collars and ladies' torn petticoat hems. Horse drawn carts were driven onto the sands and into the water in an attempt to get their passengers close to the machines; even cyclists were seen pushing their precious vehicles through the saltwater. Hundreds of hands strained to touch the two machines or write their names on the wings and fuselage while some of the more aggressive members of the crowd attempted to climb onto the fragile floats of the craft.

The rules of the race permitted the pilots 30 minutes to refuel their machines and become airborne again, after which time they started to incur time penalties, but the uncontrolled hordes either did not know or cared nothing for the time limit.

Labouret who had landed his Astra further along the beach near Beaumont, attracted a smaller but equally excited crowd, but by staying afloat 50 yards offshore in the shallows he managed to keep out of reach of all but the most determined of spectators, and at the same time make himself more accessible to his fuel boat which was amongst the flotilla of small craft that soon surrounded him.

As the tide receded the fuel boats were unable to get close to the hydro-aéroplanes and the petrol cans had to be manhandled over the sands and through the clamouring throng to the machines which were now blocked by carts that had sunk to their axles in the soft sand or even overturned.

Weymann arriving almost 30 minutes later in his Nieuport monoplane and putting down near the Astra also escaped the more aggressive attentions of the crowd and he and Labouret were able to refuel their machines almost before the Sanchez-Besa and the R.E.P. could be united with their fuel supplies. The Astra was first to take-off on the return flight, battling through the waves without undue effort until she was running along the surface and gradually lifting into the air to re-cross the finishing line at 10 hrs. 5 mins. 37 secs. having spent 50 minutes in Jersey waters and exceeding her time limit by 20 minutes. She rose steadily to about 200 feet before flying straight out to sea passing close to the *Duke of Normandy* and then banking to the east in the direction of Chausey before being lost to view. Weymann refuelled his Nieuport more swiftly than any of the other pilots and was the second to leave, getting into the air after a short glide across the water and crossing the line at 10 hrs. 16 mins., incurring a time penalty of only 4 mins. 32 secs.

The crowds watched the departure of the R.E.P. until it was lost to sight against a dense bank of purple storm clouds. The escorting French torpedo boats that had anchored outside Jersey waters, lifted their anchors and chased after their wards as the French timekeepers in Elizabeth Castle Keep were taken back to the French destroyer Belier which set off for St. Malo. As far as Jersey was concerned, the race was over, the crowds on the beach made their way back to dry land and home, and a warning cone was hoisted on the signal mast of the keep of Elizabeth Castle to indicate an approaching storm. Within an hour the thunder and lightning struck, and a deluge of rain and hail raged over Jersey. The populace now waited anxiously for news of the

Weymann flew a course following the tail of the Astra, also passing close to the Duke of Normandy, but he remained low above the water until well out to sea. This may be the only commercial image of the Nieuport in Jersey waters.

At the West Park slipway the remaining two pilots were becoming increasingly annoyed at the unreasonable and dangerous behaviour of some of the crowd who continued to delay their departure. Benoit in the stranded Sanchez-Besa was losing his temper and uttering some strong French expletives (well understood by the French speaking Jersey population) before resorting to hurling spare nuts and bolts at the unruly crowd. The timely arrival of Centenier Luxon, assisted by P. C. Jouan, restored some semblance of order, but even they found it hard to persuade the crowd to move away from the lethal spinning propeller and clear a passage to the water.

Right: At last the Sanchez-Besa began to make her laboured passage down the beach to the sea, but now the well-intentioned endeavours of the excited crowd to assist the machine were subjecting the wings and wirework to dangerous strains. Finally, to the infinite relief of both the aviators on the hydro-aéroplane and the police on the beach, the Sanchez-Besa reached the water and was soon soaring into the air, crossing the line at 10 hrs. 22 mins. 53 secs. Hindered by the crowds, Benoit's Sanchez-Besa had remained stranded on the Jersey sands for 1 hr. 18 mins. 16 secs. earning him a time penalty of 48 mins. 16 secs.

Below: The remaining hydro-aéroplane, the R.E.P., was equally impeded by a crowd that was further augmented by spectators of the Sanchez-Besa once she had left the beach. Molla, who was obviously annoyed at the delay, managed to maintain a more philosophical attitude which was attributed to a 'buxom Miss Anderson of Bay View Terrace' who rushed to greet him with a welcome jug of hot coffee.

Above: After Molla had warmed up the engine of the R.E.P. for 20 minutes, the crowd half pushed and half lifted the machine into the water where it crossed the line at 10 hrs. 44 mins. 45 secs. to chase after the other three machines. The R.E.P. had remained on the beach for 1 hr. 32 mins. 56 secs. earning Molla a time penalty of 62 mins. 56 secs.

valiant flyers and their safe return to St. Malo. The pessimistic fears of the Jersey crowd were unfounded as all four hydro-aéroplanes completed the course safely. Weymann, with the superior speed of the Nieuport, had managed to catch up and overtake the Astra on the return flight to be the first to cross the St. Malo finish line at 11 hrs. 6 mins. 47 secs. with Labouret bringing in the Astra exactly one minute later, just as the Sanchez-Besa was sighted on the horizon. Benoit crossed the line in the Sanchez-Besa at 11 hrs. 28 mins. 19 secs. while Mola in the very fast little R.E.P. managed to close the original time gap with Benoit of 22 minutes, to 8 minutes, to cross the St. Malo finish line at 11 hrs. 36 mins. 47 secs.

A MOTRICINE lubricants advertising postcard proclaims a victory for the Astra & Motricine. Labouret's Astra was the official winner of the St. Malo Concours having completed all three races and received only 9 penalty points. He also received the French Admiralty 'Ministry of Marine' prize for the machine with the most practical military application. Several navies subsequently adopted the Astra craft for military use.

WINNER WINNER WINNERS!

As far as Jersey was concerned the Sanchez-Besa biplane would always be the first aircraft to have landed on the island but within forty minutes that triumph was shared with three other machines, any of which could just as easily have been the first. The little R.E.P. was the first monoplane to land on Jersey and if Molla had not encountered navigational difficulties around the Chausey Islands he may have also stolen the crown to be the first to arrive.

Cash prizes were awarded to the first six winners of the three day 'St. Malo Concours' following calculation of the complicated handicap and time penalties.

The Sanchez-Besa piloted by Benoit was second in the Concours also having completed all three races and receiving 14 penalty points. A close third and the only other machine to complete all three races was the little R.E.P. piloted by Molla. He gained 16 penalty points, but he was a solo pilot with no passengers and the superior speed of his machine was greatly disadvantaged by the handicap rules. Renaux was fourth with his Farman and 21 penalty points, but he only completed one race and failed to make it to Jersey, while Weymann trailed in fifth place with 25 penalty points also only having completed one race following the sinking of one of his Nieuport machines at the end of the first day's trial.

The one race that Weymann managed to complete in great style was the race to Jersey and he won the 'Jersey Prize' for the fastest return flight to the island having been the last to set out from St. Malo but the first to cross the St. Malo finishing line. His total time for the return flight including the refuelling stopover in Jersey was 2 hours, 10 minutes and 21 seconds. A postcard celebrating Weymann's achievement has a vignette portrait of the pilot.

1914 – 1918 THE FIRST WORLD WAR IN THE CHANNEL ISLANDS

The First World War hardly reached the Channel Islands. Each Island supplied its quota of able men for the armed forces, both volunteers and later conscripts, but these numbers were decimated in battle with Guernsey suffering especially. The men went to the war, but for the islands there was no fear of invasion, or attack by air as it was too dangerous for German Zeppelins to fly across France, and the targets were insignificant compared to London. Even the waters around the islands were relatively safe from the predations of German U-boats as there were easier targets in the less hazardous waters of the English Channel.

The French Military Seaplane base in Guernsey

Because of the German U-boat threat to shipping in the western waters of the English Channel, ships that had crossed the Atlantic or were sailing up from the Mediterranean were marshalled into convoys for safe escort through the English Channel. Vessels destined for English ports were assembled to the west of the Scilly Isles and these hugged the English coast as they were escorted up the Channel by the Royal Navy, while ships heading for French Channel ports were formed into convoys off the island of Ushant on the north-west tip of Brittany and followed the French coast, escorted by French warships. The progress of the convoys was monitored by British seaplanes from bases along the south coast of England and by French seaplanes from bases along the Brittany and Normandy coasts. There were French seaplane bases at Camaret, Ushant, Tréguier and Cherbourg, seaplane anchorages at St. Vaast la Hougue and Port-en-Bessin and a further base at Boulogne. This seaplane coverage left a 'hole' around Dieppe and another between the bases at Cherbourg and Tréguier, a particularly vulnerable area off the Channel Islands that the German U-boats were exploiting to great effect in the winter of 1916. To combat their activities, the French Naval Ministry adopted a 'New Aviation Programme' on 9th February 1917. A seaplane base would be set up at Dieppe and another in the Channel Islands under the jurisdiction of the Préfet Maritime at Cherbourg. The British Government granted the unprecedented act of establishing a French Military seaplane base on British land, in British waters, on the island of Guernsey.

Initially the Guernsey base would have two or three seaplanes, each with a Pilot Officer and an Observer, and be commanded by a Senior Officer under the jurisdiction of the Cherbourg base. Guernsey was chosen in preference to other Channel Islands because it is the island furthest to the west and north, facing the Atlantic, on the edge of the vulnerable zone of operation by the U-boats. The British Government approved the programme, the Admiralty offered help with the construction of the base and the Lieutenant Governor of

On 30th March 1917, Ensign de Vaisseau Douillard of the Cherbourg base crossed to Guernsey and decided the model yacht pond on the Castle Cornet Emplacement at the southern side of the harbour of St. Peter Port was the most suitable location. It had a slipway where aircraft could be launched on a trolley at the half-tide, buoys close by for mooring the craft in the shelter of the harbour walls, and large workshops nearby.

Guernsey was asked to facilitate the project. The French Minister issued orders to the Préfet Maritime at Cherbourg to send an officer to Guernsey to reconnoitre a suitable location for the base and evolve a plan of construction.

The Lieutenant Governor of Guernsey ordered the yacht pond to be drained and the site prepared while personnel and stores were mustered in Cherbourg. The British garrison on the island supplied 100 Royal Engineers to construct hangars, a guardroom and other structures. Lieutenant Douillard thought it would be advantageous to increase the size of the Guernsey base to accommodate patrols as far north as the coast of England, south to the coast of Brittany and west into the Atlantic. The French Naval Ministry approved Douillard's proposals on 3rd April 1917 and decided to establish 'a large seaplane base' for possibly 12 seaplanes. Lieutenant Douillard requested that the Royal Engineers commence work immediately while the Cherbourg base mustered the aircraft, personnel and stores. The Préfet Maritime ordered the Cherbourg base to despatch a Tellier 200, two F.B.A. biplanes and a Bessoneau shed in large crates on the barge *Corail* towed by an armed tug.

Under the supervision of Ensign de Vaisseau Séguier and then Ensign de Vaisseau Dauvin, 100 Guernsey Royal Engineers assisted by French 'bluejackets' (engineers), erected the Bessoneau hangars and a heavy wire perimeter fence, a double row of accommodation huts between the harbour and the model yacht pond, workshops, stores for 5,000 litres of aviation fuel and 500 litres of aviation oil, shelters for the station's stock of ten bombs and 2,000 machine gun magazines, as well as radio and telegraph posts for a radio transmitter and a direction finder. Water and electricity services were laid on, as were telephone communications through the Guernsey Post Office and communications with Alderney via an underwater cable. Two hand-operated cranes and a trolley with a winch were built on the slipway to raise aircraft from the water, and a wheeled pigeon loft was constructed for homing pigeons trained by a French soldier to carry messages back to the base when released from aircraft. The base was also supplied with a 12-metre vedette boat, a flat-bottomed boat and land vehicles including a truck and touring car.

On 3rd June 1917 the flying personnel of the Guernsey Squadron were announced. There were to be three pilots, Lambert, Bourgault and Sylvestre, of whom one was an officer; and three observers, Rolin, Parmentier and Boissand. Enseigne de Viasseau, Le Cour Grandmaison was the officer

The Bessoneau shed built by the Royal Navy Engineers was a temporary hangar for the French seaplanes built of metal frames bolted together and covered with heavy green canvas.

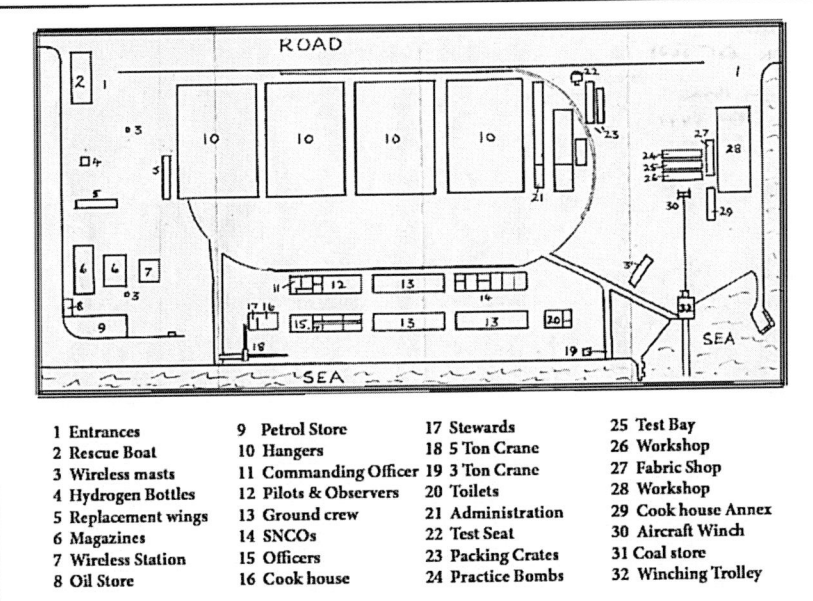

SKETCH PLAN OF THE FRENCH MILITARY SEAPLANE BASE
ST PETER PORT HARBOUR   1917 -1919

1 Entrances
2 Rescue Boat
3 Wireless masts
4 Hydrogen Bottles
5 Replacement wings
6 Magazines
7 Wireless Station
8 Oil Store
9 Petrol Store
10 Hangars
11 Commanding Officer
12 Pilots & Observers
13 Ground crew
14 SNCOs
15 Officers
16 Cook house
17 Stewards
18 5 Ton Crane
19 3 Ton Crane
20 Toilets
21 Administration
22 Test Seat
23 Packing Crates
24 Practice Bombs
25 Test Bay
26 Workshop
27 Fabric Shop
28 Workshop
29 Cook house Annex
30 Aircraft Winch
31 Coal store
32 Winching Trolley

Above photographs: Franco British Aviation (F.B.A.) seaplanes moored in the shelter of St. Peter Port Harbour.

Three Telliers and two F.B.A.s ride their moorings near the seaplane base.

An observer-gunner posing in the forward cockpit of 'G17', a Tellier 200 T3 of the Guernsey Squadron. Seaplanes of the Guernsey Squadron bore a large 'G' in front of their registration number, denoting the Guernsey base. Aircraft of the Treguier base carried the letter 'T'.

in command from the Cherbourg base. The importance of the Guernsey base escalated as on 12th June the French Naval Minister decided to equip the base with 12 seaplanes – F.B.A.s and Telliers; nine armed with machine guns and three observers carrying bombs only that were to be ready for action by 1st August.

Seaplanes of the Guernsey Squadron

The Ministerial Directive also made Guernsey an independent base working in close liaison with Treguier rather than Cherbourg. Over 100 personnel from the recently disbanded Venice Squadron of the Centre d'Aviation Maritime Francais in the Adriatic now stationed at St. Raphael, were to transfer to Guernsey by 15th July. The officers were billeted in the Hotel de France, while the men were accommodated in huts at the base. Enseigne de Viasseau, Le Cour Grandmaison was now appointed Commander of the newly enlarged Guernsey base. Weather permitting, dawn to dusk operations commenced with twelve seaplanes in August 1917, but the station only had six or seven pilots when it should have had ten and this put the men under immense pressure when in fine weather, they had to fly for many hours on long summer days. On 15th September the Squadron was increased to 16 patrol aircraft and in January 1918 it was further increased to 21 of which 11 were Telliers and ten, F.B.A.s, while a triplane from the Trieste Squadron also arrived for sea trials but was found unsuitable in the rough seas around Guernsey.

The objective of the seaplanes was to locate and bomb German U-boats. The seaplane crews would practise bomb-aiming by throwing small bags of cement at a rock located outside St. Peter Port Harbour but during one of these exercises, of 120 'cement bombs' thrown, only 81 could be observed and only nine hit the target. The location for the base was not as 'excellent' as first believed. During take-off, the seaplanes were overloaded with their machine gun, bullet magazines, full fuel load and bombs, and they required a longer take-off outside the confines of the harbour. If the sea was rough the seaplanes crashed into the waves, drenching the crew in freezing sea water and sometimes damaging the craft. The crews were in open cockpits exposed to the elements with only thick clothing and waterproof flying suits as protection. If the winds were from the east, it was impossible to even venture out of the harbour. Fog caused difficulties as the pilots had no navigational instruments and had to rely on 'line of sight'. Landing in rough weather was also problematic because the aircraft was much lighter than it was at take-off and risked being flipped over by the wind and capsizing. On 19th December the launch was lost in a storm and the Commandant des Patrouilles Alliées de

A rare aerial photograph of the Guernsey French Seaplane Base; the redundant triplane of the Trieste Squadron is to the right of the base. Jersey pilot, Flight Lieutenant C.S. Mossop D.S.C.. based at the RAF Seaplane Station near Cherbourg, was ordered to take this first ever aerial photograph of St. Peter Port Harbour on 10th August 1918, having photographed Jersey earlier in the day. He was killed two days later when his seaplane broke up in the air.

Normandie was unable to supply the torpedo boat that the base needed. The winds were tearing the canvas of the hangars and the base commander did not think that they would last through the winter. In February and March of 1918 flying was further reduced owing to damage to the crane. At the beginning of April 1918 Enseigne de Viasseau, Le Cour Grandmaison relinquished command of the base "owing to an overstrain of nerves" and his deputy, Commanding Officer Enseigne de Vaisseau Fladrin, succeeded him to the post of Commanding Officer.

Despite the weather limitations and the inaccuracy of their 'cement bomb' aiming, the pilots achieved some spectacular successes. The seaplanes flew in patrols of two and their first success was as early as 9th August 1917 when a patrol discovered a mine to the west of Guernsey. In August and September enemy submarines were sighted on three occasions but submerged before they could be engaged. One of these U-boats was sighted twice on the same day, first by a seaplane that had broken down and was taxiing back to base on the water about 20 miles north-west of the Casquets. The U-boat resurfaced off Alderney the same day and managed to shoot down a French airship that was attempting to bomb it. Extremely inclement weather greatly restricted flying at the end of 1917 and during the first three months of 1918 when the seaplanes saw little activity, only locating the enemy on one occasion in each month but failing to complete an attack. On 17th November, Ensign de Vaisseur Merveilleux Du Vignaux stayed in the air for six hours harrying a submarine and forcing it to dive twice.

At the end of January 1918 the seaplanes finally managed to get into the air on two consecutive days and the pilots' spirits rose when on 30th January a patrol located a newly laid minefield that had sunk the SS Figaro near Les Hanois lighthouse. The following day they had their first "kill" when despite a heavy sea, a patrol of two seaplanes managed to get airborne at 10.20 hours by carrying a reduced cargo of one bomb each, and very soon located a large submarine wallowing in the swell off Les Hanois. The day was bright and sunny, and the U-boat's crew initially failed to notice the seaplanes diving out of the sun. The submarine's escape was hampered by the swell and before it could complete its dive, both pilots succeeded in dropping their bomb either side of the submarine near the stern severely damaging it. One seaplane returned to base to re-arm while the other circled to keep watch on the stricken U-boat. During the next half hour the submarine tried to surface five times but eventually disappeared beneath the waves amid patches of oil, and the aviators remained in the vicinity until 12.30 hours; the U boat was considered sunk. In February 1918, for this and other actions, Enseigne de Viasseau, Le Cour Grandmaison recommended the crews of the two seaplanes, the conferment of the Croix de Guerre with palm. The pilot of one of the seaplanes was Seconde-Maitre Pilote-Aviateur, Victor Lambert who some 46 years later was to return to Guernsey as the French Consular Agent.

Frustration grew in February and March when few patrols could get into the air due to atrocious weather and the crane being out of action. The next encounter was not until 4th April 1918 when one of the patrols discovered several mines laid in the vicinity of Jersey. On the morning of 23rd April, a heavy sea mist around Guernsey was used by an audacious enemy U-boat as cover to get close to the island near St. Martin's Point where it lay in wait for a passing convoy. Fortunately, at the moment that it was approaching the lead ship to torpedo her, the submarine was sighted by seaplanes that had only just taken to the air on their first patrols of the day. Ten bombs were dropped while the submarine was below the surface in the shallow waters off Guernsey and although a hit could not officially be claimed the submarine was not seen again. Following this incident, no further Allied shipping was attacked near the Channel Islands, and the German U-boats moved further out to sea, forcing the French seaplanes to also extend their field of operations.

As the weather improved in May, so did the effectiveness of the Guernsey Squadron with five successful attacks on German submarines during the month. At the start of the month a patrol sighted a German U-boat and was able to alert a large convoy of 41 French sailing ships as they were just entering the Channel. On 6th May two patrols were working together when they saved a Cherbourg to Brest convoy from an attack by a submarine west of the Roches Douvres. All four seaplanes attacked the submarine in two sections with the second section managing to cause considerable damage. On 18th May two seaplanes dropped bombs on a submarine that had just been attacking an English convoy south of the Cornwall coast. Finally, on the 31st May two seaplanes came to the rescue of an unarmed English sailing ship, the *Dundee P.14*, that was bound from St. Malo for Portsmouth. The sailing ship was becalmed thirty miles west of the Hanois and a submarine was shelling her. The crew of the submarine were so intent on sinking their 'sitting duck' that they failed to notice the seaplanes diving on them from the sky, until it was too late. The submarine tried to crash dive, but not fast enough, and both seaplanes scored direct hits with their bombs. The submarine sank leaving large areas of oil on the calm sea. The seaplanes landed on the sea near the *Dundee* to check if anyone was injured, but the crew said that the damage was only slight.

The bad weather returned in June and only one seaplane attack was recorded on a submarine that was waiting to intercept a huge American convoy north-west of the Casquets. Despite storms in July, six successful attacks were executed on submarines while several convoys were alerted to the presence of submarines before they could attack. The seaplane observer's job became harder in August when the Germans attempted to camouflage their vessels as Allied submarines, but despite this strategy the base carried out four successful attacks on U-boats, one causing considerable damage. This was the final action for the Guernsey Squadron as the German submarine offensive was diminishing, and the weather in September and October was so bad that hardly any flying was possible. November saw the end of the war and the ceasing of hostilities, and on the 11th November 1918, Armistice Day, a lone seaplane made a commemorative flight to Jersey arriving over the island at the 11th hour. None of the French aviators was injured or killed in action although one died in a flying accident. A French pilot who was taking a shortcut across the Parish of St. Peter's instead of flying around the coast, accidentally dropped a bomb that landed in a field excavating a ten-foot-deep hole and substantially damaging neighbouring greenhouses.

Several aviators were awarded honours for their exploits during their time in Guernsey and the Croix de Guerre was awarded to the station as a whole for 25 attacks on enemy submarines and the discovery of three minefields during the year from 9th August 1917 to 11th August 1918.

A rare photo of a French F.B.A. seaplane of the Guernsey Squadron returning to St. Peter Port Harbour after a mission.

French Aviators of the Guernsey Squadron.

Carpenters at the station made a wooden model of the cross and mounted it on a wall of one of the barracks in the base. The Guernsey press encouraged local residents, who knew very little of the exploits of the base, to go and view it. The base was disbanded in January 1919. On 6th January 1919 grateful Guernsey officials gave a farewell dinner for all 150 officers and men of the Guernsey Aviation Maritime Francais who had so valiantly protected the islands and local shipping. The aviators were assured of a warm welcome should they ever return to Guernsey. Quatrier-Maitre Emile Chaplin, one of the winners of the Croix de Guerre returned three months later to marry a local girl, Miss Leah Badaire, in Notre Dame de Rosaire Church on 3rd April 1919, and Croix de Guerre winner Seconde-Maitre Pilote-Aviateur, Victor Lambert returned in 1964 as French Consular Agent. The seaplanes were re-shipped back to Cherbourg on the same barge that had brought them, and the base was dismantled. The buildings were auctioned off, attracting a crowd of 250 local residents eager to acquire sheds of various sizes. There were grumblings later in the year that the model yacht pond had still not been restored and it was estimated that it would cost between £500 and £600 to rebuild.

Either through imposed, or self-censorship, the existence of the base was never reported or commented on in the press despite the size of the construction, the billeting of some 150 French aviators and the appearance of eventually 22 French seaplanes in the harbour. Also, possibly due to censorship, very few photographs exist of the seaplanes.

1918 – A large British Felixstowe F3 passes Castle Cornet when visiting the base. No records exist of these visits and nothing was mentioned in the local press.

The War in Jersey – French Flying Visitors

The Jersey skies were silent throughout the First World War although some residents recalled seeing a French airship and the odd plane over the island, or occasionally alighting in St. Helier Harbour. Due to censorship, the local press made no mention of visiting aircraft; the St. Helier Harbour Master's office holds no records of visiting aircraft, while no diary has been found that records aircraft visits. The records of the Cherbourg and Guernsey seaplane bases were lost during the Second World War so there are no records of seaplane flights from there either. A patrol of two machines, the FPA-230 and FPA-562, set off on 26th September 1917 at 09.15 hours and flew to the L'Etacq region north-west of Jersey, returning to base at 11.35 hours. Stormy weather on 4th November probably halted flights from the Guernsey base and there must have been fears of a German submarine entering the area as two Tréguier patrols flew close to Jersey that day. A Tellier-64 flying a six hour patrol flew seven miles to the west of Jersey opposite La Rocco Tower while in the afternoon a flight of two craft, the FBA-580 and FBA-581, while on a four hour patrol descended to a height of about 160 feet to confirm the identity of a British patrol vessel in Jersey waters. The weather was still bad two days later on 6th November, when FBA-581 again flew over Jersey waters, failing to locate any enemy craft, but spotting a British steamer some seven miles off La Corbière. The last reference to Jersey for 1917 was on 18th November when a patrol of two craft, the FBA-545 and FBA-580, took off in calm seas at 11.40 hours to escort a convoy from ten miles south-west of La Corbière into St. Helier Harbour. Of the three patrols recorded in 1918 flying from the Tréguier base to the vicinity of Jersey, none located any evidence of the enemy. On the morning of 18th March a patrol of two Tellier craft, T 1 and T 6 flew a two hour patrol as far as Jersey between 10.05 hours and 12.10 hours, while another two hour patrol on 21st May flying from 10.30 hours to 12.30 hours followed a route comprising a wide loop to the south of Guernsey before passing close to La Corbière on the way back to base. The final reported patrol to Jersey took place on 29th May between 13.40 hours and 17.25 hours, again in very poor weather conditions and also again flown by Telliers T 1 and T 6. They recorded poor visibility, but as soon as they located Jersey they then turned towards St. Malo before returning to Tréguier.

The Guernsey seaplane base worked in collaboration with the Aviation Maritime Française base at Tréguier situated to the south on the Côtes-du-Nord. Reports of missions from Tréguier are extant, but Jersey is only mentioned five times in 1917 and three times the following year. Patrols from Tréguier probably only flew to Jersey when Guernsey seaplanes could not leave their base. The *Tréguier Aviation Maritime Française Tellier* 'T6' in the centre of this photograph made two patrols to Jersey in 1918.

Zodiac Airships

The French army had dirigibles that were mainly used for reconnaissance purposes over enemy lines with occasional limited bombing missions. The French Navy initially had no use for airships, but as the threat of German U-boats in the English Channel escalated, the French Naval Airship Service was initiated in 1916 to help address the problem. The newly formed service had little effect until 1917 when the French army transferred its complete fleet of airships to this new branch of the Navy.

The nearest French airship base to the Channel Islands was built in 1917 at Montebourg – Ecausseville in Normandy on the Cherbourg Peninsula some miles south and inland from the Cherbourg Seaplane Base. A huge wooden hangar, 150 feet long, 20 feet wide and 22 feet high was constructed to house airships and an even larger one made of concrete was in the course of

The concrete Montebourg Airship Hangar was only completed in 1919, survived the Second World War and was classified as a unique historical monument in 2003. The wooden hangar had been torn down in 1933 following storm damage.

construction to house the two new Zodiacs, ZD3 and ZD4, that were assigned to Montebourg Airship Base in March of 1918. The field of operations for Montebourg seldom extended to the south-west of the Cherbourg peninsula, but airships from the base were recorded passing over Jersey on two occasions in 1918. On Monday 6th May 1918, Zodiac ZD3, was ordered to escort a convoy from St. Malo into the English Channel. She commenced her patrol at 10.55 hours in hazy visibility, but after completing the mission she passed over Jersey at 19.00 hours and the Pilot Officer, Lieutenant de Font-Réaulx, recorded in the logbook "Very clear weather over the Chanel Islands". Ten days later, on Thursday 16th May, the sister Zodiac airship, the ZD4, was ordered to escort a convoy to Brest and then carry out reconnaissance in the Western Sea Zone off the Channel Islands while performing practice bomb aiming. ZD4 departed from Montebourg at 09.07 hours and having accomplished her mission in very fine weather, proceeded to Jersey where she carried out manoeuvres over St. Aubin's Bay for some time in the afternoon and this unexpected spectacle attracted hundreds of spectators. The airship returned to Montebourg Air Station at 16.35 hours.

The Zodiac Airship of the French Naval Airship Service was the newest Zodiac airship, the type ZD3, but these did not become available until the end of 1917 and the beginning of 1918. The Zodiac type 3 airship had a capacity of 21,700 cubic feet and, driven by two Renault engines each of 200 hp, had a maximum speed of 50 mph, a cruising speed of between 30 and 40 mph and a range of ten hours flying at maximum speed or double that if cruising. The Zodiac type 3 was designed for a crew of five and could carry an armament of 550 lbs of bombs.

1918 THE FIRST FLIGHTS FROM ENGLAND TO JERSEY ACCIDENTAL AND INTENDED

The Cherbourg Royal Naval Air Station

By some strange quirk of logic, while the French Navy established a seaplane base on British soil in Guernsey in 1917, the Royal Navy built a seaplane base on French soil near Cherbourg. The Cherbourg Royal Naval Air Service Station, inaugurated on 21st July 1917 with three Wight Converted Seaplanes, was not part of the French Aviation Maritime seaplane base in Cherbourg, but was situated five kilometres north-west of Cherbourg at Querqueville with a take-off and alighting area in the Bay of Sainte-Anne.

The Calshot RNAS seaplane base on the Solent was the mother station to this 'out station' RNAS Cherbourg. Calshot supplied the personnel and seaplanes and the two bases coordinated their anti-submarine patrols in the English Channel as well as operating training flights between the two bases. RNAS Cherbourg was made up of Flights 414 and 415 of the RNAS and in August 1918 they amalgamated as Squadron 243 of the newly formed Royal Air Force. This new military service, the R. A. F., had been formed on 1st April 1918 with the amalgamation of the army fliers of the Royal Flying Corps, with the navy fliers of the Royal Naval Air Services.

The First (Unintentional) Direct Flight from the UK to Jersey

On a bright morning, on 29th May 1918, a young and eager pilot, Lieutenant Sidney Burgess, and his equally keen observer Lieutenant Fox, having completed their final briefing, were preparing to make their maiden flight from Calshot to the French coast and RNAS Cherbourg at Querqueville. Unknowingly the airmen were about to create Channel Islands' aviation history by being the first people to fly directly from the UK mainland to Jersey. As the flight was unplanned there would be no reception committee, and reports of the historic event never appeared in the local newspapers. Information about the flight only became available to aviation historians with the release of the First World War records in the 1960s.

The RNAS Cherbourg base mainly flew Wight Converted Seaplanes. The Wight Converted was designed and built by Samuel White & Co. Ltd. at East Cowes on the Isle of Wight and the craft took its name from the island, not the company. The seaplane evolved from White's sole single-engined land biplane bomber of 1916. With the addition of floats, the two seater, three bay, wooden structure with fabric covering had a wing span of 65 ft 6 in., a length of 44 ft 8 in. and a height of 16 ft. The power unit, a Rolls Royce 250 hp Eagle V engine, produced a maximum speed of 84.5 mph with an endurance of 3 hr. 30 min. whilst its armament included a bomb load of up to four 112 lb bombs on under-fuselage racks and one Lewis machine gun on a 'Scarff ring' mount on the rear cockpit; this mount permitted the gun to rotate through 360°.

At 10.30 hours on the 29th May Lieutenants Burgess and Fox took off from RNAS Calshot in their Wight Converted Seaplane, N9858, armed with a Lewis machine gun and three 112 lb bombs, on their maiden flight to Cherbourg with a mission to search for U-boats en route. The craft flew from Calshot across the Solent and over the Needles at the western end of the Isle of Wight in bright sunlight, but twenty minutes into the flight they encountered an English Channel mist. With zero visibility and only a compass for navigation, the craft was steadily blown off course by a strong breeze and they missed the coast of France. With a fortunate improvement in visibility at 13.30 hours they observed land to their east and south that they believed was France, but was actually the Ecréhous rocks to the east, and the north coastline of Jersey to their south.

Jersey's north coast of cliffs and tiny bays is completely inimical to a seaplane landing. As Lieutenant Burgess flew towards the coast, fate intervened again when he detected he no longer had full control of the Wight Converted; one of the horns on the tail had become bent and was restricting the elevator control. An enforced landing was now inevitable, and he noticed the small sheltered bay of Gréve de Lecq nestling in the inhospitable coastline. Circling the bay twice, he observed a fishing boat picking up lobster pots outside the bay, a small stone pier at one end and a large building (hotel) above the sandy beach. The sea appeared reasonably calm, and descending with N9858 at half power, Lieutenant Burgess landed outside the bay and taxied towards the fishing boat, *Albert Edward*. The fishermen were Mr E. J. Prouten and Mr George Hamm from Ville Bagot, St. Ouen. Convinced he was in French waters, Lieutenant Fox shouted in his best schoolboy French asking them the location, but the reply shouted back in strong Jersey accented English, was lost in the roar of the engine.

N9858 made landfall in Gréve de Lecq Bay and the aviators were greeted by an excited group of children who had never seen a plane before and were shouting in their local Norman-French language, Jèrriais. There then occurred a farcical dialogue with

A Wight Converted Seaplane being prepared for launching from the Calshot RNAS seaplane station.

Lieutenant Fox attempting to make himself understood in French and the children jabbering away in Jèrriais. The situation was saved when eight-year-old George Baudains, the son of the owner of Gréve de Lecq mill, ran down to the beach, and hearing Lieutenant Fox asking in French if this was France, detected Fox's English accent and shouted "No…Jersey…British".

The Prince of Wales Hotel above the beach, is still open today. A Jersey merchant seaman home on leave and staying in the hotel, escorted Lieutenant Burgess into St. Helier from where he could telegram RNAS Cherbourg, while Lieutenant Fox guarded the stricken seaplane.

Gréve de Lecq Bay where the N9858 made landfall.

The Commanding Officer of RNAS Cherbourg Air Station, Captain C. W. Scott obtained the exact location of Gréve de Lecq Bay from serving Jerseyman, mechanic George W. Croad, and then ordered another serving Jersey officer pilot, Lieutenant C. S. Mossop, to execute a reconnaissance search for the Wight Converted. Lieutenant Mossop was a highly distinguished and decorated flier and he and his family make a large contribution to this narrative, commencing with this first flight by a Jerseyman to his native island. Lieutenant Mossop accompanied by Lieutenant Lindley as navigator, took off from the Cherbourg Seaplane Base at 14.45 hours in a Short Type 184 seaplane, N2805, and set course for Jersey. After locating the crippled seaplane, they circled the bay and observed that the only possible route to effect a rescue was from the sea. Lieutenant Mossop then continued his mission to search for a missing Short, numbered N2834, before returning to Cherbourg to make his report.

The Jersey tidal ranges are some of the largest in the world. As the tide rose on Gréve de Lecq Beach a struggle ensued to keep the seaplane safe as she was hauled up the beach and made secure with her own ropes and anchor. Her three bombs were unloaded, and their detonators removed and made safe before they were stored in the grounds of the Prince of Wales Hotel where Lieutenant Fox stayed overnight. Soldiers from the Jersey garrison guarded the seaplane during the night, but they could not stop the sea from damaging the tail of the craft. Mr and Mrs Charles Mossop, the parents of Lieutenant Mossop, invited Lieutenant Burgess to spend the night with them in their house, Cambray, at Millbrook. In the afternoon of the following day, Lieutenant Mossop arrived with a launch from the Cherbourg base to tow the stricken seaplane round the island and into St. Helier Harbour. The seas were too hazardous for the launch to return to base for two days, and so for two nights Lieutenant Mossop was able to billet with his parents and their unexpected flyer visitor. On 1st June with an improvement in the weather, the launch returned to the Cherbourg base with its damaged cargo in tow.

A Short Type 184 seaplane, identification number N2833, sister to the missing N2834 of the newly formed RAF Squadron 243 stationed at the RAF Cherbourg.

A Second Unintended Flight from England to Jersey

On 2nd July 1918 an experimental F 3, N4409, was sent to the RNAS station on the Isle of Grain in Kent on the Thames Estuary to carry out tests on new navigation and bomb-aiming devices. Development of the equipment required prolonged navigational experimentation and on 17th July 1918, N4409 set off for RNAS Cherbourg at Querqueville where she refuelled and then continued her journey over the Channel Islands and on to the French naval air base at Camaret, Finistère. From Camaret the F 3 departed in a south-easterly direction for the American air base at Le Croisic reaching it at 21.30 hours. The crew were intending to over-night at Le Croisic and continue their mission the following day after refuelling, but the French military authorities detained the craft and crew when no written orders could be found and none of the crew had identity cards. The seaplane was held for two days before clearance was given, and then at 14.00 hours on Friday 19th July the F 3 left Le Croisic base for a long flight north to the Scilly Isles. The seaplane sheltered at the RNAS base near the little village of New Grimsby on the island of Tresco until Sunday afternoon, 21st July, when she received orders to re-cross the Channel to Dieppe. During the flight to Dieppe, problems developed with a fuel pump and N4409 was forced to divert to Jersey where she alighted on the sea south of Elizabeth Castle Breakwater and taxied tentatively to a mooring inside the harbour. Crowds quickly gathered on the piers to watch as a mechanic climbed out onto the lower wing of the huge biplane to service both the motors. The crew did not go ashore as within fifteen minutes the mechanic completed his work and the craft revved up its deafening Rolls Royce engines and taxied back out through the harbour mouth to take-off and circle over St. Helier before setting a north-east course for Dieppe. Unfortunately, her fuel pumps failed again, and she was forced to make an emergency landing on a choppy sea some 20 miles off the French coast of Le Havre. Her crew made contact by Morse lamp with a passing convoy and a Royal Navy trawler towed her into the port of Le Havre. The rough seas during the tow badly damaged the fabric on her wings and a lengthy repair detained her for some days in Le Havre. Jersey had hosted a visit of the world's largest seaplane, but only a limited number of people saw her because her unexpected visit was so short.

The largest military seaplane on both sides of the Atlantic in early 1918 was the British Felixstowe F 3, nicknamed the 'Large America' as it derived from the American Curtiss H16. The F 3 had a length of 49 ft 2 in., a wingspan of 102 ft and a height of 18 ft 8 in.. It was powered by two Rolls-Royce Eagle VIII V12 engines, each of 345 hp giving a maximum speed of 91 mph and an endurance of 6 hours. The craft carried a crew of four and an armament of four Lewis machine guns and a 920 lbs bomb load beneath its wings.

A 'Large America' Curtiss H 12B Flying boat, sister aircraft to N4349. Lieutenants Drummond and Hanna were on board N4349 as Observers and the pilot was Flight Lieutenant Philip H. Mackworth who had joined the RNAS in 1916 at the age of 18 years and would later become Air Vice-Marshal. The passenger was Brigadier-General William Ward Warner, originally an officer in the Royal Guernsey Militia and now Director of the RAF Personal Services.

The First Intentional England to Jersey Flight

On 4th September 1918, the 'Large America' Curtiss H 12B flying boat, identification number N4349, took off from Calshot at 08.00 hours with a flight plan for a direct flight to Jersey. A high-ranking RAF officer on board the seaplane would be the first ever 'passenger' on the first ever intentional direct flight from England to Jersey. A record of the flight came to light years later, but the reason for the flight remains a mystery.

The first local knowledge of the visit of the Curtiss was when the huge seaplane arrived over St. Helier and circled low over the town before alighting in St. Aubin's Bay at 10.15 hours where General Warner was met by Captain Mainguy Robin and Mrs Harold C. Robin who ferried him by motorboat into the harbour. While the General was reporting to the island authorities in the harbour the Curtiss took to the air once again before any onlookers had time to gather, and headed for the RNAS base at Cherbourg where the crew spent the night while their craft was serviced and refuelled. The General meanwhile was driven to Rosel Manor for a meeting with Mr and Mrs R. R. Lempriere where General Warner discussed with Mr Lempriere his experience in co-ordinating local arrangements for the 1912 air race from St. Malo to St. Helier. The following day, Thursday 5th September, N4349 returned from Cherbourg, landing once more in St. Aubin's Bay and when she was made secure on her own anchors, the crew were taken off by a party that again included Captain and Mrs Harold C. Robin, to spend three hours visiting St. Helier. This time a crowd had time to gather and view the craft before General Warner and the crew re-embarked sometime between 15.00 and 16.00 hours and after taking off from the bay, the huge seaplane proceeded to make a low-level pass over the island much to the excitement of the gathered crowds. After a flight of 95 minutes, N4349 returned safely to her base on the mainland.

RAF Flight Lieutenant C S Mossop DSC
22nd June 1898 – 12th August 1918

In May and June 1918 Flight Lieutenant C. S. Mossop and his parents were very involved with the events of the first flight from England to Jersey and in the course of those events Lieutenant Mossop gained added kudos for being the first Jersey pilot to fly to his native Island, but Lieutenant Mossop was already a highly decorated wartime pilot.

Charles 'Stanley' Mossop was born on 22nd June 1898 and educated at Victoria College, Jersey from 1907 until 1914. After schooling he worked in engineering on the mainland, but within weeks war was declared on 4th August 1914 and he immediately enlisted as a 16-year-old. He gained a posting to the Royal Naval Air Service and commenced his training as a probationary Flight Officer at RNAS Redcar in Yorkshire. In March 1917 he served on the ground staff at Redcar for two weeks before going on his first flight on 23rd March. After only three hours and seventeen minutes of instruction he made his first solo flight of five minutes, on the same day! Training continued at Cranwell, Lincolnshire in May and in mid-June he moved to RNAS Calshot on the Solent. On 24th July 1917 Lieutenant Mossop made his maiden flight from Calshot to RNAS Cherbourg at Querqueville, piloting a Norman Thompson N.T.2B, numbered N1183. The N.T.2B was a new type of single pusher-engined flying boat trainer, with two seats side by side. Ten of these biplanes were ordered by the RNAS and they had been delivered to Calshot only two weeks previously on 8th July 1917.

Lieutenant Mossop was to spend the whole of his remaining flying career at RNAS Cherbourg, flying U-boat hunting patrols in all weathers. He became a proficient submarine hunter and on 18th August 1917 was the first RNAS pilot to bomb and sink a German U-boat. Then still only a Flight Sub-Lieutenant aged 19, Mossop was on patrol north-east of Cherbourg in a Wight Converted, numbered N9860, with Air Mechanic A. E. Ingledew as Observer-Navigator, when he located a German submarine, UB32, laying mines in the Cherbourg approaches. He dived on the submarine and unleashed one of his 100 lb bombs, but when he turned to drop his second bomb, he saw that it was not required as the first bomb had 'killed his quarry' by exploding on the submarine immediately in front of the periscope. The submarine sank with all 24 crew members. For this action Mossop was awarded the Distinguished Service Cross; he was not only the first British aviator to sink a German submarine, but he was the first of only seven throughout the whole of the First World War.

Captain C. W. Scott, the Commanding Officer of RNAS Cherbourg, commanded Mossop to carry out a photographic reconnaissance of both Jersey and Guernsey on Saturday 10th August 1918. Stanley asked for permission to land in Jersey waters to visit his parents, but Captain Scott officially refused his request while intimating that if he did land and the aircraft was undamaged, then he would not face a charge of insubordination. At 13.55 hours Lieutenant Mossop took off from Querqueville in a Wight Converted, numbered N9854, with Lieutenant Robert Edmund Horton as his Observer-Navigator and they soon attained an altitude of 1,500 ft flying south towards Jersey. After the island had been photographed, the Wight Converted alighted in the Inner Roadstead of St. Helier Harbour and, leaving Horton to guard her, Mossop made his way into the harbour by boat. A merchant on the Esplanade telephoned his parents to inform them their son was in his shop and very soon there was a euphoric family

A Wight Converted Seaplane on patrol; Mossop sank U-boat UB32 and made his first landing in Jersey flying a Wight Converted Seaplane.

reunion, all the more special because Stanley's older brother, RAF (originally R.N.A.S.) Captain Edward A. Mossop, was also at home on leave. The visit was fleeting and at 17.15 hours Mossop took off again to carry out the photographic record of Guernsey where he took aerial photos of St. Peter Port and the French Naval Seaplane Base. Having completed his missions, Mossop returned to his Cherbourg base to land safely at 19.05 hours.

Two days after the flight to the Channel Islands, on Monday 12th August, Lieutenants Mossop and Horton took off in another Wight Converted, N9859, on a routine patrol, unaware that their tail had sustained damage during take-off. Two hours and 55 minutes into the flight while returning along the French coast, the tail plane collapsed in mid-air and the aircraft nose-dived into the waters of Port-en-Bessin Harbour. The airmen were rescued but succumbed to their injuries later in the day. The Mossop family in Jersey were informed by telegram of the appalling news, but the shock they felt cannot be imagined considering they had only seen 20-year-old Stanley vigorously healthy and happy, 48 hours previously.

The funerals took place on Friday 16th August 1918 in the Tourlaville Communal Cemetery where the two officers were the first to be interred in a newly created British Military Cemetery. Stanley's parents and brother crossed over from Jersey in a specially chartered motorboat full of wreaths from Jersey sympathisers, friends and family.

The RAF was only established on 1st April 1918, and Squadron 243 of RAF Cherbourg was only formed a few days before Mossop's fateful crash. He and Horton were the first airmen of RAF Squadron 243 to die on active service.

Mossop and Horton were laid to rest on 16th August 1918 in the British Military Cemetery in Tourlaville Communal Cemetery.

THE "SEAPLANE SPECIAL"
NEWSPAPERS DELIVERED BY TWO AVRO SEAPLANES
THE FIRST INTER-ISLAND PASSENGER

After the war, 'joyriding', especially from the beaches around the coast, was a popular activity. Ex-Service pilots with their own war-surplus aircraft pioneered this activity and the Avro 504K Service trainer was easily converted to an Avro 504L passenger seaplane. The Avro 504L and Avro 536 that flew to the Channel Islands were different seaplane conversions of the Avro 504K with their wheels exchanged for floats. They shared the specifications of the Avro 504K with a length of 29 ft 5 in., a wingspan of 36 ft and a height of 10 ft 5 in., but the seaplanes had the more powerful 150 hp Bentley BR1 engines that gave a maximum speed of 90 mph and a range of 250 miles.

On 5th October 1919 the first 'commercial' flights from England to the Channel Islands, took place when two Avro seaplanes left Southampton for Guernsey and Jersey carrying special Sunday editions of *Lloyd's Weekly News*. The action was prompted by a railway strike that started on 27th September and included the cross-Channel steamers owned by the Great Western Railway and the Southern Railway companies, effectively cutting off the Channel Islands from the mainland. The event was a publicity stunt for *Lloyd's Weekly News*, and the Avro Transport Company, part of a struggling air transport industry trying to show its worth after four years of war. However, the Avro was a frail craft on water and the service failed to go as planned.

The Avro Transport Company flew Avro 536's joyrides from the sands at Blackpool in return for establishing Britain's first air service between Manchester and Blackpool on 26th May 1919.

The Avro Seaplane Conversions

The Avro 504L was the standard seaplane conversion and 25 were converted from old Avro 504Ks, while six were new builds.

The Avro 536 was a new design first flown in May 1919 and they were conversions from the Avro 504K where the fuselage was widened by 9 inches to accommodate four passengers in two rows in the rear cockpit. The prototype Avro 536 with registration G-EACC was the craft that flew to Jersey.

The Avro Transport Company also operated from seaside towns along the South Coast and in July 1919 positioned an Avro 504L, the seaplane variant of the 504K, at Ryde on the Isle of Wight to give 'flits' over the Solent and sky views of the Cowes Regatta Week.

The Seaplane Special Newspaper and the First Inter-Island Passenger

The railway strike from 27th September 1919 created the need for aircraft to deliver newspapers, passengers and urgent produce around the country. The Avro Transport Company saw a wonderful opportunity to promote its services with a publicity stunt flying not one, but two Avro seaplanes from its base on the River Hamble near Southampton to the Channel Islands with 'urgent' newspapers to a population deprived of English newspapers for over a week. Special Sunday editions of Lloyd's Weekly News, with an overprint "BY SEAPLANE SPECIAL EDITION" were driven by car from London to Hamble just before midday and the bundles were loaded into the two Avros. Mr A. Storey was to pilot the prototype Avro 536 seaplane registered G-EACC to Jersey, and RAF Captain H. Evans was to fly a standard conversion Avro 504L, registered G-EAFG, to Guernsey. The two seaplanes lifted off Southampton water at 12.10 hours, but immediately encountered heavy mist and low cloud obscuring the Isle of Wight.

Flying by compass bearing, they managed to maintain visual contact with each other as they flew through cloud across the English Channel. The pair made good time as their cruising speed of 60 mph was augmented by a 20 mph tail wind and the crossing was achieved in less than 90 minutes. As they neared the French coast, a break in the cloud enabled Storey in G-EACC to confirm his location when he saw Cape La Hague. He steered a course for St. Helier flying between the French coast and Guernsey, but lost sight of Captain Evans in his Avro 504L as it disappeared into low clouds over Alderney.

'SEAPLANE SPECIAL' Avro 536, G-EACC in Jersey waters.

The newspaper 'SEAPLANE SPECIAL' Avro 536, G-EACC landed safely in Jersey waters. The *Evening Post* of 6th October would describe the arrival over St. Helier under the headline:

LLOYD'S' ARRIVES BY SEAPLANE.
The Albert Pier yesterday presented an unprecedented spectacle. From 10 o'clock onwards thousands of people seemed to be making their way to the quay, the majority being anxious to witness the arrival of the seaplane which was bringing "Lloyd's Weekly" to the island, and though these had a long wait they were recompensed by witnessing the embarkation of the German prisoners and their subsequent departure. The seaplane was expected about noon, and about this time many inquiries were made of Mr Brookes, the local agent of the newspaper, as to whether the plane had left, the weather being very hazy. Though 1 o'clock passed a very large crowd waited on, and about 1.40 these were rewarded by hearing the whirr of an approaching flying machine. In a moment an "Avro" seaplane came over South Hill, and after encircling the harbour and part of the town, came gracefully down between the pier heads and breakwater, and having "taxied" up made fast to a buoy.

The Avro 536 was met by boats in front of the breakwater in St. Helier Harbour; the paper went on to describe the chaos that ensued as the papers were brought ashore in a punt to the Albert Pier slip and the crowd stampeded the waiting newsboys:

all classes seeming to be determined to have a copy. Fancy prices were offered in a large number of instances, and the newsboys in many cases must have been recompensed for the loss they had suffered during the week, by the extra prices willingly given them.

Aviator Storey was enthusiastically cheered when he came ashore, admirers demanded his autograph and local reporters interviewed him before he was finally permitted to eat a late lunch. In the afternoon he was contacted by Army Lieutenant Fulford who wanted to travel as a passenger to Guernsey. At 15.30 hours G-EACC again took to the air for Guernsey where Storey was to meet his co-pilot Captain Evans, their intention being to fly their two machines back to Hamble together the following morning.

In Guernsey the story was not such a success. Hours before the scheduled arrival time of the Avro, a large crowd congregated at the White Rock and Albert Pier in St. Peter Port Harbour eagerly awaiting the arrival of the newspaper seaplane. As the allotted hour passed and there was no sign of the craft some of the crowd drifted home, but a large contingent was still waiting at 16.20 hours when the Avro from Jersey made a graceful landing in the Pool. The crowd, thinking it was 'their' Avro, were eager to get their newspapers but were somewhat astonished when all that was unloaded from the Avro was the military kit of the passenger. Pilot Storey and Lieutenant Fulford were nevertheless given a cheering welcome when they came ashore although no one realised that aviation history had just been created with the first inter-island passenger flown from Jersey to Guernsey.

There was however no knowledge of the second Avro or Captain Evans, but in the evening, news came through that a plane had taken to the water near Alderney, and the following morning, Mr H. Le Gallez, the Guernsey agent for *Lloyd's Weekly News*, received a telegram from Captain Evans on Alderney:"Crashed through engine trouble outside Alderney. Papers destroyed. Cannot continue. Am salvaging machine."

Captain Evans lost sight of the Jersey Avro in the thick haze about an hour into the flight from Southampton. He was experiencing engine trouble and

A poor snapshot of Avro 536 in St Hellier Harbour.

when he sighted Alderney, he realised that it was imperative that he try to land there. He chose the best location he could find outside the breakwater of the harbour off the Brayes and managed a safe landing, but the seaplane was too frail to withstand the heavy sea that was running and began to break up. Two Alderney boats, *Pilot No. 1* and *Sunrise* affected a swift rescue, saving Captain Evans and towing his damaged machine into the harbour.

Initially it was reported that the newspapers on board the Avro had been lost, but the bulk of them were saved although somewhat damp. There was no chance for Captain Evans to get the papers to Guernsey quickly, so he had them overprinted with an apology and sold in Guernsey as souvenirs of his failed attempt. His overprint said:

> Message from the Pilot.
> of the Avro Seaplane.
> I regret that bad luck and the.
> weather prevented me from deliver-.
> ing this to you on Sunday.
> H.EVANS,
> Alderney, Capt. RAF.

All the *Lloyd's Weekly News* Special Seaplane Edition newspapers were sold at a high premium as souvenirs of this first attempt to deliver newspapers from England to the Channel Islands, but it is a mystery that few, if any, have survived to this day; all that is extant is this photograph of a Guernsey example.

VISIT OF THE R-36 AIRSHIP TO JERSEY

The Romance of the Airship

The British airship industry from inception had been developed entirely for military purposes to supply the army with scouting and observation platforms during military engagements. Towards the end of the First World War an alternative concept was developing, that airships could be used for long haul civilian passenger travel, but in Germany right from the outset this had always been an objective of the highly advanced Zeppelin airship industry. The first Zeppelin, LZ-1, had been built in 1899; the world's very first passenger airline, DELAG (Deutsche Luftschiffahrts-Aktiengesellschaft, or German Airship Transportation Corporation Ltd.) was established in 1909 and the world's first flight attendant, Heinrich Kubis, was employed by DELAG

The streamlined R-36 was the first British airship to carry a civil registration, G-FAAF. In 1921 there were no large passenger aircraft in existence that were capable of visiting the Channel Islands, but in the years following the First World War airships were considered a serious and viable alternative. A new airship such as the R-36 was capable of carrying 50 passengers and 28 crew as well as mail and freight by the ton. No aircraft could compete with this awesome capacity; even the largest aircraft was only capable of carrying a handful of passengers and they certainly did not enjoy the standards of comfort available in an airship.

and began serving Zeppelin passengers in March 1912. Between 1910 and the outbreak of the First World War in 1914, DELAG Zeppelins carried in excess of 34,000 passengers on over 1,500 flights.

The German Zeppelin LZ-120 *Bodensee* was one of two newly designed passenger Zeppelins that DELAG took delivery of post-war in August 1919, but before the second airship, LZ-121 *Nordstern*, could start an international service to Stockholm in 1920, both airships were confiscated as war reparations by the Allies and DELAG was forced to cease operations.

Captain, Flight Lieutenant A. H. Wann, took the R-36 on a two-hour maiden flight over Glasgow and Renfrew on 1st April 1921 and the next day she made her delivery flight to her new base at Pulham in Norfolk where she moored to her mooring mast.

In Britain, in 1917, the airship R-36 had been designed by the Admiralty for military purposes, but after long delays in construction, her design was changed, and she was completed in 1921 for the Air Ministry as Britain's first passenger-carrying airship. She had the capability of carrying 50 passengers in luxury. The only other new passenger airships flying at the time were the confiscated Zeppelins, LZ-120 *Bodensee* and LZ-121 *Nordstern*, both of which could only accommodate twenty passengers. The unique and streamlined R-36 was the first British airship to carry a civil registration, G-FAAF.

The airships were not balloons; they were termed 'dirigibles'. The dirigible had a metal skeleton structure over which was affixed a waterproofed fabric skin. Inside this structure were walkways and ladders giving access to all parts of the airship as well as to hatches that permitted the riggers to access the exterior, and the engineers to enter the engine pods that hung below the hull. Contained within the structure were envelopes for the hydrogen lifting gas, containers for water ballast and sometimes accommodation areas for the crew. The steering deck and passenger gondola hung below the ship and this permitted passengers the 'luxury of smoking' as they were far away from the highly inflammable gas envelopes.

The design for the R-36 airship was a 'stretched' version of a captured Zeppelin, the ZL-48. To attain more lift she was given an added gas bay of some 33 feet; this gave her a more sleek line and a total length of 672 ft with a diameter of 78ft 9in. Her maximum speed was 65 mph and she had a cruising speed of 50 mph. The R-36 was built at the Beardmore works near Glasgow and she was launched at 15.00 hours on 1st April 1921.

The Visit of the R-36 to Jersey

On 10th June 1921, the R-36 was loaded at Pulham for an endurance test flight and at 22.00 hours in the evening the airship slipped her mast and made her way south-west towards London. Early the next morning she altered course for Southampton and by 04.00 hours was passing over Portsmouth. The airship climbed to 3,500 feet, headed out over the Solent and set a course towards the Channel Islands, the first airship from England to have ever done this. The passengers in the airship's gondola could see France some 21 miles away, and after crossing the English Channel, Sark was seen just two miles away to starboard. The impressive cigar-shaped hull was first observed in the islands at 08.30 hours on the morning of 11th June as she slowly crossed Jersey making for St. Helier. She hovered motionless over the town before heading off towards St. Brelade and out to sea in a south-west direction.

The R-36 left Jersey and headed for Lands End in Cornwall, then over Devon and on to Bristol. She took advantage of a following wind and flew to Oxford and Hertfordshire and then Cambridgeshire and into Suffolk, finally arriving at Pulham at 01.05 hours the next day. At 04.00 hours on 12th June the R-36 was secured to her mast. The R-36's visit to Jersey had been an epic voyage completed with considerable ease over mixed conditions of land and sea. She had been in the air for 29 hours and 54 minutes, of which 446 miles were over land and 288 miles over the sea, giving a total of 734 miles. The arrival of R-36 over Jersey aroused speculation as to the reason for its journey, but hopes of an airship service to the island were seriously unfounded. A major drawback for passengers flying in the R-36 was that entry to the airship was through the nose and down a walkway along the internal keel of the craft and then down a ladder into the gondola. To gain access to the nose meant a climb of 120 feet up a ladder on the mooring mast in the open air and few sane people would be willing to attempt that in the winds of Jersey even if a location could be found to build such a mooring mast.

The unannounced arrival of the airship early in the morning had taken the residents of Jersey by surprise and as her sojourn over St. Helier was brief, it was thought there was no photographic record of the visit, until 2013 when a remarkable real photographic postcard was discovered, taken by the famous Jersey photographer Albert Smith, of the R-36 passing over Fort Regent. It is possible that other photographs by Smith and other photographers exist and are yet to be found.

The Demise of the R-36

For any airship, the most vulnerable times were when approaching the mooring mast and when entering or leaving their hangars; this was certainly the case for the R-36. On 21st June after returning from another trial flight she dropped her mooring rope that was then safely secured to the mast, but her approach was too quick and the rope fouled the bottom of the mast. The airship was jerked to a halt with such a force that two of the forward emergency ballast bags released their water and the bow of the airship shot up into the air with so much momentum that when her cable halted her ascent the bow collapsed. The ground crew managed to ease her down, but as the wind was building up it was decided to walk her into a shed as quickly as possible. As the crew tried to manoeuvre the R-36, a sudden gust of wind slammed her into the shed doors causing further damage to her port side amidships. Although not known at the time, the R-36 had made her last flight.

In 1921 the British Airship Scheme was under review and it was decided to leave the R-36 in the hangar and put off making any repairs until a new policy was formulated. With a revival as the Imperial Airship Scheme in 1924, it was thought that the R-36 could be used for testing the new Empire routes and a grant of £13,800 was made to have the ship refurbished. A replacement outer cover was put on the airship, the work was finished in August 1925, and the ship was due to fly in October of that year, but the flight was cancelled when it was recalculated that the airship did not have enough disposable lift to fly the length of the new route. Current design concepts were for even larger airships and the eight-year-old R-36 no longer fitted the latest requirements.

The R-36 remained in her hangar until June 1926 when it was finally decided that the ship should be scrapped and so she was dismantled. In her nine-year life, the longest journey that the R-36 made was her trip to Jersey in 1921.

VISIT OF AN RAF FELIXSTOWE F5 FLYING BOAT TO JERSEY

Shortly before noon on Friday 30th September 1921 a Felixtowe F5 flying boat circled over St. Aubin's Bay and the town of St. Helier before landing outside the harbour pier heads. She then taxied into the harbour and berthed in London Bay. The significance of this visit was initially exaggerated as Islanders hoped that this was the start of an air passenger service to England, and the *Jersey Evening Post* of the 30th September headed a small account with: "Arrival of Passengers by Air". The report continued:

> Shortly after midday to-day a large sea-plane arrived in the island, and after hovering about over the town for some time and circling about, alighted just outside the pier heads. It was then ascertained that she carried several passengers, who immediately on landing, drove off in motor cars.
>
> This, we think, is the first time on record that passengers have arrived here by air.

A less sensational and more accurate account was given the following day by the *Jersey Morning News* of 1st October 1921 under the headline:

FLYING BOAT VISITS JERSEY.
~~~
NO PASSENGERS ON BOARD.
</div>

This exceedingly rare photograph by Jersey photographer Albert Smith of the RAF Felixstowe F5, N4837, *Regulus* in St. Helier Harbour has the erroneous caption: "PASSENGER SEAPLANE AT JERSEY LEAVING ST HELIER HARBOUR SEP – 30 – 1921". This contributed to the mistaken belief that Jersey was about to have an air service to England.

Any Service man who had seen flying boats in the recent Great War would have recognised that this was not a civil aircraft, but an RAF machine carrying the Service recognition number N4837 and named *Regulus*.

N4837 would have probably been recognised in Guernsey as an RAF Felixstowe as a few earlier versions, notably the F3, had visited the French seaplane base in St. Peter Port Harbour during the First World War, but there had only been one fleeting visit of a Felixstowe F3 to Jersey on 21st July 1918.

N4837 had left RAF Calshot at 10.30 hours on the Friday morning for a navigation instruction tour, en route passing over Alderney and Guernsey before completing the crossing to Jersey in less than 90 minutes, arriving off St. Helier shortly before noon. The pilot, Flying Officer Hackney, flew around St. Aubin's Bay looking for a suitable landing place and his intention was to then secure to a buoy near the pier heads, but as one could not be found he decided to taxi into the harbour and berth in London Bay. The machine naturally attracted a large group of spectators including the *Jersey Morning News* journalist who interviewed

Regulus based at RAF Calshot on the Solent was a Felixstowe F5 built by Short and Co. with a wingspan of 96 feet, two 12-cylinder 250 hp Rolls-Royce Eagle engines and a maximum carrying capacity of 4,250 lbs with space for seven aircrew. The Felixstowe F5 was the last in a line of 'Felixstowes' named after the RNAS station at Felixstowe where flying boats were developed during the First World War. The prototype of the F5 appeared in 1918, but the production aircraft was too late to see operational service but became the standard RAF post-war service flying boat until replaced by the Supermarine Southampton in 1925.

the pilot, and a large group of schoolboys who quickly "divested themselves of boots and stockings" and waded into the sea to get a closer look at the craft.

The crew consisted of five British officers and one Japanese officer under training with the RAF. When the pilot had completed his interview with the *Morning News* journalist, the crew toured the town and ate lunch ashore before re-boarding the Felixstowe and leaving the harbour at 15.00 hours. They once again made a low pass over the town before heading north to return to their base at Calshot. The Felixstowe F5 was the largest plane to be seen in the islands and attracted much excitement and interest from the general population. The *Jersey Evening Post* for Monday 3rd October recorded a frightening incident when shop assistants of Woolworth Stores clambered onto the roof of the store to get a better view of the flying boat flying over the town on Friday. One of the girls who was watching the seaplane, "not heeding where she was walking, inadvertently stepped through a glass skylight". Although she sustained some rather nasty cuts on her legs, the report states that she "was otherwise more frightened than hurt."

This was to be the first of many navigational training flights over the next two decades made by seaplanes from RAF Calshot to the Channel Islands; the route afforded a long sea crossing without entering foreign air space and a safe British haven at the end of the flight.

TWO RAF FLYING BOATS VISIT JERSEY AND GUERNSEY

Four years after the Great War, the skies over the Channel Islands remained steadfastly silent. In 1922 even an RAF flight was only recorded on one occasion, albeit with two aircraft.

Felixstowe F5 Flying Boats from RAF Calshot often flew in formations of two or more craft. Two Felixstowe F 5s, numbered N4833 and N4683 (or possibly N4638), set off from RAF Calshot together at 10.00 hours on 29th May 1922 heading for Jersey and Guernsey to check the mooring facilities available for seaplanes of their huge dimensions. N4833 landed in Jersey waters outside St. Helier Harbour at 12.00 hours with Squadron Leader John C. Quinnel, D.F.C. in charge, and Flying Officer S. E. Adams piloting the F 5, while the radio operator and the engineer were Flight Lieutenants A. W. Biles and T. Q. Studd. The crew were all experienced and decorated fliers with distinguished service during the Great War. The second F 5 followed closely behind N4833 and after circling the town, also put down on the water outside the harbour. Flying Officer Adams manoeuvred his craft through the pier heads into the harbour, but was unable to find an adequate mooring buoy so resorted to his own anchors to secure his craft. Squadron Leader Quinnel ordered his radio officer to inform N4683 that navigation in and out of the harbour was too dangerous for the F 5s and as there was a lack of proper mooring facilities in the harbour he ordered the second craft to continue on to Guernsey. N4683 took off again at 13.05 hours for Guernsey, but as there are no further records for this second craft we do not know how successful her mission was. During the First World War Felixstowe F 3 seaplanes visited the French seaplane base in St. Peter Port Harbour, so we might safely assume that this second craft found adequate mooring facilities in Guernsey.

After the departure of their sister craft for Guernsey, the officers of N4833 went ashore and had lunch at the Grand Hotel in St. Helier and remained overnight. The next morning they made an inspection of the facilities in the harbour and Squadron Leader Quinnel advised the States Officials that a buoy that could hold up to 25 tons was urgently required for any future visits by military seaplanes, as well as for any commercial flying boat service that might be established in years to come. Having fulfilled their mission, the crew of N4833 embarked on the flying boat and departed Jersey waters at 12.30 hours to safely return to RAF Calshot.

A pair of Felixtowe flying boats.

THE FIRST SCHEDULED AIR PASSENGER SERVICE

Sea Eagles from Southampton

Guernsey was honoured as the first Channel Island to have a regular scheduled air service to the UK mainland in 1923, but the inauguration of the service was inauspicious while unreliability destroyed any notion of it being 'regular' or 'scheduled'. The domestic civil aviation industry was a low priority for His Majesty's Government that had faith in the existing comprehensive rail network in Britain, but in 1922 the Air Ministry issued a communiqué proposing a cross-Channel seaplane service from Southampton to Cherbourg and Le Havre. The objectives were to shorten the journey time for passengers and mail on the transatlantic steamer journey to London by flying them to and from Cherbourg, and to reduce the journey time of passengers on the London to Paris route via Southampton and Le Havre by replacing the Southampton to Le Havre steamer journey with a seaplane. An afterthought was to extend the service to the Channel Islands!

On 23rd March 1923 the British Marine Air Navigation Co. Ltd. had been registered as a private company with the declared aim:

> to establish, maintain and operate an air-service of seaworthy flying boats and flying boat 'Amphibian' aircraft between Southampton, Le Havre, Cherbourg and the Channel Islands.

G-EBFX was the first Sea Eagle to be built for B.M.A.N.Co. by the Supermarine Aviation Works Ltd. based at Woolston on the River Itchen. She was a single-engine biplane with wing spans of 46 ft and an all-up weight of 6,050 lbs The 360 hp Rolls Royce Eagle IX engine had a pusher propeller that gave a maximum speed of 93 mph; the fuel was gravity fed from tanks in the top wing. The pilot and his co-pilot, if there was one, sat in the open, while six passengers could be accommodated in a covered cabin in the boat like hull. As this cabin was forward of the engine, the passengers were seated reasonably comfortably and could almost hear each other speak! The Sea Eagle was the first amphibian design for designer R. J. Mitchell; he would be more famous for his Schneider Trophy winning aircraft and his world famous 'Supermarine Spitfire'. Because of their involvement in the Schneider Trophy air race, the Supermarine Aviation Works Ltd. were late delivering the Sea Eagles and the first to be built, G-EBFK, only received its certificate of airworthiness on 11th July 1923. The B.M.A.N.Co. colour scheme for the new aircraft was a brown hull with silver wings.

B.M.A.N.Co., as it was popularly abreviated, was the founding company of an association of the Supermarine Aviation Works Ltd., designers and suppliers of the new flying boats, and the Asiatic Petroleum Co. Ltd. who would be exclusive suppliers of all petrol and lubricating oils at the various ports of call. At the end of April, the *Observer* and the *Daily Telegraph* forecasted a 1st June start date for the Channel Islands service, flying a triangular route from Southampton to Cherbourg (83 miles), Cherbourg to Guernsey (42 miles), and Guernsey to Southampton (105 miles). Agricultural freight from the Channel Islands was important to the success of the venture as it would allow fresh produce to reach Covent Garden in London within six hours of picking in Guernsey, as opposed to 48 hours by sea and rail. B.M.A.N.Co. ordered three new amphibian 'Supermarine Sea Eagles' from Supermarine Aviation Works Ltd. that were specially designed for the cross Channel service. The Supermarine Aviation Works Ltd. based at Woolston on the Solent, had evolved from the aircraft company Pemberton-Billings Ltd.; its telegraphic address was "Supermarine". The eccentric founder of the company Noel Pemberton-Billing declared, "I will design boats that fly rather than aeroplanes that float". This certainly described the Supermarine Sea Eagle with its sea-going cabin cruiser, high-prow hull, looking more suitable for the Norfolk Broads than the English Channel.

Customs and immigration facilities for the new international flights were to be at Southampton Docks, but this was not feasible as the Docks were partly owned by the Southern Railway who were a rival of B.M.A.N.Co.. Thus, a further delay occurred while a new base was constructed beside the slipway at Woolston.

An imposing two storey 'V' shaped building housed an enquiry and booking office, a passenger waiting room, pilot's rest room, wireless room and various company offices as well as a private room for the port doctor, passport and customs offices and a baggage and bonded storeroom. When the Woolston base of B.M.A.N.Co. was finally completed with its own customs and immigration facilities it was the world's first international 'seadrome'.

The new Director-General of Civil Aviation, Sir Sefton Brancker, who was to die

B.M.A.N.Co. Seadrome at Woolston.

horrifically seven years later in the inferno of the R101 Airship disaster, toured the Supermarine Aviation Works at Woolston on 5th August and was taken on a two-hour flight in the new Sea Eagle, G-EBFK. The pilot for the flight was Captain Henri Biard, Supermarine's chief test pilot and the first pilot to be employed by B.M.A.N.Co. On 11th August 1923 the Air Council announced a grant of £10,000 for a Cherbourg and Channel Islands service subject to an annual minimum mileage of 60,000 miles being achieved by the operating airline. The Air Council would also contribute 50 per cent of the cost, up to £21,000, towards the provision of new aircraft for the project.

On 14th August 1923 Sir Sefton Brancker chartered the Sea Eagle to fly him in the cockpit with Henri Biard, while Sir Francis Shelmerdine and Mr Hubert Scott-Paine, Managing Director of B.M.A.N.Co., and an Air Ministry official occupied the forward cabin, on a flight to Cherbourg for an aviation meeting at Vauville. In the afternoon they flew to St. Peter Port where the seaplane moored to a buoy overnight off the Great Western steamer berth. The next day the party made a fifteen-minute flight to Jersey to have lunch at Government House with the Lieutenant-Governor and attend a conference in the afternoon at the Chamber of Commerce with aviation-minded Jersey businessmen. When the party was ready to return to Woolston, the departure of the Sea Eagle from St. Helier Harbour was blocked by the Southern Railway steamer *Alberta* lying in the Roads waiting for the tide to allow her to berth. Whether this was a deliberate act by the rival transport company remains debatable but eventually at 18.15 hours, Captain Biard was able to taxi G-EBFK out of the harbour where she rose sharply into the air to arrive safely back at Woolston at 20.45 hours. These flights on 14th and 15th August had been the first proving flights of a Sea Eagle to Cherbourg, Guernsey and Jersey and some reports, including the Air Council's own Annual Report, heralded it as the start date for the new Southampton to Guernsey service. This was the first and only time that B.M.A.N.Co. ever flew to Cherbourg and the extension of the service to Le Havre appears to have been completely forgotten, so the originally declared aims of the new airline were never to be fulfilled.

Sea Eagle G-EBFK taxiing on its charter flight to Cherbourg.

B.M.A.N.Co. advert in the *Southampton Docks Magazine* of Sept. 1923.

The First Scheduled Air Passenger Service

The first 'commercial flight' with a fare-paying passenger, (there was only one!), took place on 24th August when G-EBFK left Woolston at 14.15 hours and arrived at a buoy off Cambridge Pier in St. Peter Port Harbour at 16.50 hours to be met by a motor launch to bring the passenger and crew ashore at the steps near the Weighbridge. There were more crew than passengers on this flight because the pilot Henri Biard was accompanied by Flight-Lieut. Frank J. Bailey, who was to become one of the regular pilots on the Channel Islands route. Two passengers boarded for the flight back to Woolston at 18.00 hours. The next commercial flight to Guernsey was not for another week, on 31st August, and the first commercial flight to Jersey took place the following day on 1st September, again with only one fare-paying passenger, although for the return journey there were three passengers each of whom had paid a fare of £3-18s-0d to fly to the mainland. These arrivals and departures were a cause of great excitement and crowds gathered whenever the Sea Eagle was sighted landing off the harbours, but the arrivals were still a rarity and the promised daily service was yet to materialise. There were several legitimate reasons why the regular service could not start; the facilities at Woolston were not yet completed, the two pilots employed by B.M.A.N.Co. needed to get accustomed to the ports, bad weather and rough seas would interrupt the service and there was only one aircraft flying the service as the Supermarine Aviation Works Ltd. had still not delivered the remaining two Sea Eagles.

B.M.A.N.Co. finally took delivery of the second and third Sea Eagles (G-EBGR and G-EBGS) on 2nd October and G-EBGR made her maiden flight to Guernsey on the same day piloted by Frank Bailey and carrying 90 lbs of the *Daily Sketch* newspapers.

On 13th October G-EBGS, flown by Henri Biard, made her maiden flight to Guernsey accompanied by G-EBGR, piloted by Bailey. They were the intended stars of an official inauguration ceremony of the new "daily" service between Southampton and Guernsey, but G-EBGR had engine trouble on the flight from Southampton which delayed her arrival at the ceremony.

The fiasco of the naming ceremony was followed by a disastrous attempt to fly back to Woolston when both seaplanes were nearly lost. *Flight* magazine of 18th October 1923 gave an amazingly blasé account of what was actually a very serious incident:

> On Saturday afternoon Cpt. F. J. Bailey, accompanied by a mechanic named Linsdale, left St. Peter Port, Guernsey, on the return trip to Southampton. Capt. H. C. Biard, with five passengers and a mechanic, followed on a second machine two minutes later. When about five miles off Alderney, Bailey's machine (G-EBGR) was compelled to descend owing to engine trouble. Seeing his colleague's plight, Biard also descended, with the object of rendering assistance. Being unable to give help, however, and observing that the other machine was riding the water well in spite of a very choppy sea, Biard decided to put back to Guernsey, which was accomplished safely. Shortly after, a motor

A double Christening had been planned for the two seaplanes, but in the event only G-EBGS was photographed officially being named *Sarnia*, the old name for Guernsey. G-EBGR that had arrived too late for the ceremony and would have probably been given the old Jersey name, *Caesarea*, was forevermore confusingly called *Sea Eagle*; this was bizarre as all three planes were Sea Eagles. G-EBFK failed to make the flight to Guernsey because at this time B.M.A.N.Co. still only had two pilots, and consequently never received a name.

boat was sent off to assist the other machine, which in the meantime had cast out a sea-anchor and was patiently awaiting help. Bailey fired S.O.S. signals at intervals, and after five hours, during which time the machine rode the rough sea in fine style, the motor boat Lita rescued the captain and "crew" and towed the machine, safely and undamaged into Alderney Harbour.

The incident was much more dramatic. When the Sea Eagles left Guernsey, it was late in the day and a gale was blowing up. The pilots were concerned about G-EBGR's engine which was still giving trouble so Linsdale the mechanic flew with Bailey while five passengers along with another mechanic were on board *Sarnia*. As they flew between Alderney and the Casquets, G-EBGR's engine completely failed forcing Bailey to take to the water. The sea was rough, but initially the plane was safe in the lee of some large rocks off the Casquets. They deployed a sea-anchor, but this could not stop them from drifting into the open heavy seas. Biard flew low to see if he could help, but the seas were too dangerous for him to attempt a landing and he flew to Alderney, managing to land in the shelter of Braye Harbour. Biard learned that Alderney did not have a boat strong enough to make the Casquets in the gale and so decided that he would return to Guernsey for help.

Braye Harbour was too small for *Sarnia* to attain lift off, so Biard had to take her out into the rough water to get airborne. That was when disaster struck. A fifteen-foot-high wave hit *Sarnia* as she was taking off, bouncing her 40 feet into the air. She had not attained flying speed so crashed down onto the crest of the next wave before being bounced into the air again when she was finally able to lift herself into the air. When Biard, who was sitting in his open cockpit in the raging gale, was able to survey the damage, he found that a wing tip float had been smashed off along with all the under surface of the plane, the ribs were naked, and some were splintered or broken, and part of the tail plane was lost. The cabin was a scene of total devastation with all the passengers thrown to the floor and one of them unconscious. Biard eventually managed to get *Sarnia* back to Guernsey and the relative calm of St. Peter Port where she landed with the mechanic lying

A dramatic illustration in *The Graphic* magazine of 20th October 1923 fails to adequately depict the serious peril that the two Sea Eagles were in during the gale on 13th October 1923.

on the wing to make sure that wing tip float hit the water first. Meanwhile G-EBGR continued to drift for hours between the treacherous rock outcrops of the Casquets being battered by the heavy seas, while all the pilot and mechanic could do was fire off Verey lights at regular intervals in the hope that a ship would find them. A Southern Railway cargo boat, alerted by Biard, set off from Guernsey in an attempt to locate the seaplane but failed; eventually the motor launch *Lita* from Alderney found them in the vicinity of Les Etacs. After a very difficult manoeuvre in which their borrowed punt capsized, the crew of *Lita* managed to get a line onto the seaplane and tow her into Longis Bay on Alderney where they waited for calmer seas before being towed round to Braye Harbour.

On Monday 15th October Bailey managed to fly G-EBGR back to Guernsey where the engine was overhauled, and she eventually made it back to Woolston on 17th October. G-EBGS *Sarnia* was not as lucky because she was completely out of action. She was pulled up onto the careening hard in St. Peter Port, but the damage was too great for repairs to be made on the island. She remained there looking a very sorry sight until the end of the month when she was shipped back to Southampton for a refit at Woolston. The

G-EBGR in calm waters at Woolston.

original Sea Eagle, the un-named G-EBFK, was the only plane left available to keep the newly inaugurated service going throughout October. A daily service was attempted in November when Captain Bailey made frequent trips to Guernsey, weather and fog permitting. On 30th November a double crossing to Guernsey of the two Sea Eagles, G-EBGR and G-EBGS *Sarnia* was made, and this was *Sarnia's* first crossing since the disaster of her christening day. This time the two seaplanes returned home without mishap. In December the service became purely 'on demand'. It was advertised in both Guernsey and Jersey that a seaplane would be arriving on 7th December carrying copies of the *Daily News* and *Daily Sketch* featuring results of the mainland General Election, but none put in an appearance, probably hampered yet again by the weather.

Both Bailey and Biard flew Sea Eagles to Guernsey in January 1924, but there was little demand for the service and the pilots often found themselves stormbound for days either in St. Peter Port or at Woolston. February saw little improvement until the second half of the month when a strike by dockers increased business considerably and a new pilot was appointed, Captain John H. Horsey, who made his first flight to Guernsey on 22nd February.

Freight

The speedy transportation of fresh Island produce was always considered the major contributor to the success of the service, but as most flights had taken place in winter out of the growing season, B.M.A.N.Co. benefited very little from this market. The first commercial merchandise to pass through customs was a consignment of hams from a company in Bath that was flown to Guernsey on 5th September

A private snapshot of Sea Eagle G-EBGS, *Sarnia*, exiting St. Peter Port Harbour in 1923.

1923. Frank Bailey carried 90 lbs of newspapers on the maiden flight of G-EBGR on 2nd October, but it was not until the dockers strike in February 1924 that the Sea Eagles started to regularly carry the London newspapers to Guernsey; the first time ever that residents of the islands were able to read a mainland newspaper on the day of publication. On Saturday 23rd February two Sea Eagles carried a large consignment of newspapers to the island and on Sunday 24th one returned to Woolston with the very first consignment of fresh produce carried by air from Guernsey, it consisted of 54 boxes of flowers and two packages of beans. Unfortunately, the unreliability of the service meant that it could never be considered for the transportation of the mails. The weather and mechanical problems continued to hamper flights in March. On 2nd March a Sea Eagle piloted by Horsey was almost swamped when attempting take-off and had to return to St. Peter Port Harbour to try again the following day. G-EBGR arrived in Guernsey on 4th March only to be immediately taken out of service because of more engine problems. The following day she was hoisted out of the water on to the dock side where on 8th March a new engine was fitted. She finally managed to return to Woolston in the afternoon of 10th March. Fog continued to disrupt flights for the rest of the month and the local press reported that the Sea Eagles arrived or departed from Guernsey on only sixteen days during the month.

As with the first flight of the service, the last flight of the Woolston – Guernsey service also passed ignominiously unrecorded. Just a year after it was registered as a Company, the British Marine Air Navigation Co. Ltd. ceased to exist at midnight on 31st March 1924 when it was replaced on 1st April by the newly amalgamated and H.M. Government sponsored giant, Imperial Airways Ltd..

The only known commercial photographic postcard of a Sea Eagle in B.M.A.N.Co. colours is this example produced by "The Regent Series".

A FRENCH NAVAL SEAPLANE EMERGENCY LANDING IN JERSEY

The entrance to the Centre d'Aviation Maritime de Cherbourg with a Georges Levy G.L. 40 HB2 hydro aeroplane on the slipway. Although constructed by Georges Levy, the aircraft was designed in 1917 by Blanchard and Le Pen and was also known as a Levy-Le Pen. She was a three-seated biplane hydroplane with a length of 40 ft 8 in., a wingspan of 60 ft 8 in. and a height of 12 ft 7½ in. Her powerplant was a Renault 12Fe v-12 pusher engine of 300 hp that could achieve a maximum speed of 90 mph and a cruising speed of 71 mph over a range of 248 miles. She had a crew of three and an armament of one machine gun and a 440 lb load of bombs.

At the beginning of August 1923, Georges Levy G.L. 40 HB2 hydro aeroplanes from the Centre d'Aviation Maritime de Cherbourg had been engaged for eleven days in aerial manoeuvres and exercises along the Brittany coast in the area of the Côtes-du-Nord, now more romantically renamed the Côtes-d'Amor, west of St. Malo. On Tuesday 14th August the pilots were intending to return to base, but fog forced a stopover in St. Malo until Thursday 16th August. Thursday dawned bright and clear with perfect flying conditions, good visibility and light cloud on a westerly breeze across a choppy sea. At 10.30 hours three aircraft set off, their assents off the water at Saint Servan passed without mishap but one of the craft, officially identified as C-35, was experiencing vibration due to corrosion of one of the blades of its propeller. C-35 was in the charge of a crew of three with 'Aspirant' Chupin as Pilot Aviator, 'Seconde Maitre' Le Bozec as Observer and 'Matelot' Entzmann as Mechanic. As they passed over Les Minquiers, the large group of rocky islands 9.3 miles south of Jersey but part of the Balliwick, C-35 was flying at an altitude of 1,650 ft when her engine started to behave erratically, and the revolutions dropped dramatically. Low tide at Les Minquiers exposes an area of rocky outcrops greater than the total surface area of the landmass of the island of Jersey; it is an extreme hazard for shipping and not an area where a seaplane could land. Thankfully, the engine stabilised and C-35 managed to clear Les Minquiers.

The crew hoped that they could continue to Cherbourg without further mishap, but a few minutes later when they were about three miles south-east of Jersey another mechanical fault developed resulting in an appreciable loss of power and speed. Pilot Chupin maintained a controlled descent passing below one of his accompanying aircraft, C-44, but its crew were totally unaware of the emergency developing beneath them. Chupin headed for the sheltered waters of St. Aubin's Bay passing over the Noirmont headland at an altitude of barely 160 ft. He safely put down on the water close to the beach at 11.35 hours before taxiing ashore immediately below Millbrook railway station. The crew examined the engine and soon discovered an overheating induction pipe and faulty connectors. They were able to accomplish these repairs on the spot, but a more exhaustive check identified problems with the magnetos that they could not rectify on the beach. Pilot Officer Chupin and Seaman Entzmann proceeded into town to locate the French Vice-Consulate and telegraph their Cherbourg base, while Second Mate Le Bozec was left to guard the craft.

The middle of August is the height of the tourist season in Jersey and very soon large crowds were hurrying along the sands to see what they thought was the return of the 'Sea Eagle' that had visited the island the previous day. As word spread more spectators were attracted to the stricken craft, many conveniently arriving by train at Millbrook Station from St. Helier and St. Aubin. The mob crowded round the aircraft and one local resident clambered on to the fuselage of the craft with a lit cigarette in his mouth, completely oblivious of the vapours seeping from the damaged engine and unaware that the craft was carrying thirty gallons of aviation fuel. The agitated screams of Second Mate Le Bozec alerted the smoker who rapidly descended from the craft, averting a tragedy.

An element of farce now entered the narrative. When Pilot Officer Chupin and Seaman Entzmann arrived at the French Vice-Consulate the building was locked as Thursday was a holiday; the Consul was staying in France and nobody knew where a responsible consular officer might be found. The French aviators went to York Street Police Station to enlist the help of the island police, but it was not until after four o'clock in the afternoon that a consular official was finally located who undertook to telegraph the Centre d'Aviation Maritime de Cherbourg and alert them to the situation and also arrange accommodation for the crew overnight in the Finsbury Hotel on the Weighbridge. Before they received the telegraph from the consular official, senior officers at Cherbourg base despatched a search and rescue party of two seaplanes, C-41 and C-46, to retrace the route from Cherbourg to St. Malo in an attempt to locate missing C-35. While skirting the Jersey coastline the search party observed the craft safe on the St. Aubin sands. Signals passed between the disabled craft and the search party and when they ascertained that the crew were also safe, the rescue craft flew back to base. As Chupin and Entzmann were returning to Millbrook Station they watched the search aircraft making their passes along the beach, but they were of course unable to communicate with them. When they re-joined Second Mate Le Bozec waiting on the sands with the stricken craft it was decided that each would take it in turn to guard the craft throughout the night. Later that evening Pilot Officer Chupin was honoured with an invitation to visit the Lieutenant-Governor of Jersey.

On Friday 17th August further efforts by the crew to repair the aircraft engine proved in vain and a telegram was sent to the Cherbourg base requesting a naval tug to tow C-35 back to base. French Naval Tug *Chasseur 55* was despatched from Cherbourg and arrived off Jersey at 16.45 hours locating the position of the stricken craft from a red flare fired by the crew. The tug docked in St. Helier Harbour where Pilot Officer Chupin reported to Lieutenant de Vaisseau Remusat on board and apprised him of the situation. The weather had deteriorated, and it was decided not to attempt to attach a towline that evening but unfortunately the unsettled weather continued throughout the Saturday and thwarted any attempt of recovery. On Sunday 19th August the seas were calmer, and the crew were able to re-float the craft with the aid of rollers and planks and a tow from *Chasseur 55*. The tug towed C-35 into St. Helier Harbour at 13.25 hours and the crew set about making her secure for the journey back to Cherbourg. On Monday their departure was defeated again by the weather and Lieutenant Remusat ordered the stripping of the canvas from the wing framework to reduce the wind resistance when the craft was under tow. Tuesday 21st August was a calmer day and *Chasseur 55* weighed anchor with C-35 in tow, but her problems were not yet over. On manoeuvring out of the harbour her port wing was damaged striking the pier head and then during the voyage the towline broke and she was only saved by an emergency dragline. She eventually made Cherbourg at 15.30 hours without further mishap. On proper inspection, her damage proved not to be extensive and she was back in service four days later.

Two holiday snapshots of C-35 stranded on the sands of St. Aubin's Bay.

IMPERIAL AIRWAYS FLYING TO THE CHANNEL ISLANDS

The Birth of Imperial Airways Ltd

In August 1923 the British Marine Air Navigation Co. Ltd. had been awarded a £10,000 subsidy for the UK to Cherbourg and Channel Islands air service, but the Air Council soon realised that developing air services with hand to mouth subsidies was not the way to proceed. Sir Herbert Hambling, deputy-chairman of Barclay's Bank and the Ocean Marine Insurance Company, was asked to head up a committee to advise on the development and financing of civil aviation. The Hambling Committee recommended that from the existing cross-Channel airlines a single airline should be formed with an H.M. Government guaranteed capital of one million pounds with nominees on the governing board. The resulting monopoly airline was virtually state nationalised, even if it was registered as a public limited company and sought shareholders. On 3rd December 1923 a merger agreement was signed by the four cross-Channel airlines; Handley Page Transport Ltd., Instone Air Line Ltd., Daimler Hire Ltd. and the British Marine Air Navigation Co. Ltd.. The name suggested by the Hambling Committee for the new airline was British Air Transport Service with a launch day of 1st April 1924. Fortunately, somebody noticed that the airline acronym was 'BATS', and the start date was April Fool's Day! A new name would be decided before the company was formally registered.

The terms of the merger agreement were published on 28th December and included:

> ...a Heavier-than-Air Air Transport Company to be called the Imperial Air Transport Co. Ltd.... should operate an efficient air service...between London and Paris, London and Brussels, London and Amsterdam, and Southampton and the Channel Islands or such other places ...",

and that the air service:

> "between Southampton and the Channel Islands, or alternative places respectively, shall be operated by sea-going marine aircraft...".

The airline eventually employed nineteen pilots from the pre-amalgamation companies including two of the original B.M.A.N.Co. pilots, Frank J. Bailey (left) and John H. Horsey (right); the third Henri Biard, returned to Supermarine Aviation Works Ltd. as a test pilot. Imperial Airways produced postcards of their aircraft and signed postcard portraits of each pilot, awarding them the charisma of film stars.

The emphasis on "sea-going marine aircraft", but the vagueness of the actual route and destination indicates that pioneering a regular air service to the Channel Islands was less important than gathering data on the value of seaplanes for civil airline purposes.

The agreement came into force on 1st April 1924, with the airline named Imperial Airways Ltd., but there were no celebratory inaugural flights because the new airline had no pilots! The proposed new terms and conditions for the pilots were much less generous than with their previous companies and none of the pilots would sign them; they were effectively on strike. The dispute lasted until the beginning of May during which time no aircraft flew for the new Imperial Airways.

Imperial Airways Ltd. paid compensation to the amalgamated airlines but inherited their assets. For B.M.A.N.Co. these included the seadrome at Woolston, an office at 1 Glategny Esplanade in Guernsey, a new passenger launch, *Laura*, and two of the Sea Eagles, G-EBGR and G-EBGS valued at £5,600 each. The original prototype Sea Eagle, G-EBFK, is not listed in the acquiring assets and as its registration was cancelled on 21st May 1924 it was probably dismantled for spares during the last days of B.M.A.N.Co. to keep the other two Sea Eagles flying.

The Hambling Committee required that all the acquired aircraft undergo a thorough overhaul before they could fly for Imperial Airways, so when the month-long dispute was resolved there was a fleet of newly refurbished aircraft immediately available to commence services. During their refurbishment the two Sea Eagles were repainted in the Imperial colours of a blue hull and white wings with the name 'IMPERIAL AIRWAYS Ltd' emblazoned in white on each side of the prow.

The Imperial Airways timetable optimistically advertised two return trips every weekday for the Southampton to Guernsey route with one return flight on Sundays. Captain Horsey made the first Imperial Airways flight to Guernsey in G-EBGR on 1st May 1924 to position Office Manager, Mr Drury-Hudson, in the Guernsey office. Then on the 4th May, even though it was a Sunday, he commenced the regular passenger service with two return flights to Guernsey from Woolston. Monday 5th May saw one trip each made by Captains Bailey and Horsey and on Tuesday 6th May, Frank Bailey made his first double crossing in one day. It was not long however before mechanical failure and fog decimated the service. G-EBGR was out of action by 10 May and on 14th May Bailey, who was returning from St. Peter Port in G-EBGS, ran into fog in the Channel that was so dense he could not fly over it and had to land on the sea and 'cruise' back on the water to Woolston via the Needles.

The service limped on through June, July and August, but seldom with two Sea Eagles flying at the same time. There were no operations during September and October and although a new reduced service was advertised in October with only one return flight each day, the service was not actually resumed until 3rd November.

A decision was made to modify the Sea Eagles and fit them with more powerful 450 hp Napier Lion engines and larger top wings to give them a cruising speed of 90 mph with a maximum all-up weight of 6,500 lbs The extra 100 hp and modified wings would give them more lift and a shorter take-off run which it was hoped would be advantageous in the heavy winter seas off Guernsey. The capacity of the passenger cabin

Imperial Airways Sea Eagle G-EBGS exiting St. Peter Port Harbour at full throttle.

was also reduced from six to four; instead of six loose chairs there was now a comfortable double seat forward and two wicker armchairs.

G-EBGR was already installed with the new engine when she resumed the lapsed service on 3rd November, and she continued the service single handed throughout November and December while G-EBGS was being modified.

Captain Bailey made the first recorded visit of an Imperial Airways Sea Eagle to Jersey on 12th December when he flew direct to St. Helier with Air Council officials, but another official Air Council flight round Guernsey on 22nd December went disastrously wrong when Bailey forgot to wind in the trailing wire radio aerial of the Sea Eagle before landing. When the radio aerial's plumb weight hit the water, it rebounded into the spinning propeller with such force that it split the blades and put the Sea Eagle completely out of action. B.M.A.N.Co., during its short existence had made over 100 return trips to the Channel Islands, but in 1924 Imperial Airways had only managed to fly 73 passengers to Guernsey during its longer tenure and ended the year with both the Sea Eagles out of action.

Imperial Airways Sea Eagle G-EBGS resting on her buoy in St. Peter Port Harbour, Guernsey.

Lifting Sea Eagle G-EBGR from the water at Southampton for her modification.

1925 Silent Skies over the islands

Probably not since before the Great War was there a quieter time in the Channel Islands for aviation than in 1925. There were no visits by any Service aircraft and although Imperial Airways Ltd. still had a legal obligation to service the Channel Islands, the Sea Eagles were seldom seen.

A surprise announcement was made on 5th March that the service would be suspended indefinitely at the end of the month due to the expiration of the lease on the seadrome at Woolston that was owned by the Supermarine Aviation Company. A new seadrome

A superb Imperial Airways publicity photograph of Captain Bailey at the controls of the Sea Eagle G-EBGR. G-EBGR made her first appearance of the New Year on 5th January 1925 with a few more flights later in the month, but bad weather defeated her until 21st February when she visited both Guernsey and Jersey. She reappeared the following day but was again halted by gales.

would have to be built elsewhere on Southampton water. Drury-Hudson, the manager of the Guernsey Office closed the office and returned to the mainland. The service remained suspended and it was not until September 1925 that the Guernsey office was again opened with a new manager. A new Imperial Airways marine airport had been built at Durham Wharf on the River Itchen just south of the floating bridge and by the end of October, G-EBGS was finally refitted with her Napier Lion engine and ready to join G-EBGR on the service.

Captain Frank Bailey was now the manager of the new Durham Wharf Seadrome, but he was also now the only Imperial Airways flying boat pilot as John Horsey had transferred to the London to Paris route while the Sea Eagles were in hibernation. The reopened Guernsey service finally commenced on 11th November when Captain Bailey set out from Durham Wharf piloting the newly refurbished G-EBGS, but a snow blizzard forced him to return and the weather did not improve until 10th December when the Sea Eagle made its first appearance in Guernsey since 22nd February that year. According to States of Guernsey records, Imperial Airways carried three fare paying passengers in 1925!

London. That Imperial Airways were attempting to maintain a service for only four passengers a week confirmed the belief that the seaplane service to Guernsey was run purely for experimental reasons and to enable Imperial Airways to claim the Government subsidy. The new timetable was announced in January, but it was not until 24th February that Captain Bailey managed to make the first crossing of the year in G-EBGS, and with improved weather maintain the weekly service through March and April.

Britain's first General Strike was called by the TUC at midnight on 3rd May in support of a miners' strike and although it was called off on 12th May, the miners' strike continued into November. The dockers in Jersey and Guernsey supported the strike, but freight transport within the islands was uninterrupted. Imperial Airways saw an opportunity to develop a freight service to the islands and announced a "special flying boat" could be chartered for Guernsey or Jersey. The return flight to Jersey cost £48 and the seaplane could accommodate four passengers or 750lbs of freight. There is no record of a charter taking place during the strike, but tantalisingly there exists a photo postcard of a Sea Eagle moored to a buoy off the Great Western Railway berth in St. Helier Harbour, with the handwritten caption on the reverse stating: "The seaplane that went between England and the Channel Isles during the strike May to June 1926. Photographed in St. Helier Harbour".

The discrepancy in the end date for the strike quoted in the caption on the postcard may mean that the photo is actually of an emergency flight of G-EBGS piloted by Captain Bailey to St. Helier Harbour that took place on 17th May, just after the strike. Emergency and ambulance flights were to become a feature of Imperial Airways' services to the islands with this emergency charter to St. Helier being the first of several in the coming years.

1926

The new year of 1926 commenced with Imperial Airways Ltd. announcing that the recently re-inaugurated Southampton to Guernsey service would be reduced to one return journey a week on Wednesday mornings. The hope was that they would be able to maintain this 'regular service' now that the Sea Eagles were more powerful which in turn had shortened their flight time for the crossing by ten minutes to one hour and forty minutes. This new timetable was met with increased scepticism especially as there was no mention of a previously announced connecting flight to

Captain Bailey pilots G-EBGS through the pier-heads of St. Peter Port Harbour, Guernsey.

A Sea Eagle Emergency Flight, 17th May 1926

An eighteen-year-old Jersey girl, Miss Ena Single, who was an actress in London, was in a serious car accident on Sunday 16th May on the Great West Road near Hounslow when she was thrown from the 'dickey seat' of a Morris Cowley on a trip to Brighton. She received a compound fracture of the skull and her life was thought to be in the balance. An S.O.S. was broadcast at the end of the 6 o'clock evening news bulletin by the BBC requesting any known relatives of Miss Single to travel urgently to Hounslow Hospital. In Jersey the parents of the girl were informed of the S.O.S. broadcast and chartered a seaplane 'at the earliest opportunity' via Imperial Airways' Jersey agents, the Jersey General Engineering Co.. On Monday 17th May a gale was blowing hard in the Channel, but Captain Bailey brought G-EBGS to St. Helier in the late morning and then battled back across the Channel in the afternoon with the parents and a sister of Miss Single. Imperial Airways were granted special permission to land another machine at RAF Gosport which was the nearest airfield to the seadrome on the Itchen and as soon as the Sea Eagle landed, a waiting car rushed the three passengers to Gosport to board the waiting aircraft. An hour later they landed at Croydon Airport where they were whisked, this time by police car, to Hounslow Hospital. A press photographer was conveniently on hand to photograph the family standing by Ena's bedside and certainly, the 'unsolicited' publicity in the national newspapers did Imperial Airways no harm! Happily, Ena recovered and was able to return to her career in the theatre.

On 26th May G-EBGR extended the regular weekly Wednesday Guernsey service to Jersey when it flew direct to St. Helier with two passengers. The return journey in the afternoon was via Guernsey, but as the seaplane passed Corbière Captain Bailey noticed that the water in the radiator was boiling. He reached Guernsey safely, but a mechanical check revealed that a new radiator was needed and consequently the Sea Eagle was once again stranded. The passengers were forced to continue their journey by steamer and on 4th June G-EBGR was herself shipped to Southampton on board the *S.S. Fratton*.

A Sea Eagle moored to a buoy with the Great Western Railway berth in St. Helier Harbour in the background. The caption on the back of this card states 'the seaplane that went between England and the Channel Isles during the strike May to June 1926'. However, it may be that it is is actually a photograph of an emergency flight of G-EBGS piloted by Captain Bailey to St. Helier Harbour that took place on 17th May, just after the strike.

First Flight of the Supermarine Swan

On 30th June 1926 a new Supermarine Aviation seaplane made its maiden flight to Guernsey from Woolston piloted by Frank Bailey; it was the Supermarine Swan, registered G-EBJY. The Swan took 91 minutes to make the crossing arriving for the first time in Guernsey at 12.35 hours.

The Supermarine Swan had made its debut on the River Itchen in 1924 as Supermarine's first twin-engined amphibian. It was a heavy looking machine with an incongruously large cockpit standing high above the hull and was built to an Air Ministry specification, given the RAF serial number N175 and went under trial at RAF Calshot. The Swan was much larger than the Sea Eagle, with a wing span of 69' and was initially fitted with two Rolls Royce IX engines that gave it a cruising speed of 83 mph. Following modifications and evaluation, the Air Ministry ordered an even larger version of the Swan that became the RAF's very successful Supermarine Southampton.

Supermarine Swan, G-EBJY.

Supermarine Swan before and after its rebuild.

No longer required by the Air Ministry and always thought a contender for the cross-Channel service, the Swan was further modified and fitted with two 492 hp Napier Lion IIB engines giving an improved cruising speed of 87 mph and a maximum all-up weight of 13,710 lbs Its conversion included the capacity to carry ten passengers and two crew and in this new form Henri Biard took her on a test flight on 9th June with Frank Bailey and representatives of Imperial Airways. She was loaned to Imperial Airways and on 30th June given the civil registration G-EBJY when she received her Certificate of Airworthiness for passenger carrying. Frank Bailey piloted the Swan's maiden voyage to Guernsey that same day with four passengers.

The incongruously named Swan was big and ugly compared to the Sea Eagle but maintained the Supermarine concept of a 'boat that flies'. The designer was again Supermarine's R. J. Mitchell and it is a strange anomaly that he designed one of the ugliest amphibian aircraft but also the sublimely beautiful Spitfire. 'The luxurious new Swan', as an advert in the *Guernsey Evening Press* called her, took over from the Sea Eagles for the weekly service throughout the summer of 1926 and on 31st July she was chartered for a weekend trip to Dinard via Guernsey with a full complement of ten passengers. Her flight on 2nd September was prevented by fog and the airline

The perilous process of boarding the Swan from the slipway of the Imperial Airways seadrome at Durham Wharf on the River Itchen for a flight to Guernsey. The Swan returned to Guernsey on the 8th and 9th February 1927 but this was to be her last visit. During March and April, she was reported "laid up", and she was scrapped later that year.

announced that in future if there was a disruption on Wednesday then the flight would leave on Thursday and if the problem persisted then the flight would be on Friday. The Swan made a crossing on 29th September, but this was her last recoded visit in 1926; the following week the service was resumed by the Sea Eagles.

Death of a Sea Eagle

The Sea Eagles took over the new winter timetable of 1926 with one seaplane leaving Woolston every Tuesday at 11.30 hours, staying overnight in St. Peter Port Harbour and returning on the Wednesday morning at 09.15 hours in time to connect with the 11.14 am Southampton to Waterloo restaurant train. During the stop-over the Sea Eagle would make afternoon flights around Guernsey, Herm and Jethou at a price of £1. 5s. 0d. The Sea Eagles maintained this service throughout October and November, but on 1st December when Captain Bailey was returning from Guernsey in G-EBGS, engine failure forced him to ditch in the Solent and he was ignominiously towed back to Woolston.

On Tuesday 14th December Bailey made the crossing to Guernsey in the repaired G-EBGS, but next morning when he went to St. Peter Port Harbour with a mechanic, the men were appalled to discover that during the night she had sunk at her mooring. The Sea Eagle was hoisted on to Castle Emplacement and presented a very sad sight; it was obvious that a large boat must have collided with her during the night as

Wreckage of Sea Eagle G-EBGS recovered from St. Peter Port Harbour.

two feet of her tail was smashed off. A reward of £10 was offered to locate the culprit, but when it was announced that the service would be suspended while a mooring buoy that was too near the Imperial Airways' mooring was to be moved, it became evident that the incident may have been the innocent fouling by a ship on the adjacent buoy. G-EBGS was shipped back to her base but was never repaired and the service had to rely solely on G-EBGR.

Even though the service in 1926 had only been weekly, 67 passengers arrived in Guernsey during the year, the slightly healthier figures being attributed to the greater seating capacity of the Supermarine Swan flying during the summer months.

1927 A Lone Sea Eagle Maintains the Service

G-EBGR was the last remaining Sea Eagle flying for Imperial Airways Ltd. in 1927. The January, *Guernsey Evening Press* newspapers continued to carry advertisements for the weekly service and Captain Bailey tried to maintain it when not thwarted by the weather. On 11th January he flew the Sea Eagle to Guernsey and on 8th February he flew the Swan for the last time. He was back on the island again on 8th March with the Sea Eagle and managed to maintain the weekly service until 6th April, but then the *Guernsey Evening Press* reported that on 12th April a mechanical inspection at Southampton prior

A painting by Koike Shigeo of the last remaining Sea Eagle G-EBGR.

Imperial Airways first timetable for the Channel Islands service.

Henri Biard.

to departure had discovered a 'structural defect' that necessitated the stripping down of the whole machine. Imperial Airways published an apology for the unforeseen suspension of the service over the busy Easter holiday period, but it was not until the end of June that the Sea Eagle attempted to re-establish the weekly service to Guernsey.

The First Channel Islands Timetable

At the end of September, a new winter timetable was published when the departure days were changed. From the 6th and 7th October the Sea Eagle would now leave Woolston on Thursdays and return from St. Peter Port on Fridays. Imperial Airways even went to the effort of producing a little 'Time Table' of the 'Winter Service' that consisted of one entry for this sole return flight each week.

This very attractive folded card was Imperial Airways' first published timetable for a single route; it is therefore a very rare and sought-after item. Unfortunately, the timetable is illustrated with a photograph of the 'Swan' seaplane G-EBJY that was already scrapped!

Captain Frank Bailey, the only Channel Islands pilot and manager of the seadrome, left the Channel Islands service in December 1927 to fly seaplanes on the Nile for Imperial Airways.

His old colleague, Henri Biard returned to fill his place flying the route from December 1927 until April 1928, even though he was also still employed as senior test pilot for the Supermarine Aviation Works Ltd.

The records for 1927 show that the Sea Eagle only managed to bring 43 passengers to Guernsey by air.

The New Short S8 Calcutta replaces the Sea Eagle

Imperial Airways Ltd. intended to maintain their cross-Channel service to Guernsey with Henri Biard flying the sole Sea Eagle, G-EBGR, once a week. It was a purely cynical exercise that enabled them to claim the subsidy for a domestic seaplane route. The only deviation to the weekly service took place at the beginning of March when Biard made a rare visit to Cherbourg via St. Peter Port to meet up with the transatlantic liner, *RMS Olympic*. Two passengers on the *Olympic*, Mr and Mrs Mackie, needed to connect with a Union Castle liner, *RMS Balmoral Castle*, leaving Southampton that same day for Madeira, and the flight in the Sea Eagle saved them a six-hour Channel crossing on the steamer.

Frank Bailey returned to the Guernsey service in March after his interlude on the Nile and Henri Biard then left the service and continued with his flight testing for the Supermarine Aviation Works Ltd. A new timetable was announced for 1st June when the Sea Eagle would leave Woolston every Friday morning at 11.30 hours and return from Guernsey in the afternoon at 16.00 hours. She was timetabled to connect with the express trains running to and from Waterloo, and her Friday afternoon in Guernsey was available for around the island joyrides. On 3rd August Captain Bailey extended her service to Jersey for the last time, with one passenger. This was probably her final flight to the islands as on 9th August Imperial Airways officially took delivery of their stunning new Short S.8 Calcutta flying boat and had no more use for the Sea Eagle. G-EBGR, the last Sea Eagle, was relegated to private charter commissions from Woolston and in 1929 was finally recorded as 'withdrawn from use'.

The Short S8 Calcutta Flying Boat

Imperial Airways had learnt all they wanted from the Channel Islands experiment and were far more interested in developing flying boats for the eastern Mediterranean link of their Royal Airmail service to India. The Short Bros. Seaplane Works at Rochester on the River Medway had been commissioned to design a large and powerful all-metal seaplane that could accommodate fifteen passengers in comfortable armchairs served by an in-flight steward. On 13th February 1928 the prototype Short S.8 Calcutta flying boat, G-EBVG, was launched at Rochester. 'Calcutta', the name given to the seaplanes by Shorts, indicated Imperial Airways' intended destination.

Short S.8 Calcutta flying boat, G-EBVG.

The prototype Short S.8 Calcutta, G-EBVG, made her first flight from the River Medway on 21st February 1928 piloted by Short's Chief Test Pilot John Lankester Parker and with Major Herbert G. Brackley of Imperial Airways as co-pilot. They flew her to Felixstowe for stringent testing prior to her obtaining her Certificate of Airworthiness. The Short Calcutta was more than twice the size of the Sea Eagle and with its all-metal streamlined hull and classic lines, it was an icon of Art Deco and far removed from the Supermarine ethos of 'boats that fly'. Her hull was a stressed-skin construction, made entirely of the new metal duralumin with fittings of steel. She had a wingspan of 93 feet and a length of 67 feet and the spars and ribs of the wings were made of the same duralumin and covered with fabric. Her cruising speed of just less than 100 mph was achieved by the immense power of three 540 hp Bristol Jupiter XIF engines geared to lift her maximum all-up weight of 22,500 lbs Passengers enjoyed the "height of comfort" and the concession of smoking in-flight as well as being served drinks by an air-steward. They were also issued with little hygienic packs of cotton wool to put in their ears to suppress the engine noise!

G-EBVG, making her first flight from the River Medway.

Calcutta G-EBVG and RAF Supermarine Southampton S1231 make their maiden flights to Jersey

On 29th May Calcutta G-EBVG made her maiden cross-Channel flight to the Channel Islands; this was an official H.M. Government flight as she was not yet in the service of Imperial Airways. A Supermarine Southampton RAF flying boat, Registration No. S123 accompanied the Calcutta and photographed her flying over the Needles at the west end of the Isle of Wight. On board for the two days' flight, visiting Jersey and Plymouth, were Sir Samuel Hoare, the Secretary of State for

G-EBVG on her maiden cross-Channel flight to the Channel Islands photographed flying over the Needles.

Air, his wife Lady Hoare, and various other government officials. G-EBVG and the Supermarine Southampton left RAF Calshot on the Solent in fine weather at 11.00 hours and passed over Alderney an hour later. On reaching Jersey, both aircraft made two circuits of St. Helier before alighting in the Inner Roads at 12.45 hours and making fast to two buoys that had previously been specially positioned to take the seaplanes. They were greeted by the States' tug *Duke of Normandy* with a party of Jersey dignitaries on board and then conveyed to Government House for a grand luncheon.

The party returned to the harbour at 15.30 hours after a tour of the island and the Supermarine Southampton was the first to leave her moorings at 16.15 hours. Hundreds of spectators had assembled on Albert Pier for a close view of the seaplanes and thirteen minutes later they watched the Calcutta take to the air. The RAF serving officers piloting the seaplanes were Flight Lieutenant Martin in the Calcutta assisted by Flying Officer E. Chilton; flying the Supermarine Southampton was Flight Lieutenant Cross. This had been a 'double first' for Jersey as it was also the first visit to the island by a Supermarine Southampton. The two seaplanes had a good return crossing over the Channel and arrived off the RAF Cattewater Air Station and flying boat base at Plymouth at 18.50 hours. They stayed at Cattewater overnight and returned to RAF Calshot the following day.

On 27th July the Calcutta made a second attempt to cross the Channel, this time to Guernsey on an official flight with Imperial Airways dignitaries including Major H. G. Brackley ('Brackles') who was Imperial Airways' air superintendent, and eleven other passengers. Major Brackley acted as co-pilot to Captain Bailey who was piloting the craft for his first Channel crossing in a Calcutta and although he found the craft far more robust than the little Sea Eagle, it was still just as vulnerable to fog. As they passed the Needles at the western end of the Isle of Wight they were enveloped in low cloud, while out in the Channel they found that visibility was down to 200 yards. When the wireless operator on board the Calcutta received a message from Guernsey that visibility on the island was only 100 yards there was nothing Bailey could do but turn back for home.

The Calcutta Finally Reaches Guernsey

The Calcutta G-EBVG was officially handed over to Imperial Airways Ltd. on 9th August and finally managed to reach Guernsey piloted by Bailey with Major Brackley as co-pilot. She was photographed in Guernsey waters for the first time on 10th August 1928.

A new summer timetable was announced with bi-weekly departures on Tuesdays and Friday and for

G-EBVG on her first visit to Guernsey.

Imperial Airways summer 1928 timetable.

An Imperial Airways signed publicity postcard of Captain Donald Drew.

their new Summer 1928 service to the Channel Islands, Imperial Airways published an attractive four-page, pocket timetable with a photograph on the front of the Calcutta in flight, but it was obvious that this timetable was a temporary measure as it had an end date of 28th September 1928. The Calcutta flying boats had not been built for the Channel Islands route; Imperial Airways were only waiting for more of the Calcutta fleet to be completed so they would be able to start their eastern Mediterranean service. The timetable even stated:

> The "Calcutta" Flying Boats used on this Service are the largest All-metal Commercial Flying Boats ever constructed in the British Isles, and have been designed to operate long sea links of Empire Air Routes. They will shortly be transferred to the IMPERIAL AIRWAYS London-India Mail Service.

There was no mention of what would replace them on the Channel Islands route!

For the time being however, Captain Bailey was the established pilot and the Calcutta managed to achieve its scheduled timetable. Because of increased activity towards the end of the month when the Calcutta was charted for other flights as well as Guernsey, Captain Bailey was joined by his old colleague John Horsey and a new pilot to the Channel Island service, Donald Drew.

On 12th September the second Calcutta flying boat, G-EBVH, named *City of Athens* was delivered to Imperial Airways at Woolston. She did not immediately join the Channel Island service as on the

Second Calcutta flying boat G-EBVH *City of Athens*.

Holidaymakers' snapshots of Calcutta G-EBVG in Guernsey waters during the late summer of 1928.

14th September she flew a party of family and friends of Imperial Airways' Chairman, Sir Eric Geddes, to Scotland. When she made it back to Woolston she was still not required on the Guernsey service as the timetable had been reduced to one flight a week every Wednesday. The demand for joyrides round the island in the afternoon had also disappeared along with the summer tourists. While Bailey and Brackley had been enjoying their tour of Scotland in G-EBVH, John Horsey and Donald Drew were maintaining a good Guernsey schedule with G-EBVG. The service had improved because the Calcutta had a larger capacity than the Sea Eagle and could cope better with rough seas, but she still had no defence against fog.

The number of air passenger arrivals in Guernsey in 1928 was recorded at a healthier 160.

1929 Goodbye Imperial Airways

Imperial Airways Ltd. announced that on 28th February it intended to relinquish its Government-backed monopoly air service to the Channel Islands. The *Guernsey Evening Press* of 27th February stated that the air service was suspended until further notice and went on to say: "To-day was to have been the final flight but the weather prevented a departure.".

The final flight of the Imperial Airways service to Guernsey had therefore been made by G-EBVH the week before on Wednesday 20th February without anybody realising or marking the occasion. Just as had happened for its predecessor, the British Marine Air Navigation Co. Ltd., the ending of the Imperial Airways service came quietly without notice.

The two Calcutta seaplanes flew to their intended station of operations in the eastern Mediterranean and the Woolston seaplane depot was put up for lease. With the departure of Imperial Airways from the Channel Islands route there was no longer any legal constraint preventing private companies from attempting to establish a service to the islands. The stylish Calcutta had given Guernsey a frisson of modernity in the summer of 1928, but by the spring of 1929 Imperial Airways Ltd. finally left the island with no air service at all.

An aerial view of the Imperial Airways base at Durham Wharf, Woolston. This publicity photograph shows a Calcutta being launched from the slipway of the Woolston seadrome into the River Itchen. The shadow of the second Calcutta from which the photograph was taken can be seen on the water, whilst the two steam ferry boats of the Itchen chain ferry floating bridge are visible in the top of the picture. The year 1929 dawned with both of the Imperial Airways new Short S.8 Calcuttas stationed at Durham Wharf, and available for use on the Channel Islands service, but they were never seen together except perhaps for when this photograph was taken.

On 16th January 1929 the second Calcutta G-EBVH took over the service from G-EBVG and made her maiden flight to Guernsey. This stunning study of the new Calcutta G-EBVH was taken in Guernsey waters but few photographs exist of her in Guernsey as the service only continued for a little over a month and G-EBVH only managed a handful of flights to the island.

THE FIRST REGULAR PASSENGER SERVICE FROM JERSEY

Establishing a reliable air passenger service to the Channel Islands was never the prime goal of many entrepreneurs; the two real prizes of a daily air service to the islands were:

1) Delivering the Royal Mails on the same day as posting.
2) Receiving the London newspapers on the morning of issue instead of a day late.

Lord Alfred Northcliffe, the Publisher of the *Daily Mail*, was always in the vanguard of sponsoring pioneer aviation, regularly offering cash prizes for challenges. In the summer of 1926, at the height of the Jersey tourist season, the *Daily Mail* saw an opportunity to outmanoeuvre their rival London newspapers by vastly enhancing their sales in the islands and performing a stunt that would give them great publicity. For the month of August, they secured the services of an amphibian Vickers 60 Viking Mk IV, registration G-EBED, that would leave Woolston and fly to Jersey carrying copies of the *Daily Mail* as soon as they were collected from the London to Southampton early morning mail train.

The crossing would take about 90 minutes, culminating with the seaplane landing near St. Catherine's Breakwater on the east end of the island, where it would taxi onto the beach of Anne Port to be met by newspaper agents.

The service was inaugurated on Bank Holiday Monday 2nd August when the craft was due to leave Woolston at about 06.30 hours, but fog in the Solent delayed its departure by an hour. Once under way, flying conditions were perfect and the Vickers Viking made the crossing to Jersey in one hour and twenty minutes piloted by Captain Leslie Hamilton and with a Captain Cooper as navigator. G-EBED made a "graceful" taxi into Anne Port and the newspapers were unloaded and distributed around the island. However, the event was not initially very well

Anne Port, Jersey.

publicised in Jersey and it took the public a while to appreciate what had happened. Anne Port was a quiet little bay on the east of the island, and it is doubtful if many people would have seen the craft land, if the Vickers Viking had flown over St. Helier and landed on the sands of St. Aubins, then the story may have been very different. As the *Evening Post* of Tuesday 3rd August reported in Jersey:

> Unfortunately the fact had not been made generally known, and it took some time for the public to fully appreciate the wonderful achievement, but when once it got noised about, "The Daily Mail" was eagerly sought after, and ere long all the copies were disposed of.

The same report stated that the voyage on the morning of 3rd August had taken one hour and twenty minutes and this seems to have been the pattern for the rest of the holiday week. There are no records to show if the service continued successfully for the whole of the month, but it seems doubtful as the service never became a permanent fixture and no attempt was made to repeat it in subsequent years. There is no record of the newspapers bearing any special imprint to indicate that they were carried on the seaplane service, so it seems unlikely that it would be possible to identify an August 1926 *Daily Mail* carried on the service. Intriguingly, both the *Jersey Morning News* and the *Evening Post* carried the following announcement in their editions during the August Bank Holiday week:

FLYING TO SOUTHAMPTON.
A seaplane will leave Anne Port daily, weather permitting, at 2.15 for Southampton, the approximate duration of the journey being 1 hour and 20 minutes. There is accommodation for five passengers with light luggage, the fare being £3.6s. per passenger. Those desirous of travelling thus should telephone Fairbanks Hotel, Gorey 125.

Holidaymakers pose in front of Vickers Viking G-EBED as she rests in the shallows of Anne Port.

The Viking was Vickers' first venture into flying boats and was designed by Rex Pierson as an amphibious biplane. The prototype, built during the war mainly by women workers within only two months, first flew at Brooklands on 21st November 1919. Of the thirty-one Vikings built, twenty-three were exported to foreign countries. G-EBED was a Viking Mk IV built in 1922 with a length of 34 ft and wingspan of 50 ft, powered by a 450 hp Napier Lion 'pusher' engine and with space for six passengers. She had originally been built as a reserve machine for Keith and Ross Smith's round-the-world flight in 1922, but when that flight was abandoned following Keith Smith's death at Brooklands in another Viking, Vickers Aviation Ltd. used G-EBED as a demonstrator.

G-EBED lives on as a replica machine at the Brooklands Aviation Museum. She was originally built in the early 1970s by Fairey Marine Ltd. at Hamble for the film *The People that Time Forgot*. Later acquired by Thorpe Park Amusement Centre at Chertsey, she was on the lake painted in the Argentine Navy colours until she was capsized by severe storms in 1987. She was subsequently purchased by VAFA (Brooklands)

Captain Hamilton's Vickers Viking G-EBED had accommodation for six passengers, but with one seat taken by his navigator Captain Cooper, this left the five available seats mentioned in the announcement. This was probably not part of the *Daily Mail* enterprise and was more likely a perquisite of Hamilton to earn extra cash on his return flight to Southampton each day. It was certainly the first ever regular passenger service from Jersey to the mainland, but unfortunately there are no records of the numbers of passengers carried, if any, nor how long the service functioned.

Aerophil for the Brooklands Museum, dismantled by volunteers and delivered to the museum by British Aerospace on 27th October 1987. She is now fully restored as G-EBED with a gleaming varnished hull.

Captain Leslie Hamilton bought her for charter use and she regularly ran a winter sports service between Croydon, St. Moritz and Nice where she could be seen guarded by French Gendarmes. She was scrapped in December 1929.

THE FIRST LANDPLANE TO LAND ON JERSEY

During the 1920s Surrey Flying Services Ltd., based at Croydon Airport, were renowned for their stunting, joyriding and aerial photography using Avro biplanes flown from holiday beaches around Britain. On 16th July 1927 an Avro 536 arrived in the afternoon on the beach in St. Aubin's Bay, piloted by Captain S.F. Woods and carrying two employees of Surrey Flying Services Ltd.. The Avro biplane, G-EBOY, had left Croydon Airport in the morning taking the shortest route across the Channel before following the French coast until Jersey was in sight. G-EBOY landed on the sands of St. Aubin's Bay setting a precedent for landplanes visiting Jersey for the next decade.

The Avro 536 was a development of the Avro 504 military training biplane that had proved so popular for conversion immediately after the Great War for joyriding purposes. The Avro 536 was designed and first flew in the summer of 1919 and was similar to the Avro 504 but with the fuselage widened by 9 inches to accommodate four, instead of two passengers. G-EBOY first flew in August 1919 as G-EAKL, but was withdrawn from use on 14th November 1920 and written off in August 1921. She was rebuilt five years later as G-EBOY and received her certificate of airworthiness on 28th June 1926. G-EBOY was principally intended for joyriding, and her wingspan of 36 ft 9 in. and 150 hp Bentley BR1 engine were powerful enough to lift the pilot and four passengers.

Captain Woods when interviewed by Jersey reporters gave a serious intention for his visit to Jersey. Surrey Flying Services wanted to make Islanders 'air-conscious' and they would be giving exhibitions of flying to the school children. The children would be invited to write an essay on the topic of aviation and the winners would be rewarded with flights in the Avro. Surrey Flying Services would also take aerial photographs of the island and were available for any 'special commissions that might be entrusted to them'. Captain Woods would also undertake 'instructive demonstrations' during the exercise and manoeuvres of the Jersey Royal Militia; perhaps he was going to drop bombs on them! He was also of course available for joyriding flights.

A beach base was set up at Bel Royal and Captain Woods started joyriding trips the next day, Sunday 17th July 1927. A large crowd congregated and some of the wealthier members availed themselves of this exciting mode of transport taking brief flights round St. Aubin's Bay. Unfortunately for publicity conscious Woods, a mishap occurred when the aircraft was landing after its final trip of the day and business was interrupted for a few days for repairs.

Tides and weather permitting, the Avro flew from 10.00 hours until dusk with a flight round St. Aubin's Bay costing 7s. 6d. per person. As the holiday season came to a close, this fare was reduced to 5s. on 27th August. The Avro could be hired for a trip round the island at a cost of four guineas, to Gorey for three guineas or by the hour for eight guineas.

A performance of 'wonder stunts and crazy flying' happened every Saturday, Sunday and on August Bank Holiday Monday above Bel Royal, but as it was impossible to charge admission fees, Woods invited local charities to make benefit collections from the

Built in 1919, Avro 536, G-EAKJ with a 130 hp Clerget engine was a sister Avro 536 to G-EAKL (later rebuilt as G-EBOY).

crowds. The aims of these stunt flying demonstrations were to advertise the joyriding flights and to display the stability of the Avro to any sceptical member of the public. One of the daredevil antics carried out during these demonstrations involved the mechanic walking along the lower wing to the tip and back while the aeroplane skimmed over the sands. Captain Woods received an unexpected publicity boost on 2nd August when Mrs Robins, a 95-year-old lady from St. Helier, went on a spin round the bay. She declared that she wished that she could have remained aloft all day.

Woods anticipated a flying season of sixty days, but the weather took its inevitable toll and although there were no serious mechanical failures, days were lost at the start when a cylinder connecting-rod failed in the engine. There was also a brief suspension of joyrides from 15th to 18th August when the Avro had to be overhauled for a compulsory Air Ministry inspection. Woods was congratulated on the maintenance of his machine, but this did not compensate for the loss of four days' revenue.

With the rapid decline in tourists at the start of September, joyriding was no longer an economic proposition and the decision was made to return home. G-EBOY left Jersey on the morning of 10th September flying via Caen, Dieppe, St. Inglevert and Lympne and arrived safely back at her base at Croydon in the late afternoon.

Surrey Flying Service, Croydon – The Jersey Avro 536, G-EBOY photographed during a previous stunt delivering newspapers.

AN RAF SEAPLANE MISHAP OFF GUERNSEY

At noon on Tuesday 6th March 1928 a flight of three RAF Vickers Supermarine Southampton twin-engine seaplanes set off from RAF Calshot on the Solent for a navigational training flight to Guernsey. Shortly before 15.00 hours two of the machines reached St. Peter Port and entered the harbour, but the third seaplane with registration No. 1 failed to arrive. This machine had developed engine trouble and was forced to alight on the sea at 15.45 hours, ten miles north of Guernsey. She could generate power from one engine, and this allowed her to taxi slowly on the sea towards Guernsey. The crew of the States of Guernsey dayboat were on duty at the Platte Fougère lighthouse and they towed her into the St. Peter Port Harbour pool at 16.30 hours where she was made fast to a buoy. The crew of six including Pilot Officer G.I.L. 'Gil' Saye and Navigation Officer W. Andrews went ashore and found accommodation for the night at the Royal Hotel. When it was confirmed that craft and crew were safe the other two Supermarine Southamptons returned to their base.

The RAF Supermarine Southampton seaplane registration No. 1 was stranded at Guernsey from 6th March 1928.

The problem with the engine was major as the disabled craft was still moored in St. Peter Port pool on Saturday 10th March until another Supermarine Southampton arrived from RAF Calshot at noon and moored near the stranded craft. This machine brought vital engine parts and after some mechanical work on the disabled craft, both seaplanes were able to leave for England later in the afternoon. Unfortunately, there is no record of the serial numbers of any of the other seaplanes.

Vickers Supermarine Southampton MK I.

The metal-hulled Supermarine Southampton MK II; flights of these RAF seaplanes would make navigational training exercises to the Channel Islands in subsequent years.

The Supermarine Southampton

The Vickers Supermarine Southampton MK I replaced the RAF's wartime Felixstowe F 5 and was the first flying boat designed after the First World War to enter RAF service. Its designer was Reginald Mitchell, whose work included the Supermarine's Sea Eagle, Swan and the sublime Spitfire. It would become the second longest serving RAF flying boat, with over ten years of service. The design of the Southampton was based on the unique Supermarine Swan that flew to Guernsey in 1926. The Swan, designed as a passenger craft, was not intended for the RAF, but when offered to the RAF as a prototype for the Southampton she was so impressive in tests that the RAF ordered six Supermarine Southamptons straight off the drawing board in August 1924 without any further testing.

The Supermarine Southampton was a 2-bay biplane with a distinctive triple fin rudder, similar to that of the Swan. The first 18 aircraft to be produced were designated MK I and had wooden hulls and were powered by two Napier Lion V engines. The subsequent MK II versions were metal-hulled, and this made them 500 lbs lighter. A further 400 lbs was saved from no water seepage: this was a problem with wooden hulls immersed in the sea for any length of time. The MK II was powered by two of the more powerful 500 hp Napier VA W-12 engines that, combined with the weight saving, greatly increased the range of the craft. Supermarine converted the majority of the MK I's in 1929 to the improved specifications of the MK II.

The Southampton had a crew of five with a pilot and co-pilot sitting side by side, a gunner in the nose of the craft and two more gunners amidships, behind the pilots. The wingspan of the seaplane was 75 ft, the length was 51 ft 1 in. and the height was 22 ft 4 in.. She had a speed of 95 mph at sea level and a top speed of 108 mph while her range varied with the specification from 473 miles to 540 miles or even 770 miles and an endurance of 6.3 hours. She was armed with three Lewis machine guns and could carry a 1,100 lb bomb load.

The Supermarine Southampton proved to be a very reliable craft and she became famous for long distance formation flying typically in flights of four or five where she would 'show the flag' around the empire.

THE FIRST TERRA FIRMA LANDING ON GUERNSEY

The topography of Guernsey with sea cliffs, hills and hedged small fields greatly inhibited aeroplanes from making a landing. Flights to the island had historically only been by seaplane with landings on the relatively calm waters outside St. Peter Port Harbour.

On Thursday 26th April 1928 the first terra firma landing by an aeroplane was made on Guernsey. The privately owned, blue painted, De Havilland D.H. 60 Cirrus Moth with the registration G-EBOU, made a safe landing at 13.00 hours on Fort Field at Fort George after a flight from England piloted by RAF Flight Lieutenant Frank Ormond Soden. The *Guernsey Weekly Press* proclaimed the event with headlines:

AIR PIONEERS.
The Coming of the First Aeroplane.
April 26 unique in history of Guernsey.

The Cirrus Moth had made a dawn departure from Croydon at 06.00 hours, taken the short Channel crossing to Calais arriving at 07.30 hours and then flew across France to Deauville where it alighted at 09.20 hours. Flight Lt. Soden took refreshment at Deauville before flying on to Guernsey at midday. A lady passenger accompanied the pilot and in the afternoon they visited St. Peter Port in order to purchase 20 gallons of motor spirit and a gallon of oil to refuel the plane at a total cost of £2 10s 0d. The machine was the object of much interest and large crowds travelled to Fort Field on Thursday afternoon and all day Friday to view the craft where it rested near the Morley Chapel.

Early on Saturday morning, 28th April, the couple, along with friends, made their way to Fort Field and at 09.50 hours Soden taxied to the south end of the field and took off over Fort George. The Cirrus Moth circled over the town and came back over the Fort flying so low over the field that the fliers were able to shout "Goodbye" to their friends. The plane then rose rapidly and, according to the *Guernsey Weekly Press* report of 5th May 1928, "headed for Jersey where they intended to land on the racecourse," but it has not been possible to corroborate this statement.

Flight Lt. Soden would later fly to Jersey in July 1929 as the pilot of a flagship craft of four Supermarine Southampton seaplanes making an official RAF visit to the island. This made him the first pilot ever to fly both a land and seaplane to the Channel Islands. Flight Lt. F.O. Soden was based at RAF Wittering and had only bought the Cirrus Moth four months earlier in December 1927, but he sold it in less than a year in November 1928. Following this visit of G-EBOU in 1928, there was only one other successful land landing of an aircraft on Guernsey four years later in 1932, and no others until the establishment in October 1934 of Guernsey's first airfield at L'Eree on the west coast.

The first aeroplane to land in Guernsey. The de Havilland Moth, piloted by Flight-Lieut. F. W. Soden, which alighted on the Fort Field on Thursday, April 26.

In this newspaper cutting from the *Guernsey Weekly Press* of 5th May 1928, the top photograph shows the Cirrus Moth with her wings folded back, and Flight-Lieutenant Soden servicing the engine after refuelling. The bottom photograph portrays Soden and his lady passenger in front of G-EBOU. (Photo reproduction in newspapers was very poor and the originals of these photographs have never been found.)

The prototype of the De Havilland D.H. 60 Cirrus Moth first flew on 22nd February 1925 and Flight Lt. Soden's craft, G-EBOU, was built the following year. It was a two-seat biplane of wooden construction, with plywood covered fuselage and fabric covered wings. The Cirrus Moth had a wingspan of 30 feet, but a feature of the design was its wings folded to allow owners to hangar the aircraft in smaller spaces. Production Cirrus Moths were equipped with a 60 hp (45 kW) ADC Cirrus engine, but in order for G-EBOU to participate in the Lympne Air Race Trials that were to take place the week after she received her Certificate of Airworthiness on 8th September 1926, she was fitted with the more powerful 75 hp AS Genet 1 engine.

VISITING FLIGHTS OF RAF SUPERMARINE SOUTHAMPTONS

A flight of three RAF Supermarine Southamptons from RAF Calshot visited Guernsey on Tuesday 6th March 1928 and a flight of four visited Jersey at midday on 22nd June 1928. Few details are recorded regarding the visits as the Harbour authorities denied any prior knowledge of the RAF's intentions. The Jersey press records three of the craft on 22nd June 1928 bearing the registrations S-1123, S-1142 and S-1162. The fourth craft's markings went unrecorded and there is also some debate about the registration "S-1142" as this is the registration of a Fairey IIIF Mk.I. (This registration number was probably S-1042 as this Calshot craft would visit Jersey in 1929.)

The seaplanes were probably on a navigational training flight and Jersey may not have been their ultimate destination but a stopover on their route home, as they approached the island from the south flying towards St. Aubin. The pilots dispensed with strict RAF protocol as the seaplanes circled St. Aubin's Bay, St. Helier Harbour and Fort Regent several times before one of them made such low passes over the docks that onlookers thought that the Southampton would take away the parapet of Albert Pier or the masts of the Southern Railway mail boat that had arrived that morning. Two of the Southamptons landed in the bay but took off again almost immediately and flying in a north-westerly direction were joined by the third craft. The fourth Southampton continued cruising around for some time before eventually flying off in the same direction. At 13.00 hours another seaplane appeared and flew over the island, also circling St. Aubin's Bay. As there is no record of its registration markings it is not known if this was a fifth machine or one of the original four having returned. This machine also disappeared in a north-west direction only to reappear half an hour later, again circling the bay. The reason for the repeated flights round the bay is unknown; it may have just been the bravado of young pilots looking at the girls on the beach!

Supermarine Southampton MK II's from RAF Calshot flying from their base in formation over the Solent. The photograph was taken from a third Southampton MK II of the flight.

THE TOUR AND TRAVEL ASSOCIATION 'SEAGULL' OVER JERSEY

With the exit of Imperial Airways Ltd. from the Channel Islands arena at the end of February 1929, the skies around the islands were free for anyone wishing to develop a service to the islands. There was, however, no rush of entrepreneurs eager to fill the gap and indeed there were no new civil airlines established anywhere on the mainland. When an interest did develop, it came from Jersey. The focus of attention moved away from Guernsey and for the next six years that Island seldom saw an aircraft.

The local Channel Islands newspapers announced the inauguration of a new service to start in May 1929 from Southampton to Jersey with the involvement of the Southern Railway but May passed without any signs of a new service or any Southern Railway initiative. The announcement came from the new 'Aviation Department' of the travel agency, Tour and Travel Association, run by Captain Richard Taylor of the Jersey and French store, Orviss Ltd.. Captain Taylor intended to establish a regular daily service from Southampton to Jersey with a 'stop-over' at Guernsey when required, as well as a charter service to France.

The only link with Southern Railway was that the flights would connect with convenient trains from Waterloo to Southampton West Station, and the conveyance of passengers and baggage from the station to the seaplane base would be included in the cross-Channel ticket price.

The mainland base of Tour and Travel Association was initially Brooklands Airfield, but this was a temporary measure until a lease was signed for the redundant Imperial Airways' seadrome at Woolston. With a viable mainland base, Captain Taylor now appointed a manager, Mr George W. Higgs, an ex RAF pilot with considerable war and peacetime flying experience. Although inauguration of the service was re-announced for 9th June, that date also passed without a flight as the factor still lacking in the enterprise was an aircraft!

The aircraft of choice was a converted RAF Supermarine Seagull, and the Supermarine works were confident of being able to supply a fleet of these flying boats to satisfy the requirements of the Tour and Travel Association. The Seagull was a deck-landing

The craft purchased by Tour and Travel Association was the unique Supermarine Seagull IV which was a modified version of the production model Seagull II, but with Handley Page leading edge wing slots that gave it greater lift and the ability to fly more slowly without stalling. It was also fitted with new twin fins and rudders but retained the 492 hp Napier Lion IIB engine of the Seagull II. Its RAF registration had been N9605, but when it was sold to Tour and Travel Association it was further modified as a "luxuriously appointed, six seater (pilot plus six passengers) passenger craft" with the civil registration G-AAIZ.

amphibian with a wingspan of 46 feet used for gunnery reconnaissance. The prototype took to the air in 1921 and several versions followed. The Tour and Travel Association service to the islands failed to materialise in June because the newly converted seaplane was not delivered by the Supermarine works until 28th June when there were further delays before a Certificate of Airworthiness could be issued by the Air Ministry. As a result of the wrecking of an Imperial Airways air liner *City of Ottowa* in the English Channel on 17th June with the loss of seven lives, the Air Ministry was being extra cautious about granting certificates. When Bellingham's, the local agents in the islands for Tour and Travel Association, passed on this excuse for the delay to the islands' press, Imperial Airways, mindful of the bad publicity, demanded a retraction be published in the *Evening Post*. There was, however, no other logical reason why it would take twelve days to issue a Certificate of Airworthiness to the Seagull, a craft that had already been flying for a year with the RAF and had only undergone a cosmetic change to its interior. Eventually the Seagull's Certificate of Airworthiness was signed on 10th July. George Higgs, the Woolston manager, lost no time in putting it into service and on 11th July 1929 at 14.00 hours, the Tour and Travel Association's Supermarine Seagull G-AAIZ took to the air from Woolston on her maiden flight to the Channel Islands. Although this was essentially a proving flight for the pilot to survey the route and acquaint himself with the landing areas in the islands, the Seagull was decorated with

The Seagull landed outside the breakwater of St. Helier and taxied into the harbour to its new permanent mooring opposite the Great Western Railway steamer berth.

streamers and old shoes as it had also been charted to convey newlywed RAF Captain Grant and his young French bride to Jersey. Two other passengers were with the couple as they flew to Guernsey where they were to pick up two more travellers for Jersey. St. Peter Port was reached at about 16.00 hours and after a two hour stop-over G-AAIZ, now with a full complement of passengers, left the harbour and arrived off Jersey forty-five minutes later.

Earlier attempts to establish an air service to the islands had commenced in winter, but the Tour and Travel Association had the good fortune of a summer start. They initially achieved a regular daily return service from 13th July, and on 15th and 17th July they even managed an extension of the service to St. Malo, but it was not long before the perennial problems of fog, bad weather and mechanical failure began to take their toll. Early in the morning of 28th July the flying boat arrived at St. Helier with only one passenger but could not make a return flight for two days because of inclement weather. On 30th July the pilot, J. Oliver, attempted to return to Woolston at 06.35 hours, but after taxiing out of St. Helier Harbour he was forced to return ten minutes later with engine trouble. The engine could not be repaired on the water and the following day the aircraft was hoisted out of the harbour onto the Albert Pier for closer inspection. G-AIZZ was finally able to leave for Southampton at midday on 2nd August, but on 6th August storms again forced her to seek shelter in St. Helier for two more days. The weather moderated on 8th August and with four passengers on board J. Oliver set off once again for Woolston at 17.00 hours. The tide was abnormally low and the wind had dropped to give a flat calm. Without a headwind to lift off into, the pilot had to use full throttle on the engine and travelling at high speed across the water he failed to notice a submerged rock lying just below the surface of the water. A large hole was torn in the lower part of the wooden hull and with water flooding in, the pilot managed to race the craft back to her mooring buoy and get the passengers safely ashore. Full of water and beginning to sink the Seagull was again hoisted onto Albert Pier. On 9th August George Higgs sailed over from Southampton to assess the damage and he soon realised that the aircraft would have to be shipped back to the Supermarine works for repair. Her wings were folded back and on Saturday 17th August she was loaded on board the *S.S. Haslemere* and shipped to Southampton. The experience appears to have dampened Oliver's interest in seaplanes as he left his employment with the Tour and Travel Association and returned to his old job as a flying instructor.

After a complete renovation, the Seagull resumed service on 30th August now piloted by a new head pilot, Mr Stanley Siegfried Kirsten, an ex RAF pilot, who was to fly for the Tour and Travel Association for only about a week, but he would make a much greater contribution to the development of air services to the islands when he was a partner in yet another new venture in the following year.

The resumed service on 30th August arrived in Jersey at 11.00 hours with two passengers and left again at 13.00 hours with five passengers before returning once again that evening at 19.10 hours with another three passengers. For two days the service appeared to be picking up, but on the evening of 2nd September Kirsten left Jersey for Woolston at 18.30 hours with a lady passenger and halfway into the flight the Seagull developed engine problems. Kirsten was forced to reduce speed so much that daylight was fading as he passed over the Isle of Wight. Drifting off course and unable to reach Woolston Marine Airport before darkness he alighted on the sea off Southsea at 22.00 hours and taxied onto the beach. A mechanic joined them and was left on board the Seagull while Kirsten and his passenger completed their journey to Woolston by car.

This was the last flight of Tour and Travel Association and the last visit of the Seagull G-AAIZ to Jersey; the service had lasted all of seven weeks and yet again ended without any announcement.

Shortly afterwards, George Higgs acquired the aviation department of the Tour and Travel Association along with the Seagull flying boat, but the craft was only available for charter flights. Higgs relocated his new company 'Air Transit' to Brooklands and the Seagull ended her days there when she was withdrawn from service and her wooden hull burnt in December 1933.

The Tour and Travel Association Seagull G-AAIZ at Jersey – but not for long.

A BUSY DAY IN JERSEY

Wednesday 17th July 1929 was busy in St. Aubin's Bay in Jersey as in the course of the day no less than five seaplanes landed. The Supermarine Seagull of Tour and Travel Association made its scheduled visit to St. Helier Harbour with an extension of the service to St. Malo, and a flight of four RAF Supermarine Southamptons landed in the bay at the end of an instructional flight from RAF Calshot; this was the first time that five seaplanes were recorded together in Jersey waters. Although the impending arrival of the RAF Southamptons was unannounced to the Jersey public, the authorities on the island were aware of the RAF visit as the launch, the *Lady Diana* was cruising in the bay with Captain H.G. Benest M.C. on board ready to convey the aviator officers and men ashore after their landing. The flagship aircraft was S-1161 with high-ranking officers, Group Commander W. H. Primrose and Squadron Leader F. O. Soden on board. Two of the other craft were recorded as S-1162 and S-1042, the latter having visited the island the previous year. The registration of the fourth Supermarine Southampton was unrecorded.

The four Southamptons anchored in St. Aubin's Bay and the RAF officers were transported by the *Lady Diana* to Elizabeth Castle where officers of the Royal Channel Islands Yacht Club welcomed them ashore. Also waiting to greet them were His Excellency the Lieutenant-Governor of Jersey, Major-General Edward Henry Willis, C.B., C.M.G., Harbour Master Captain Le Scelieur and other local officials. Later in the afternoon, the launch *Lady Diana* transported the party into St. Helier Harbour where the officers had tea in town before returning to their flying boats at about 17.30 hours. The unidentified Southampton was the first to leave in an easterly direction across the island and then the remaining three circled the bay in formation as a parting salute before they also departed in an easterly direction flying low over Gorey and Mont Orgueil Castle at about 18.00 hours and heading, not for Calshot, but for the coast of France.

A flight of four RAF Supermarine Southamptons from RAF Calshot; sister flying boats to the Jersey visitors.

A NEW AIRLINE – KIRSTEN AND MACE LTD
THE *SARO CUTTY SARK* BECOMES A *SILVER BAT*

Kirsten and Mace Ltd

On 29th October 1929 the stock market crash on Wall Street heralded the meltdown of the economies of the western world. In the United Kingdom, 1930 saw the new decade start without any commercial air service to the Channel Islands and Britain's sole remaining domestic airline had gone with the demise of the Channel Islands' Tour and Travel Association Ltd. the previous summer. For the first five months of 1930 there was no intimation of a replacement Channel Islands service, but then at the end of May, the *Jersey Morning News* announced the probability that a new Jersey–Southampton air service would start in a few weeks. The focus was now firmly on Jersey, with the aircraft positioned on the island rather than the mainland.

The new company, Kirsten and Mace Ltd., was formed by Mr R. B. Mace and Mr Stanley Siegfried Kirsten. An ex-RAF officer with eight years experience of military and commercial flying, Kirsten would be the chief pilot for the new venture, as he had been for a week for Tour and Travel Association Ltd. The new company intended to fly their service from Jersey to Woolston, having rented the office and marine landing space at Durham Wharf. A passenger leaving Jersey at 09.00 hours would be at Woolston by 10.30 hours and could catch a Southern Railway express train to be in London by lunchtime. The fares were £3 10s for a single trip and £6 10s for a return journey. The new service was planned to run on two days a week, but as the aircraft was based in Jersey it was available for charter on other days or for collecting passengers from the transatlantic liners at Cherbourg. When not engaged with scheduled services or charters, it would be free for joyriding flights around the island from the beach of St. Aubin's Bay. Bellinghams Travel Office in Mulcaster Street in St. Helier was the local agent for the airline and Messrs H.G. Benest & Co. were the Guernsey agents in St. Peter Port. The craft that Kirsten and Mace were acquiring for their service was the *Saro Cutty Sark*. This was the first craft to be built by the new embryonic company from Cowes in the Isle of Wight, of Saunders-Roe Ltd. (Saro), a combination of S.E. Saunders Ltd. and Sir Alliott Roe, who was the ex-owner of the Avro Company. The Cutty Sark registered G-AAIP had first flown as a prototype seaplane on 4th July 1929 with two 105 hp Cirrus Hermes I engines. It was a four-seater monoplane with its engines mounted well out of the sea spray on pylons above the wooden Fokker-type wing that was bolted on top of a simple boat-shaped hull formed from an aluminium coated alloy called "Alclad".

G-AAIP received her Certificate of Airworthiness on 13th September 1929 and was converted to an amphibian with retractable landing gear, the weight of which necessitated an increase in the power of the engines to 120 hp Gipsy engines. She had a length of 34 ft 4 in., a wingspan of 45 ft and a height of 11 ft 2 in.; her maximum speed was 107 mph and her cruising speed 90 mph with a range of 315 miles. The *Manchester Guardian* described the Cutty Sark as being "one of the prettiest exhibits" at the 1929 Olympic Aero Show. She was sold to a Mr Holden before returning to Saunders-Roe for refurbishment as a coupé machine, one of the few craft at the time licensed for smoking in the cabin, and capable of carrying four passengers with luggage or six passengers without. In this new guise her Certificate of Airworthiness was renewed on 12th June 1930 when she was taken over by Kirsten and Mace.

Siegfried Stanley Kirsten, Chief Pilot of Kirsten and Mace.

With Stanley Kirsten at the controls, *Saro Cutty Sark*, G-AAIP, made her maiden flight to Jersey on an inauspicious Friday 13th June, alighting in St. Helier Harbour just after 11.00 hours. She remained in the harbour overnight and returned to Woolston on Saturday at 13.15 hours. On Sunday 15th June Kirsten flew her back to Jersey at 12.55 hours and two and a half hours later started the first fare paying joyrides from the sands near First Tower. Joyriding took place from the beach at West Park, but on occasions the *Cutty Sark* flew from First Tower and one day from Millbrook. The flying started at 10.30 or 11.30 hours until 14.00 hours. If there were afternoon sessions these could continue to 19.00, 20.00 or even 21.00 hours on particularly fine days. Mr Mace assured the Jersey press that there would be no joyriding on Sundays before noon "so that no possible offence will be given to church-goers". The high tide also restricted flying for two hours each day when there was not enough beach available for passengers to board the seaplane safely. 'Round the island' joyrides cost £1 while 'Short Trips' were available for 10s.

During June 1930, Kirsten and Mace failed to initiate their bi-weekly schedule to Woolston on Mondays and Fridays, although they made two unscheduled flights to the mainland, and their first inter-island flight to Guernsey was executed on 17th June when four passengers from Jersey arrived in St. Peter Port Harbour at 13.15 hours and the *Saro Cutty Sark* returned later in the afternoon with three passengers. The following day, 18th June, Cutty Sark made an unscheduled flight to Woolston and returned via Guernsey in order to pick up two passengers for Jersey. She landed outside St. Peter Port Harbour at 20.50 hours but 35 minutes later when she was due to depart, she failed to take-off for some unspecified reason and instead taxied into the harbour to wait safely in the Pool overnight before taking off for Jersey the next morning. Throughout the whole month of June, the Cutty Sark only managed to complete two official scheduled flights to the mainland on the subsequent Mondays of 23rd and 30th June.

The *Saro Cutty Sark* becomes a *Silver Bat*

For reasons known only to themselves, possibly publicity, Kirsten and Mace decided to re-christen the *Cutty Sark* in a ceremony on the sands at Millbrook on 3rd July 1930. Lord and Lady Trent of Nottingham, the founders of Boot's the Chemists, preceded the ceremony with a tea party in their home, Villa Millbrook, held for various invited local dignitaries including the guests of honour, His Excellency Major-General E.H. Willis C.B., C.M.G., the Lieutenant-Governor of Jersey, and his wife Mrs Willis. After tea, the party made their way to the beach at Millbrook where the amphibian was drawn up on the sands and had already attracted a huge crowd requiring the control of local police officers. Under a beautiful hot summer sky, Kirsten delivered a brief speech to the assembled gathering and then presented Mrs Willis with a bouquet of sweet peas before inviting her to christen the craft. Mrs Willis broke the obligatory bottle of champagne over the prow of the aircraft and named it *Silver Bat*, a somewhat incongruous name for a seaplane and certainly not as evocative as her original name, *Saro Cutty Sark*. His Excellency, the Lieutenant-Governor and his wife were then the first of the local dignitaries to be treated to a series of short flights over the island.

The Christening of the *Silver Bat*.

Four days later on Monday 7th July, the *Silver Bat*, as G-AAIP was now named, commenced the regular scheduled bi-weekly service to the mainland as originally planned, leaving Jersey at 10.30 hours and Woolston at 14.30 hours, but there was considerable flexibility in the service as the second scheduled flight on Friday 11th July left an hour late for the convenience of the passengers while an extra flight departed Jersey on the same day at 19.00 hours with more passengers for Southampton. The following week adverts appeared in the local press for midweek day return flights to Granville on the French coast, departing at 10.00 and 11.00 hours in the morning and returning at 17.00 and 18.00 hours in the evening with joyriding during the hours between the flights, while a Guernsey excursion, the only one in July, was advertised for Saturday 19th July. The month of July ended with the *Silver Bat* taking part in the 'Battle of Flowers' on 31st July, passing several times low over Springfield Stadium during the parade of floats and dropping flowers on the heads of the spectators; another well devised publicity stunt by Kirsten and Mace.

August continued with the same routine of bi-

Starting up the engines of the *Silver Bat*. This and the christening are two of a series of postcards recording the naming of the *Silver Bat*.

weekly scheduled return flights on Monday and Friday to Woolston with joyrides as frequently as was possible at other times. The *Silver Bat* only flew a couple of special charters during the month; once on 14th August when it flew to Reading at 10.30 hours, returning to the island at 17.30 hours in time to make another special flight with Dr Halliwell to Guernsey at 18.30 hours, and the other on 20th August when she made a charter flight to Woolston.

At the end of August, the *Silver Bat* returned to the Saunders-Roe factory at Cowes for a routine service and overhaul, but this was the last that the island would hear of the craft. On 10th September 1930 at 06.00 hours she left Cowes on a charter for Renfrew Aerodrome in Scotland and was never seen in the Channel Islands again. As with previous airlines the service ended unannounced without any explanation. It can only be assumed that charter flights were too few; there had been none to France despite the various advertising efforts; and the profits from scheduled flights were not enough to maintain the service through the bleak months of winter when there would be no subsidy from joyriding. One more Channel Islands air service had failed and there would be no attempt to establish another for three years.

A holidaymaker's snapshot of the *Silver Bat* on the sands in St. Aubin's Bay; everybody wanted to be photographed with the *Silver Bat*.

THE AIRSHIP R100 VISITS GUERNSEY

On Saturday 26th July 1930 the world's largest and most stately aircraft, the R100 Airship, visited Guernsey on a final test flight preparatory to her epic voyage across the Atlantic to Montreal, Canada, on 29th July 1930. She had left the mast at her base at Cardington the evening before at 19.02 hours for an 805-mile return flight lasting 24 hours and 16 minutes with Guernsey as her southern-most destination. Her arrival over the island at 14.30 hours on the Saturday afternoon generated massive excitement amongst the Guernsey population as she spent 45 minutes flying over the island and making two passes over the centre of St. Peter Port. Jersey was not honoured with a visit and the only people who were able to view her from Jersey were the Corbiere Lighthouse keepers who reported seeing a huge airship passing between Sark and Grosnez Point at 14.45 hours, but glinting in the sun, she was too far away for them to be able to identify her.

The *Guernsey Evening Press* of Monday 28th July printed a very romantic report of her visit:

> First a mere silvery grey blob in the sky, she came up slowly, against the fresh south-west wind. Then her full length and handsome lines became perceptible as she drew close to the

R 100 tethered to the mast at Cardington Airfield, Bedfordshire.

Harbour of St. Peter-Port. Her upper structure gleamed in the sun, and for a few minutes was partially merged with loose cloud. On her under structure appeared "R100" and the letters "F.A.A.V." the three gondolas were vividly outlined below the hull. The impression was of a great whale heading in an ocean of air. The spectacle was un-usual and beautiful. The only symptom of "force" was the busy whirr of the motors when she passed over the Town.

The R100 and R101

The British Government decided in 1925 to instigate the Imperial Airship Scheme to develop an airship that was capable of reaching India. The Government felt that if it had two prototypes built by different design teams and companies then it would get twice the level of innovation. The R101 would be built by the Royal Airship Workshops at Cardington while the contract for the R100 was awarded to the private sector, skilled airship constructors, Vickers at Howden. Vickers' design was the inspiration of Barnes Wallis and Neville Shute-Norway (later Sir Barnes Wallis of the Dam Busters bouncing bomb fame and Neville Shute the famous novelist.) Because the airships were Government financed, they would be called H.M. Airships. Construction of the two airships began in 1927 and the prototype R100 made her maiden voyage from Howden to the Royal Airship Workshops base at Cardington on the morning of 16th December 1929. Over the following months the R100 made a further six trial flights culminating in her flight to the Channel Islands on the 25th and 26th July 1930.

R100 over the Town Church Guernsey 26th July 1930. This is the only known image of the R100 over Guernsey published as a photo postcard.

Prior to her intended flight to India, the sister ship R101 required extensive modifications to improve her lift by adding an extra hydrogen gas bag to the centre of the ship that increased her length by 35 feet. On 1st October she emerged from No. 1 shed at Cardington and was moored to the mast while the R100 was removed from shed No. 2 and walked to No. 1 shed where it was intended that she would receive similar alterations. This was the last time the two airships were seen together and the last time the R100 would ever see the light of day. She had only made ten flights, covering 11,135 miles in twelve flying days.

The R100 and R101 Airships in the sheds at Cardington Royal Airship Works.

Three days later, on 29th July 1930 at 02.48 hours, the airship slipped its moorings from the Cardington mast and flew across the Atlantic heading for the Newfoundland coast. She arrived at the newly-erected mast in Montreal on 1st August 1930 at 05.37 hours having covered 3,364 miles in 78 hours and 49 minutes. Half an hour before midnight on 13th August the R100 set off again on her return flight to Cardington and aided by winds from the Gulf Stream, she achieved the 2,995 mile journey in 57 hours and 56 minutes knocking 21 hours off her outward journey time. She arrived at her Cardington mast on 16th August at 11.06 hours and on 17th August was moved into No. 2 shed for inspection. She was never to fly again.

The developing Imperial Airship Scheme only had a small group of fully trained officers and crew. These crew members had to cover the operation of both airships and on the return of the R100 from Canada, the majority of her crew were transferred to the preparation of the R101 for her intended flight to India. The Air Minister, Lord Thompson of Cardington, was to be a passenger on the R101 and there was pressure from the Government to make the flight to Karachi as soon as possible as Lord Thompson was required back in London for an Imperial Conference on 20th October.

On 1st October 1930 the R101 made her only trial flight in the new configuration in perfect weather conditions, but it was curtailed after only 17 hours following an engine failure. As there was a serious risk of engine failure that would put the whole voyage to India in jeopardy, it was bizarrely agreed that the flight could go ahead but that her cruising speed would now be the recommended maximum speed for the journey. On 4th October the race was on to depart before the deteriorating weather conditions could cancel the flight. The R101 slipped her mast for the last time at 18.24 hours in darkness and misty rain and as the ship was fully loaded with fuel it was worryingly noted that she had to drop 4 tons of ballast before she could gain any height. The airship made the 60 mile crossing of the English Channel in two hours, but as the airship reached the Beauvais ridge, notorious with aviators for dangerous gusting winds, a rent occurred in the rain-soaked outer skin of the upper part of the nose, and the forward gas bags, damaged by the gusting winds, suffered a critical loss of gas.

The captain made an almost perfect emergency landing but the hot exhaust fumes from an engine ignited the free hydrogen gas from the torn gas bags and the ship was immediately enveloped in fire; very soon all that remained was the skeleton of the once majestic ship, now twisted and broken by heat and explosions

Of the entire roll call of fifty-five crew and passengers of the R101, only eight men were able to escape from the wreck although one later died from injuries. Forty-eight crew and passengers died in the inferno. Two of the more famous passengers were the Air Minister, Lord Thompson, and Sir Sefton Brancker, Director of Civil Aviation, who had previously flown in the Supermarine Sea Eagle to Jersey in 1923. The disaster was the largest air fatality known. The victims were given full state honours and over a million mourners lined the funeral route. Memorial services were held in every town and village in the country as well as in the Channel Islands. The service in Guernsey was especially poignant as people remembered that many of the dead were the same crew who had given them such excitement earlier in the year when they

Wreckage of the R101 near Beauvais, about 50 miles north of Paris.

brought the R100 to the island in July. After a service in St. Pauls Cathedral, the 48 coffins were laid to rest in a special mass grave in Cardington Village.

The End of the Imperial Airship Scheme.

Following the R101 disaster, all future flights of the R100 were halted and planning of the R102 was put on hold until the outcome of the R101 inquiry.

With the country emerging from a global financial depression there was no longer any desire to continue with the project. The R100 was seen to be deteriorating in her shed at Cardington so the decision was made to sell her for scrap. Work to dismantle her began on 16th November 1931 and was finished in February 1932. Britain's flirtation with the giant airship was finished, but Guernsey would always remember a sunny summer afternoon when the world's largest airship spent 45 minutes gracefully dipping and cruising over the island.

The Stately Visitor to Guernsey

The photo postcard of the R100 over the Town Church in Guernsey is thought to be the only known image of the airship in the Channel Islands. It is all the more amazing that a short film of the visit also exists. Roger Dawson, a member of The Airship Heritage Trust, has posted on the Trust's Facebook Page a film made by his grandfather, Stuart Carmell, that shows the R100 flying over Castle Cornet and the Harbour Weighbridge clock tower.

Stills from the film made by Stuart Carmell of the R100 over the town of St. Peter Port, Guernsey

VISIT OF THE PROTOTYPE SARO CLOUD TO JERSEY

Although Kirsten and Mace finally gave up trying to run a Jersey service with the *Silver Bat*, they still maintained a desire to establish a service to the islands and had hoped to acquire a much larger amphibian craft being developed at East Cowes on the Isle of Wight by Saunders-Roe Ltd., the Saro Cloud. As early as July 1930, Kirsten had written to Saunders-Roe recounting their activities in Jersey:

Saro Cloud, G-ABCJ on the beach at West Park following her maiden flight to Jersey 26th September 1930.

> We are writing to give you some information regarding the air service which we have opened between England and the Channel Islands with your Cutty Sark type amphibian aircraft. As you know, we are running special trips to places on the French coast, Guernsey, etc, in addition to scheduled trips to England and we have found your Cutty Sark to be the ideal type for such operations, which, as you will readily understand, entail our making the fullest possible use of the amphibian properties of this splendid little machine....
>
> We would like to take this opportunity of saying how pleased we are with the machine, and how well it is standing up to the work it is being given to do. ... so delighted are we with our experience of the Cutty Sark that we hope to take a very early delivery of the Flying Cloud in order to cope with the demand the Cutty Sark has set up...

Sir Edwin A. V. Roe and Mr John Lord, the directors of Saunders-Roe Ltd. had watched with interest the efforts of Kirsten and Mace in establishing an airline from Jersey with their diminutive Cutty Sark. Hearing of the safe landing facilities on the island for an amphibian aircraft they decided to visit Jersey with their new large Saro Cloud and seek the opinions of Kirsten and Mace while seeing for themselves the possibilities of establishing a service with the new machine. On Friday 26th September Sir Roe and Mr Lord set out from the Sanders-Roe base at East Cowes in the prototype *Saro Cloud*, G-ABCJ, with Captain S. D. Scott as pilot, Squadron Leader Underhill as navigator and a mechanic and lady passenger. The *Saro Cloud* was the largest amphibian flying in English waters and the steady roar of her two 300 hp Wright Whirlwind J-6 engines that towered above her wings attracted a large number of curious spectators as the shimmering machine circled St. Aubin's Bay before landing on the water at 17.15 hours having accomplished the journey comfortably in only 70 minutes.

After meeting Kirsten and Mace and viewing the facilities of St. Helier Harbour and St. Aubin Bay the

The Saro Cloud amphibian was a much larger version of the Saro Cutty Sark as it carried a crew of two and had space for eight passengers. The prototype, G-ABCJ, that flew to Jersey in 1930 had a length of 50 ft 11½ in., a wingspan of 64 ft and a height of 16 ft 5 in.. Her power plant was two 300 hp Wright Whirlwind J-6 radial engines generating a cruising speed of 95 mph with an endurance of four hours.

party were preparing for their return journey when a thunderstorm broke. They waited in vain for an up to date weather report and then decided to attempt the flight back to the Isle of Wight despite the poor visibility. The wind increased to gale force, but during the flight home the visibility improved enough for them to observe the Channel Islands ferry battling through the waves a hundred feet below them while they were flying along in relative comfort and certainly much faster. Flying into the wind, the flight took them two hours compared to their outward flight of 70 minutes and although they were relieved to see the Isle of Wight when it came into view, they were all very impressed with the fine performance of the *Saro Cloud* in the worst possible conditions.

Sir Roe, Mr Lord and Captain Scott were convinced that a regular service to the Channel Islands was a distinct possibility using the Saro Cloud, as the craft had a range of almost 400 miles and could take its daily complement of passengers between Jersey, Guernsey and London in real comfort at a cruising speed of 95 mph in about 2 hours. What was required was a sound commercial company with sufficient capital to purchase at least two of the big amphibians in order to make the project a success. Kirsten and Mace planned to take delivery of two of the Saro Clouds and after operating a service for three months they then intended to apply for the lucrative mail contract. Unfortunately they did not have the financial resources to purchase the craft and with the deep recession starting to bite in the UK, they could not find any backers to support them. As Saunders-Roe were in no position to help, they had to finally give up the idea.

Saro Cloud G-ABCJ went to Canada to become CF-ARB. She returned to Saunders-Roe in 1934 when she was fitted with two 340 hp Napier Rapier IV engines that increased her speed to 102 mph. She was loaned to Guernsey Airways in August 1935 in this guise for a short period, but was withdrawn from use in 1936.

This rare postcard produced by SAUNDERS-ROE, COWES, I.O.W. shows the interior of the Saro Cloud cabin with eight rattan passenger armchairs in the salon, and the two-seater pilot's cabin.

THE SECOND LANDPLANE TO LAND ON JERSEY

A Moth in Winter

On 31st January 1931 a somewhat foolish attempt was made to fly to Jersey from Heston in a De Havilland Gipsy Moth 60G in the depth of winter. This was only the second attempt at a terra firma landing on Jersey and the first successful flight three and a half years previously, had been in summer. The pilot, RAF Flying Officer Donald Vernon Ivins had over five years' service. In 1929, he had suffered serious injuries in an aeroplane crash at RAF Henlow and when he went to Jersey to recuperate, he met Mrs J. G. Pontius of Queens Road, St. Helier and it was she that he was visiting. He had previously travelled to the island by mail boat, but this was his first flight to the island, and he had no definite idea where to land.

Ivins had hired the De Havilland Gipsy Moth 60G two-seater biplane, registration G-AAYL, from the famous airwoman, Miss W. E. Spooner. The blue painted plane was only 23 ft 11 ins. long with a wingspan of 30 ft It had a Gipsy engine capable of 105 mph and a cruising speed of 85 mph that gave it three and a half hours endurance.

Ivins set off from Heston at 10.15 hours on Saturday morning, but met gale force head winds over the English Channel. Blown off course and with fuel left for only 30 minutes flying, Ivins was forced to make a landing at 13.15 hours on the Cotentin coast of France at Barneville, 2 miles south of Carteret. Ivins had only passed his Civil Pilot's Certificate six weeks previously and was not certified for international flights. His illegal landing in France did not seem to concern the local authorities as with the weather unabated, Ivins was able to stay overnight in the small fishing village. The weather moderated during the night but he still experienced difficulties taking off from France because of mechanical problems with the plane. He finally got airborne at 09.50 hours on Sunday 1st February and landed safely 25 minutes later on the windswept sands between First Tower and Millbrook to be met by Mrs Pontius. Ivins had achieved the second ever England to Jersey flight by a landplane, albeit with an illegal detour to France. Ivins' visit caused great excitement amongst the Islanders as told by the *Jersey Morning News* for Monday 2nd February 1931 under the headline:

RAF Wing Commander Donald Vernon Ivins 2nd October 1906 – 18th May 1945.

> RAF Officer's Moth Arrives Despite strong gale. –.
> ROUGH WEATHER FORCES A LANDING NEAR GRANVILLE.

The story starts:

> Intense interest was caused about 10 o'clock yesterday morning among many thousand inhabitants, by a small moth seaplane flying over the island.
> It alighted on the sands near First Tower and was towed by car to Mr. W. B. Stevenson's Garage in Seaton Place, where it was visited by many people throughout the day.
> Residents on the Victoria Avenue were mildly surprised to see a car towing a plane along the road, at a time of year when flying crafts are not seen in Jersey. Many people in fact were seen to stare open-mouthed at the unusual sight.
> The plane was piloted by Flying Officer D. V. Ivins, who was its only occupant. During his stay in the island the Flying Officer is residing at No.2, Les Chalets, Queen's road, the residence of Mrs. J. G. Pontius.

The story concludes:

> …He hopes to fly here again, but the only difficulty is the landing. A certain amount of difficulty is experienced in the hiring of a 'plane when there is no recognised landing ground, and Flying Officer Ivins intends looking for a suitable field when he flies over the island on the return journey.
> If the weather moderates he will leave St. Aubin's Bay at low tide to-day, and attempt to fly direct to London, stoppages on the journey proving very costly.

As there were no refuelling facilities on the beach at Millbrook, the Gipsy Moth, with one of its wings folded, had to be towed by car and manhandled to Stevenson's Garage where it was "hangared" overnight and refuelled next morning.

Ivins refuelled the De Havilland Gipsy Moth 60G at Stevenson's Garage, he can be seen standing above the engine filling the fuel tank on top of the wings.

The reporter's limited knowledge of aviation is evident by his description of the craft as 'a small moth seaplane'! Even the most uninitiated should notice that it had wheels not floats.

After safely taking off again, Flying Officer Ivins gave an exhibition of stunt flying to the large group of spectators who had gathered to see his departure, before heading off for England. The *Jersey Evening Post* for Monday 2nd February stated in its "LATE NEWS" that:

> Flying Officer Ivins in his Gipsy Moth plane arrived safely at Heston Aerodrome at 3.30 this afternoon.

Even *Flight* magazine was intrigued by the incident and reported:

> Will this sight become common? A DH Gipsy Moth filling up at a Shell pump in a Jersey street. Jersey has no landing ground, so F.O. D. V. Ivan landed on the beach between First Tower and Millbrook, then folded the wings and brought the machine to a local garage, where he had it refuelled from a Shell pump. Aeroplanes do not attract much attention today, but judging from the crowd that gathered about the machine whilst refuelling, the novelty of fuelling a machine in the same way as cars are fuelled aroused considerable local interest.

Donald Ivins frequently visited Mrs Pontius throughout 1931 and 1932 when he would take friends for "flips" round the island and always give a display of his stunt flying skills before departing for home.

The Gipsy Moth 60G hired by Ivins was first registered as G-AAYL in June 1930 and acquired new by Miss Spooner who lived in Reading and was a famous aviator who flew G-AAYL in the Kings Cup Air Race in 1932. G-AAYL was then sold to a fellow aviator, Miss E. Battye and passed through several companies until it was impressed into war service with the RAF on 3rd August 1940 as BK835. It was scrapped a year later at St. Athan and removed from the records on 1st April 1942.

Miss W.E. Spooner preparing G-AAYL for the start of the 1932 King's Cup Air Race.

THE FIRST GERMAN VISITOR

Aircraft visiting the Channel Islands started with French aircraft to Jersey in the 1912 air race and French seaplanes in Guernsey during the First World War. French and British service craft made visits after the war, but it was not until the 1920s that English civil aircraft started visiting. Service aircraft still accounted for the majority of visits and civil craft were piloted by serving or retired RAF officers. It is unsurprising then that the first German aircraft to visit the islands came from England piloted by an RAF crew. Early in the morning of Sunday 17th May 1931, Flight Lieutenant Richard Hugh Barlow, accompanied by two fellow officers on the Air Force Reserve List, took off from RAF Worthy Down Aerodrome near Winchester intent on visiting Jersey in what was regarded as a 'veteran' aircraft, having had its sixth birthday the day before. The aircraft was a Fokker F III, Puma engine powered, monoplane that first flew in Germany on 16th May 1925 and now bore the British civilian registration markings G-AARG. Because of its venerable age and this registration, the craft was affectionately known as *Old Jarge*.

G-AARG arrived over Jersey at about 07.00 hours, but the pilot could not locate the 'seadrome' he was looking for, which is unsurprising as high tide was at 07.02 hours and the sands of St. Aubin's Bay were covered by water. The Fokker was not a seaplane and as Lieutenant Barlow could not find any safe landing on Jersey, he decided to make for Montebourg Airfield on the Cherbourg peninsula. Unfortunately, the Fokker was running low on fuel and Barlow was forced to land at 07.45 hours in the grounds of the Trappist monastery at Bricquebec. Much of the Cherbourg peninsula was a Military zone forbidden to foreign aircraft and Bricquebec was within this zone. The local police detained the aeroplane and its three British flying officers while they consulted with higher authorities in Cherbourg. The party were soon released and given permission to continue their journey and, after purchasing some cans of petrol, they thanked their Trappist hosts and flew on to what had been the First World War RAF British seaplane base at Querqueville near Cherbourg, where they arrived at 16.35 hours. Querqueville was now back in French Navy hands and in 1925 had become a training and research base for *Aèronavale*. Monsieur Loubry, the representative of Air-Union (soon to become Air-France), arranged for the craft to be fully refuelled and at 18.00 hours Lieutenant Barlow took off once more, heading across the Channel to arrive back at Worthy Down 75 minutes later.

Old Jarge – Fokker F III G-AARG at RAF Worthy Down.

The Fokker F III was a strange single-engined, cantilever high-wing monoplane with fixed undercarriage and unusual square section fuselage that provided enough directional stability for it to sport only a rather unattractive 'token' stub of a fin. It was 38 ft 3 in. long with a wingspan of 52 ft 10 in. and a height of 12 ft. The craft was designed to carry a pilot and four passengers with a fifth passenger or navigator sat next to the pilot in the cockpit. The powerplant was one Armstrong Siddeley Puma 240 hp engine that gave a maximum speed of 93 mph and a cruising speed of 75 mph with a range of 750 miles. Such a large range should have permitted Barlow to make the journey to Jersey and back with ease but he must have set off for Jersey rather recklessly with a petrol tank less than quarter full.

ONLY THREE OTHER FLEETING VISITORS TO JERSEY IN 1931

Besides the frequent visits of Donald Ivins and the abortive attempt of *Old Jarge* to visit Jersey, there were only three other aerial visitors to the Channel Islands in 1931 with Jersey the destination. Two visitors stayed for just a few hours while the third did not even land.

Jesse Boot, 1st Baron Trent of Nottingham: 2nd June 1850 – 13th June 1931

Jesse Boot, Baron Trent of Nottingham, died in his residence Villa Millbrook, at Millbrook, Jersey on 13th June 1931. Founder of Boots the Chemists, he was elevated to the peerage only two years before on 18th March 1929. In 1930, he and his wife had generously hosted a tea party for the dignitaries attending the christening ceremony on the beach at Millbrook, of the Kirsten and Mace, *Saro Cutty Sark*, to be named *Silver Bat*.

The funeral and interment in the cemetery of St. Brelade's Church was on 16th June, and at 09.15 hours an air-taxi chartered by photographers from the *Daily Mirror* and *Sunday Pictorial* national newspapers, left Croydon Aerodrome for Jersey in time for the photographers to capture pictures of the funeral. The machine in the red livery of Air Taxis Ltd. of Stag Lane, Edgeware, Middlesex, was one of the latest De Havilland 80A Puss Moths with registration G-ABMC. Piloted by Captain Birkett, it landed on the sands between Bel Royal and Millbrook at 12.55 hours and as soon as the funeral ceremonies ended, the photographers flew back to Croydon and raced to Fleet Street to get their photographs printed in the newspapers the next day.

Colonel, The Master Of Sempill

The notorious deeds of the Master of Sempill, as well as some of his many visits to Jersey, are chronicled later (*see* AVIATION IN SARK – A SPY COMES TO LUNCH *page 83*) and during these visits he would usually pilot his De Havilland D.H. 80 Puss Moth, registration G-ABJU. His flights to Jersey were to meet with Lady Houston, the rich widow resident of Beaufield, St. Saviour, to discuss financing private aviation. She was an eccentric millionaire aviation enthusiast who was financing the British entry for the Schneider Trophy Air Race and who would later finance a British aerial photographic survey of Mount Everest.

On Sunday 12th July 1931 the Master of Sempill arrived in Jersey for a meeting with Lady Houston unusually not by aeroplane, but on the GWR mail boat steamer. He determined to return to the mainland that evening and summoned a National Flying Services Ltd. air-taxi from their headquarters at Hanworth Park Aerodrome in Middlesex. Captain J. B Wilson, the pilot of the air-taxi, a diminutive Desoutter I, flew from Hanworth to Jersey where he had tea at St. Peter, and after a 25-minute rest, returned to the mainland with the Master of Sempill.

The National Flying Services Ltd. (NFS) was an organisation proposed in November 1928 to co-ordinate a national network of flying clubs and aerodromes on a commercial basis. The Air Ministry controversially supported the proposers and in June 1929 the British Government gave the NFS an exclusive Government subsidy. The first project of the NFS was to develop Hanworth Park as a functioning aerodrome for their headquarters. The aerodrome was reopened on 31st August 1929 and renamed London Air Park after which they opened aerodromes over the entire breadth of England.

Initially their flying activities were limited to training, but in 1930 the NFS started operating an air-taxi service using the Desoutter I monoplane. The NFS placed a large order for the Desoutter I and received 19 of the total 28 craft built by the

The Air Taxis Ltd. Puss Moth G-ABMC (photographed at a later date with a different pilot and passenger) had only been registered on 7th May 1931 and received its Certificate of Airworthiness on 11 May. It was resold on 5th November 1934 to Aircraft Exchange and Mart Ltd. and passed through several owners. On 17th September 1936 it was intriguingly sold to Richard V.D. Beaumont of Sark who was refused permission by the Dame of Sark to land it on the island and so based it at Croydon Airport. G-ABMC was impressed for war service but was unfortunately damaged beyond repair on 29th April 1942 when another aircraft ran into it at RAF White Waltham.

company; each NFS craft was painted in a bold black above bright orange NFS livery.

Following financial losses in the first year, famous names were co-opted onto the board of the NFS; Sir Alan Cobham joined, and the Colonel, the Master of Sempill was appointed Chairman. Despite the arrival of these 'heavy weights', the NFS continued to make financial losses in 1932 and the British Government withdrew its subsidy. In June 1933 the NFS went into receivership but continued to function until October 1934.

The designer and maker of the Desoutter I was a Dutch company named Desoutter Aircraft Company Ltd. The prototype, the Desoutter Dolphin, with registration G-AAGC, was first displayed at the Olympia Aero Show, London in July 1929 and then sold to South Africa. 'Dolphin' was dropped from the name and the production craft were known just as 'Desoutter I', the bulk of which were purchased by the NFS. The Desoutter I was a small fixed carriage monoplane with a crew of one and one passenger. Its length was 26 ft 0 in., wingspan was 35 ft 8½ in., and height only 7 ft. The powerplant was one Cirrus – Hermes I, 60 hp engine with a maximum speed of 125 mph, a cruising speed of 99 mph and a range of 498 miles.

Desoutter I aircraft G-AANB operated by National Flying Services.

RAF Training Flight

The only other recorded flight to Jersey in 1931 was on Thursday 12th November at 13.00 hours when a RAF twin-engined Supermarine Southampton II flying boat, S-1301, visited the island. This aircraft was from RAF 201 Squadron stationed at Calshot and after circling St. Helier Harbour the craft did not land but departed out to sea and back to the mainland.

Jersey Visitor – Amy Johnson CBE

In 1930 Amy Johnson became internationally famous for being the first woman pilot to fly solo from England to Australia in her second-hand de Havilland D.H. 60 G Gipsy Moth, G-AAAH, named *Jason*

On Sunday 8th September Amy arrived in Jersey not by air, but on the GWR mail boat *St. Helier*. She was giving a lecture the following evening to an audience of 1,300 Islanders. Her thrilling and humorous lecture that recounted exciting adventures flying over exotic countries received a thunderous response from her enthralled audience. Asked why she had not flown to the island, she explained that she no longer owned an aircraft as *Jason* had been acquired as a permanent exhibit at The Science Museum in South Kensington, London. G-AAAH, *Jason* can still be seen on display in the 'Flight Hall' of The Science Museum today.

Another of Amy Johnson's aircraft, the famous Puss Moth, G-ACAB, The *Desert Cloud* did fly to the Channel Islands in 1935 although not piloted by Miss Johnson. The story of this visit and also Amy's short life is recounted in a later chapter.

Amy Johnson photographed beside her Gipsy Moth *Jason*, during a stopover in Kolcata (Calcutta).

A SECOND SARO CLOUD VISITS JERSEY

Another new year dawned in 1932 without any promise of an air service to any of the Channel Islands. Indeed, during the first few months of the year there weren't even any air visitors to the islands until early March when Guernsey and Jersey each received one.

The first air visitor of 1932 was to Jersey in the afternoon of Tuesday 8th March 1932 when Captain S. D. Scott, senior pilot for the Saunders-Roe Company, took off from the Saunders-Roe base at East Cowes in their latest craft, the powerful twin-engined amphibian monoplane, 'Saro Cloud' A 19/2, and headed for Jersey. Captain Scott had brought the original prototype Saro Cloud A19/1, registration G-ABCJ to Jersey in 1930. This second Saro Cloud built by Saunders-Roe carried the registration G-ABHG and received her first Certificate of Airworthiness on 3rd December 1930. She was a unique variant of the Saro Cloud and for some unknown reason was named *Flying Amo*. In later life she was bought by Imperial Airways Ltd. before ending her days in 1941.

Scott guided his Saro Cloud safely down onto the beach of St. Aubin's Bay; he was only carrying two passengers and they quickly alighted onto the sands and made their way to the Palace Hotel. His passengers were both Welshmen, one a Mr H. Evans and the other the Conservative M. P. for Limehouse, the Honourable Evan Morgan, who succeeded in 1934 to the title of Earl of Tredegar. Despite Evan Morgan's known homosexuality, he married twice, once to the daughter of a Baron and the second time to the beautiful Russian Princess Olga Sergievna Dolgorouky.

Once Scott's passengers were safely disembarked, he revved up the engines of the Saro Cloud and taxied the amphibian out to sea, around Elizabeth Castle and through the mouth of St. Helier Harbour to moor opposite Albert Pier, before re-joining his passengers in the Palace Hotel. The reason for the visit to Jersey by Evan Morgan and his friend is not known, but it was brief as two days later the party re-embarked the Saro Cloud in St. Helier Harbour and once again Scott returned her safely to her base at Cowes.

The gleaming silver craft attracted much attention for two days as she rode her mooring in the harbour, and the visit of Evan Morgan was eagerly reported in the local press so if he had intended the visit to be a private romantic tryst with his companion, then arriving in a Saro Cloud, the most modern of seaplanes, was perhaps not the most discreet way to achieve it. Despite the interest in the Saro Cloud G-ABHG, *Flying Amo*, no photographic record of her visit has been discovered.

Saro Cloud, G-ABHG was the second Cloud to be built and the first variant of the class designated A19/2. When first built, she was powered by three 215 hp Armstong Siddeley Lynx NC engines at the request of the purchaser, the Honourable A.E Guiness, who wanted the third engine "for extra safety". Saunders-Roe experienced problems with three engines, and the Cloud was re-engined with two powerful 425 hp (317 kW) Pratt & Whitney Wasp C radials before delivery to the owner. To accommodate the increase in power she was fitted with an unique auxiliary aerofoil above the engines and twin tail fins and rudders to improve directional control. No similar machines were built by Sanders-Roe except for the 'SARO WINDHOVER' and G-ABHG remained a unique variant of her class.

Saro Cloud *Flying Amo* in front of the Saunders-Roe slipway at Cowes.

THE MONOCOUPÉ 70 – SECOND LANDPLANE TO LAND ON GUERNSEY

The first landplane to land in Guernsey alighted on Fort Field at Fort George in 1928. Four years were to pass before another intrepid pilot would attempt the Channel crossing to Guernsey in a landplane.

The plane making the flight in 1932 was a Monocoupé 70, a small two-seater cabin monoplane with the registration G-AADG, of American manufacture. The owner-pilot was Mr Ronald W. H. Knight who was on the staff of Shell-Mex Ltd. and he was accompanied by his fiancée, Miss N. Ainslie. The couple were visiting Mr Knight's uncle, Mr F. W. A. Knight of La Fosse, St. Martins.

Monocoupé 70 G-AADG, the second plane to land on Guernsey.

They set out from Hereford at 09.00 hours on Good Friday, 25th March, and although the aircraft had a range of 500 miles, they flew in stages, first stopping after 130 miles at Old Sarum and then 60 miles later at Hamble. From Hamble, they set off on the 110 mile stage to Guernsey passing Alderney on the way, but strong head winds slowed the craft's normal cruising speed of 95 mph and they did not arrive until after 14.00 hours. Mr Knight intended to land on Fort Field at Fort George, but Fort Field was occupied with people playing ballgames and Knight had to circle the island looking for a suitable place to land. The sight of the small plane circling low over the island excited locals and the large number of Easter weekend holidaymakers so that when the machine finally made a perfect landing at 14.15 hours in a large field on Mr Albert Gavey's farm, Friquet de Hout, bordering the Candie Road at Castel, it was soon inundated with spectators. The pilot and passenger seemed quite unconcerned by the excitement they were creating and gathering their luggage, quickly left for St. Martins in a taxi.

Mr Knight's intention was to spend the holiday weekend giving 'joyrides' to paying passengers from Vazon Bay. He flew 40 passengers on Easter Saturday, but on Sunday high winds and rain made flying impossible and the machine remained in the field at Castel, secured by ropes and surrounded by a temporary wire fence. Despite the inclement weather, large numbers of visitors were willing to pay 3d admission to the field to get a close look at the plane. Incredibly, this is another instance of there being no photographic record of a rare aircraft visit to Guernsey, despite the large number of spectators with cameras.

The departure of the Monocoupé 70 on Bank Holiday Monday, 28th March, was recorded in the *Guernsey Weekly Press* of 2nd April 1932. The weather cleared and was ideal for the return flight to England. Mr Knight had an easy take-off at 10.55 hours and with a fresh wind on his tail, the machine made a very fast Channel crossing. Mr Knight's uncle received a telegram stating that the monoplane and its passengers had arrived safely at Hamble at 12.20 hours. Although the plane had been built in 1928, it was a recent purchase for Mr Knight who flew 120 hours with it before this epic flight to Guernsey, which was the longest the pilot had ever made across water.

Guernsey Weekly Press of 2nd April 1932 report on the departure of the plane.

The Monocoupé 70

The Monocoupé 70 was a diminutive wood framed, doped fabric covered monoplane with a two seat (pilot and passenger) enclosed cabin. It had a wingspan of 30 ft and length of 19 ft 9 ins.. Her range was 500 miles with a maximum speed of 100 mph, using 6 gallons of fuel per hour. The Monocoupé was originally designed by the Central States Aircraft Co. of America, but the company was reorganised in 1928 as the Mono-Aircraft Corp. of Moliné, Illinois and it was this company that built G-AADG with a serial number 154. Although officially designated as a Monocoupé 70, G-AADG was fitted with a larger 5 cylinder 80 hp Armstong Siddeley radial engine.

G-AADG was owned by two other pilots after Ronald Knight, and with the outbreak of the Second World War the craft was commandeered, but proved unsuitable for any military role and was stored along with other redundant aircraft at Gatwick Airport. She never flew again and in 1947 was broken up at Gatwick.

A Monocoupé 70.

IMPERIAL AIRWAYS AIR-TAXI FLIGHTS TO JERSEY

Imperial Airways Ltd. was famed for developing Empire routes using the biggest airliners in production, but the company also maintained a full-time domestic service with smaller craft. This service did not run to regular destinations or a daily timetable but was a twenty-four-hour charter service, available out of Croydon Airport to anywhere in the United Kingdom or the north of Europe. Imperial Airways titled their service an 'Air-Taxi Service,' but they only maintained a small permanent fleet of aircraft as they would hire other aircraft according to demand.

The Westland IV and the Westland Wessex aircraft

The first air-taxi of Imperial Airways was the three-engined Westland IV 'Limousine',G-AAGW. A prototype Westland IV, G-EBXK, powered by three 95 hp Cirrus III engines, first flew on 21st February 1929. The Imperial Airways' craft was a second prototype with more powerful 105 hp Cirrus Hermes engines and a metal rear fuselage, that first flew in April 1929. Westland failed to obtain any orders for the craft and re-engineered it with three 105 hp Genet-Major 7 cylinder rotary engines. This new craft, the Westland Wessex, was a high-winged monoplane with a cruising speed of 95 mph, a top speed of 105 mph and a landing speed of only 65 mph making it ideal for a taxi service as it could land in small fields. In 1932 the Westland Wessex was (erroneously) credited with the safety features of the ability to fly on only two engines if one failed and being able to find a safe landing location with only one engine. Imperial Airways acquired two more of the craft, G-ABEG and G-ACHI, for their taxi service in 1933 and upgraded G-AAGW to Wessex standards. Other charter companies chose the Westland Wessex including the Portsmouth, Southsea, and Isle of Wight Aviation Ltd.. The safety features of three engines later proved unjustified with tragic consequences in 1935 when a Cobham Air Routes' Wessex was lost in the English Channel flying from Guernsey to Bournemouth.

Air-Taxi Flights to Jersey

The Imperial Airways air-taxi service was not cheap. Its clientele were primarily wealthy managers in the private and public sector whose air fares would be financed by their company or the public purse. The air-taxi service also fulfilled a vital role as an emergency service for important doctors, nurses and medicines as well as the next of kin of the seriously sick and dying, but this service was not philanthropic; it was still the prerogative of only the very rich. It was as an emergency service that an Imperial Airways air-taxi

Westland Limousine, Imperial Airways first air-taxi.

visited Jersey for the first time on three occasions during in1932.

Nancy, the young daughter of the Jersey contractor, Frank Le Quesne, of Les Vagues, Pontac, was taken critically ill and on 17th June, two London specialists, Dr Pearce-Gould and Dr Boldero were summoned to attend the young patient. The doctors flew from Croydon Airport late in the afternoon in the Imperial Airways Westland IV air-taxi, G-AAGW.

With the renowned Captain Olley at the controls and Imperial Airways Flight Engineer Buxton in the cockpit, G-AAGW arrived over Jersey at 18.00 hours, but the tide was up and from the air the Olley could not detect a suitable landing place. A smoke signal was lit on La Moye golf course, but when Olley reconnoitred the area he saw that although they would be able to make a safe landing, there was insufficient space to take-off again with a full passenger load. There was nothing to do but fly to an aerodrome in France and wait for the tide to recede. After about 95 minutes, G-AAGW returned and Olley landed on the beach at Millbrook where the machine was hauled up the slipway to spend the night out of reach of the next high tide. The doctors attended the child who had been moved to the Bon Air Nursing Home and her condition thankfully improved enough that the following morning Captain Olley was able to take-off in the Wessex at 10.05 hours with the specialist doctors and return to Croydon.

Four days later Captain Olley was called into service with G-AAGW when on the night of Wednesday 22nd June two girls living in London received a telephone call from Jersey to say that their father, Mr Richards, living at Ramona in Bel Royal was seriously ill. The two girls rushed to Croydon Airport at 04.00 hours on 23rd June and were flown by Captain Olley to Jersey where the Westland IV made a smooth landing on the sands of Millbrook two hours later at 06.00 hours as the tide was fully out. Luckily the Westland IV landed on the sands near Bel Royal slipway opposite the Richards' house and the girls were immediately able to see their father. The return flight is unrecorded, but it doubtless took place that morning as the girls remained in Jersey with their father.

On Sunday 17th July, Captain Olley again flew G-AAGW from Croydon to Bel Royal slipway, this time arriving at the civilised time of 13.30 hours following a journey of 105 minutes. On board were a family; father, mother, son and daughter who only a few hours previously had disembarked from a transatlantic liner. The father was an American, Mr Octave Vlamynck from New Jersey and his wife was from Jersey, C.I. and was racing to visit her mother, Mrs L. Herpe of Six Rues, St. Lawrence who was seriously ill. As soon as they alighted, the party were driven to St. Lawrence in a waiting car and Olley refuelled his craft before making the return flight at 16.00 hours.

Captain Olley and the Imperial Airways air-taxi Westland IV, G-AAGW never made another flight to Jersey. When G-AAGW was re-engineered as a Wessex she returned in 1933 and there were several other Imperial Airways air-taxi flights to Jersey in other aircraft with different pilots, but Captain Olley did not return to the islands until he made flights to Guernsey in aircraft belonging to his own airline in 1935.

AVIATION IN SARK – A SPY COMES TO LUNCH

Aviation in Sark

To attempt landing a fragile aircraft on Sark, an island only some 2.1 miles square, with small fields totally surrounded by 100+ foot high cliffs and lacking the luxury of any flat sandy beach, might be regarded as foolish if not impossible and yet on 21st August 1932 a De Havilland D.H.80 Puss Moth, registration G-ABJU, with a famous pilot and an illustrious passenger achieved the feat not once but twice in the same day. Sark was an island unique in the western world as being the last vestige of feudal government with laws originating from Norman times. The island of Sark was a Royal fief governed by a Seigneur who wielded absolute power. In 1565 when the island was a haven for pirates, Queen Elizabeth I endowed Helier de Cateret as first Seigneur in perpetuity, on condition that he keep the island free of pirates and continuously populate it with at least 40 loyal subjects.

By 1932 the population of the island was about 580 'loyal subjects' and the Seigneur was a lady, the indomitable Dame of Sark, Sibyl Hathaway (1884 – 1974). She was a widow with six children when she succeeded her father in 1927 to become the feudal lord

Sibyl Hathaway, the Dame of Sark from 1927 to 1974. The title Dame is the female form of the male Seigneur.

of the island. The Dame remarried an American, Robert Hathaway in 1929 and although he was legally her co-ruler and Seigneur, she remained the benevolent dictator of Sark until her death in 1974.

Foremost amongst the Dame's archaic rulings, she forbade any combustion engine on the island. The only form of transport was equine, including the famous Sark ambulance carriage, and there was no electric power. Given her aversion to the combustion engine, it is a puzzle why the Dame should permit such a disruptive and noisy machine as an aeroplane to alight on her land in 1932. (In 1936 she would refuse permission for one of her subjects, Richard V.D. Beaumont to land his Puss Moth G-ABMC on the island and he was obliged to base it at Croydon Airport.).

The clue to the conundrum is found in the rank of the pilot and the purpose of his passenger's visit. When the Dame acceded to her title in 1927 she was already heavily in debt, and rents from her tenant farmers would not alleviate her situation. She believed that to generate income she must promote tourism and she embarked on a publicity campaign for Sark. She wrote a 19-page article published in the July 1932 edition of the *National Geographic* magazine, accompanied by 21 photographs of island life, but she realised that she needed to reach a wider and more commercial audience through the national press. The Dame would not countenance any 'common journalist' with the task, but instead invited James Wentworth Day (1899 – 1983) to write an illustrated article about the island.

Wentworth Day had fought in the First World War and became a journalist after the war working for *Express* newspapers and *Country Life*. He was a high Tory of extreme right-wing views, a supporter of Benito Mussolini although suspicious of Hitler, a racist and xenophobe who thought homosexuals should be hanged. He had a career as an author writing articles and books on country life, his most famous being *Farming Adventure* published in 1943 detailing his horseback journey around the farms of East Anglia during the Second World War. The book was later reprinted with a new title, *Wartime Ride*. After the war he became a small-time broadcaster for radio and TV, but was eventually shunned by the broadcasting companies because of the extreme views that he aired. He was a close associate of another extreme right sympathiser and prominent aviator, the Master of Sempill (Colonel the Hon. William Frances Forbes-Sempill, later Lord Sempill, 1893 – 1965) and it was he who piloted Wentworth Day on his visit to Sark. Wentworth Day's article was published in the London *Evening Standard* where he described the flight from London, leaving Hanworth Aerodrome and flying over Surrey, Hampshire and the Isle of Wight, crossing the English Channel and flying past Alderney, Herm and Jethou before landing in the Seigneurie grounds. He wrote in a very lyrical style:

> Out of a mackerel sky our airplane descended on the last feudal state in Europe, the island of Sark. In two hours fifteen minutes of flying time Colonel the Master of Sempill had piloted us from the sprawling complicated London to this compact domain ruled by an Englishwoman and her America-born husband who have their own army (the 40 tenants), summon their own parliament, and make their own laws.

Of this first landing of a plane on Sark he wrote:

> People ran, cows looked to the skies whence came this new vision, and we glided down into a long, narrow field filled with clover.

The article was illustrated with a photograph of Sark Harbour and a 'Chief Pleas' member being sworn-in by candlelight but although he eulogised on the many virtues of Sark, what he failed to mention was that no other tourist would be permitted to fly to the island; if you wanted to visit Sark you could only reach it by boat!

It is uncertain if the Dame was acquainted with either of the flyers but the pilot, the Master of Sempill, was certainly of her class and only he was ever afforded this unique privilege of landing an aircraft on Sark, a privilege refused to her own loyal subjects. Sempill

The Master of Sempill. Colonel the Hon. William Frances forbes-Sempill, later Lord Sempill. (1893 – 1965).

landed his DH 80 Puss Moth, G-ABJU, on Sark at 12.45 hours and he and Wentworth Day were promptly greeted by the Dame and invited to take lunch at the Seigneurie.

After their meeting and lunch, Sempill flew on to Jersey for a meeting with the extremely wealthy, if not slightly eccentric, philanthropic widow, Lady Houston. The philanthropy of this resident of the Parish of St. Saviour had already made it possible for Britain to retain the Schneider Air Race Trophy in 1931 and Lady Houston was now intending to finance the first aerial photographic survey of Mount Everest; Sempill would not be one of the pilots, but he was a senior member of the Committee of the 'Houston – Mount Everest Expedition'. His landing on Jersey after this flight from Sark had been effected at Don Bridge where the boys of the Rotary Club who happened to be holding their summer camp, were given an exciting aerial display and salute on his departure two hours later. Sempill and Wentworth Day did not return directly to the mainland as Sempill had left his coat behind at the Seigneurie (perhaps the lunch was a little too 'liquid') and so they made a second landing on Sark and another visit to the Dame before their return flight to Hanworth.

Sempill was a very famous and courageous aviator, but he was also an infamous and naive spy for the Japanese who, because of his status in society, never faced a reckoning for his treachery during his lifetime. The full damming extent of his treachery never became known until the release of classified documents into the public domain at the Public Record Office in Kew after the expiration of the 60-year ruling in 2011. Sempill had worked and spied for the Japanese before the Second World War and even after the attack on Pearl Harbour he was caught sending British aviation secrets to Japan. Spying during wartime is high treason and punishable by firing squad, but because his father was equerry to the King, he was protected by Winston Churchill and the Establishment and shipped off to Canada out of harms' way where he led a safe and protected life until after the war ended.

De Havilland DH 80 Puss Moth, G-ABJU

The plane that flew to Sark

Although Sempill had access to hundreds of aircraft during his lifetime he only owned one, his de Havilland D.H. 80 Puss Moth, G-ABJU, in which he flew to Sark on 21st August 1932. He had acquired the new G-ABJU a year earlier, and its Certificate of Registration No. 3062 shows it was registered on 30th March 1931. Sempill was issued with a Certificate of Airworthiness for the craft a month later. G-ABJU was based mainly at Hanworth and it was from there that the flight to Sark took place, but in later years it was based at Gatwick and also at a private airstrip at The Lizard, Cornwall.

The de Havilland DH 80 Puss Moth, G-ABJU, was heavily modified and enhanced for Sempill's return flight to Australia in 1934 and 1935 and it remained in his possession until the Second World War when private flying was banned. On 27th March 1941 Sempill sold G-ABJU, and it was impressed into military service as ES918 on 31st May 1941. It was used by RAF '4 Ferry Pilots Pool' and later '1 Ferry Pilots Pool' based at RAF White Waltham. On 24th August 1941 ES918 departed Prestwick Airport, Ayrshire with two pilots on board bound for White Waltham, but she crashed at RAF Dumfries, Tinwald, Dumfriesshire following brake seizure. The pilots escaped unharmed, but ES918 was written off and struck off the register on 3rd September 1941.

Did any other plane land on Sark?

In a later chapter, mention is made of the visit of a Gipsy Moth to Guernsey on 27th July 1935 piloted by two Cambridge University students who were returning home from a flying excursion round Europe. The account is described in the paragraphs headed *A Gipsy Moth on Sark?* and was reported by a journalist at the time for *The Star* newspaper in Guernsey. This reporter frustratingly ends his report with the throwaway comment: "It is understood that they landed in Sark and called on La Dame." We may never know the validity of his statement and as there is no other evidence to corroborate his comment, it seems very unlikely.

A Second World War Crash-landing on Sark

German forces occupied all the Channel Islands during the Second World War, but the isolated and tiny island of Sark only warranted a token occupation force and the invaders never attempted to land an aircraft on the island.

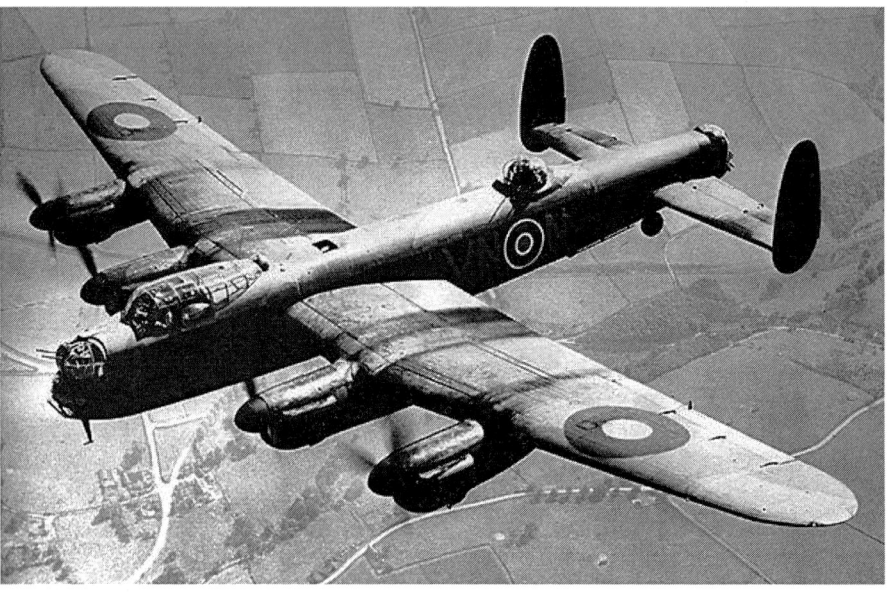

An Avro Lancaster Bomber.

On the night of 22nd November 1942, a massive Allied bombing raid took place on Stuttgart in Germany with over 200 bomber aircraft flying from various airfields and bases around Britain. After dropping their bombs, the aircraft received return fire and an Avro Lancaster bomber, W4107, from RAF 49 Squadron at Scampton in Lincolnshire, with seven crew on board, took several direct hits setting fire to the starboard inner engine and inside the fuselage. Fearing an imminent explosion, four of the crew were ordered to bail out which they did successfully but then the pilot, Flight Sergeant Eric J. Singleton, decided to get the damaged aircraft back to England. The two remaining crew successfully extinguished the fires in the fuselage and somewhat miraculously the engine fire extinguished itself. Sergeant Singleton was now flying without his navigator who had bailed out, and when he reached the coast, he thought that he was north of the Cherbourg Peninsula crossing the Channel for England. When he saw land beneath him, he imagined that it was friendly terrain and determined to bring the Lancaster down. He landed "wheels up" and bumpily skidded some 500 feet ploughing through the hedge bordering one field and coming to rest at right angles in another.

When Singleton and his remaining crew members clambered out of the aircraft they were met by a reception party that they assumed were the local Home Guard; that was until they were ordered in German to put up their hands. They realised that their welcoming committee were some rather startled German troops and they were informed that they had landed on Sark in the Channel Islands. Singleton and his crew, including the four who had bailed out and had been captured, spent the rest of the war in a P.O.W. camp.

The Dame of Sark with her husband Robert Hathaway and their two poodle dogs, are photographed inspecting the wreckage of the Avro Lancaster (part of which is behind them in the photograph) in a field on Sark. The Dame is accompanied by a group of the German Occupation Forces billeted on Sark. The Avro Lancaster bomber was too large for the Germans to remove from the island and pieces of wreckage can still be found today in what has affectionately become known by the Sark locals as 'Aeroplane Field'.

FLYING OFFICER DONALD IVINS, JERSEY'S MOST FREQUENT VISITOR

Bristol F.2B Type 14 Fighter.

Flying Officer Donald Vernon Ivins was only the second pilot ever to execute a terra firma landing on Jersey on Sunday 1st February 1931. After this initial visit he bought his own aeroplane, a vintage Bristol Fighter F.2B Type 14 with registration G-EBIO, made several more visits with it in 1931, and became Jersey's most frequent air visitor in 1932.

Ivins maintained his Bristol F.2B at RAF Henlow in Berkshire and most of his visits to Jersey were made at weekends when he would land on the Millbrook sands. He carried a collapsible boat in the aircraft in case he was forced to ditch in the sea, and he always gave a display of stunt flying on his departure for home.

There is no accurate log of Ivins' visits in 1932, but visiting aircraft were still newsworthy events and the first visit recorded by the local press took place on Saturday 16th April when he cleared customs at Heston at 07.30 hours and arrived in Jersey at about 09.30 hours, returning to Heston on the following Monday. He visited on Saturday 7th May and again on Friday 13th May. Ten days later a friend of Ivins had a parent who was dangerously ill in Jersey and Ivins brought his friend to the island on Monday 23rd May and returned home the next day. He carried another passenger on Friday 3rd June and returned again to Jersey on Thursday 18th August for a summer holiday of ten days. There is no mention of other visits until a Christmas excursion on Wednesday 21st December when he stayed until Friday 30th December. His visits to Jersey were by far the most frequent of any pilot; he was undeterred by weather conditions and his flights were more regular than some previous commercial ventures.

The Bristol Fighter

Ivins' Bristol Fighter F.2B Type 14 was a First World War vintage machine; the prototype first flew in October 1916 and his craft was built for the RAF in 1918. The Bristol F.2B Type 14 Fighter was a two-seater biplane built as a reconnaissance aircraft but capable of carrying a machine gun that fired through the propeller. The craft was a fixed wing landplane with fixed undercarriage and was a product of the Bristol Aeroplane Co. Ltd.. The Fighter had a wingspan of 39 ft 3 in., a length of 26 ft 2 in. and a height of 10 ft 1 in. and the power plant was a Rolls Royce Falcon III V12 engine of 275 hp, although Ivins' machine had a 300 hp Hispano-Suiza engine. The range of the aeroplane was 369 miles and the maximum speed was claimed to be 123 mph, but Ivins never managed to attain that speed.

The Bristol F.2B was a popular aircraft nicknamed "Brisfit" and when first built in 1918 Ivins' Brisfit had the service registration, H1254. It remained with the RAF until November 1923 when the Aircraft Disposal Co. Ltd. obtained its civil registration, G-EBIO. It became the most well-known Brisfit built, as it was used as a demonstrator for nearly eight years until sold to Ivins in 1931. Ivins tested it to its limits with long flights to Jersey and air races on the mainland.

Despite Ivins' frequent visits to Jersey, a photograph of the Bristol Fighter on the island has yet to be discovered.

At the opening of Speke Airport (Liverpool) on 1st July 1933 Ivins flew to victory in a race from Blackpool and back attaining a speed of 114.25 mph.

THE PORTSMOUTH CONNECTION

In 1928, the Air Ministry wrote to all towns in the United Kingdom with a population greater than 20,000, promoting the advantages of owning an airport. Portsmouth City Council considered such a scheme for Portsmouth and it won immediate approval; there were only seven other municipal airports in the country at Blackpool, Hull, Norwich, Liverpool, Nottingham, Manchester and Bristol; Portsmouth intended to be the eighth and best.

Portsmouth Airport

The Council purchased 276 acres of land to the north-east of Portsea Island, including a farm and government land with old fortifications built to repel a Napoleonic invasion, all for a sum of £77,000, and they allocated a further £52,000 for the construction work of the airport. Construction involved blowing up 103,000 cubic yards of fortifications, levelling the ground and seeding it and erecting essential buildings, all of which was put out to tender. The finished airport covered 204 acres with grass landing strips of 4,500 ft and 2,500 ft, two hangars, a customs office, control tower and refreshment chalet while the old farmhouse was converted into the premises of a flying club.

The official opening of the airport took place on 2nd July 1932 when 50,000 spectators were entertained by an air pageant involving over 100 aircraft. The highlight was the arrival of the giant German airship Graf Zeppelin that sedately cruised low over the city, but there was subsequent embarrassment with questions in the House of Commons when it was realised the German aviators had been given an excellent opportunity to spy on the Royal Naval Dockyard. On 8th July, the airfield was chosen to be the finishing point for the King's Cup Air Race and then a month later, on 10th August, another huge pageant was held to honour National Aviation Day with the air ace Sir Alan Cobham and his flying circus attending. Sir Alan said that Portsmouth was the best aerodrome on which he had ever landed.

Portsmouth Airport was operational prior to its official opening, and a new company, Portsmouth, Southsea and Isle of Wight Aviation Co. Ltd. (PSIOWA) were 'quick off the mark', securing the rights to run a passenger service to the Isle of Wight from the airport and occupying one of the two new airport hangars. The PSIOWA had evolved from Inland Flying Services Ltd., a company originally from Romford in Essex. PSIOWA started services from Portsmouth with a specially commissioned Westland Wessex, G-ABVB, that flew joyrides from the airport while waiting for Ryde Airport to be developed to accommodate the Wessex. Once operational, the Portsmouth to Ryde service quickly became a huge success and was known affectionately as "Spithead Ferry" or "Solent Ferry – the World's Shortest Airline." Before the end of June 1932, PSIOWA had flown over 1,000 people and at the summer season height were flying 26 return flights a day to Ryde.

PSIOWA offered aircraft maintenance and over the years their air services expanded with an increasing fleet of aircraft. At the start of the Second World War the company was ordered to stop flying and concentrate on the manufacturing and repair of military aircraft, while their fleet of planes and pilots, who by then included the famous Amy Johnson, joined the National Communications Service. After the war PSIOWA never regained their aircraft fleet but developed their manufacturing base and in 1946 changed their name to the more user friendly, Portsmouth Aviation.

Official opening of Portsmouth Airport.

PSIOWA's Unique Westland Wessex

PSIOWA's first aircraft was a specially commissioned cabin monoplane Westland Wessex, chosen because the Portsmouth to Ryde route was all over water and the Wessex had three engines, but reputedly could fly on two in the event of an engine failure. The Wessex, G-ABVB, was built to order and delivered on 7th May 1932. It had three 7 cylinder Armstrong Siddeley Genet Major engines that were modified to increase its speed by 4 mph The fuselage was larger both by height and width and after reducing the luggage space the craft could accommodate six passengers rather than four, while the pilots' cabin was raised by 18 inches to allow them to see sideways over the wings. This unique Wessex also had tubular steel spars in the wings instead of wood, and an all-over metal skin. G-ABVB was the only Wessex bought by PSIOWA, as they mostly required faster craft, but she gave excellent service and was featured on all their advertising until she crashed at Ryde on 30th May 1936.

PSIOWA's first aircraft Westland Wessex G-ABVB.

In 1932 the States of Jersey watched with envy the developing Portsmouth Airport and the success of the PSIOWA, and the Chamber of Commerce decided to invite Lionel Balfour, the managing director of PSIOWA, to visit Jersey and undertake a tour of inspection of the island in order to locate a suitable site for an airport. Balfour was only too willing to offer his services as he hoped to obtain a contract to build the airport and wanted to develop a regular air service between Portsmouth and the new Jersey Airport.

PSIOWA Westland Wessex G-ABVB visits Jersey

On Monday 17th October Lionel Balfour and his wife, the former Lady Myrtle Jellicoe, took off from Portsmouth Airport in the company's Wessex G-ABVB and flew to Jersey for a three-day inspection. On arrival, they first touched down on the sands of St. Aubin's Bay and then took off again to view a landing site at Les Quennevais but Balfour quickly dismissed it. The party put up at the Grand Hotel and the next day Balfour was taken on an extensive tour of the island by the President of the Chamber of Commerce, Mr John Le Marquand. They saw the racecourse, the old prisoner-of-war camp, Les Landes, Les Platons, Mont La Mare and an area north-east of St. Peter's Barracks which Balfour considered the most favourable. He spent most of his third day writing a detailed submission to the Chamber of Commerce before flying back to the mainland. His lengthy report recommended two possibilities, Mont La Mare at St. Ouen, and the more favourite option, the land at St. Peter's Barracks. Although the report Balfour wrote was thorough, the Chamber of Commerce failed to make any decision except to use the report as a basis for further deliberations by a special committee. Neither of Balfour's ulterior objectives ever came to fruition as the Ministry of Aviation would not recognise the PSIOWA as a competent company to contract for the construction of the airport and a year later at the end of 1933 Jersey's own new airline would establish a service between Portsmouth and Jersey. Portsmouth Airport would feature greatly in the development of an airline service to Jersey but unfortunately for Balfour the PSIOWA would not be involved with it.

G-ABVB featured on all the posters of PSIOWA. The posters had different wording for various locations; this is an exceedingly rare version for use in Jersey.

NUMEROUS FLIGHTS TO JERSEY BUT NONE TO GUERNSEY

1933 saw the sky over Guernsey as empty as it had been before the First World War. There would have been no aviation activity on the island in 1933 if it were not for the efforts of one man working in a garage in St. Peter Port designing, building and eventually flying his own miniature aircraft named the *Wee Mite*. (*See* THE FIRST AIRCRAFT BUILT IN GUERNSEY *page 111*).

By contrast in Jersey, 1933 was to be one of the busiest and most significant years. There was an RAF service flight, Imperial Airways Air Taxi and Air Ambulance flights, charter flights by new airline companies, joyriding, repeat visits by regular visitors, flights to survey the island for a new airport site, a spectacular air pageant, and even the first aeroplane crash. Finally, in the last bleak days of December against all odds, the most important chapter in Channel Islands' aviation history was written when Jersey's own commercial airline was established flying from a beach 'airfield zone' prior to construction of the airport.

3rd February 1933 – The first visitor of the year, an RAF aeroplane from RAF Northolt

Despite the plethora of reporting on air activity in Jersey some accounts are woefully incomplete, this is especially frustrating when the visit had some significance. On 3rd February 1933 at about 14.00 hours an RAF aeroplane from RAF Northolt landed on Jersey after a flight lasting two hours and twenty minutes. The initial local press reports failed to record the type of aircraft that landed or the reason for the visit because the journalist was more excited that the second pilot of the craft, Sergeant F. W. Otter, was an 'Old Victorian', an ex-pupil of Victoria College, St. Helier; with his father still living in Gorey Village. The reporter failed to mention the name of the first pilot and conjectured that the plane was on a routine training flight, but the aircraft was a landplane from RAF Northolt and an R.A.F landplane would not make a training flight almost entirely over water.

Northolt Airfield in South Ruislip was established for the Royal Flying Corps and opened in May 1915 making it the RAF airfield in longest continuous use. RAF Squadrons based at Northolt in 1933 were No. 41 Squadron that arrived in April 1923 and No. 24 Squadron that arrived in January 1927. No. 24 Squadron was a Communications Squadron, but also became the only RAF 'Air Transport Unit', tasked with transporting high-ranking officers, Air Ministry officials, Government Ministers, dignitaries and even members of the royal family. Sergeant Otter boasted of his considerable experience flying statesmen to France and Geneva and it seems probable that the pilots were members of this 'Air Transport Unit'. It is especially frustrating that the type of aircraft was not recorded as this was the first visit by an RAF landplane from Northolt to the Channel Islands and it reportedly only remained in Jersey for a few hours before returning to its base at Northolt. A more measured report appeared in the *Jersey Weekly Press* of Saturday 11th February 1933 and here we learn that the first pilot officer was none other than Jersey's most 'frequent flyer', Donald Vernon Ivins and the craft was his vintage Bristol Fighter G-EBIO. Furthermore, he had not returned to Northolt that same evening as originally reported but remained in the island over the weekend and made his return flight to England from Bel Royal at 14.30 hours on the following Sunday.

This was the first flight to Jersey of an aircraft from RAF Northolt, but it was not an official RAF flight. Ivins made frequent visits to Jersey in 1933, but second pilot and Jersey 'Old Victorian', Sergeant Otter, never flew to Jersey again in an RAF aircraft.

Frequent Return Visitors to Jersey

Jersey's most 'frequent flyer', Donald Vernon Ivins had attained the rank of Flight Lieutenant when he continued his visits to the island through the winter months of early 1933 in his vintage Bristol Fighter, G-EBIO. Following this visit from RAF Northolt, Ivins visited again on Wednesday 15th February, returning after five days from the sands at Bel Royal at 09.40 hours. He visited over the weekend of Sunday 12th March and later that same week on Friday 17th March for nine days when his return flight in 100 minutes was a record. On Friday 31st March, Ivins left Heston for Jersey with two passengers and his last recorded arrival was a 'late in the day' landing at 20.00 hours on Friday 19th May in St. Aubin's Bay. This appears to

A Bristol 'Brisfit' Fighter F2B Type 14, similar to Ivins' machine.

have been his last visit, but he flew in air races on the mainland during the summer of 1933 before selling his Brisfit the following year.

The other regular visitor was Colonel the Master of Sempill who made visits to Jersey to meet with Lady Houston. On Tuesday 7th February 1933 Sempill's De Havilland D.H.80 Puss Moth, G-ABJU, cleared customs at Heston Airport shortly after lunch, but his passage across the Channel was bumpy and the flight took 3 hours before he landed at Les Quennevais Racecourse at 15.35 hours. He had intended to call in on the Dame of Sark and make the first landing on Herm but the high winds prevented this. Capt. G. MacDonald M.C., Staff Captain, on behalf of the Lieutenant Governor, along with Mr R.C.F. Maughan, Chairman of the Jersey Centre of the Royal Empire Society met Sempill when he landed. Sempill's visit was to inspect the site at St. Peter for Jersey's proposed airport and report his recommendations to the States' representatives. Sempill was national deputy chairman of the Royal Empire Society and the second reason for his visit was to deliver the inaugural lecture to the newly formed Jersey Centre of the Royal Empire Society on Wednesday 8th February at the Palace Hotel in St. Saviour. The meeting was presided over by the local chairman, Mr R. C. F. Maughan and guests of honour included the Lieutenant Governor and the Bailiff. Membership of the Royal Empire Society, especially of the Jersey Centre, was notoriously right

The Master of Sempill's De Havilland D.H. 80 Puss Moth G-ABJU. Two lady friends are attempting to fold back the wings of the craft for storage at Hanworth Aerodrome in 1933.

wing, so Sempill was very at home in the company. The title of his lecture "Aviation and Its Importance to the Empire" appeared innocuous as he charted the history of aeronautics in Britain through to the developing Imperial Airways routes of the British Empire, but even his most right wing listeners must have felt a little uncomfortable when Sempill concluded his lecture by projecting a German Third Reich Nazi propaganda film of the ten day return journey of the Graf Zeppelin dirigible between Friedrichshafen in Germany and Pernambuco in Brazil. Sempill had travelled on the Graf Zeppelin and paraded a guest companion that he had brought to Jersey – a very young German sailor who had served on the Graf Zeppelin from the age of fifteen!

Lady Houston and her Jewellery

The philanthropic Lady Lucy Houston was not a native of Jersey, but a seventy-six-year-old tax exile resident. When she wished to buy some diamonds and jewellery from the London jewellers and medal makers, Spink and Sons, she engaged the charter services of Imperial Airways to bring Captain and Mrs Spink to Jersey with a selection of gems and jewellery. At 08.15 hours on Tuesday 21st February the Imperial Airways three-engined Westland Wessex,

Imperial Airways Wessex G-AAGW in front of the Imperial Airways hangar at Croydon Airport.

G-AAGW, left its base at Croydon Airport piloted by Captain Lionel Louis Leleu, with Flying Engineer Casely as crew and their two passengers carrying their valuable cargo. G-AAGW landed on the beach of St. Aubins Bay at 10.00 hours and Captain Spink and his wife proceeded straight away to the home of Lady Houston while Captain Leleu, who happened to be a Channel Islander, paid a personal visit to the Palace Hotel to meet an old friend, Mr R. G. Miller, who was employed there. Lady Houston took some time to make her selection because it was late afternoon before the Wessex made its return flight to Croydon.

Pilot Captain Lionel Leleu had made his home on the mainland and joined Imperial Airways in 1926 after previously piloting for Berkshire Aviation Tours. This visit to Jersey was his last as a month later his Armstrong Whitworth Argosy II, registration G-AACI *City of London*, on a flight from Brussels to Croydon on 28th March, developed an on-board fire and crashed near Diksmuide in Belgium killing the three crew and twelve passengers.

The Imperial Airways Air-Taxi and Air-Ambulance Services

The managers of Imperial Airways could never have imagined that a famous old and exceedingly rich Jersey resident, Lady Houston, would use their air charter service to buy jewellery from London, but the Air-Taxi and Air-Ambulance Services of Imperial Airways were an invaluable development of the air charter business that enabled an aircraft to be summoned almost at a moment's notice to fly anywhere. If Imperial Airways did not have a suitable craft available, then they would charter one from the numerous small companies or private owners that proliferated the airfields of England. There existed the reassurance that if a person needed to travel urgently, they could fly to any destination they wanted, but this reassurance was expensive and was the prerogative of the very rich, such as Lady Houston.

Messrs. Bellingham's Ocean Travel Office on Mulcaster Street in St. Helier, Jersey was the only travel agent on the island in 1933. It had been established as a shipping agent in the mid eighteenth century and can rightly claim to be the oldest travel agency in the world. With the arrival of the aeroplane and the Imperial Airways Air-Taxi service, Bellingham's was thrust into the twentieth century to cope with the new technologies of radio, telegraph and the telephone, and the requirement to satisfy the immediate demands of aerial passengers by procuring an aircraft from the mainland at a moment's notice.

The First Air Ambulance Flight

On Sunday morning, 9th April 1933, at 07.00 hours, Captain Harold Benest, manager of Bellingham's, received urgent instructions to procure an air-ambulance to transfer a patient from "Oaklands" at Mont-au-Prêtre to a London nursing home for an immediate operation. Captain Benest telephoned Croydon Airport where Imperial Airways arranged for a four-passenger seater De Havilland D.H.83 Fox Moth craft with the registration G-ABUT, belonging to Surrey Flying Services Ltd., to undertake the charter from Croydon piloted by Imperial Airways' Captain Woods; who already had a good knowledge of the island having landed the first landplane on Jersey in 1927.

Captain Woods set off from Croydon Airport mid-morning, but soon encountered fog over the English Channel and was twice forced to land G-ABUT on the French coast near Cherbourg, but eventually managed to land safely on the sands of St. Aubin's Bay near First Tower at 15.05 hours. The patient, accompanied by his

Captain Woods' De Havilland D.H.83 Fox Moth on the sands of St. Aubin's Bay.

wife, a doctor and a nurse, was brought to the aircraft by private ambulance and G-ABUT took off again an hour later. The return journey was uneventful, and the patient was safely delivered to the London nursing home by 19.00 hours. Despite the weather conditions, the first air-ambulance flight from Jersey had been initiated and completed successfully within twelve hours, but unfortunately the patient died within the week.

On Monday 10th April, Captain Benest again received a request to charter a plane, this time to bring a family of three to the island from London during the morning of Thursday 13th April. On Tuesday 11th April, Imperial Airways once again arranged for G-ABUT to undertake the charter from Croydon, piloted this time by Imperial Airways' Captain Hancock, while on the island, Bellingham's were advertising for passengers for the return flight; they managed to book three. On the Thursday Captain Hancock took off from Croydon Airport at 12.10 hours and landed his three passengers on the beach at Millbrook at 14.14 hours. After 90 minutes on the beach, G-ABUT took off again at 15.49 hours carrying three Jersey businessmen for her return flight to Croydon Airport where she arrived in the early evening.

G-ABUT was the first of 98 production models of the De Havilland D.H.83 Fox Moth. The prototype, designed by A. E. Hagg, flew for the first time in March 1932. It had an unusual structure for a single engine biplane as the open cockpit for the pilot was located well aft, behind the wings, on a plywood-covered fuselage. A small cabin for four passengers was enclosed within the fuselage ahead of the pilot. The wingspan of the craft was 30 ft 10½ ins., the maximum speed was 110 mph

D.H. 83 Fox Moth G-ABUT in the Surrey Flying Services Ltd. colours. Below the cockpit she sports the legend: "SURREY FLYING SERVICES LTD. AIR PORT OF LONDON" and above this the inscription: "Winner of the King's Cup Race 1932".

and the endurance was 375 miles. This was achieved with a diminutive power plant; either a 120 hp Gipsy III or a 130 hp Gipsy Major engine.

Less than a week after G-ABUT's visits to the island, Bellingham's were again urgently contacted at 09.45 hours on Wednesday 19th April, this time by the manager of the Bonne Nuit Chalet Hotel, who had a wealthy English resident, Mr R. A. Dagenhardt, in need of immediate repatriation to London. Within twenty minutes a suitable craft was found with the Portsmouth, Southsea and Isle of Wight Aviation Company Ltd. at Portsmouth Airport who informed Bellingham's that their aeroplane would arrive from Portsmouth on the beach at St. Aubin's Bay at noon.

Amazingly, precisely at 12.00 hours the PSIOWA General Aircraft Monospar ST- 4 Mark 1 with registration G-ABVN landed on the beach piloted by ex RAF Lieutenant C.A. Eckersley-Maslin. (Eckersley-Maslin would become a very famous flier and his next post was as Superintendent of Jersey Airways Ltd. after its formation later in the year.) They cleared customs with the Jersey Bureau des Impôts officials on the beach, and Mr Dagenhardt with his daughter departed Jersey at 13.16 hours, arriving at Croydon Airport at 15.29 hours. After disembarking his passengers, Eckersley-Maslin flew G-ABVN back to Portsmouth that evening.

This was the first and only visit to the Channel Islands of a Monospar ST- 4 Mark 1, and G-ABVN was then only seven months old. The aircraft incorporated the new design

PSIOWA General Aircraft Monospar ST- 4 Mark 1 G-ABVN.

technique, invented by the Swiss-born designer Helmit J. Steiger, of a single girder spar for the wings and in the case of the ST – 4, a single girder for the body also. Steiger set up his factory, General Aircraft Ltd., in Croydon, Surrey to build various craft all based on the Monospar principle.

There was one prototype of the ST – 4 MK 1, registered G-ABUZ, that first flew in March 1932 and G-ABVN was one of five Mark 1 production aircraft all of which were also built in 1932. The Monospar ST – 4 Mark 1 was a lightweight, twin engine, four-seater, low wing monoplane with a sleek appearance likened to "a silver bullet crossing the sky". It had a short body of 26 ft 4 ins. compared to a big wingspan of 40 ft 2 ins.. Its maximum speed of 130 mph and cruising speed of 115 mph was generated by two 85 hp Pobjoy R radial engines. It had an extensive range of 540 miles and a duration of 4 hours 30 minutes.

Prototype Monospar ST – 4 MK 1, G-ABUZ.

Hillman Airways' De Havilland D.H.80A Puss Moth, G-ABVX.

Hillman Saloon Coaches and Airways

The next air-taxi flight to Jersey and the next air-ambulance flight from Jersey were linked as both were undertaken by Hillman's Airways of Romford, flying out of their own privately leased Maylands Aerodrome near Harold Wood in Essex.

Mrs Elizabeth Hidden, aged 71 years, from Holland-on-Sea near Clacton was on vacation in Jersey with her daughter, Mrs F. E. Pratt, staying at the Aberfeldy Hotel in St. Helier, when Mrs Hidden became seriously ill on 30th May 1933 suffering a cerebral haemorrhage. She was taken to Jersey General Hospital and her son, Mr C. F. Hidden, was urgently summoned from England, as his mother was not expected to live.

On Wednesday 31st May, Mr Hidden charted a De Havilland D.H.80A Puss Moth, registered G-ABVX from Hillman's Airways. The pilot, Mr J. H. Lock, had never visited Jersey before, but managed the journey from Maylands in less than two hours, flying via Croydon, out across the Channel and then hugging the French coast until he saw Jersey. Lock touched down at noon on Grouville golf links as Grouville Common appeared to him to be the only suitable landing area that he could find as when he arrived the tide was up and he was unable to make a beach landing. Mr Hidden, visited his mother and was reunited with his sister, while the pilot spent the night on Jersey and after refuelling G-ABVX, returned to Maylands Aerodrome the next day.

Against all expectations, Mrs Hidden made considerable progress and within a couple of weeks was considered well enough to transfer by air to a mainland hospital. Mr Hidden again contacted Hillman's, and this time they supplied one of their newly designed De Havilland D.H.84 Dragon twin-engine biplane passenger craft that was large enough to take a stretcher in the cabin after the removal of two seats. The Hillman's D.H. 84 Dragon G-ACBW, named *Gidea Park*, was flown on 16th June from

Maylands Aerodrome by Pilot F. E. Flowerday with Mr Hidden as the only passenger and landed on the sands at Bel Royal in the early afternoon. The patient was sedated for the return journey and accompanied by her daughter and son. G-ACBW made an intermediate stop at Maylands Aerodrome to clear Customs in the late afternoon and then made the final hop to Clacton Aerodrome to disembark its patient and passengers to a waiting ambulance.

Hillman's D.H. 84 Dragon G-ACBW in 1935 when she was converted to a permanent Air-Ambulance.

The owner of Hillman's Airways was Edward Hillman who started his charter business with small twin seater craft, but gave a specification to De Havilland for a larger passenger craft and when the De Havilland D.H.84 Dragon was designed to his specification, he bought the prototype and first five production models. He was very much a self-publicist and christened all his craft with the names of his six children, and then with famous place names. The Puss Moth G-ABVX that flew to Jersey was named *Gilford* after his son.

His airline became the second largest in the country after Imperial Airways, but sadly he died on 31st December 1934 at the young age of 45 and in less than a year his company merged with two others to become British Airways (not to be confused with the identically named modern company which formed in 1974).

The famous flier Amy Mollison (née Johnson) named Hillman's first D.H.84 Dragon *Maylands* in December 1932, while G-ACBW was named *Gidea Park*.

The *Daily Mirror* Air-Cargo Charter

The final air-taxi flight of the year was the only 'cargo flight' to be made to the island. Until this time, the London daily newspapers were taken by train to Southampton or Weymouth and brought to the Channel Islands by the mail boat always arriving a day late in the islands and if there was fog in the Channel the news could be held up even longer. On 17th July the supply of the *Daily Mirror* for Jersey missed the departure of the mail boat from Southampton and the *Daily Mirror* managers chartered an aeroplane to fly the newspapers from Heston Aerodrome straight to Jersey.

The aircraft was a German built Junkers F-13 with registration G-ABDC, belonging to Brooklands Airways Ltd.. The pilot brought G-ABDC down on the sands in St. Aubin's Bay at 17.30 hours and after quickly unloading his cargo into a waiting van, he immediately departed on his return flight to the mainland.

The Junkers F-13 was designed by Otto Reuter and developed in Germany immediately after the First World War. It was the world's first 'all metal' transport aircraft, the structure and skin being made from "duralumin", the lightweight aluminium alloy favoured for the construction of British airships and German Zeppelins. It had an advanced design and shape and was a cantilever low-wing monoplane without any external bracing and with a single engine, behind which was a semi-enclosed cockpit for two crew, roofed but with no side glazing, and a further enclosed and heated cabin for four passengers. The aircraft was a very useful machine as the landing gear could easily be converted to skis for snow and ice, or floats for water landings.

German built Junkers F-13, G-ABDC.

G-ABDC was a Junkers F-13ge, first registered in July 1930. It had a wingspan of 58 ft, a length of 34 ft and the power plant was a 310 hp Junkers L5, six cylinder, upright water cooled, piston engine, capable of producing a speed of 107 mph over an extensive range of 870 miles.

The visit of a German Junkers F-13 to Jersey was especially rare because although 322 planes were built, only five were registered in England.

HMT Air Services?
There is a report of one other charter flight to Jersey in 1933, but the details are nebulous. The local Jersey press reported that on the afternoon of Friday 4th August, an aircraft was cleared by Customs at Heston and flying without passengers or cargo, landed in St. Aubin's Bay. The reason for the flight and very quick turn-round by the pilot remains unknown.

The unidentified aircraft is reported as belonging to HMT Air Services, but despite extensive research I have been unable to locate any such airline. It is probable that the name of the 'airline' was derived from the pilot's initials, Mr H. M. Tod, and that he was a 'one-man airline'. The pilot is much easier identified as he was uniquely named 'Hamish Muir Turner Tod', born in Glasgow in 1905. He was a Scottish civil pilot between the World Wars, who obtained his first service commission when he volunteered with the RAFV.R. on 6th September 1940.

It seems that Tod only ever purchased one aircraft, a Comper CLA.7 Swift, registration G-ABPR, and this was delivered to him at Renfrew in September 1931, but the Swift was a small stubby single seater craft built for racing and totally unsuitable for long cross-Channel flights. Tod is not registered as owning an aircraft in 1933 so the aircraft that he used must have been on hire or loan.

I thought it unlikely that I would ever discover the type and registration of the aircraft that Tod flew to Jersey on the 4th August 1933 or what his mission was, but subsequent research at the British Library has revealed in a Jersey newspaper an insignificant comment that identified Tod's craft as G-AAWE. The craft with registration G-AAWE was a Klemm L25 1A, a German two-seater low wing monoplane with two open cockpits, similar in size and looks to another Klemm already in the island. This other Klemm was a Klemm L27A that on this same day, was flown from Jersey to Alderney by Mr Gerald Guy Farquharson, to be the first landplane to land there.

A Klemm L25 1A, similar to Tod's G-AAWE.

JOHN GRIERSON VISITS JERSEY IN THE *ROUGE ET NOIR*

In 1933, RAF Pilot Officer John Grierson (2nd January 1909 – 21st May 1977), aged twenty-four, was already a famous long-distance flier who would rise to the rank of Wing Commander, become a jet test pilot, author, lecturer and civil aviation administrator. On 10th June 1933 Grierson made an experimental flight to Jersey aboard his De Havilland D.H. 60G Gipsy Moth, G-AAJP, named *Rouge et Noir*, that he had converted to a seaplane.

Grierson took flying lessons at Brooklands Aerodrome as a schoolboy, and graduated from RAF Cranwell in 1929, aged twenty. In August 1930, he bought his D.H. Gipsy Moth, G-AAJP, repainted it startlingly red on one side and black on the other, and named it *Rouge et Noir*. He also modified the craft with doors on both sides of the cockpit. When he was posted to RAF 11(B) Squadron, in Karachi, India, he flew there in his Gipsy Moth and returned to England the following year in a record time of 4 days 10 hrs. 30 min.. On 21st May 1932 he came second in the *Morning Post* Air Race and in September and October he flew 8,800 miles through Russia to Samarkand via Moscow and Astrakhan, but his cavalier attitude to regulations earned him a Soviet air space ban for his "inexplicable propensity for landing in prohibited areas".

In 1933 Grierson's plans to fly around the world by the 'Arctic Route' were thwarted by the Soviet ban and he determined to attempt a 'First Flight' from London to New York on the 'Northern Route' via Iceland, the Greenland ice cap, the Canadian Arctic and Ottawa. He converted G-AAJP into a seaplane and decided to test the newly invented Marconi-Robinson 'homing' navigational equipment during the enterprise. He first had to learn how to use the equipment and fly on floats, thus on the morning of 10th June 1933 he embarked from the Hamble slipway on an experimental flight to Jersey. He had the accomplished airwoman, the Honourable Mrs Westenra on board simulating the weight of an additional fuel tank, but

John Grierson.

she must have been perturbed when Grierson barely managed to get the Gipsy Moth off the water in time to avoid ramming a cargo boat crossing their path. They enjoyed a speedy 75-minute flight to Jersey and after Grierson brought the *Rouge et Noir* safely down on the water near Elizabeth Castle she was towed to a secure mooring inside St. Helier Harbour. Grierson and Mrs Westenra went ashore for lunch but were met by surprised harbour officials who had not been expecting their arrival and were concerned that they had not obtained customs clearance before leaving England. The Jersey Impôts officials accepted Grierson's naïve excuse that he thought Jersey formed part of the United Kingdom. With a tail wind blowing, the afternoon flight back to Southampton Water was even quicker, but when the *Rouge et Noir* landed at Hamble, the English Customs and Excise officers were far less indulgent than their Jersey colleagues and Grierson later received a letter of reprimand from the Air Ministry.

To fly across the Canadian Arctic, the Canadian authorities insisted the *Rouge et Noir* carry a substantial amount of survival equipment which greatly added to the weight of the craft already heavy with extra fuel tanks and the Marconi equipment. Grierson set off from Brough in Yorkshire on 5th August 1933 but crashed on landing at Reykjavik in Iceland on 7th August. The plane was repaired, but when he attempted to continue his journey on 20th August, the underpowered, overloaded seaplane capsized on take-off. A ship rescued him and the Captain

De Havilland D.H. 60G Gipsy Moth, G-AAJP, *Rouge et Noir*, after conversion to a seaplane.

commented that it was lucky he did capsize, as he would have killed himself trying to fly such an underpowered 'plane in those conditions. Grierson shipped the *Rouge et Noir* back to Brough to rebuild as a landplane while he sought a more powerful craft for the attempt.

On 10th July 1934 Grierson bought a new De Havilland D.H. 83 Fox Moth, registration G-ACRK, named it *Robert Bruce* and had it specially modified with floats by Short Bros. of Rochester. On 20th July he departed Rochester on his second attempt at the 'Northern Route', but again on reaching Reykjaik he damaged the craft and had to return to England. His third attempt on 22nd August was finally successful and he arrived at Ottawa on 30th August, but six days later crashed in the Ottawa River and only reached New York on 11th September 1934.

In later life Grierson lived in Guernsey where he continued to fly his own aeroplane. He was interested in polar flying and flew to the South Pole in November 1966. He wrote and lectured on early aviation and on Charles Lindbergh who he met in Reykjavik during his first abortive attempt at the 'Northern Route' in 1933. He died on 21st May 1977 having just lectured on Lindbergh at the Smithsonian's Air and Space Museum's symposium on the fiftieth anniversary of Lindbergh's solo New York to Paris flight.

THE FIRST LANDING OF A LANDPLANE ON ALDERNEY

In the summer of 1933, Gerald Guy Farquharson, a partner in the Malcolm & Farquharson Ltd. aircraft agency at Heston Airport, was operating joyriding flights in Jersey from La Pulente at the southern end of St. Ouen's Bay Beach. His aircraft was the German built Klemm L27A, a three-seater variation of the two-seater L 25 monoplane constructed entirely of wood with two open cockpits and a large low cantilevered wing that gave the craft a spectacularly low landing speed of only 32 mph. The Klemm L 25 had numerous variations with over 600 units produced, several of which were sold to pilots in England, but in 1934 it was also to be built under licence by the British Klemm Aeroplane Co. Ltd. at Hanworth Aerodrome, Feltham as well as in America. English versions would be the British Klemm 'Swallow' and a three-seater, enclosed cabin version named 'Eagle', while Farquharson's company were the "Agents for British-Klemm Aeroplanes".

On the morning of Friday 4th August 1933, a Jersey architect, Mr A. B. Grayson and his assistant, Mr A. Le Sueur, hired Farquharson for a chartered flight to Alderney for the weekend. The expedition was ill conceived as neither pilot nor passengers had ever visited Alderney, and nobody had knowledge of a safe landing site.

Farquharson made two unsuccessful attempts to take-off at La Pulente when his overloaded aircraft, with two passengers and their luggage, sank in soft sand before he eventually managed to get it airborne. Arriving over Alderney, Farquharson made several low passes over the beaches but was dismayed to find that Alderney beaches consisted of steeply sloping shingle, not flat sand. Eventually he spotted the fairly level upper section of Platte Saline Beach and managed to bring the aircraft down to a bumpy, but safe landing thanks to the incredibly low landing speed of the Klemm.

Platte Saline Beach, Alderney.

His passengers alighted with their rucksacks filled with provisions for their weekend while Farquharson inspected the beach for a suitable take-off strip for his return journey, but the only safe take-off area was a patch of grazing land above the beach. He enlisted the help of quarrymen from the nearby stone-crushing works who had probably never seen an aircraft before but were only too eager to get involved with this wondrous machine. Carrying the Klemm up to the field was no problem for these brawny workers who then herded the cows out of harm's way and marked any hidden ditches with sticks and their waistcoats and shirts. Several of the strongest men then held the wings and tail of the Klemm while Farquharson revved up the engine to full shattering power. At his signal the men 'let go' and the craft catapulted into the air for the return flight. Farquharson had no intention of repeating the enterprise, and his passengers were compelled to return to Jersey by sea.

Not only was this the first time a landplane had landed on Alderney, but it was also the first direct aerial link executed between Jersey and Alderney. Unfortunately, there is no record of the registration of the Klemm and Farquharson is not recorded as owning his own Klemm, so the craft must have been on loan or hire. It is unlikely that photographs were taken of the aircraft on Alderney, but numerous holiday snaps must exist of it joyriding from La Pulente that would give identification.

On Thursday 31st August, Farquharson is mentioned taking part in the first Jersey Air Pageant along with seven other pilots and their craft. We have to assume that he was flying the Klemm, but frustratingly, there is no record of the aircraft that he flew, or any photograph despite extensive coverage and photographs of the other participants and their aeroplanes.

The standard Klemm L25 had two open cockpits and was a two-seater craft (pilot in one cockpit, passenger in front in the other) but the class L 27A had a larger passenger cockpit and was capable of carrying a pilot and two passengers. Only eight of these larger German craft were built and of these, only three, G-ABJX, G-ABOP and G-ABOR were registered in England; Farquharson's Klemm had to be one of these three. We can only conjecture which as it was unlikely to be G-ABOP as she was in full time employment with Aerofilms Ltd.. The craft may have been G-ABJX of the PSIOWA, but it is unlikely that Farquharson would go to Portsmouth to hire a machine when he could hire G-ABOR from Airwork Ltd., the owners of Heston Airport where he was based, making it the most likely candidate.

G-ABJX was a Klemm L27A III with a 95 hp Cirrus III engine. She was first registered on 27th March 1931 to E.F. Stephen at Heston as G-ABJX and promptly went to A.G. Murray at Shanklin on the Isle of Wight. When the Portsmouth, Southsea and Isle of Wight Aviation Co. Ltd. was formed her base became Portsmouth. She was then sold to Ms P.M. Beardmore at Hanworth Aerodrome and finally moved to Mrs M. Templeton at Heston Airport. G-ABJX was impressed for war service and scrapped in 1946.

Klemm G-ABJX in PSIOWA colours, photographed on the Isle of Wight.

G-ABOP was a Klemm L27A VIII with a 105 hp Cirrus Hermes IIB engine and she was first registered on 21st August 1931 also to E. F. Stephen at Heston. She then went to Aerofilms Ltd. at Heston and finally to A.A. Bathurst (for Lord Apsley) at the small airfield at Yate near Bristol. She was scrapped at Yate in 1939.

Klemm G-ABOR photographed in South Australia where she was re-registered as VH-USZ. It was a Klemm L27A IX with the larger 120 hp De Havilland Gipsy III engine. This craft was registered in England on 25th August 1931 to Jeffery John Archer Amherst, the 5th Earl Amherst, who based it at Heston Airport. It then passed to Airwork Ltd. the owners of Heston Airport who also ran a flying school there. She was eventually sold to R.W. Groper from Norwood, South Australia who took possession of her in June 1936 and shipped her to Australia where she was re-registered as VH-USZ. She had a short life in Australia as she crashed and was destroyed at Salisbury, South Australia on 13th March 1937.

AERIAL RECONNOITRES OF THE PROPOSED SITE FOR JERSEY AIRPORT

Guernsey and Jersey initially only established full Impôts and Customs facilities in their respective capital harbours of St. Peter Port and St. Helier for shipping and later for seaplanes. These arrangements became increasingly farcical as landplanes arriving from the U.K. could not land on the water, but by landing elsewhere were running the risk of being impounded. As the number of landplanes arriving increased, the authorities realised that without a proper airport, they had to establish recognised landing areas where Impôts and Customs formalities could be completed. The only stretches of flat, firm land not in private ownership were the beaches and so in Jersey the sole recognised landing area was a strip of sand between Elizabeth Castle and West Park in St. Aubin's bay governed by the state of the tide. An airport was needed in Jersey, but there were still people in authority who thought it a "wildcat scheme" while others wanted to wait to see if the newly invented helicopter might be the way forward. There were also debates whether an airport should be a private or States' venture and if built by the States of Jersey, should they also run it, or lease it out?.

Aerial Reconnoitres by the Master of Sempill

In October 1932 the States of Jersey had approached Mr L. M. J. Balfour of the Portsmouth, Southsea and Isle of Wight Aviation Co. Ltd. for advice on the location of an airport. His extensive report recommended the area north-east of St. Peter's Barracks.

On Tuesday 7th February 1933 Colonel, the Master of Sempill visited Jersey in his D.H. 80 Puss Moth aircraft, registration G-ABJU, and landed at Les Quennevais Racecourse at 15.25 hours. He had been asked to inspect and report on Balfour's recommendations for an airport site. He overflew the proposed airport sites and then inspected them from the ground, and he concurred with Balfour that the only viable site was the St. Peter's Barracks location. Sempill agreed to submit a report to the Air Ministry in London, and the States commissioned a survey of the proposed site to establish the costs of acquiring the land involved.

The St. Peter's site had the added advantage that it would be adjacent to the barracks, which was strategically sound for security and the deployment of military aircraft. The War Department had no objection to the airport or to selling War Department land for the project, providing it was replaced on a quid pro quo basis. The specification for the new airport was modest as the States of Jersey officials had no intimation of the explosion of flying interest that would be engendered following the establishment of Jersey Airways Ltd. later in the year. A surveyor's report stated some 64 acres would be required to facilitate a grass landing strip, a surfaced apron with terminal and tower and a medium sized hangar to accommodate one medium-sized airliner, an amphibian air-taxi, a Moth, and other visiting small craft. The States officials had the unenviable task of negotiating the compulsory purchase of 70 fields of private farmland that had been owned by families for generations.

Aerial Reconnoitres by Captain JCC Taylor of the British Petroleum Company

With the decision confirmed to build the States of Jersey Airport near St. Peter's Barracks, the site engendered interest from various parties. The airport would require a fuel depot, and Captain Joseph Carey C. Taylor, born in 1896 and resident in Jersey until 1926 when he became Aviation Manager of the British Petroleum Company (BP), was immediately interested. On 15th May 1933 Captain Taylor flew his Company's De Havilland D.H. 80A Puss Moth, G-AAXY, resplendent in the company's yellow and green livery, from Hatfield in Hertfordshire via Lympne Airfield in Kent and Berck on the Pas de Calais in France, to Jersey, landing at the evening low tide at Bel Royal. The Puss Moth could not be left on the beach overnight and so with its wings folded it was trundled along Victoria

The Master of Sempill's Puss Moth, G-ABJU.

Avenue to Le Marquand's Garage, the local BP outlet, where it was hangared overnight. Next morning, Captain Taylor made an aerial survey of the St. Peter's Barracks site and took photographs for his own use and that of any interested party. Captain Taylor executed ten flights in G-AAXY over the island during the day either from Bel Royal or from St. Ouen's Bay when the tide was low. He carried a total of eighteen passengers that day including Mr S. Chapple, the local manager of Shell-Mex & BP, and Victor Simmons, honorary secretary of the Jersey RAF Association. Having obtained all the insight possible on the proposed landing site from his passengers, Captain Taylor flew the BP Puss Moth back to England that evening.

BP's De Havilland D.H. 80A Puss Moth, G-AAXY, was new when first registered to Shell-Mex Co. Ltd. at Croydon in June 1930. It was re-registered to Shell-Mex & BP Ltd. at Heston in February 1932 when it obtained its BP livery. It was re-registered to Brooklands Aviation Ltd. at Brooklands in March 1936. G-AAXY changed hands several times over the next few years, but always remained at Brooklands where it acquired the nickname *Jacksie* from its registration. It was impressed into war service with the registration DJ711 on 25th March 1941 and operated as an air-taxi by the Air Transport Auxiliary at White Waltham. On 10th July 1942 it was sent to Witney, Oxfordshire for an overhaul but its condition was so poor that on 1st August 1942 it was reduced to spares and parts.

Aerial Reconnoitres by the Portsmouth, Southsea and Isle of Wight Aviation Co Ltd

Mr L. M. J. Balfour of the Portsmouth, Southsea and Isle of Wight Aviation Co. Ltd. maintained his interest in the proposed airport and air services to and from the mainland and was accordingly invited to attend States of Jersey discussions related to the plans. In June 1933 he and his associates made several flights to Jersey to attend meetings and inspect the site.

On the morning of Thursday 8th June PSIOWA pilot, Fl Lt C. E. Eckersley-Maslin, flew from Portsmouth to Jersey in just 72 minutes despite heat haze over the Channel. Passengers on the flight were two PSIOWA Directors and Mr Hunter, an aeroplane designer from Chester. The pilot circled the proposed airport site for several minutes before landing on the sands of St. Aubin's Bay. In the afternoon, while his passengers were in talks with members of the Chamber of Commerce, Eckersley-Maslin intended to fly joyrides from the beach, but his plans were thwarted when Jersey's H. M. Receiver-General refused to grant him permission. This was unusual as there was normally a totally cavalier attitude to joyriding from the beaches. With the conclusion of their talks the party flew back to Portsmouth that same evening.

At 12.10 hours on Wednesday 21st June, after a flight lasting 90 minutes, the PSIOWA new De Havilland D.H. 83 Fox Moth landed at First Tower with Messrs' Balfour, Luxmoore and Murray on board. They did not remain on the island for very long but were back again the next day in the same aircraft for more meetings with the States' Committees, only returning home late in the evening.

The PSIOWA aircraft that made these commutes was the airlines' new De Havilland D.H. 83 Fox Moth, G-ACCA. The D.H. 83 Fox Moth was a small, low cost, light

Not yet in PSIOWA colours, the Company's De Havilland D.H.83 Fox Moth, registration G-ACCA on the sands at First Tower with the name 'W.D. Campbell' painted beneath the cockpit.

passenger biplane with a wingspan of 30 ft 10.5 in. and powered by a single De Havilland Gipsy Major 1 in-line, vertical engine. The pilot sat in an open, raised cockpit behind and above a small, enclosed cabin for four passengers. The prototype craft (G-ABUO) first flew in March 1932 and G-ACCA was built at the end of that year. It was sold on 24th January 1933 and first registered to the Hon. Brian E. Lewis at Heston who obtained its Certificate of Airworthiness on 2nd February 1933. Brian Lewis & Co. are recorded as selling it in July 1933, but it must have been on hire to other pilots and the PSIOWA prior to that date as a photograph of G-ACCA on the beach at First Tower on 21st June 1933 shows that it is not yet sporting the PSIOWA livery and near the rim of the cockpit is the painted inscription of a famous pilot's name, 'W. D. Campbell'!

The PSIOWA made plans with the States Committee members for reciprocal luncheon meetings whereby executives of the Portsmouth company would fly to Jersey early in the morning in the unique PSIOWA triple-engine Westland 'Wessex', G-ABVB, and the craft would return to Portsmouth Airport with the Jersey committee members who would inspect the Portsmouth facilities. In the afternoon the Wessex would return the Jersey contingent to Jersey and fly home the PSIOWA executives in the evening. In the event, bad weather frustrated the arrangements as when the Wessex arrived over Jersey at 09.30 hours dense fog obscured not only the landing area, but the whole island. The aircraft circled the island until 10.45, but when no break appeared in the fog, it was forced to find a safe landing site on the French coast. The pilot obtained a meteorological report that conditions would deteriorate, and the project was abandoned and never repeated.

De Havilland D.H.83 Fox Moth, registration G-ACCA, repainted in the colours of PSIOWA in August 1933. G-ACCA remained with PSIOWA until 1935 when it was sold to Australia and registered as VH-UTY on 4th June 1935. She remained in service for another twenty years until she crashed into a swamp on Lake Myola, Papua New Guinea on 17th November 1953, when on a mail and cargo flight for Papuan Air Transport Ltd. The plane was a write-off, but the pilot survived with only minor injuries and was rescued a few days later.

An Official Air Ministry Aerial Reconnoitre and Visit to Jersey

The Greffier in Jersey, H. E. Le Riche Edwards, was directed by the States' Committee to officially inform the Air Ministry of the proposed establishment of Jersey Airport and to seek approval for it to be a 'Customs Aerodrome'. The Air Ministry arranged for an official inspection of the site by two RAF Supermarine Southampton flying boats with the Chief of Air Staff, Air Chief Marshal Sir Edward L. Ellington, K.C.B, C.M.G., C.B.E., and his A.D.C. in attendance. On 24th July 1933 two RAF Supermarine Southampton flying boats, the S-1042, that had visited Jersey on 8th July 1929, and S-1645, took off from RAF Calshot at 11.00 hours and landed on the waters in St. Aubin's Bay at 12.30 hours. S-1042 dropped anchor and remained near Elizabeth Castle Breakwater while S-1645, carrying Sir Edward, taxied into the harbour to be met by a pinnace carrying Colonel H. H. Hulton, D.S.O., the Government Secretary of Jersey. Colonel Hulton disembarked Sir Edward from S-1645 and escorted him to the Albert Pier steps where the Lieutenant Governor of Jersey,

Westland Wessex, G-ABVB.

Major General E. H. Willis was waiting to greet his old friend; for Sir Edward had been General Willis' best man at his wedding when they were on a posting together in India. The pinnace then returned to collect Flight Lieutenant Saye from S-1042 and Flight Lieutenant Waring from S-1645. After lunch at Government House, the two officers were driven to St. Peter to inspect the site of the new airport. At the end of the visit the two officers were transported back to their craft in the pinnace and Sir Edward was taken, this time to S-1042, for the return flight to Calshot. Both flying boats took to the air at 15.45 hours and circled the bay for 15 minutes in the course of which they overflew the St. Peter's Barracks site before departing over Noirmont Point to head north for England.

This needless exercise was a waste of both U.K. and Jersey taxpayers' money, and an extravagant way for two old army chums to meet and have lunch. The two Flight Lieutenants, who were the only people to do any work during the visit, could have flown themselves to Jersey in a more modest way to carry out their inspection. Eventually, the States' Committee received a letter from the Air Ministry giving its approvals for the proposed airport.

Rare private snapshots of the RAF Supermarine Southampton S-1645 in St. Helier Harbour.

THE BLUE FOX – THE FIRST AIR ACCIDENT IN JERSEY

The Blue Fox

A new 4-seater De Havilland D.H. 83 Fox Moth, G-ACGW, was registered to Captain Charles Lloyd of L'Etacq, Jersey on 24th May 1933 and issued with a Certificate of Aviation on 27th May. Lloyd painted the aircraft pale blue and christened her *Blue Fox*. A month later, Captain Lloyd, with Mr F.E. "Boom" Chasemore a business manager, and Mr C. Burgess, a mechanic, both ex-employees of De Havilland Aircraft, flew *Blue Fox* from London for Jersey on Saturday 24th June 1933. Bad weather forced a diversion and overnight stop in France at St. Inglevert, but on the Sunday, they completed their journey and landed safely on Bel Royal Beach. The aviators had arrived to organise Jersey's first Air Pageant planned for 31st August 1933 under the joint direction of the famous airwoman, the Hon. Mrs Victor Bruce, RAF Squadron Leader P.R. Burchall (Ret'd), and Captain Lloyd.

While preparing the Pageant, Captain Lloyd seized the opportunity to operate joyrides in the *Blue Fox*. Adverts were placed in local newspapers announcing aerial excursions from L'Etacq and St. Ouen's Bay. Tickets cost 5 shillings, 10 shillings and one pound and there was a special 25 minute 'Round the island Trip'. Passengers would fly to a height of 2,000 feet at around 80 to 90 mph The aviators operational base for the Pageant and the joyriding venture was in the L'Etacq Hotel that had a telephone installed especially.

Captain Charles Lloyd's De Havilland D.H.83 Fox Moth, G-ACGW named *Blue Fox* photographed on Quennevais Racecourse, Jersey; Lloyd is seen fitting a cockpit cover to the craft.

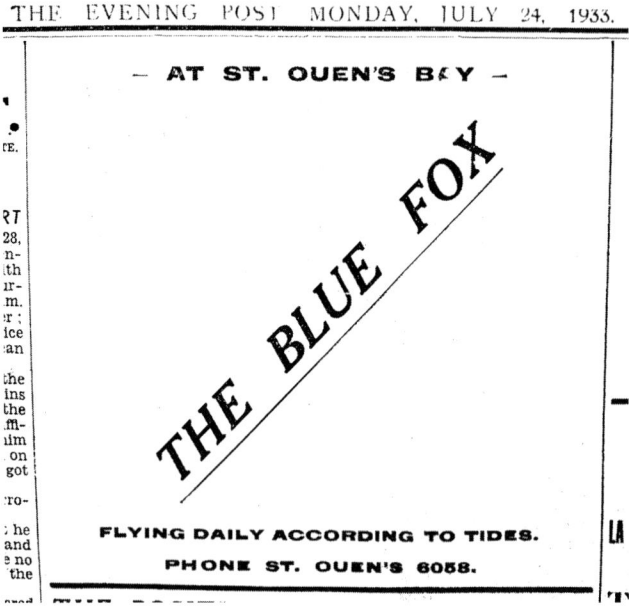

An advert for joyrides in the *Blue Fox*.

The Jersey Photographic Map

Pilots had previously taken aerial photographs of parts of Jersey, but at the beginning of August 1933, Captain Lloyd and "Boom" Chasemore carried out the first aerial photographic survey of the whole island from G-ACGW. In 1929, Colonel G.A. Beazeley commenced a mammoth survey of the Sudan and Uganda from the air, and Captain Lloyd completed it in 1932. Colonel G.A. Beazeley became a resident of Jersey in 1933 and with his old colleague Captain Lloyd, and Squadron Leader P.R. Burchall, they evolved the "comparatively simple" plan to photograph the 72 square miles of Jersey, which was considerably less than the Sudan and Uganda. Captain Lloyd acquired the Williamson Eagle camera, used to make the first aerial survey of Mount Everest, that automatically took a continuous strip of overlapping 5 inch square photographs, and "Boom" Chasemore managed to photograph the whole island from a steady height of 6,000 ft during a two-hour flight. With all the photographs laid out in order, the mosaic formed a perfect photographic map of the island that was later presented to the Société Jersiaise.

A Race for a Car, Motorbike and the *Blue Fox*

On Thursday 10th August, the Caesarean Motor Cycle and Light Car Club was staging a series of races for cars and motorbikes on the sands of St. Ouen's Bay near La Pulente. A highlight was a novelty race from a standing start between the fastest car, the fastest motorcycle and an aeroplane. The car was an MG belonging to Mr W. Mauger from Guernsey; the Club President, Mr G.L. Boudin, owned a Norton, the fastest motorcycle; while the *Blue Fox* piloted by Captain Lloyd was the aircraft. Predictably, the Fox Moth taking to the air had been the slowest off the start line, but after racing round the course, it won by half a lap with the Norton motorcycle coming in second.

A Beautiful Widow

Despite his Air Pageant involvement and joyriding venture, Captain Lloyd also found time to give flying lessons to a beautiful young widow. Mrs Ursula Hanson had been the wife of Charles Reginald Francis Hanson, a company director and son of City of London Alderman, Sir Charles Hanson. Charles junior had recently lost his life aged 29, in a boating accident on the River Thames in June 1933. To console herself, his young widow sailed to Jersey for the summer and initially stayed at the L'Etacq Hotel where she met Captain Lloyd who suggested flying as a distraction for her sorrow. A strong friendship developed and although Mrs Hanson moved to the grander Palace Hotel, she maintained her constant association with Lloyd and became a keen amateur pilot, making numerous flights under his instruction.

When the Hon. Mrs Victor Bruce visited Jersey for the Air Pageant, she persuaded Captain Lloyd to participate with his *Blue Fox* in an air display and garden party that she was organising at Hook Aerodrome in Surrey in aid of the Surbiton Hospital. On Tuesday 5th September, Lloyd and Mrs Hanson flew to Heston to clear Customs and then proceeded to Hook for the display. The charity event on Wednesday 6th September was a great success with a programme similar to the Jersey Air Pageant except that Mrs Bruce managed to obtain far more aircraft and flying personalities. Captain Lloyd made a solo return flight to Jersey on the following Friday, and on Saturday 9th September he flew back to Jersey with Mrs Hanson. Mrs Hanson was now a passionate aviator; she assisted Lloyd with the Jersey Air Pageant, presented her own cup for the first craft to reach Jersey on the day of the show and was very involved with promoting the establishment of a Jersey Aero Club. In the following weeks Mrs Hanson and Captain Lloyd planned a return flight to India, organising air pageants en route; their final departure from Jersey in the *Blue Fox* would be on Sunday 1st October.

The First Air Accident in Jersey

Sunday 1st October 1933 arrived, and a few spectators gathered on Quennevais Racecourse to watch the final departure of *Blue Fox*. Mr G.G. Farquharson was waiting for Captain Lloyd to get into the air so that he could follow. Mrs Hanson and Mr A. "Peppar" Fletcher were already seated with their luggage when Captain Lloyd climbed into the cockpit of the D.H. Fox Moth. Lloyd took off into the wind but failed to clear the wooden rail that encircled the racecourse, the landing wheels caught the rail, and a length broke off. The *Blue Fox* failed to get airborne and ploughed through a ten-foot-high wire net fence before landing in a depression and breaking its back. Lloyd skilfully applied a full left rudder that brought the tail round and enabled him to land the machine on the lower fuselage. The manoeuvre prevented the aeroplane from nose-diving into the ground and although the fuselage was wrecked, the cabin and cockpit remained intact saving the lives of all three occupants.

Smoke pouring from the engine started to penetrate the passenger cabin, but Mrs Hanson and Mr Fletcher were able to grab their suitcases and jump out of the burning craft. Looking back through the smoke, they could just make out that Lloyd appeared unconscious in his cockpit. They managed to pull him out and he regained consciousness just as Mr Farquharson arrived with a fire extinguisher. A local resident, Mr George Boudin, ran over to help and retrieved the remaining baggage except for the pilot's flying coat and raincoat.

The propeller had sheared off during the impact and, now without its resistance, the engine was roaring out of control and quickly overheated and burst into flames. Attempts to quell the flames with the fire extinguisher and sand proved fruitless and were abandoned when the fuel tank exploded, and the entire machine was consumed by the blaze. Miraculously, although very shaken, the passengers were unhurt, and Captain Lloyd only suffered minor injuries; even all their luggage had been rescued except for Lloyd's two coats.

Some days after the crash, Mr Boudin received a request to dismantle the engine and mechanisms from the wreck and forward them to London, but it was a forlorn hope as souvenir hunters had already stripped everything after the fire.

Captain Lloyd and Mrs Hanson could no longer make their long-distance flight to India and instead, a few weeks later, the couple were married in a London Registry Office and Captain Charles and Mrs Ursula Lloyd made their way to Ireland to start life as a married couple.

De Havilland D.H. 83 Fox Moth, G-ACGW, the *Blue Fox*, had a very brief but eventful career spent almost entirely in Jersey. She was regarded as Jersey's first resident aircraft; unfortunately, she also had the dubious distinction of being the first aeroplane to crash in Jersey. The official registration of the *Blue Fox* was cancelled on 4th February 1934.

On the *Blue Fox* crash site there is nothing left for Mr Boudin to salvage.

THE FIRST JERSEY AERIAL PAGEANT

There were few resident pilots on Jersey and no permanent aircraft, so it is uncertain who instigated the idea of a Jersey Aerial Pageant. Doubtless the project won favour with aviation enthusiast, Lady Houston, who had the status to gain the support of the Bailiff for the event to take place. She also had influence with the Colonel the Master of Sempill and the Hon. Mrs Victor Bruce, who were joint Vice-Presidents of the newly formed Thames Valley Aero Club, and this may explain why this mainland-based club was perversely tasked with arranging an aerial pageant on an island almost 200 miles away.

A triumvirate of directors for the project was established of the Hon. Mrs Victor Bruce aided by RAF Squadron Leader P.R. Burchall (Ret'd), and Captain Charles Lloyd. Mrs Bruce (née Mildred Mary Petre) was the glamorous figurehead as she held 17 world records for motoring including the longest lone drive of 2,164 miles in 24 hours by man or woman. As a pioneering pilot, she made the first solo flight from England to Japan, the longest solo flight from India to French Indochina and the first round the world flight by a woman. Mrs Bruce even held maritime records including the fastest crossing of the English Channel in a speedboat. Despite her world travels, Mrs Bruce never visited Jersey until the day of the pageant as her task was to procure entrants from the mainland who would fly across the Channel to Jersey. It was hoped twenty pilots might take part, and Mrs Bruce approached over forty, but in the event only five brave aviators made the crossing, Mrs Bruce being one of them, while two others were already on the island with their aircraft.

The bulk of the preparation for the Aerial Pageant had to be executed in Jersey and therefore on Saturday 24th June, Captain Charles Lloyd, set off for Jersey in his new De Havilland D.H. Fox Moth, G-ACGW, named the *Blue Fox*, with two passengers on board. They were ex De Havilland Aircraft Company employees; mechanic C. Burgess and business manager F.E. "Boom" Cashemore. Bad weather forced the party to stop-over for a night at St. Inglevert in France. On the Sunday they resumed their flight to Jersey and the *Blue Fox* landed safely at Bel Royal to clear Customs before flying on to L'Etacq where the three men set up their headquarters for the next three months in the L'Etacq Hotel.

Lloyd placed regular adverts in the Jersey newspapers for the "Jersey Aerial Pageant at La Moye Race Course –Thursday, Aug. 31st – The First Time In Jersey". The adverts gave the start time as 2.30 in the afternoon and the prices of admission were 1s. 6d., 2s. 6d. and 5s. with a charge of 1s. for the car park or 2s. 6d. to take a car onto the racecourse. Two sites had to be prepared for the pageant. One was Quennevais Racecourse at La Moye where the displays would take place and the aeroplanes land for the spectators to view, while the second was the beach at Bel Royal where the visitors would land after their flights from England and where they could refuel before their performances over the racecourse.

Quennevais Racecourse, although fairly level, was rough ground and Mr E. Farley, a local contractor, was contracted with a large group of men to work twelve hours a day to construct a safe landing area, as well as levelling the ground in the spectator and car park enclosures. Messrs Goldsmith erected loudspeakers around the ground and on the day Captain Griffin kept the crowds entertained with an informative and humorous commentary. Refreshments were provided by Messrs Orviss; the Caesarean Motor Cycle and

Captain Lloyd's De Havilland D.H. Fox Moth, G-ACGW, named the *Blue Fox*, on the beach at L'Etacq.

Light Car Club supervised the car parks; St. John's Ambulance members were in attendance, and Jersey Militiamen and visiting Scouts on summer camp helped with the stewarding of the crowds. At Bel Royal the Paid Police kept the landing area safe and clear of spectators, and a refuelling area was established where the local Jersey representatives of the oil companies had their fuel lorries parked Mr S.J. Chapple with Shell-Mex B.P., Mr D. Woods with Duckham's oils and Messrs Gordon Benett with supplies of XXL Castrol. The public transport companies were approached to lay on additional services in the afternoon of the pageant. The Jersey Railways and Tramways Ltd. put on special trains to Don Bridge Station advertising a joint ticket for rail travel plus entry to the show, while Jersey Motor Transport and The Safety Coach Service supplied extra buses and coaches from all parts of the island. On the day the attendance was estimated well in excess of 10,000 people of which over 7,000 arrived by train at Don Bridge Station, a true bonanza day for the J.R.&T. Ltd.

Not everybody was as welcoming or helpful. The Parish Officials of St. Brelade were dismissive of the event and made no provision for the increase in road traffic. The Constable of St. Brelade, Mr W. Benest, refused to declare the main road from St. Aubin to Corbière a one-way thoroughfare for the afternoon saying such a plan was "unreasonable". On the day, traffic jams from the eastern parishes and St. Helier started to build up from midday and in the afternoon the road from St. Aubin to Don Bridge became gridlocked with an unmoving queue of cars, buses and motorbikes; only people walking could make any progress. The situation was exacerbated by 59 drivers who abandoned their vehicles, effectively blocking one lane of traffic all afternoon. The police issued fines to all 59 drivers, a record in itself, but not a measure that relieved the situation. Some people decided to just watch the displays from the roofs of their vehicles while hundreds who still tried to get to the racecourse arrived after the displays had finished.

The aircraft from England were expected at Bel Royal between 11.30 hours and 12.30 hours and the crowds were so large that the Paid Police had difficulty keeping them off the landing area. Promptly at 11.30 hours a plane was seen flying in overland from the west and a huge cry went up although the more knowledgeable were confused by the direction that the craft was coming from as it was opposite to the expected direction. The plane was identified as the *Blue Fox*, the resident Jersey plane of Captain Lloyd who had flown in from La Moye to inspect the beach reception. After the Captain's return to La Moye the crowd had to wait for almost another hour before the first aeroplane from England was observed coming in from the correct direction, over St. Helier.

This first machine was the giant of the party, a two-seater Bristol F 2B Fighter, registration G-ACFP, piloted by Flying-Officer John N. Addensell who was accompanied by Mr George East. These two aviators had left Lympne Aerodrome in Kent at 06.30 hours intending to arrive in Jersey early, but they encountered fog over the Channel and were forced to put down in Le Havre for three hours, which meant that they did not arrive in Jersey until 12.20 hours.

Fifteen more minutes passed before the crowd were treated to the exciting sight of three machines approaching in spearhead formation, a manoeuvre not witnessed before in Jersey. These three machines were the De Havilland D.H. 60X Cirrus II Moth, registration G-EBWI, piloted by the Hon. Mrs Victor Bruce, the unique diminutive single seat Miles M.1 Satyr aerobatic, red and silver biplane, registered G-ABVG, piloted by Ft Lt Flying Officer John B.W. Pugh, and the peculiar autogiro two seater Cierva C 19. IV with registration G-ABUH, piloted by Mr J. H. Barringer. He flew the autogiro across the Channel from the Kent Flying Club at Bekesbourne and had met the other two machines from the Thames Valley Aero Club at Deauville. On arrival in Jersey Mrs Bruce said that although the weather for the cross-Channel flight had been favourable they met thin fog along the French coast so had taken things calmly and stopped twice in France for coffee. Mrs Bruce liked the way they made coffee in Deauville and believed that: "an air trip should be as full of itinerary as a motorcar tour".

With the pilots refreshed and their aeroplanes refuelled the four craft made the short hop to Quennevais Racecourse for the show to commence. They failed to make the official start time of 14.30 hours, but at 15.00 hours the Pageant began with a flypast in front of the grandstand by all

Two-seater Bristol F 2B Fighter, registration G-ACFP

Left: De Havilland D.H. 60X Cirrus II Moth, registration G-EBWI, piloted by the event organiser the Hon. Mrs Victor Bruce, has just landed on the beach at Bel Royal.

Right: The single seat Miles M.1 Satyr aerobatic, red and silver biplane, registered G-ABVG, piloted by Ft Lt Flying Officer John B.W. Pugh is under guard by an officer of the Paid Police.

Right: The third of the trio to land was the peculiar autogiro two-seater Cierva C 19. IV with registration G-ABUH, piloted by Mr J. H. Barringer.

Below: An Autogiro is not a helicopter and is incapable of a vertical take-off or landing because the rotor is free spinning and unpowered. The rotor aids lift but is only effective when the machine is moving forward (much like a conventional wing). The rotor will not start to spin unaided; Cierva C 19. IV, G-ABUH, had a clutch mechanism linked to the engine to start the rotor spinning.

Formation flying over Quennevais Racecourse at the opening of the first Jersey Aerial Pageant.

the aircraft. The Hon. Mrs Bruce led in the Cirrus Moth and reports state that she was closely followed by Mr Farquharson, but there is no record of the craft that he was flying and bizarrely he does not appear in any photographs of the event. It is to be assumed that he was flying the three-seater Klemm 27A in which he flew to Alderney, but it is also possible that he had access to another craft that was not recorded. The order of the craft that followed him was, the autogiro piloted by Mr Barringer, Captain Lloyd in the *Blue Fox*, the Bristol Fighter with Flying-Officer Addensell and finally the little Satyr piloted by Flight Lieutenant Pugh.

A short time later, a twin engine RAF flying boat appeared out of the sky and flew over the racecourse at low level before mooring in the harbour. The Hon. Mrs Bruce had approached the Air Ministry to send any available military craft to the Pageant, but was told it was impossible to release service machines for such a purpose. It can safely be assumed that a Supermarine Southampton from RAF Calshot had made a "training flight" to the island.

At 15.30 hours another late arrival landed on the racecourse. This was the white De Havilland D.H. 60G Gipsy Moth, registration G-ABDV that, when new, had been Amy Johnson's first aeroplane. The pilot of G-ABDV was Flying Officer John Frederick Lawn of the RAF Reserve and with him was parachutist, Mr F. George. Dare devil parachutist G. du Greeuw should have attended and attempted to break John Tranum's world record of 3.5 miles for a delayed parachute descent, but he was suddenly called upon to take part in the Aerial Tour and Pageant for British Hospitals due to the fatal accident of their parachutist! Mr George rather blithely explained that he was replacing Mr du Greeuw although he had only taken up parachuting the previous year!

With all aircraft present the afternoon's entertainment commenced with each craft showing its individual attributes and then jointly taking part in stunting, aerobatics, 'crazy' flying, aerial combat and an eight-mile race. There was a competition for the spectators to guess the height at which Flying Officer Lawn was flying his Gipsy Moth, the successful entrants winning a free flight in the *Blue Fox* from L'Etacq. The audience were hoaxed when the pilots did aerial sharp shooting at bottles and all scored 'direct hits'; an official obligingly smashed a bottle with a hammer when he heard a blank cartridge fired from a passing aeroplane. Mr George's delayed parachute descent from Flying Officer Lawn's Gipsy Moth was eagerly anticipated; the breeze blew him slightly off course, but he landed safely. The finale was a

De Havilland D.H. 60G Gipsy Moth, registration G-ABDV.

Above: A section of the estimated 10,000 plus spectators with some of their vehicles on Quennevais Racecourse at the start of the proceedings

Scenes during the performances of the aircraft over the racecourse culminating in a spectacular aerial battle and bombing finale.

spectacular battle involving all the aeroplanes and the Jersey Militia. An enemy wireless station was bombed, its officer captured, and defensive enemy aircraft driven off.

Jersey's First Aerial Pageant had been a resounding success, with the whole programme devised without rehearsal and with most of the pilots never visiting Jersey before the day.

An Aviation Ball was held at the Palace Hotel in the evening and the aeronauts danced with the same abandon that they had shown in the skies over Jersey earlier in the day. Speeches were made and prizes awarded; Flying Officer Addensell won a silver cup given by Mrs Ursula Hanson for the first aeroplane to reach Jersey, and the Hon. Mrs Victor Bruce was presented with a cup that was quickly filled with champagne and passed around. The ball continued into the early hours of the following day so there were no early departures back to England. The visiting craft left individually between 14.30 hours and 17.00 hours in the afternoon of Friday 1st September.

Mrs Victor Bruce (right) standing with Mrs Ursula Hanson beside the D.H. Cirrus Moth, G-EBWI on Quennevais Racecourse.

Fight Lieutenant Flying Officer John B.W. Pugh with the Miles M.1 Satyr, registration G-ABVG.

THE FIRST AIRCRAFT BUILT IN GUERNSEY

The *Wee Mite*

At 09.15 hours on 15th September 1933 Sarnian aviation history was made when the first Guernsey built aeroplane, the *Wee Mite*, made a perfect take-off and landing on the sands of Vazon Bay; the culmination of years of research and design by the pilot, Cecil W. Noel.

Noel was a First World War pilot, and Royal Flying Corps N.C.O who would continue serving in the RAF in the Second World War. After the war, he was desperate to fly in Guernsey but was well aware of the restrictions imposed by the terrain. He experimented with a glider and in 1929 he was building wing and aerofoil sections to his own designs. In 1931 he acquired an A.B.C. Motors Ltd. (All British {Engine} Company) Scorpion engine – a 2 cylinder, radial, air-cooled, aero-engine of 30 hp, and set himself the task of designing a two-seater, miniature aircraft powered by this engine and capable of flying from the restricted spaces available on Guernsey. The craft would have dual control so that Noel could train other enthusiasts. Noel designed the *Wee Mite* in five months and in April

Cecil W. Noel "Father of aviation in Guernsey".

1932 he was ready to build. He was fortunate to be joined by Harold Le Parmentier who not only brought finance to the venture but also, as the Manager of Motor House Ltd. at Doyle Road, had the necessary tools and machinery for fashioning metal structures, and a large shed where the *Wee Mite* could be built. Apart from the engine, every part of the *Wee Mite* was designed and manufactured in Guernsey. Propellers are notoriously the most difficult part of an aircraft to produce and working to Noel's specifications, two other enthusiasts, Mr R. Edmonds and Mr R. E. Le Lacheur, joined Noel in constructing experimental props. Harold Le Parmentier ingeniously fitted up an old Ford chassis as a test bed for the engine and props for experiments on the sands of Vazon Bay. The sight of this contraption running along the beach prompted local sceptics to rename the project 'We Might'.

When the sheet metal, tube and wood for the fuselage was sourced, the team were joined by two more enthusiasts, Messrs Harry Kaines and E. Gould. First the tail plane, elevators and rudder were constructed, then the fuselage, wings and struts were formed and finally the engine and propeller were fitted to the fuselage. The completed craft was a high wing, 'Parasol Monoplane' with detachable wings, 18 ft in length and with a 30 ft wingspan.

The aeroplane was carried on a specially created cradle to the sands at Vazon Bay for testing and on 12th February 1933 the machine rose 12 feet into the air and flew for 45 yards, but the engine was not powerful enough for it to get properly airborne.

Adjustments were made to the undercarriage and wing position, and on 10th April the *Wee Mite* made its first sustained flight over the sands, one year after construction had started. Although the plane was out of trim, Noel had proved that flight was possible with such a low powered engine and a locally manufactured prop. He set about re-gearing the Scorpion engine to increase revs and designed a new hollow metal prop, but the outcome was disastrous as the stresses generated resulted in the prop 'bursting'. The explosion hurt nobody, but there was extensive damage to the front end of the fuselage. Harold Le Parmentier saw the disappointment of Noel and the team and secretly purchased and had shipped from England, a more powerful, new 9 cylinder, 50 hp, British Salmson Aero Engine. He presented it to Noel, and work commenced on accommodating it in the newly built nose unit; the construction was only completed on the morning of the first flight.

At 08.00 hours on 15th September 1933 the team conveyed the *Wee Mite* from Doyle Road to Vazon Bay. After last-minute adjustments to the new engine, Cecil Noel taxied the craft over the sands and took to the air at 09.15 hours. *The Star* newspaper later reported that Noel had one (unidentified) passenger on board; it was undoubtedly Harold Le

Cecil Noel observing Harold Le Parmentier adjusting the propeller of the *Wee Mite* at Vazon Bay.

Parmentier. After flying towards St. Peter Port and then over the sea and circling Fort Houmet, the *Wee Mite* attained considerable height before making a perfect landing back on the beach at Vazon. Further adjustments were made before the main test flight of the day at 10.30 hours when Noel set out alone. After a take-off run of 150 yards, he attained an altitude of 1,000 ft and flew directly to Pleinmount where he circled before making for St. Peter Port. He twice circled the town at 1,800 ft and a *Guernsey Evening Press* reporter gleefully reported that the plane passed over the 'Press' offices at five minutes to eleven. Noel then flew to L'Ancresse over the golf links and circled Vazon Bay at 2,500 ft before making another perfect landing at 11.20 hours. Many spectators had turned up in the morning at Vazon Bay to observe the first flight of the *Wee Mite*, but all the aerial activity over the town encouraged hundreds more to descend onto the Bay. They were not disappointed as they observed the team re-tuning the aeroplane and replacing the four-blade propeller used for the morning flights with a new two-blade propeller for the afternoon flight. At 17.00 hours Noel took the *Wee Mite* on another twenty-minute flight and announced that the new two-blade prop increased the speed of the machine by at least 10 miles per hour. The *Wee Mite* had attained a take-off speed of 40 mph in a shortened take-off distance of only 120 yds., while her landing speed was 28 mph. The all-metal fuselage and tail weighed 5 cwt, she travelled 80 to 90 miles to a gallon of fuel and during her speed test reached 93 mph.

Cecil Noel and Harold Le Parmentier, although partners in the *Wee Mite* venture, approached it with different objectives. Cecil Noel had wanted to produce an aircraft for a price of £300 (the average price of a family saloon car) that would make flying available to Guernsey enthusiasts. Harold Le Parmentier the entrepreneur, could see the commercial potential of such a cheap and small aircraft but success had come at the wrong time, the western world was in serious economic decline and commercial production of the aeroplane was untenable.

Cecil Noel continued his crusade to make flying possible for the Guernsey enthusiast by turning his attention to the formation of the Guernsey Gliding Club and later the Guernsey Aero Club while Harold Le Parmentier appears to have taken over the *Wee Mite* as it was registered in his name on 24th April 1934 and

Cecil Noel in the cockpit of his *Wee Mite* preparing for her attempted flight from the sands of Vazon Bay.

received the identification G-ACRL with its 'Usual Station' listed as Robais, Guernsey. Flight literature of the period refers to it as the 'Parmentier *Wee Mite*' with no mention of Cecil Noel's contribution.

Little more is recorded about the *Wee Mite* until Tuesday 22nd January 1935 when *The Star* headlined an article:

"WEE MITE" CRASHES AT VAZON
Pilot escapes with bruises and a shaking
Plane Badly Damaged

The newspaper article reports that the morning before, on Monday 21st January, Harold Le Parmentier and Mr W. L. Stranger were carrying out tests on the plane on the sands at Vazon Bay in a blustery wind. Several successful flights had been made before Harold Le Parmentier took the plane up at about 12.35 hours, but when he was at a height of only 60 ft the plane faltered and he tried to land, but a gust of wind slipped the plane sideways and he crashed to the sand and the craft turned over. The machine had hit the ground broadside completely smashing the port side and wing. The prop was in splinters, a wheel was torn off and the fuselage buckled badly. A small crowd who had been watching helped to extricate the shaken pilot from the wreckage who, apart from a few bruises, was amazingly uninjured. A forlorn group loaded the wreck of the *Wee Mite* onto a lorry and it was driven back to its shed at Doyle Road. *The Star* reporter rather pointedly commented that "Mr Noel was not assisting with the tests".

The *Wee Mite* was never repaired or took to the air again and in March 1936 it was officially recorded as 'broken up' and its registration withdrawn.

THE BIRTH OF JERSEY AIRWAYS LTD

In October 1933, Mr L.T.H. Greig visited Jersey by boat with a friend, but the friend became ill and, eager to get him back to England quickly, Greig approached a travel agent's office in St. Helier where he saw air travel advertised. He was told that there was no air service to England, but a charted aircraft from Portsmouth would cost £30 (almost £2,000 by the prices of today). They could not afford such a fare, but Greig, despite having no experience of aviation, decided that Jersey should have an air service. On his return to England, he contacted a wealthy friend, Mr Walter (Bill) L. Thurgood, with his proposal and it took Greig a month to convince Thurgood of the prospects of the proposed venture and he finally agreed to provide the capital to establish Jersey Airways Ltd.

W.L. Thurgood had an early career that closely mirrored Edward Hillman's of Hillman Saloon Coaches and Airways whose charter planes from Romford, Essex had visited Jersey in May of 1933. Both men had a history of coach building and private bus services and both had been forced to sell their bus fleets and routes to London Transport following the rationalisation of the Nation's bus services, and with the proceeds, both men set up airlines.

Greig returned to Jersey to negotiate with Major Giffard the Receiver-General, permission to land the company's aeroplanes on the beach, there being no viable land strip available. On 9th December 1933 "Jersey Airways Ltd." was registered by the Jersey Royal Court, with two directors and a company office at No. 1 Mulcaster Street, also the home of Messrs W.G. Bellingham, passenger and shipping agents who would be the booking agents for the company. Directors, W.L. Thurgood and L.T.H. Greig announced their intention to establish a regular daily air service between Jersey and Portsmouth with the latest passenger air liner, the De Havilland D.H. Dragon. The flight would, optimistically, be approximately one hour, with a single fare costing 32s. 6d. and a return fare being 55s.; the planes could carry freight as well as passengers. The proposed timetable was a 10.00 hours departure from Portsmouth with 75 minutes allowed for the flight to Jersey and a return flight from Jersey at 11.30 hours. Although the airline was registered in Jersey, its base would have to be Portsmouth Municipal Airport, recently opened in 1932, as the beach at St. Helier was subject to high tides and it would be impossible for the planes to stay there overnight.

Thurgood would eventually order a fleet of eight D.H. Dragons for the airline and at dawn on Friday 15th December he took delivery of his first, G-ACMJ, named *St. Aubin's Bay*, from De Havilland's factory at Stagg Lane Aerodrome, Edgeware. The company's first pilot was "a dour Scot", Mr W.B. (Bill) Caldwell and he made a proving flight in G-ACMJ to Portsmouth and then on to Jersey with three passengers, Thurgood, Greig and a Mr Sharpe. With a favourable tailwind the crossing only took 54 minutes and G-ACMJ landed on the sands of its namesake bay, St. Aubin's Bay, at 10.30 hours.

On the return journey the party had two additional passengers, Captain H. Benest, M.C. and a reporter from the *Jersey Morning News*. The reporter wired back to Jersey that they had landed at 16.38 hours just as dusk was falling, but that the flight had been a "trifle bumpy" and had taken longer than expected because of a head wind. Greig later confessed that this was his first and rather upsetting experience of air travel.

Jersey Airways Ltd.'s scheduled flights were due to start on Monday 18th December 1933, but advance bookings were so good that Thurgood had to hire two extra Dragons, G-ACCE from Brian Lewis Ltd. and G-ACET from Scottish Motor Traction (Bill Caldwell's previous employers), to cover the service until his own new craft arrived. On the historic inaugural flight two craft were used; G-ACMJ, *St. Aubin's Bay* was piloted by "Bill" Caldwell, but it is not recorded which of the other hired craft escorted him. The second pilot was Mr E.A. Swiss who, like Caldwell, had previously been employed by Scottish Motor Traction. The two Dragons left Portsmouth on time at 10.00 hours with only one passenger between them and landed at St. Helier about an hour later. The return flights left 20 minutes late at 11.50 hours with seven passengers in one machine and five passengers in the other, but because of a strong head wind across the Channel, they did not land in Portsmouth until 13.30 hours. A Portsmouth Corporation bus was booked to coordinate with the flight to take passengers into town where most of them caught the Southern Railway express train to London.

A very attractive painting by Frank Wootton celebrates the moment of arrival with the Dragon flying low over the sands of St. Aubin's Bay searching for rocks and rivulets before making its first landing.

The passenger demand on that inaugural day took Thurgood and Greig by surprise as one of the reasons for establishing their airline in winter was the belief that demand would be low, and they would be able to gradually build up on their expertise without pressure. They were partly justified as the day following the inauguration was quiet with only one Dragon arriving from Portsmouth late at 11.30 hours with one passenger and leaving Jersey an hour late of the scheduled departure time, at 12.30 hours, with just two passengers.

The saboteur of all previous air services appeared the following day when dense fog in the Channel and over Southern England saw the service cancelled and while the three planes, two pilots and the ground engineer, Mr Stanton, were trapped at Portsmouth their woes were further compounded by the arrival of an Air Ministry Inspector who observed several points of concern. Passengers and baggage needed to be weighed for each flight but the scales were inadequate, no load sheets were compiled for the flights, there was only one ground engineer and he was not licensed "in compass swinging or turn indicators" and neither of the pilots held a navigator's licence, a requirement if the journey exceeded 100 miles over the sea.

The Air Ministry informed Thurgood that load-sheets should be initiated at once, that Mr Stanton was not qualified to sign daily certificates for aircraft operating beyond a radius of 20 miles from the point of departure if he was not licensed for the adjustment of the compass and turn indicators, and the pilots required navigator's licences. The pilots intended to obtain their navigator licences they explained, but because they flew over land over the Isle of Wight and again over Alderney, although they did not land there, their flights over water were only 78 miles between the two islands.

On 21st December the service was again cancelled

G-ACET has been restored and preserved and is still flying today in the original silver and blue livery of Scottish Motor Traction. Unfortunately there appears to be no existing image of the third D.H. Dragon G-ACCE belonging to Brian Lewis Ltd.

with visibility only 50 yards. The following day the skies cleared, and two Dragons flew to Jersey with three passengers and brought back twelve while on 23rd December one passenger left Portsmouth and eleven returned, but on Christmas Eve two dragons took off, but again encountered fog and had to return to Portsmouth. There was no attempt to fly on Christmas Day or Boxing Day and although they tried twice on the 27th, they again failed and had to return to Portsmouth. They managed to run a service on the 28th, failed on the next two days, but improved on New Year's Eve with two Dragons landing at Jersey at 14.40 hours with seven passengers and returning two hours later with thirteen; almost a full complement!

There were wagers in Jersey on the new airline; not on whether it would succeed, but on how long it would take to fold. What absolutely nobody could foresee was that 1933 was the turning point for aviation in the Channel Islands and, in Jersey, the pioneer days were over. The new airline would be a resounding success in the following year and agreement was made for the building of an airport even if as yet, not a clod of earth had been turned on the site.

The first aircraft of Jersey Airways Ltd., D.H. Dragon G-ACMJ, *St. Aubin's Bay* on the sands at Jersey.

THE RAPID EXPANSION OF JERSEY AIRWAYS

Dragons in the Sky over Jersey

In 1933 and 1934 the De Havilland D.H. 84 Dragon was the most desired civil passenger aircraft. Edward Hillman of Hillman Saloon Coaches and Airways claimed to have designed the craft for his projected service to Paris although when he approached De Havilland with his specifications the company already had a design of the De Havilland Dragon as a light inexpensive bomber for the Iraqi Air Force. De Havilland offered Hillman a civil version of the Dragon bomber and he immediately ordered four to be ready for the opening of his Paris service on 1st April 1933 with two more to follow at a later date. The prototype, registration G-ACAN, made its maiden flight from the De Havilland factory at Stag Lane Aerodrome on 24th November 1932 in the very smart blue and white Hillman colours.

Jersey Airways' first machine that went into service on the 18th December 1933 was a Dragon 1, registration G-ACMJ and named *St. Aubin's Bay*.

The D.H. 84 Dragon was a twin-engine biplane capable of carrying a pilot and six or eight passengers. The craft had a length of 34 ft 6 in. and a wingspan of 47 ft 4 in., which reduced to 25 ft 4 in. when the wings were folded. The power plant was two Gipsy Major I engines, each of 130 hp, producing a cruising speed of 110 mph and a maximum speed of 130 mph, with a 50 mph landing speed. The wooden craft had fabric-covered wings and a three-ply timber, box shaped fuselage. The fuel capacity of 60 gallons gave a range of 545 miles, but most importantly, even with a full load the Dragon could maintain height on only one engine and, without any power, it could glide for 17 miles from 1,000 ft.

1933 Dragons were 'version 1' and 64 were sold by De Havilland in that year. Walter Thurgood ordered eight D.H. Dragons for Jersey Airways Ltd. and each was named after a coastal bay in Jersey.

From the 2nd January 1934, the Jersey Airways winter timetable between Portsmouth and Jersey was revised so that the departure time of the aircraft from Portsmouth related to the 08.50 hours Southern Railway express departure from Waterloo rather than the inconvenient 06.30 hours train. The planes left Portsmouth Aerodrome at 11.40 hours to arrive in Jersey at 12.55 hours and returned at 14.00 hours for a 75-minute flight to Portsmouth, the only deviation being when a midday high tide covered the St. Aubin's Beach.

The weather in the first week of the year played havoc with the new timetable. On 2nd January "Bill" Caldwell in G-ACMJ, *St. Aubin's Bay*, failed to leave Jersey until 14.15 hours and arrived in Portsmouth at 15.30 hours, while fog on 3rd January caused a late arrival in Jersey with six passengers, but a quick turnaround achieved an on-time departure with a full complement of eight passengers. He was not so lucky the following day as he had to return to Portsmouth after flying through fog for an hour. On the 5th January the weather cleared, and Mr Swiss was able to land *St. Aubin's Bay* on the beach exactly on time at 12.55 hours.

The 1934 D.H. 84 Dragon was a 'Dragon 2'. It had cosmetic changes that replaced the continuous passenger compartment window with separate windows with streamlined frames, while the two undercarriage vertical struts were 'faired together' into one streamlined strut. Improved engine performance increased cruising and maximum speeds by 4 mph and increased the maximum load to eight passengers with baggage, while the price was reduced.

Gales interrupted the service in mid-January with a complete cancellation on 17th January. The first month anniversary of the inauguration of the service on 18th January saw the two Jersey Airways Dragons leave Portsmouth together at 12.30 hours, but they immediately ran into a rain squall off the Isle of Wight. The planes lost sight of each other, but Caldwell in *St. Aubin's Bay* pushed on to Jersey with his six passengers while *St. Brelade's Bay*, returned to Portsmouth. Despite fog and gales, the service was only cancelled on three days during January and 120 passengers were flown to Jersey and 176 flown from Jersey. (This imbalance would be the norm and was attributed to bad experiences of passengers on the mail boat crossing to the islands who decided to return to the mainland by air.).

On 9th January Thurgood collected Jersey Airways' second machine G-ACMC, *St. Brelade's Bay*, seen here on West Park Beach. G-ACMC was a 1933 D.H. 84 Dragon 1 'converted' to a D.H. Dragon 2, but this photograph shows that she did not receive the cosmetic changes to her windows and wheel fairings that later Dragon 2's received.

A New Service from Heston

Thurgood and Greig were not content that the isolated Portsmouth Aerodrome was their only mainland base; the real prize was London, and on 28th January 1934 they inaugurated a service from Heston. The route was via Portsmouth to link up with the Portsmouth departure so that both planes could cross the Channel and land together in Jersey, also returning from Jersey at the same time. This kept to a minimum the amount of time the beach needed to be kept clear, and also the time the Customs, police and airline staff were employed on the beach. With perfect weather, the opening day went well and a new pilot, W. E. Knowlden, landed *St. Brelade's Bay* at West Park at 12.45 hours after a flight of only 1 hr. 55 min. that included waiting time at Portsmouth for *St. Aubin's Bay* to depart. There was only a slight delay before both planes made their return departures at 14.15 hours for their respective airports.

Thurgood and Greig had chosen Heston as it was much cheaper than the international airport at Croydon. The aerodrome was owned by Nigel Norman (later Sir Nigel) and Alan Muntz, a two-man company named Airwork Ltd.. Before Jersey Airways moved in, Heston had only been home to the Spartan Airways' summer service to the Isle of Wight, and a charter firm, British Air Navigation Co., flying the large American Ford Trimotor. With the arrival of Jersey Airways, Airwork Ltd. improved the aerodrome facilities by building a Customs Traffic Hall, a waiting hall with luggage-counter and newspaper kiosk, as well as offices for the airlines. Jersey Airways opened a London office in the Canadian National Railway building near Trafalgar Square and offered free transport to and from Heston from their offices 75 minutes before their plane's departure to Jersey and after arrival of incoming planes. With the passing of January, Jersey Airways had survived the worst time of the year and loads increased.

The developing strength of the airline was causing concern to the railway companies and other airlines that hoped to establish services to the Channel Islands. Thurgood and Greig wanted to extend their empire to include Guernsey, and on 16th February 1934 they left Heston in a craft piloted by Caldwell and headed for Guernsey. They passed over St. Peter Port at 10.45 hours in the direction of L'Ancresse Common and landed at Vazon Bay at 11.00 hours. Thurgood and Greig met various Island officials and visited L'Ancresse by car while Caldwell made two flights round the north of Guernsey and over L'Ancresse Common to assess it as an airport location. They left Vazon Bay for Jersey at 15.15 hours, but it would be several years before an airport was built on Guernsey.

Without an aerodrome, the airline was forced to land on the beach, but this would always prove problematical as the high tide progresses an hour each day and to be safe, an aeroplane could not be on the beach two hours either side of the high tide as the water rushes across the sands at an alarming rate. Despite knowledge of the tide table, some Jersey Airline pilots got caught out by high tides and the first was Chief Pilot, "Bill" Caldwell, on 12th February. He had taken off from West Park on time at 14.00 hours, but after passing the French coast at Cap de La Hague he encountered a heavy fog bank in the Channel; he climbed above it, but still could not locate the Isle of Wight or Portsmouth. He decided to turn back for France where the weather was clear and 're-fix' his position for another attempt, but he again encountered fog on the south coast and decided to return to Jersey. The tide was already coming in with a high water of 32 feet due at 17.30 hours that would entirely cover the sands to the sea wall. As soon as the craft put down and was unloaded, all the available Jersey Airways staff with some willing members of the public dragged it up the Millbrook slipway as the tide lapped at their heels and there it had to remain until the following morning.

March 1934 saw three new pilots join the airline; Jenkins, Glyn Roberts and Eckersley-Maslin who had been the former Chief Pilot of Portsmouth and Isle of Wight Aviation Ltd.

On Sunday 4th March the airline received an S.O.S. request from Mr J. M. Mark of Jerbourg, Guernsey, to divert a Portsmouth-bound plane via Guernsey to collect Mrs Mark whose father, Sir Cecil Herslet, K.B.E., J.P. was seriously ill in Bristol. The only comparable landing place on Guernsey was Vazon Bay, but the grey sand is deep and not as firm as the sand of St. Aubin's Bay. There was concern that a heavily loaded machine might sink into the sand and so the empty 'spare' Dragon, G-ACMP *St. Clement's Bay* was sent to collect the lady. The pilot was Eckersley-Maslin, and Miss McFarling from the agent, Bellingham's, was on board to complete the paperwork. *St. Clement's Bay* left Jersey at 13.35 hours, flew at 120 mph to Guernsey and landed safely on the sand of Vazon Bay only fifteen minutes later, the engines were left running and within five minutes the plane was on its way back with Mrs Mark. The Portsmouth-bound machine was held until Mrs Mark could transfer and it departed at 14.15 hours, only fifteen minutes behind schedule. Despite a desperate dash from Portsmouth to Bristol, Mrs Mark unfortunately arrived too late as her father died just before she arrived.

Jersey Airways' third machine was delivered on 1st February and was the first production model of a D.H. 84 Dragon 2 (as opposed to a 'converted' machine). G-ACMO, *St. Ouen's Bay* is seen here at Portsmouth being prepared for her flight to Jersey. *St. Ouen's Bay* seems to have been very camera shy as no portrait of her on the sands in Jersey has been recorded.

St. Aubin's Bay faces south with a high sea wall behind it that can cause problems for aeroplanes attempting to land when the wind is from the south as they are flying at right angles to the wind. On 14th March the Portsmouth machine set out for Jersey, but it was driven back by the winds. *St. Clement's Bay*, flying from Heston, managed to get through, but had a very tricky landing being tipped over sideways twice before the pilot succeeded in landing safely. The take-off was equally dangerous but with an 80 mph gale force tailwind *St. Clement's Bay* returned to Heston in a record breaking 50 minutes.

The second production model of a De Havilland D.H. 84 Dragon 2, G-ACMP became Jersey Airways' fourth machine, *St. Clement's Bay*, delivered on 27th February. This unusual 'reverse silhouette' image of G-ACMP illustrates well the individual window panes and the faired together struts of the undercarriage of the Dragon 2.

Expansion to Southampton

Thurgood and Greig continued to spread their reach when on Sunday 18th March the Portsmouth service was extended to Southampton. Mr Swiss arrived at Southampton from Jersey with an empty *St. Ouen's Bay* at 16.15 hours having dropped off all seven passengers at Portsmouth en route. Although the Southampton planes flew every day, it was not until 29th March that the first through passengers flew from Jersey to Southampton, and the first Southampton to Jersey passenger did not travel until 3rd April. Southampton Aerodrome was originally a First World War U. S. Navy air station called "Atlantic Park", but it was reopened in 1932 by Southampton Corporation and renamed "Eastleigh". It had no Customs facilities and the extension to Southampton by Jersey Airways seemed a doubtful move as it cost more to fly the extra 'hop' and passengers still had to clear Customs at Portsmouth, but Thurgood was looking to the future when he hoped Eastleigh would have its own Customs facilities.

Initially the planes left Southampton 15 minutes before the Portsmouth departure time, but when passengers started to make the through journey in April while still needing to clear Customs in Portsmouth, half an hour had to be allowed to complete the extra hop. Eastleigh had a large hangar and until Portsmouth Airport built one for Jersey Airways, the Dragons were housed overnight in hangars at Eastleigh and Heston rather than on the open aerodrome at Portsmouth.

Four More Dragons

The next four Jersey Airways D.H. 84 Dragon 2's were all completed in the De Havilland factory at the end of February and received consecutive production numbers and sequential registration identities in March. They all received Certificates of Airworthiness during the last week of March, but the exact dates when Jersey Airways took possession of each craft is vague.

Above: D.H.84 Dragon 2, G-ACNG, named *Portelet Bay* received its C. of A. on 23rd March 1934, and was Jersey Airways' fifth aircraft.

Right: D.H. 84 Dragon 2, G-ACNH, named *Bouley Bay* received its C. of A. on 26th March 1934, and was Jersey Airways' sixth aircraft. Both *Portelet Bay* and *Bouley Bay* were with Jersey Airways by the busy Easter weekend when Easter Sunday was 1st April.

D.H. 84 Dragon 2, G-ACNI, named *Plemont Bay*, Jersey Airways' seventh Dragon, was flying with the Jersey Airways fleet in May 1934. She is seen here on the sands of St. Aubin's Bay in a photograph taken from the top of the sea wall looking out to sea. (Every early resource identifies G-ACNI as *Bonne Nuit Bay* but there never was such a craft.).

D.H. 84 Dragon 2, G-ACNJ, named *Rozel Bay*, Jersey Airways' eighth and final Dragon was purported to have been delivered on 8th June 1934, but it remains a mystery where the last two craft were during April and most of May. Jersey Airways loaned at least one of their D.H. 84 Dragons to the government testing centre at Martlesham Heath for safe loading assessment that may explain the late arrival. The final two Dragons both received their C. of A.'s on 28th March, but the date they joined Jersey Airways is unrecorded.

The West Park Beach seadrome over the Easter weekend 1934.

The Rapid Expansion of Jersey Airways

There now appeared the spectacle of the Jersey Airways 'Air Armada'. The landing window on the beach in Jersey was so limited by the tides that all the planes had to fly together in formation and land one after the other.

This stunning sight was the only place in the world where aircraft could regularly be seen flying in convoy and lined up on a beach awaiting departure. It gave Thurgood much free publicity as newspapers around the world printed photographs of his unique Air Armada.

The fleet on the beach.

Sea Rescue

On Sunday 22nd April 1934 an aircraft piloted by Flight-Lieut. Eckersley Maslin on a routine service from Jersey to London, was involved in a dramatic sea rescue. The motor yacht *Cormorant* cruising towards Jersey, developed engine trouble in the English Channel and began to take water. News of her plight was flashed by morse to shore by the Italian steamer *Camparia* at the same time as Eckersley Maslin spotted the yacht some 22 miles south of St. Catherine's Point. He wirelessed the yacht's state and position to the mainland and all shipping and then came down to about twenty feet and circled over her much to the excitement of his passengers including Mr R.E. Knight of Stockwell who told the story to the *Daily Express* newspaper. "...We rose then and left the yacht and when we sighted a cargo steamer we fired Verey lights to show that a ship was in distress.".

Eckersley Maslin cut across the bows of the steamer and headed back in the direction of the yacht followed by the steamer. When the steamer signalled that it had sighted the yacht, the Jersey Airways craft headed for the mainland as she was now running low on fuel and managed to land safely at Heston with her tanks almost empty. Eventually an American steamer, the *Arizpa*, rescued the six passengers and took the *Cormorant* in tow to St. Catherine's Point.

The beach on Jersey lacked any facilities so a refuelling tanker was provided, and a Tillings 32-seater coach, built by Thurgoods' coach building business, was converted into a mobile office and waiting room that could be driven down the slipway and onto the sands for the duration that the aeroplanes were landing and taking off.

Improvements

In May Thurgood decided to improve some of the facilities of his airline and announced that he intended to equip four of the Dragons with radio. Quite why only four was not explained although the aircraft involved in the rescue of the *Cormorant* was obviously already equipped with radio, so perhaps some of the others were also.

In London on 1st May, Thurgood moved his London office to Elizabeth Street, SW1, on the north side of Victoria Coach Station and opposite Samuelson's Garage from where the free Heston bus service would now run.

A few days later on 4th May the summer timetable was implemented with an optimistic twice-daily summer service. Fitting this around the high tides was problematical at times especially if there were other calls on the aircraft such as, when following the loss of a French airliner in the Channel on 9th May, one of the Dragons was sent on a fruitless search and rescue mission over the Channel for two consecutive days.

Two American Ford Tri-motors Arrive in Jersey

On 12th May there was an exciting new visitor to Jersey. A new pilot, Mr Hay, flew *Portelet Bay* from Portsmouth and embarked seven passengers for the return flight. As he taxied along the beach the tail wheel of the craft locked and he proceeded to career around in erratic circles. Rather than abandoning his take-off, Hay made several more futile attempts before he was ordered to remain on the ground by the ground crew. *Portelet Bay* was withdrawn from service and Hay was never heard of again, but there was now a backlog of passengers and Jersey Airways was forced to hire a replacement machine.

Ford 5-AT-C Tri-motor monoplane, registration G-ABHO.

They turned to their neighbours at Heston, The British Air Navigation Co. Ltd. (BANCO), and BANCO pilot, Mr Morton, made a return trip to Jersey in a large 17 seater Ford 5-AT-C Tri-motor monoplane, registration G-ABHO. The arrival of the Ford Tri-motor caused huge excitement as it was the largest aircraft seen on the beach at West Park. Jersey Airways director Mr Greig was resident in Jersey, and he 'spun' Pilot Hay's mishandling of *Portelet Bay* and its replacement with the Ford Tri-motor by claiming the airline was carrying out experiments with the giant Ford as they were anticipating operating larger capacity machines. The Ford Tri-motor carried nine passengers in each direction for Jersey Airways, a load that would require two Dragons had they been available.

There are few contemporary records of the daily running of Jersey Airways, but accounts of more exceptional incidents or first use of unusual aircraft are

Ford 5-AT-C Tri-motor monoplane, registration G-ABHF.

found in the island's press and Britain's *Flight* magazine that regularly reported on all the airlines in Great Britain. They reported the visit of BANCO's Ford 5-AT-C Tri-motor aircraft, registration *G-ABHO*, but this research has uncovered the photographic record of another Ford 5-AT-C Tri-motor on the sands of West Park Beach at this time. This second visiting Ford Tri-motor was G-ABHF. She was the property of H. S. Cooper at Heston, the importer and agent for Ford Tri-motors in England. Cooper acquired G-ABHF as a demonstrator in October 1930 when she was registered on 14th October 1930 with the next available registration, G-ABFF. Cooper re-registered the craft on 7th January 1931 when the more significant registration G-ABHF became available; the last letters of the registration being the initials of Henry Ford, the maker. Although G-ABHF was not owned by BANCO she was probably on long hire from Cooper, and BANCO must have used both these Ford tri-motors, G-ABHO and G-ABHF, when Jersey Airways called on them for assistance.

The American Ford 5-AT-C Tri-motor

The scale of the Ford 5-AT-C Tri-motor was immense compared to a Dragon; it had a wingspan of 77 ft 10 in., a length of 50 ft 3 in. and a height of 12 ft 8 in. The power plant was three 420 hp Pratt and Whitney Wasp C radial engines with nine cylinders that produced a maximum speed of 150 mph and a cruising speed of 90 mph The construction of the craft owed much to Junker's designs as the Ford Tri-motors had all-metal bodies constructed from corrugated aluminium alloy that was structurally strong and did not corrode. This corrugated metal body gave the craft its nickname, *The Tin Goose*. The Ford 5-AT-C was the largest of a long development line of Ford Tri-motors and had seats for 17 passengers as well as a crew of two pilots and one cabin assistant. G-ABHO was first registered in November 1930 and sold to BANCO in 1933 where she was stationed at Heston. Both she and another Ford Tri-motor belonging to BANCO, G-ABEF, along with Cooper's G-ABHF, were all sold and exported to Australia in 1934 and 1935.

Jersey Airways Flies to Paris

On 4th June 1934 Jersey Airways extended its range even further when it inaugurated its first international service with a twice-weekly flight on Mondays and Thursdays to Le Bourget Airport four miles north-east of Paris. The timetable was subject to the tides at West Park, but the inaugural flight on 4th June by *Bouley Bay* left Jersey at 10.00 hours to arrive at Le Bourget by 12.15 hours and after a 30-minute turn round it arrived back on Jersey sands at 15.00 hours. Eckersley-Maslin was the dedicated pilot for the service and on the inaugural flight he flew one passenger to Paris and returned with two. The Dragon for the Paris service was the 'spare' machine kept in reserve for charters and emergencies. In order for it to be immediately available in Jersey, the company had been granted permission to store it on Quennevais Racecourse and although this was not licensed for passengers, they were able to erect a canvas hangar and later a corrugated iron hangar to house the machine and act as a workshop for a ground engineer.

The Revised Summer Timetable

Following the introduction of the new Paris service and increasing flights to and from the mainland, Jersey Airways Ltd. issued a new and revised timetable for the summer months of July, August and September. Thurgood was acutely aware of 'brand image' and employed a good graphic

Herbert J. Williams design for the summer 1934 timetable.

artist, Herbert J. Williams, to design the thin card covers of the timetable.

Williams designed a dramatic front cover with an engraving of a Dragon bursting out of sun-rimmed clouds, while the back cover had a motif of three silhouetted Dragons flying in formation, a nod to the unique Jersey Airways 'Air Armada'. Williams would continue to design all future covers of the Jersey Airways timetables and his colourful Art Deco designs became much more famous than the prosaic designs of other provincial airlines.

Onlookers and staff work to free a Dragon after it ran into the surf.

A Complete Fleet of Aircraft but with some Problems!

On 8th June 1934, Thurgood finally had his complete fleet of eight Dragons in service following the delivery of G-ACNJ, *Rozel Bay*. On 9th June a record number of Dragons were flying to Jersey as with the airline's eight craft was a hired machine, G-ACCR of Commercial Air Hire Ltd., but on 10th June, the craft taking off from Quennevais Racecourse developed engine trouble and had to make an emergency landing on the beach. Even with his full fleet, Thurgood found that he would still have to hire craft if he was to maintain his busy schedule. The 18th June was the six-month anniversary of the airline's founding and they had flown over 5,400 passengers and made over 1,000 Channel crossings. Two more pilots joined the company, Blythe and Duggan, while Eckersley-Maslin was appointed Air Superintendent with control of Jersey, and Caldwell was confirmed as Chief Pilot.

The end of June was less buoyant as the optimistic summer timetable clashed with summer high tides. There was a 34 foot tide due at 18.39 hours on 26th June and when three machines arrived late in the afternoon they found that the incoming tide, assisted by the prevailing wind, had already covered most of the beach with water. The first machine attempted to land, but once it was down its port wheel ploughed into the water and it was immediately swung through 90 degrees and ran into the sea.

All the Jersey Airways staff, assisted by the usual ever-eager onlookers, managed to drag the craft back out of the water to the remaining dry land where the passengers were quickly disembarked, and the plane immediately took off again from the diminishing strip of dry beach.

The other two machines circled the bay observing the beach but were ordered away by the ground crew and flew to Quennevais Racecourse to unload their passengers. These unfortunate passengers waited over an hour before the Customs officials arrived from St. Helier, and the two machines stayed on the racecourse overnight.

On 26th July another high tide scored a devastating hit when the Tilling-Stevens coach, Jersey Airways' mobile office and waiting room, developed engine trouble on the beach. Before any help could be summoned, the coach sank into soft sand and was engulfed by the incoming tide and battered by the waves. The vehicle could only be rescued the

Tilling-Stevens coach caught by the sea.

next day after the sea had receded, but by then it was a very sorry sight.

Thurgood's belief in Eastleigh Airport paid off when on 30th July his rival, the Railway Air Services, opened a route from Cowes to Birmingham calling in at Southampton (Eastleigh) and Bristol. Without any effort, Jersey Airways had a direct connection with the Midlands, the west and the north-west. Thurgood had more good fortune when it was revealed that La Genetière, a farm property in Sark had been sold to a Guernsey resident on condition that he leased some of the fields to Jersey Airways Ltd. to erect an aerodrome in the near future. Even Herm was contemplating an aerodrome, but nothing came of either venture.

**A Spectacular August,
but a Devastating Bank Holiday Weekend**

High summer, and Jersey Airways was now carrying nearly 1,000 passengers a week, while on 4th August the 10,000th passenger was flown. On busy days during August and especially at weekends all eight of the Jersey Airways Dragons plus one or two hired Dragons could be seen together on the West Park Beach. Unfortunately, Jersey Airways could not cope with its own success over the August Bank Holiday week. Increasingly, pressure was placed on the pilots and the craft to achieve more flights in the limited time periods available between the tides and inevitably disasters struck with devastatingly increasing magnitude. On Friday 24th August all eight Jersey Airways Dragons arrived in Jersey on schedule at 16.15 hours and because a 36 ft tide caused by the full moon was predicted for 19.16 hours the passengers were disembarked and the turn round completed as hastily as possible. The tide could be seen rising faster than expected and seven machines got away safely, but the eighth, *St. Aubin's Bay* piloted by Mr Orchard was too late. The pilot opened his throttles to full as the craft dashed along the ever-decreasing strip of dry sand, but the port landing wheel was caught by the incoming tide and the drag on the wheel swung the craft through 90 degrees, straight into the sea. As it was a summer evening many spectators and bathers were on the promenade watching the planes and there was an immediate rush onto the sands when they saw what had happened. Within a few minutes the bathers safely carried all five passengers to dry land. Mr Whelan, a manager of Jersey Airways was on the beach and he immediately ordered the mobile coach office to be driven as near to the stranded plane as possible. A towrope was tied to the Dragon and the coach hauled it out of the water, aided by the large crowd of very willing helpers. Without such quick-thinking *St. Aubin's Bay* would certainly have been lost to the sea, but once she was on dry land, she was towed by a car along the sand to First Tower slipway where the wings were folded, and she was stored until next morning. Mr Greig, ever the company's 'spin merchant', issued a statement to the *Jersey Evening Press* asserting that the pilot was forced to go near the rising tide to avoid some bathers on the beach.

Jersey Airways and hired Dragons at West Park Beach. Dragon G-ACCR was hired from Commercial Air Hire Ltd.

Saturday 25th August should have been the pinnacle of success for Jersey Airways, but it became a very bleak day with two accidents, the second, fatal and especially sad. Because of the heavy load of weekend bookings, two extra Dragons had been hired to augment the Jersey Airways fleet.

A Provincial Airlines' Dragon from Croydon Airport, registration G-ACKD, named *Saturn*, was parked on the beach alongside *St. Clement's Bay*. As the two were readying for take-off, for some unknown reason *Saturn* spun round on one wheel and collided head-on with *St. Clement's Bay* denting the noses of both craft. Fortunately, nobody was injured, and the damage was not serious, but both machines were withdrawn from service and returned empty to the mainland that evening for repair.

Dragon G-ACKD *Saturn*.

The second incident was considerably more serious and confirmed all the dire prophesies in the Jersey press that to use a public swimming beach in high summer as an air landing strip was a disaster waiting to happen. The 18.00 hours departure time on Saturday 25th August had been brought forward by 30 minutes because there were eight Dragons waiting to take-off and high water was expected at 20.05 hours. G-ACMO, *St. Ouen's Bay* was the last to depart, but it was almost 17.45 hours before it could take-off. A newly appointed relief pilot Geoffrey Wood was flying the aircraft on his first day of service with the airline. He had previously completed five years' service with the RAF with 690 flying hours, but all were on single engine aircraft. Eight months after leaving the RAF, Wood had taken his 'B' licence, but did not fly for twelve months until his second period of RAF Reserve training just before joining Jersey Airways. He had his first and only 2 hours 40 minutes practice flying a D.H. 84 Dragon at Heston just four days before this first day of public service with Jersey Airways Ltd.

On the Saturday, Wood made his first scheduled return flight in the morning from Heston and returned to the island again in the afternoon. The weather was perfect with no wind at sea level and he was last to take-off from the beach in a westerly direction with the sea wall on his right. As he opened both throttles the aircraft began to swing to the right, he applied full left rudder to check the swing, but the craft failed to respond and so he throttled back on the port engine, but the swing continued, and an accident was inevitable. He throttled down both engines and pulled on the wheel brakes, but it was too late to avoid a collision.

A group of young children were playing at the base of the sea wall in an area that would normally be out of harm's way. *St. Ouen's Bay* hit the sea wall with a mild impact and neither the pilot nor passengers were injured while the machine only received minor damage to its nose and propellers, but the wheels of the craft struck two little boys. A ten-year-old, Denis Dutot and his friend Raymond Potigny were hit, but Raymond's younger sister miraculously escaped unharmed. Mr Greig who was watching the planes depart, immediately rushed

Visitors play games beside Dragon the *St. Brelades Bay*.

down with his car and took the boys to hospital, but there was no doctor on duty. Raymond who had a serious hand and arm injury was admitted, but Denis sadly died before a doctor could be summoned. Police guarded the crashed plane until investigators could make an inspection the following day and the passengers were sent to a hotel for the night and flown to the mainland the next morning. Nothing was wrong with the machine, and the Air Ministry Accident Report issued in October found that the accident was due to errors of judgement on the part of the pilot arising from his lack of experience in handling twin-engine aircraft. Although the pilot was blamed for the accident, the Directors of Jersey Airways Ltd. were just as culpable for employing an inexperienced pilot to master a new craft while in service with the public on the busiest day of the year.

Sunday 26th August thankfully passed without mishap, but on Monday 27th August the other hired Dragon, G-ACCR of Commercial Air Hire Ltd, had to return to the beach at West Park after it had just passed over Alderney. The pilot announced rather tactfully that he was being recalled to Jersey "by wireless" when in fact he was low on fuel, only having petrol in one tank. This was an easy mistake to make on a Dragon as there was only one petrol gauge for both tanks and this always read zero until switched to a tank and then switched on to check the fuel level. The plane returned to the beach at 15.00 hours and rumours soon spread that it had been in trouble. Greig endeavoured to bluff it out by saying that "The machine is only on hire to us and apparently the pilot was not satisfied with something and came back. There was no danger." He failed to mention that the craft had been on hire for the whole of the summer. The *Evening Post*, while making no comment, concluded its report cryptically by saying: "After refuelling, the machine was to leave again for Heston."

The St Ouen's bay after it hit the sea wall on Saturday 25th August.

Numbers flown over the August weekend were stunning with over 400 flown on just the Saturday and Sunday, but the Bank Holiday was not Jersey Airways' finest hour, with four major incidents, three machines out of service, and one child badly injured and another killed. The month concluded with ten pilots in full time employment, they were: Caldwell, Jenkins, Eckersley-Maslin, Swiss, Knowlden, Israel, Oakley, Orchard, Blythe and the novice Wood.

Attempting to thwart more incidents, the September timetable was adjusted to give even wider margins either side of high water. A minor mishap happened on 4th September unrelated to the tide, when *St. Clement's Bay* landed safely, but as she was

Dragon G-ACCT which Jersey Airways hired from Commercial Air Hire Ltd.

taxiing to the mobile office for Customs clearance of the passengers, a wheel spat and tyre were torn off by a depression in the sand. The craft was towed up the beach clear of the reach of the 25 foot tide so that a repair could be effected. A more serious incident happened at Heston when Pilot Israel was carrying out a test flight with *St. Aubin's Bay* after her overhaul. As he was taking off, one of the engines cut out and the craft dived into the ground. Israel had a lucky escape with only minor injuries, but *St. Aubin's Bay* required a more extensive overhaul and repair.

The Winter Timetable

The old winter timetable was reintroduced on 17th September when the service was reduced to one flight a day from Heston and one a day from Southampton via Portsmouth, both scheduled to arrive in Jersey at 12.30 hours and depart an hour later except when high water forced a change. This now happened on more days than in the previous winter and so the safety margin was increased to 2½ hours either side of the high tide. The Paris service closed on 27th September although confusingly the timetable still advertised the journey time to Paris.

Most of the marketing for the airline was aimed at the mainland promoting return services to Jersey for a sunny break, but in the winter months from November a new strategy was instigated offering weekend excursions to London from Jersey for events such as the Armistice Day services, the Lord Mayor's Show and Christmas shopping and the theatres.

Thurgood made a dramatic statement in November that the Jersey Airways fleet of D.H. Dragons, which were not even a year old, would be replaced in the following year by a new fleet of six D.H. 86 Express, four engine machines. These machines could carry two pilots and twelve passengers and could fly on any two of their four Gipsy Six engines thus removing the possibility of failure during the sea crossing. Another announcement followed on 24th November that a company called Guernsey Airways Ltd. had been registered in Guernsey as a wholly owned subsidiary of Jersey Airways Ltd., and Thurgood formed Channel Island Airways Ltd. on 1st December as a holding company for both the airlines. Thurgood was no nearer establishing a Guernsey service, but his action was pre-emptive to stop anyone using the names "Channel Islands", "Guernsey" and "Jersey" when the proposed aerodromes in each of the islands became operational. Thurgood realised that the residents of each island would prefer their 'own' airline rather than a single airline with a generic title.

Despite the wide safety window in the winter timetable, the tide could still be unpredictable. On 15th December a relatively safe tide of 29 feet was expected at 13.30 hours so the two machines scheduled to arrive at 10.15 hours should have had ample time to land and turn round, but a strong and gusty head wind was blowing from the south and they did not arrive until 11.00 hours. On their first pass of the beach they saw that the southerly gale was piling the tide up the beach making their normal landing place by West Park impossible and the mobile office coach had already moved towards the First Tower slip where there was still a narrow viable landing area. Even here the landing was not easy as they were landing at right angles to the wind on a very narrow strip of beach. One of the machines landed right on the water's edge, but the pilot managed to skilfully spin his craft on the up-shore wheel and safely bring it to a halt facing away from the sea. The passengers were hastily disembarked, and the outgoing passengers embarked while the sea continued its race towards the machines. With the gale blowing straight into the bay from the south, the Dragons had to take-off seawards immediately after their taxi in order to become airborne. Both machines managed it, but one machine was seen to skim the water with her wing tip as she turned into the air.

By December 1934 Portsmouth had a mobile radio station and the Dragons were equipped with radio receiver-transmitters, but these could not help with fog. There was not the blanket fog of the previous Christmas, but on 22nd December Heston was shut down and the passengers were taken by coach to RAF Kenley in Surrey where Dragons from Portsmouth had come to collect them. Six plane loads left Portsmouth for Jersey that day and on 23rd December the fog cleared enough for four to leave from Heston and another four from Portsmouth, but on Christmas Eve there was only one aircraft departure from each of the aerodromes. The fog returned over London on Christmas Day and the only departures were from Portsmouth when two Dragons took two passengers to Jersey and returned with fourteen.

1934 was a spectacular year for Jersey Airways and its two directors who had never flown in an aircraft before December 1933. The company had made a profit of £5,150 with 19,7361 passengers carried, the Heston route accounting for some 7,000, but only 105 used the Paris service.

GUERNSEY VISITORS, CRASHES AND MORE

Guernsey Weekly Press photograph of three Supermarine Southamptons, Nos. S-1044 and S-1043, and a third unidentified aircraft.

The First Visitors of the Year

The *Guernsey Weekly Press* of 17th March 1934 printed a photograph of three large Coastal Defence aircraft from RAF Mount Batten, Plymouth visiting Guernsey on Thursday 15th March on a navigation exercise; they arrived at 12.40 hours and departed at 16.00 hours. The aircraft were Supermarine Southamptons, S-1044 and S-1043, and a third unidentified.

It was unusual that they were from Plymouth, not RAF Calshot, and entered St. Peter Port Harbour so early in the year and stayed late requiring a return journey in the dark.

The aircraft were from what was originally First World War, Royal Navy Air Station, RAF Cattewater on the Mount Batten Peninsula in Plymouth Sound. Little used after the war, it had an extensive rebuild in 1923 and reopened as RAF Mount Batten in 1928. The name Mount Batten did not derive from the Mountbatten family, but rather the Mount Batten Peninsula location. Incongruously, RAF Mount Batten's motto "In Honour Bound" was also the Mountbatten family motto.

Two 'Moths' Crash on Guernsey

Aviation history was created on Tuesday 20th March 1934 when a visiting De Havilland D.H. 80A Puss Moth was the first aircraft to crash on Guernsey when she nose-dived while landing on the island. The event was recreated less than three months later on Monday 11th June 1934 when another, this time unintentional visiting De Havilland D.H. 60G Gipsy Moth executed a similar manoeuvre. In both instances the aircraft suffered considerable damage and had to be shipped back to England by cargo steamer for repair, but fortunately neither the pilots nor passengers were seriously injured.

The First Guernsey Air Crash

A D.H. Puss Moth piloted by Mr F. Woods with mechanic Mr R. Anderson on board, was visiting from London on 20th March 1934 and expected at 15.30 hours on Vazon Bay Beach where a *Guernsey Evening Press* reporter and party of several hundred people were waiting.

The 'Moth' left Heston Airport at noon and the pilot flew via the French coast, but head winds delayed his arrival. At 15.55 hours the craft was observed approaching the island from an easterly direction. Woods had never flown to Guernsey before and was uncertain if the sands at Vazon Bay were a hard enough landing surface. He made low passes several times over the beach looking for a suitable landing area and was not yet intending to land, when his engine cut out. He desperately tried to gain height to clear the reef of rocks in the centre of the bay, but his undercarriage struck a projecting outcrop and the aircraft nosedived into soft sand with its tail projecting skywards.

The crowds rushed forward to help the crew escape from the wreck uninjured and then assisted in righting the machine that had suffered serious damage to the undercarriage, both wheels broken, a stay smashed and torn fuselage. Mr Geo. S. Robilliard's lorry was driven onto the beach and Mr Terry Bougourd and his men from Motor House Ltd. in St. Julian's Avenue raised the machine onto the lorry and moved it off the beach before the rising tide claimed it. The tail of the craft extended beyond the back of the lorry and had to be supported by men walking slowly with the lorry. The Puss Moth was accommodated in a nearby field overnight and then transported to the harbour the next day for transhipment to England by cargo steamer.

The Second Guernsey Air Crash

A young Guernsey airman from St. Martins, Lloyd Stranger, piloted the second Moth that crashed when he was accompanied by another pilot, John Engar A'Bear from Transvaal, South Africa. The two pilots left Brooklands Airfield at 16.20 hours on Monday 11th June in the Brooklands Aero Club's De Havilland D.H. 60G Gipsy Moth biplane, registration G-ABWL, on a flight to Bristol.

The little red and black craft with silver wings headed west and landed at Portsmouth Airport at 17.00 hours, but when Stranger set off again, he immediately encountered thick fog and was forced to climb to 4,000 feet over the Isle of Wight to escape it. When the fog cleared, the pilots were lost over the sea. They flew for some time until Stranger, being a Guernsey man, recognised the Casquets Islands off the port wing. He contemplated flying to Jersey, but noticed that it was high tide and knew the sands of St. Aubin's Bay would not be exposed. As his fuel was getting low, he headed for his home, Guernsey, that he knew well.

Stranger knew he would not be able to land on the sands of Vazon Bay, so he circled the island looking for a suitable field. Thousands of Islanders watched the little aircraft flying along the northern coast and parishes, but Stranger could not find anywhere. It was now 20.00 hours, the wind was not favourable for landing at Fort George and he no longer had enough fuel to reach Jersey so he decided to come down in a promising looking field at The Marais in Victoria Avenue next to the cycling ground. He carried out a perfect landing, but what he had failed to see was that the grass was very long. The wheels became entangled in this grass and the craft was so violently arrested that it went down on its nose and overturned. Stranger quickly released himself, but his co-pilot was trapped and only escaped with the help of Mr T. Gill who was working in the field.

The Gipsy Moth lacked the luck of the pilots; the propeller was damaged, the rudder bent, both top and bottom starboard wings were broken, and the engine casing was buckled. It was 21.00 hours in the evening when Mr W. Head, a carting contractor, arrived with a lorry and a group of men who were able to fold the wings and tow the aircraft from the field to the White Rock in St. Peter Port Harbour. The pilots stayed in town overnight and on Tuesday stripped the plane down for shipment to England on the evening Southern Railway cargo boat.

G-ABWL was written off on 23rd May 1936 when it crashed on Lancing Hill near Shoreham. The pilot was not as lucky as Stranger as although he escaped, he was seriously injured.

Brooklands Aero Club's De Havilland D.H. 60G Gipsy Moth biplane G-ABWL flying over the Brooklands Racing Circuit. Painted by Richard Wheatland.

A Spartan Airways Ltd Cloud over Guernsey

Within a few months Jersey Airways Ltd. had established itself as a leading domestic airline and the sole airline serving Jersey. Five passenger transport companies were monitoring Jersey Airways Ltd. as they were directly affected by the Airways' success. The railway companies, Great Western Railway and Southern Railway were losing a thousand boat passengers a week. The four mainline railway companies amalgamated to establish their own airline, Railway Air Services Ltd. (R.A.S.) on 21st March 1934 with shares divided between the railway companies and Imperial Airways. Imperial Airways had no desire be involved in a Channel Islands service, but Jersey Airways Ltd. was disseminating their air-taxi service to the islands. Portsmouth, Southsea and Isle of Wight Aviation Co. who had made such a big contribution into researching a site for an aerodrome on Jersey and had hopes running a service were completely wrong footed by the establishment of Jersey Airways Ltd. and could only watch the success of Jersey Airways Ltd. on their own home aerodrome at Portsmouth. The fifth company Spartan Airways Ltd. saw Jersey Airways

Ltd. as a threat to their future aims of obtaining the lucrative mail contracts and passenger services when airports were built on Guernsey and Jersey.

Spartan Airways approached the SR with an idea for a Channel Islands service and at a meeting between the SR, the GWR, Imperial Airways and Spartan Airways it was agreed that Mr W.D.L. Roberts of Spartan Airways should act as their representative and approach the States' officials in Jersey and Guernsey to investigate the status of the planned airports and the possibility of monopolies.

On 6th April Roberts met in Jersey with Major Giffard the Receiver-General, Mr Duret-Albin the Solicitor General and Captain Allix the Harbour Master. At the meeting he was informed that the only approved airport was the seaplane base at St. Helier and when Major Giffard had extended the airport regulations to cover Jersey Airways' craft landing on the foreshore at West Park he had not realised that this was outside the approved zone. He had also failed to appreciate the scale of Jersey Airways' operations; that two aircraft daily in winter would become eight craft twice a day by summer. Major Giffard could not cancel his permission as Jersey Airways Ltd. was now an enormous benefit to the travelling public, but he realised that loosely controlled landings of aircraft was dangerous and he would not issue any more permits. Jersey Airways Ltd. had the monopoly on West Park Beach and there was no alternative landing ground that he could offer Spartan Airways.

Mr Roberts reported back to the R.A.S. his concern about a rumour in the island that Jersey Airways was intending to build its own aerodrome that would give it a monopoly. Thurgood had no intention of building an aerodrome, but he also made no effort to contradict the rumour. Roberts stated the only way to break the monopoly held by Jersey Airways Ltd. was to immediately start a rival service with seaplanes or amphibians that could land in the established seaplane airport areas of Jersey and Guernsey.

On 20th July 1934 Saro Cloud amphibian, G-ABXW, named *Cloud of Iona,* on loan from Saunders-Roe, arrived in Jersey with two directors of Spartan Airways and remained moored in the harbour overnight before returning to the Solent the next day. On 27th August *Cloud of Iona* returned, this time to Guernsey, and at 17.30 hours landed outside the harbour and taxied into the Pool where she was secured to a buoy for the night. The seaplane was piloted by Captain Scott and was bringing Messrs' Harrington of the SR, Biggs of the GWR., Roberts of Spartan Airways and Lord for Saunders-Roe to confer with Guernsey States' officials about a proposed service between Guernsey and Jersey and eventually Alderney and Sark. The service would use a Saro Cloud amphibian based in Guernsey. *The Star* newspaper published on Tuesday 28th August 1934, erroneously stated that the contemplated service was being considered "in conjunction with Jersey Airways Ltd." when in fact it was in direct competition. The conference took place on 28th August and the *Cloud of Iona* returned to the Saunders-Roe base on the Solent on 29th August.

Roberts discovered that Thurgood had been inspecting proposed landing sites in Guernsey,

L'Ancresse Bay was one of the proposed Spartan Airways Ltd. landing sites.

Alderney and Sark and if these did not come to fruition, he was considering starting his own flying boat service. Roberts took the threat seriously and immediately chartered the *Cloud of Iona* from Saunders-Roe for Spartan Airways as she was the only amphibian available at the time. Saunders-Roe had two more Saro Clouds in production and Roberts took out options on both of these as well to thwart any attempt by Thurgood to obtain a seaplane for Jersey Airways Ltd.

The Star on Saturday 1st September 1934 reported that the Royal Court had sanctioned coastal landings and had given Spartan Airways Ltd. permission to land a machine at Vazon, Grand Havre and L'Ancresse. Spartan Airways Ltd. was going to experiment with an amphibian in Guernsey until 30th November.

On Friday 12th October *Cloud of Iona* returned to Guernsey to commence the experiments. The pilot was Flying Officer R.C.H. Monk who had previously flown for Saunders-Roe and PSIOWA. Supporting Captain Monk was Mr Haigh, a qualified ground engineer who would service the machine. Buoys had been laid for the craft in St. Peter Port Harbour and at Grand Havre to provide alternative landing sites and she would try landing at various bays in different weather conditions. Her mainland base would be Portsmouth where passengers could link up with existing airline services. To obtain income while carrying out the experiments, *Cloud of Iona* was available for charter, as well as pleasure flights from Vazon Bay on Sundays.

Vazon Bay, the proposed landing site for Sunday pleasure flights. The first pleasure flight was advertised for Sunday 21st October but hundreds of people waited in vain to see it as the weather prevented the craft from leaving her mooring in the harbour.

Captain Monk had no success hiring the Cloud for charter flights. Spartan Airways was allocated a mooring buoy in London Bay in St. Helier Harbour, but the value was limited as the buoy was high and dry at anything below half tide. If Monk carried passengers to Jersey at the right state of the tide, he could not wait long enough to make the journey worthwhile for the passengers and it was uneconomical to make a return journey to pick them up.

The First commercial Flight to Alderney

Captain Monk had greater success with a commercial flight to Alderney.

On Friday 26th October 1934 there was a large gathering of spectators at the Cambridge sheds on the harbour quay to witness the departure of *Cloud of Iona*. The crew of two were carrying eight passengers with business in Alderney. *The Star* newspaper was very involved in promoting the flight, their reporter was a passenger, and a special "Alderney Edition" was printed and flown on board the *Cloud* for the first time. The reporter wrote a fulsome account of the flight headed:

Guernsey to Alderney in 14 Minutes
Eight Passengers Make First
Commercial Flight
'THE STAR' Goes By Air

Cloud of Iona beached at her mouring bouy in London Bay.

It was a fine day when the flight took place and the duralumin hull of the *Cloud* glistened in the sun as she taxied out of the harbour at 10.50 hours to be in the air in less than five minutes heading for Alderney. Visibility was excellent with a ride free of "bumps" and as they neared Alderney the passengers could see the mail boat in the distance and the steamer *Courier* beneath them that had left St. Peter Port for Alderney some hour and a half before their own departure. Captain Monk circled Alderney before taking a line straight inside the breakwater and cutting his engines to make a long steady glide for a perfect landing.

Within a few minutes the seaplane was secured to the buoy that had been specially prepared for her and as the *Courier* berthed, the air passengers stepped ashore to be met by Judge Mellish OBE (Leader of Alderney). Photographs were taken to record the occasion and then the party was conveyed into town by cars. Within fifteen minutes of landing, posters outside newspaper agents selling *The Star* proclaimed:

THE STAR".
COMES TO.
ALDERNEY.
BY AIR.

There was an immediate demand for all the special Alderney editions carried by plane.

With their business completed, the party gathered at Belle Vue Hotel for a formal luncheon to mark the unique occasion. After lunch Captain Monk was taken to the Blayes, a high flat area of land, to inspect it for a possible aerodrome location which he thought was admirable. By 16.20 hours the party once more embarked into the *Cloud of Iona* and less than 20 minutes later they were back in St. Peter Port Harbour. This first commercial return flight to Alderney by Spartan Airways Ltd. had been a resounding success but it was never repeated and at the end of November the *Cloud of Iona* returned once again to her Solent base. The efforts of Spartan Airways and the R.A.S. came to nothing while the fortunes of Jersey Airways Ltd. went from strength to strength.

The Guernsey Aero Club on L'Erée Aerodrome

After designing, building and flying the *Wee Mite* in 1933, Cecil Noel, Guernsey's first resident pilot, turned his attention to establishing a Guernsey Aeronautical Club. An inaugural meeting was held with six of the members of Noel's flying classes on 13th December 1933, but they did not have sufficient finances to buy a plane or to form a proper aero club. A meeting to generate new members on 17th January 1934 produced more interest, but only enough to establish the Guernsey Gliding Club. Noel diverted all his efforts into this new club, but they could only afford to purchase one glider that subsequently spent most of its time in the repair shop because the novice pilots continually crashed the craft. Dispirited by the failure, Noel's desire to establish a proper aero club on a firm financial footing, returned.

With a core group of directors including H. H. Randell, C. H. Smith and B. Bartlett, Noel re-founded the original Guernsey Aero Club and in July 1934 the directors advertised the sale of shares in the venture. The proceeds from the share issue enabled them to acquire a rectangle of poor agricultural land behind the headland and bay at L'Erée on the extreme west

Two very rare photographic postcard images of the *Cloud of Iona*, G-ABXW, pulled up on Braye Beach, Alderney.

of the island. In October 1934 they were granted permission by the States of Guernsey to use the land as an airfield for pleasure flying within a three-mile radius and the club members set about attempting to clear the rough terrain to make runways. The initial work entailed the removal of stone buildings and granite outcrops, often rather dangerously with dynamite, but a 75 foot high hillock in the centre of the north side of their parcel of land defeated them and the runways had to skirt it. Eventually three grass runways were created, the longest being 450 yards, and 'L'Erée', the Bailiwicks' first aerodrome was built.

Avro 594 Avian IV, G-AACF, Guernsey's first acquired aircraft.

Guernsey's First Acquired Aircraft – The Avro Avion

Once the Guernsey Aero Club had a serviceable airfield, Noel turned his attention to acquiring an aircraft that could be used for training the members. In December 1934 the club purchased a three-year old Avro Avion from Aircraft Exchange and Mart Ltd.. The two-seater biplane was an Avro 594 Avian IV, G-AACF. The craft had a wingspan of 28 ft, was 24 ft 3 in. long, and with a 95 hp Cirrus III engine, had a cruising speed of 85 mph and a top speed of 100 mph. Furthermore, it was licensed for full aerobatic performances.

The Avro Avian G-AACF had been built in 1928 and had its Certificate of Airworthiness issued on 22nd October 1928. On 10th May 1929 it was sold to Northern Air Line (Manchester) Ltd. and in April 1930 it moved to National Flying Services Ltd. at Hanworth.

While it was with N.F.S. Ltd., it was flown to the Goodwood Estate and photographed in front of Goodwood House with the 9th Duke of Richmond, the famous racing driver, Freddie March, (also titled The Earl of March), who set up the Goodwood Racing Circuit on his estate.

Noel travelled to England and on Sunday 23rd December he set out to make a solo flight in the Avro Avion back to the club's aerodrome at L'Erée. He took off from Hanworth at 10.40 hours and arrived at Portsmouth Airport at 11.15 hours to clear Customs. At 12.43 hours, he took to the air again from Portsmouth and headed out over the Channel, but encountered head winds and heavy rainstorms throughout the flight. When Noel sighted Cap La Hague he headed for Alderney and then flew to Guernsey making a perfect landing in front of his welcoming committee at L'Erée Aerodrome at 14.38 hours.

Noel had created yet another aviation 'first', having delivered Guernsey's own first 'imported' aeroplane. Christmas could not impede Noel's enthusiasm; he did not yet have a licence that permitted him to carry passengers, but he was in the air again on Boxing Day giving exhibition flights from the Club's airfield at L'Erée.

G-AACF photographed in front of Goodwood House with the 9th Duke of Richmond, Frederick Charles Gordon Lennox, also known as Freddie March, after his title the Earl of March. When he became Duke of Richmond in 1935, the earldom passed to his son.

On New Year's Day 1935, he flew the Avro Avion back across the Channel to the mainland in order to complete his 'B Licence' which would permit him to pilot passengers on flights and carry out instruction. He passed his RAF tests and on Thursday 3rd January 1935 he returned to L'Erée and embarked his first passenger; she was somebody who had never flown before, his mother. They took to the air at 14.45 hours and for 20 minutes flew from L'Erée Aerodrome to Icart, then over the sea towards Herm, circled over St. Peter Port, flew out to L'Ancresse and finally over the western coast and back to L'Erée. Mrs A. A. Noel had no idea of her son's intentions, but afterwards she said: "I had no fear, it was the thrill of my life and I want to go again.".

G-AACF on the airfield at L'Erée.

Noel immediately took to the air again with Mr Carl H. Toms of St. Martin's who was later to become a famous Guernsey historian and photographer. Toms took his camera with him and their flight of 15 minutes duration saw them fly from L'Erée to the south coast, over St. Martin's Town and back to L'Erée over the middle of the island. Noel flew as often as possible with various club members as passengers, but these halcyon days were soon curtailed when disaster struck on the morning of Friday 25th January 1935. The Avro Avian was anchored to the ground with ropes to stop any gust of wind turning it over when not in use and it was housed in a temporary hangar to protect it from the elements and salt sea air. On the morning of the 25th January a heavy winter squall ripped the hangar apart and it collapsed onto the anchored machine. The hangar was of lightweight canvas construction and in consequence the Avro Avian was not badly damaged. There was no damage to the fuselage or engine of the machine, but the leading edge of both planes suffered extensive damage and the elevator was smashed. The damage was severe enough that Air Ministry requirements might demand that the plane be shipped to England for repairs and re-certification so the Guernsey Aero Club members sent for a rigger-inspector to visit the island and give a report. The Avro Avian was repaired and Noel, the Guernsey Aero Club's Chief Flying Instructor, made at least four return trips to the mainland in her throughout the summer of 1935 as well as Aero Club training flights every weekend.

The Guernsey Gliding Club had permission to use L'Erée Aerodrome for its SCUD 1 glider flights and the two craft were anchored together in a new canvas hangar on the perimeter of the airfield when not flying. On the night of Saturday 16th November 1935 devastating gale winds of 75 mph roared across the L'Erée Peninsula and tore the hangar to sheds. The two aircraft were anchored to the ground, but the gale was of such force that it picked up both craft and smashed them to the ground. The Avro Avian was hurled across the hangar and landed with its nose in the earth; the top wing was badly buckled, several ribs were broken and the tail was torn off. The SCUD 1 glider was also violently thrown into the

A *Guernsey Weekly Press* photograph with the caption: THE GUERNSEY AEROPLANE – Flight Lieut. C. W. Noel and his mother, Mrs A. A. Noel in the 'plane just before taking off for Mrs. Noel's first flight last week. Pilot Noel is sat behind his mother.

corner of the hangar where the wreck lay huddled with its wings completely smashed. Both aircraft were so badly damaged that neither was worth repairing and as they were not insured there was no money available to replace them. The Avro Avian was stored in a garage in Upland Road in the hope that she might be repaired, but as she was incapable of flight, it was still there when the Germans occupied the Channel Islands in 1940. They eventually discovered the Avro Avian and she was seized and shipped to Germany in March 1941; whether they ever managed to get her to fly again is not recorded. The Avro Avian was the only remotely serviceable aircraft to be found and seized by the occupying forces in Guernsey during the war.

The Establishment of L'Erée Aerodrome

Without an aircraft to fly, one of the prime objectives of the Guernsey Aero Club was defeated. The members never acquired another aeroplane but turned their attention to developing their airfield at L'Erée into an international aerodrome that would attract visiting aircraft. At the time Customs clearance could only be processed at the seaplane mooring in St. Peter Port Harbour that was of no practical use to landplanes. If L'Erée could attain full international aerodrome status Customs officers would be stationed there and this would save the Customs Officials having to travel across the island to L'Erée each time an aircraft landed. Cecil Noel once again put all his efforts into the venture, becoming the manager of the aerodrome and running it virtually single-handed, even down to reseeding the grass runways. The venture would require a massive infusion of funds to improve the airfield to Ministry of Aviation standards. The Aero Club managed to attract the interest of both Sir Alan Cobham of Cobham Air Routes Ltd. and Captain G. P. Olley of Olley Air Service Ltd., but the Guernsey States Aerodrome Committee would not support the L'Erée project and instead recommended a new site for an island airport at La Villiaze. Noel doggedly continued to improve the conditions and facilities of L'Erée in competition to La Villiaze and the airfield did manage to attract visiting private aircraft, but it never achieved the status that the club had hoped for.

Arrest of the first two aircraft to visit L'Erée Aerodrome

The arrival of the first two aircraft to test the new airfield in September 1934 was an act of pure drama, starting as a total farce but ending as a near tragedy. Flying at L'Erée would always prove to be a great spectator attraction and the opportunity to see the first two land-based aircraft officially testing the new airstrip generated huge crowds who gleefully witnessed not only the spectacle, but also the farce that ensued.

The two aircraft left London on Saturday 8th September 1934 from Hanworth, cleared Customs at Portsmouth Airport and landed at L'Erée earlier than expected, just after 11.00 hours. One aircraft was an Avro Cadet, G-ACJZ, piloted by Mr Sidney Turner and the other was a Puss Moth, G-ABMC, piloted by Captain A. Naish; both pilots worked for Aircraft Exchange and Mart Ltd.. Mr H. H. Randell, the Chairman of the Guernsey Aero Club Ltd. was a passenger. The planes made several short test flights,

The bay at L'Erée with the sea wall to the left, behind which L'Erée Airfield was built.

landing and taking off from the airfield; hundreds of onlookers enjoyed the spectacle, and the pilots described the airfield as 'better than the average mainland aerodrome'. When the pilots were about to return to England, Guernsey Police and Customs Officials arrived in force at L'Erée and promptly impounded both aircraft, detained the pilots and refused them permission to leave the island. The reasons given were that the aircraft were on an unlicensed aerodrome, the only official aerodrome in Guernsey for landings was the seaplane base in St. Peter Port and it was also the only permitted location where they could clear Customs. The irony that these were landplanes and that Guernsey only had a seaplane aerodrome was not lost on the crowds of amused onlookers. Eventually officialdom saw sense and the pilots were permitted to clear Customs on the field at L'Erée and leave for England at 17.45 hours. It was then that the farce turned to near tragedy.

The aircraft set off for England in sight of each other on the clear September evening heading across the Channel for the City Airport at Portsmouth, but when they were within twenty miles of the Isle of Wight the weather deteriorated, visibility dropped drastically and the pilots lost touch with each other and could see neither land nor sea. Captain Naish in the Puss Moth, G-ABMC, got through to Portsmouth safely, but there was no sign of Sidney Turner in his Avro Cadet, G-ACJZ. At 21.55 hours the airport controller at Portsmouth telephoned Guernsey asking if G-ACJZ had returned to the island as it had not arrived at its home airport. When the reply was negative the alarm was raised, and the Admiralty initiated a search and request for all shipping to keep a look out for the missing aircraft. As it was now dark and visibility was restricted by the bad weather, the chances of finding the missing aeroplane were nil especially as the search coordinators had no idea where the craft may have come down in an area that spread from Guernsey to France and across the Channel to the Solent.

Where was G-ACJZ? When Turner in the Avro Cadet lost contact with Naish in his accompanying Puss Moth and he was unable to make out any landmark or even see the sea, he turned downwind and headed back to Guernsey to try and out-run the storm. He reached Guernsey, but still could not land because the visibility was now equally bad over L'Erée. He realised that a beach landing at West Park in Jersey would be impossible because of the storm and determined to try and make a landing on Alderney. A window of visibility enabled him to locate a field in which to land and his skilful piloting brought the Avro Cadet down undamaged, coming to a standstill four feet from the stone wall that surrounded the field. He had landed on Alderney at about 20.00 hours but could not inform anybody that he and his craft were safe as there was no telephone link to either Portsmouth or Guernsey. He chartered an Alderney fishing boat and set out for Guernsey where he arrived at 02.00 hours on Sunday morning. As soon as he located the harbour authorities, news of his safe arrival was transmitted to Portsmouth and to his anxious wife, and the search was called off. Mrs Turner flew to Jersey and Turner caught the mail boat from Guernsey to Jersey where he met his wife and they returned to Portsmouth on a regular commercial Jersey Airways Ltd. flight.

Turner returned to Alderney on Wednesday 12th September to collect the Avro Cadet and experienced no difficulty in taking off from the field where he had made his forced landing. He was low on fuel and so was forced to return to L'Erée to refuel. Even though the airfield was still unlicensed the authorities did not

Avro Cadet, G-ACJZ.

detain him again and the Customs officials did not delay his departure because although he had flown within twenty miles of the English coast, they deemed he had only landed on Alderney, which was part of the Bailiwick of Guernsey and so he had not technically left the Bailiwick! His flight back to Portsmouth was uneventful and he arrived safely at his home port that evening, albeit four days late.

The following month, in early October 1934, Aircraft Exchange and Mart Ltd. with their pilots, Naish and Turner, requested permission to land on West Park Beach in Jersey to inaugurate a regular Guernsey to Jersey service from L'Erée. Jersey Airways Ltd. would not countenance another operator using the beach, and the permission was denied. There was also a block to the project in Guernsey. L'Erée had received its licence and was finally no longer an illegal airfield, but the licence that was granted was not the commercial licence hoped for, but only a club permit for flying within a three mile radius of the aerodrome, with the caveat that no flying should take place during chapel hours on Sundays.

The De Havilland DH 80A Puss Moth G-ABMC

When the DH 80A Puss Moth G-ABMC landed on L'Erée Aerodrome on Saturday 8th September 1934 it was its first visit to Guernsey, but not its first flight to the Channel Islands as the craft had made an air-taxi flight to Jersey on 16th June 1931.

G-ABMC had received its first Certificate of Airworthiness on 11th May 1931 when it was registered to Air Taxis Ltd. at Stag Lane Aerodrome, Edgeware. When she was flown to Guernsey by the Aircraft Exchange and Mart Ltd. pilot Captain Naish on 8th September 1934 she was still registered to Air Taxis Ltd. although the registration would change to Aircraft Exchange and Mart Ltd. at Hanworth two months later on 5th November 1934. G-ABMC then passed through a rapid series of owners until she was registered to R.V.D. Beaumont of Sark on 17th September 1936, but the Dame of Sark refused permission for the Puss Moth to land on the island and Beaumont was forced to base it at Croydon where it was re-registered two months later on 26th November 1936 to H.L.& B.W. Harrison at Croydon. G-ABMC was impressed for war service on 25th March 1941 as DP849 and went to RAF 1 Ferry Pilots Pool at White Waltham. Unfortunately, she was 'Written Off' by Mustang AG523 while parked on the runway at White Waltham on 29th April 1942.

Testing with a Monospar – The fastest flight to L'Erée

On Friday 4th January 1935, Captain Naish returned to L'Erée Airfield to carry out more tests, this time with a larger commercial aircraft with a view to establishing a passenger service between Guernsey and London via Portsmouth. His Aircraft Exchange and Mart Ltd. machine was the newly designed four-seat Monospar ST-10 with registration G-ACTS. The aircraft was the latest and fastest version of the Monospar design built by General Aircraft Ltd. with two powerful Pobjoy Niagara engines. It had a length of 26 ft 4 in. a wingspan of 40 ft 2 in. and a height of 7 ft 10 in.. The Monospar was a streamlined aerodynamic low winged design with manually retracting landing gear; a newly invented aerodynamic enhancement used by only one other aircraft.

Captain Nash left Hanworth Air Park at 14.24 hours accompanied by two passengers; Dr. Mc. Gregor, and Major H. S. Shield M.C., the local Aircraft Exchange and Mart Ltd. representative. G-ACTS landed at Portsmouth Aerodrome to clear Customs and was in the air again at 15.10 hours, landing again on L'Erée Airfield at 16.01 hours. This was the fastest aeroplane journey ever made from London to Guernsey via Portsmouth and the record would last for another decade. The whole journey had been completed in 1 hour 36 minutes and the crossing from Portsmouth to Guernsey was accomplished in 51 minutes. The approximate total distance flown

DH 80A Puss Moth G-ABMC

Monospar ST-10 G-ACTS.

G-ACTS went on to achieve greater fame later in the year when on 14th July 1935 she won the King's Cup Air Race at Hatfield completing the course at an average speed of 131.16 mph.

from Hanworth to L'Erée via Portsmouth was 210 miles. The following day, a Saturday morning, the Monospar made three trips to and from L'Erée Airfield with two passengers on each occasion and Naish was very pleased with the take-offs, completing each in a run up of 80 to 90 yds. with 90 ft clearance at the end of the airfield.

When the aircraft returned to the mainland, Major Shield went to Southampton to confer with Sir Alan Cobham, who was due to make the same journey to Guernsey the following Saturday. They were discussing their intention to use Monospar planes on a service being considered for a new company, Channel Airlines Ltd. that was expected to take over Guernsey Aero Club Ltd. and the L'Erée Airfield. Sir Alan Cobham made his visit to L'Erée on Saturday 12th January, but on 18th January, the States of Guernsey Aerodrome Committee recommended that the new Island Airport should be sited at La Villiaze and Cobham's plans were thwarted.

THE GLIDING CLUBS OF GUERNSEY AND JERSEY

The Guernsey Gliding Club

Cecil Noel, the 'Father' of aviation in Guernsey held, on 13th December 1933, the inaugural meeting of the 'Guernsey Aeronautical Club' with enthusiasts from his flying classes. The group advertised for new members, and on Wednesday 17th January 1934 it held its first general meeting at Rectory Hall in St. Peter Port. The *Guernsey Weekly Press* announced:

"GUERNSEY TO GLIDE.
ISLAND CLUB FORMED".

With Cecil Noel chairing the meeting, thirty members voted Mr Osmond Priaulx their President and Noel, Vice President. The club was renamed more accurately, 'The Guernsey Gliding and Sailplaning Club', abbreviated to 'The Guernsey Gliding Club' with objectives 'to promote interest in gliding, sailplaning and soaring.' The annual subscription was two guineas, and it was agreed that the club should acquire a machine to be used as a glider and then later as a 'semi-soar-plane'. Cecil Noel previously approached the President of L'Ancresse Commons Committee for permission to use the common as a flying field and he was in correspondence with Messers E & D Abbott Ltd. of Farnham, Surrey, purveyors of gliders. A membership of 60 or 70 people would require two or three machines, but the subscriptions only permitted the purchase of one inferior plane. One of the lady members offered a loan of £20 to purchase a better craft and Messers Abbott Ltd. offered Noel a shop-soiled machine listed at £65 for a cash payment of £45; Noel managed to get them to include an elastic launching rope in the deal.

With limited members and finance, The Guernsey Gliding Club was doomed from the start. The single seat SCUD 1 sailplane was not a trainer because once the student had left the ground there was no way for instructor and pilot to communicate. Nor was L'Ancresse Common an ideal flying field, its uneven terrain had rocky outcrops, and was susceptible to unpredictable gusts of wind. The club had its first outing on Sunday 4th February 1934, but a strong gusty wind immediately put the SCUD 1 out of action. The craft had only risen a few feet when the wind

The craft sold by Messers E & D Abbott Ltd. was the popular, small, cheap, single-seat glider 'SCUD 1' Sail Plane.

The SCUD 1 weighed one hundredweight, had a wingspan of 25 ft and a length of only 13 ft 4 in. It was launched by catapult, which entailed two very strong elastic ropes being stretched manually while the tail was held and then at maximum stretch of the ropes, the tail was released and, in theory, the craft would take to the air. Within a week of purchase the craft was in the island and on Wednesday 31st January 1934 gliding was inaugurated with trials of the SCUD 1 on L'Ancresse Common. Initial trials restricted flights to manoeuvres along the ground, but Noel was able to thrill people by demonstrating the possibility of rising to 20 feet.

Right and below: On Saturday 10th February the *Guernsey Weekly Press* carried a photo spread of the new SCUD 1 glider being manoeuvred by members of the Guernsey Gliding Club and piloted in the air by Noel.

slammed it back to earth damaging the skid and the front of the fuselage. During the following week, the members, under Noel's direction, repaired the damage and redesigned the nose to improve access to the cockpit. The following Sunday the club members were again at L'Ancresse attempting to control the craft, but the next Sunday, 18th February, 250 spectators and 20 motor cars turned out to witness an all-day meeting when several novice pilots took to the air and attained heights of six and eight feet. Noel made three inspirational flights at a considerable height, but the machine also sustained more damage although this was repaired on the spot.

Flight magazine published this photograph of the Guernsey SCUD 1 in action with the information that the club proposed to build a similar machine.

During the last week of February, the club acquired new headquarters in Doyle Road when they took over the lease of Messers Huberts' office and workshops. Now the business, construction work, lectures and social meetings could be conducted here as well as the construction of a new glider. This was not to be, however, for on 11th March 1934 *The Star* of Guernsey reported 'Glider crashes again' and the workshops were occupied with yet another repair of the SCUD 1.

It was incredible that nobody was injured in the repeated crashes especially on 1st April when a meeting at L'Ancresse culminated in a spectacular mishap. Several members made small hops and Noel made his inspirational high altitude flights, then Mr J. P. Seideman took up the SCUD 1 in a wind gusting between 20 and 30 mph. Seideman was preparing to land when, near the Bungalows at L'Ancresse, at about 30 feet a dramatic 'flip' occurred. A gust caused the wing tip to hit the ground and the SCUD 1 soared sideways into the air describing a perfect arc before crashing on its back. Seideman was uninjured, but the SCUD 1 was badly damaged with both wings smashed. The craft would require a two month rebuild.

Cecil Noel still remained The Guernsey Gliding Club's instructor, but his ambition was powered flight from a Guernsey airfield. He relaunched 'Guernsey Aeronautical Club' (later shortened to 'Guernsey Aero Club') and acquired land at L'Erée for an airfield. When the SCUD 1 was rebuilt, the Guernsey Gliding Club members took it to the emerging airfield at L'Erée on Sunday 3rd June for an exhilarating evening of flying in ideal conditions with a steady wind of about 20 mph. Cecil Noel and two of the club pilots, Hollis and Adey made several flights and Noel soared to over 60 feet in a demonstration flight.

The Guernsey Gliding Club limped through 1934 repeatedly crashing and repairing the SCUD 1 and on Tuesday 29th January 1935 held its annual general meeting at their headquarters in Doyle Road, but Noel was no longer an official of the club. A vote of thanks was given to Mr J. Stacey who had stored the glider in his premises during the winter, and a decision was made to open the club to non-flying members at a nominal subscription to generate more interest and funds. The club had given up the dangerous L'Ancresse flying field but intended 'to resume operations as soon as a suitable ground is found'. Without a permanent flying field and with the SCUD 1 under constant repair, the membership dwindled to six people in August 1935. The

HAPPIER TIMES – The Guernsey Gliding Club's entry in the 1934 Guernsey Battle of Flowers. The SCUD 1 is small enough to sit on the back of a small truck with its wings located under the fuselage

gliding magazine *The Sailplane* recorded the club's demise with the short statement:

> The Guernsey Gliding Club is now defunct, having held its winding-up meeting. Contrary to expectations, the club proved to be solvent and the balance in hand is to go towards the building of a 'Flying Flea'.

The only 'suitable ground' that the Guernsey Gliding Club could use was the new airfield under construction at L'Erée. What remained of the SCUD 1 after winding up the club was stored in the Guernsey Aero Cub's hangar at L'Erée on the night of 16th November 1935 when a gale tore across the airfield, ripped the hangar to shreds and destroyed both the Guernsey Aero Club's Avro Avion two-seater aircraft and the SCUD 1. The glider was not worth repairing and it could not be replaced as it was uninsured.

Plans for the Scud 1 glider.

The Jersey Gliding Club, 1931-1936

There is very little record of the 'Jersey Gliding Club' although it was far more prosperous and successful than its Sarnian sister, lasted longer and had more aircraft. The concept of a gliding club originated in Germany as early as 1920, and gliding clubs were established in Britain later in the decade. The 'British Gliding Association' formed in 1929, published a list in 1930 of all known gliding clubs in Britain. A Jersey club did not feature, but the list did not claim to be comprehensive. The 19th June 1931 issue of *Flight* magazine listed all the then known gliding clubs in the country, publishing contact details for each club, and an entry appeared for a "Jersey Gliding Club – Secretary, Meadow Bank, St. Lawrence, Jersey, C.I.", so we can be sure that a gliding club was functioning in Jersey in 1931, if not earlier.

As with the Guernsey Gliding Club, the first craft owned by the Jersey Gliding Club was a SCUD 1. The club did not buy their machine, but instead a member of the club, Mr K. J. Carter, purchased a copy of the original plans from Abbot Boynes Gliders of Wrecclesham, Farnham, (Messers Abbot Ltd.) and the club members built an improved version of the sailplane over a period of 12 months, giving it a finish of silver and blue.

A photograph of the Jersey Gliding Club with their machines in 1936 shows at least two SCUD 1 sailplanes, but we do not know if the second craft was purchased or built. Messers Abbott Ltd. only built twelve SCUD 1's and 2's combined, and it is not known how many clubs built machines, but the Channel Islands' contingent must have been a high proportion of the final total.

It is recorded that the club owned an RFD Type 3 Dagling Primary Glider designed by Reginald Foster Dagnall of R.F.D. Co., Guildford. 'Primary' gliders were low performance, crude machines of simple structure with basic controls for use by novice pilots. The Dagling Primary had a wingspan of 33 ft and a length of 17 ft 10 in., but it had no fuselage, the pilot sat in the open on the skid while the tail was attached to the body by four poles and the wings were supported by cables from a central vertical pillar. The structure was so simple that the club might easily have built their own craft, but it is not recorded if they did, or whether they purchased one from the R.F.D. Co.

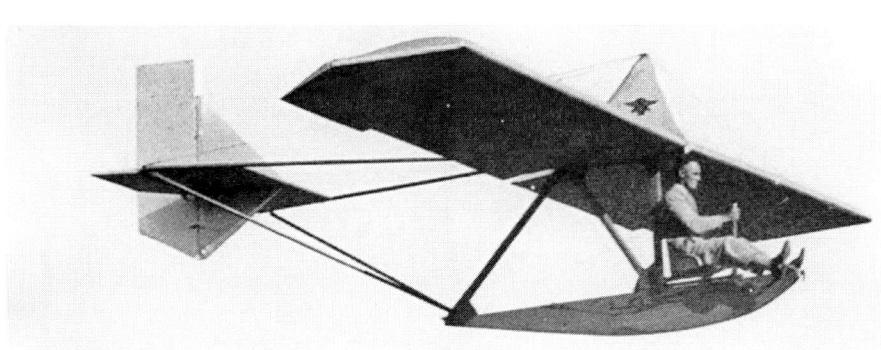

RFD Type 3 Dagling Primary Glider

The Jersey Gliding Club used a safe landing site at St. Peter near St. Ouen's Bay and on 26th September 1935, the *Jersey Evening Post* sent a reporter to learn about the club and their machines. He was especially interested in the "intrepid nature" of the amateur glider pilots and their method for launching the gliders into the air:

> One man acts as an anchor and holds the tail of the machine down, another the wing level. Four more tail on to the two ends of a long elastic rope which is attached by a ring to the nose of the machine. When the pilot is ready he calls out 'walk'. The towing team walk outwards, taking the strain on the rope. 'Run' comes the command, the towing team starts to run, the strain of the rope is increased. 'Let go' sings out the pilot, the plane starts to move, rapidly gains speed until it drops its rope and soars over the heads of its towing team. After that it depends on the wind and the pilot.

A proud Mr R. Wagstaffe in the cockpit of his new Kirby Kite T.6 glider at St. Peter in October 1936

The *Evening Post* reporter recorded that the weather conditions were poor on 26th September and that Mr Carter in his SCUD 1 only managed to fly 400 yards in the air with a flight time of 22 seconds. This must have been an early outing for Mr Carter as by November 1935 he was a competent pilot, achieving a flight of over 40 minutes at an average speed of 35 mph.

In 1936, members of the Jersey Gliding Club acquired at least two more craft. The most advanced machine was a high performance Kirby Kite T.6 purchased by Mr R. Wagstaffe in October 1936. Slingsby Sailplanes Ltd. of Kirbymoorside built a total of 25 Kirby Kite T.6 gliders that were of the new graceful 'gull wing' design with a length of 20 ft 4 in. and a wingspan of 46 ft 7 in. Unfortunately, Wagstaffe had little use of his Kirby Kite T.6 for within a few weeks the Jersey Gliding Club were forbidden to use St. Peter as the land was acquired for the new States' Airport to open in March 1937. The club members were unable to find any other safe landing site and the Jersey Gliding Club was soon disbanded. The fate of the club's gliding fleet is unrecorded, but the craft were probably sold to the mainland.

Pilots and members of the Jersey Gliding Club pose by their gliders in the winter of 1936. This is the only known photograph of the Jersey Gliding Club and may have been taken at their final meeting in the winter of 1936 before the club was disbanded. On the far left of the photograph is the RFD Type 3 Dagling Primary Glider and next to it are two SCUD 1 machines. Beyond these can be seen the elegant 'gull wings' of Mr. R Wagstaffe's Kirby Kite T.6, while to the right is an even larger unidentified glider. When this photograph was taken, work on the new Jersey Airport had been in progress for two years and within a few weeks all the land in the photograph would be enclosed to become the new airport

JERSEY AIRWAYS LTD GOES FROM STRENGTH TO STRENGTH

Jersey Airways Ltd growth

Within one year, Jersey Airways Ltd. was established as the premiere U. K. provincial airline and it approached 1935 with orders to replace its fleet of D.H. 84 Dragon aircraft with six machines of the latest De Havilland D.H. 86 Express design; a larger, faster, more streamlined, four engine biplane, equipped with the latest navigational and radio equipment. Both Portsmouth Aerodrome and the Jersey Airport site already had functioning radio stations in temporary wooden sheds, and they would soon be furnished with direction finding equipment. Jersey Airways Ltd. began 1935 in a strong financial position, they had made a profit of £5,150 in 1934 and they now had the backing of Whitehall Securities Corporation (W.S.C.). In January the internal British airline group run by the railways, Great Western Railway and Southern Railway, previously rivals of Jersey Airways, now took out a one-third interest in the airline with the remaining two thirds being equally divided between Thurgood and his associates, and the W.S.C.. Jersey Airways Ltd. timetables now appeared in the *Railway Air Services General Time Table of the four main line Railway Companies and Imperial Airways*, through-flights could be booked to any destination on the mainland, and combined tickets purchased for cross-Channel travel by air or the railway mail boats, while air passengers could send heavy luggage in advance by rail and mail boat.

A New Service to Rennes

The winter timetable was single daily services from Portsmouth/Southampton and Heston, but on Tuesday 8th January 1935 a continental service was inaugurated to Rennes in Brittany to run every Tuesday and Friday. Rennes was a rail centre 85 miles south of Jersey and the link offered substantial time savings for travellers to Western France, Bordeaux, Biarritz, Spain or even Paris. The Rennes timetable had to vary with the high tide in St. Aubin's Bay, and the aircraft would slot in ahead of the U.K. services for use of the beach. The scheduled time for the inaugural flight on 8th January was 11.00 hours, an hour before the arrival of the flights from the mainland, and two Dragons had stayed overnight on Quennevais Racecourse rather than flying over from Portsmouth that morning. The schedule failed to adhere to the 2½ hour landing embargo either side of high tide and a spring tide of 37.2 ft had only started to ebb at 08.44 hours. When the two Dragons flew from the racecourse at 10.30 hours the sea was still high up the beach with no space for them to land. The two machines circled the bay waiting for the tide to recede and when eventually Eckersley-Maslin made the first landing, one wheel of his Dragon was observed to be on the water's edge while the opposite wing tip nearly scraped the sea wall. Blythe piloting the second craft had to make two attempts before he found enough beach to land on. Despite the tide, the Dragons still managed to leave on time with five passengers each and they arrived at Rennes eight minutes ahead of their scheduled 50-minute flight.

The Rennes arrival was far more auspicious than the Jersey departure as they were greeted by the President of the Rennes Chamber of Commerce and a large crowd of residents while the airport was decorated with red, white and blue bunting, the French tricolour and Union Jacks. The service was a great success with passengers bound for Switzerland arriving in ample time for the 12.49 hours Paris express train. Unfortunately, the Rennes service was halted at the end of March by the Jersey States Assembly who were lobbied by concerned Jersey potato growers alarmed at the thought of a Colorado beetle hitching a ride on an aircraft and infecting the Jersey crop. Rennes was in the Colorado beetle zone and although the creature is dormant in the winter months it becomes active in the spring. In the twelve weeks that the service ran, 4,000 miles were flown, and 1.2 tons of freight and 93 passengers were carried.

The Jersey Airways Ltd
De Havilland DH 86 Express Air Liner Fleet

The D.H. 86 Express airliner was a larger, more streamlined version of the D.H. 84 Dragon with four engines instead of two. The prototype was designed and built in under four months to meet an Australian Government specification for an airliner for the Singapore to Australia sector of the England – Australia airmail route that had to be available by the last day of January 1934; the prototype D.H. 86, G-ACPL, received its certificate of airworthiness on 30th January! The prototype accommodated ten passengers, two crew, baggage storage, and a lavatory. It was not dual–control as the pilot sat in the nose and the second pilot, acting as wireless-operator, sat on the starboard side, behind the pilot. Only four single-pilot versions were built, all subsequent 86's were dual-control with the pilots sitting side by side in an elongated nose. An unintended advantage of the elongated nose was that the craft was more streamlined and flew faster.

The six D.H. 86's supplied to Jersey Airways Ltd. in 1935 were all dual-control streamlined versions. Their fuselage was wooden box construction as on the D.H. Dragon, but with plywood skin on the inside of the frames and sound-proofing material between this and an outer fabric skin. Like the Dragon, the wings were made of wood, but their shape was more streamlined with a strong curving taper to the tip that was supported by a single strut. The major difference in construction was an all-metal undercarriage in streamlined Elektron fairings. The power plant of four newly designed 200 hp Gipsy Six in-line engines produced a cruising speed of 145 mph and maximum speed of 170 mph, with the 114-gallon fuel capacity giving a range of 760 miles. The wingspan was 64 ft 6 in. and the length 43 ft 11 in. while the height was 13 ft. The latest navigation equipment included a Kollsman sensitive altimeter giving an altitude to within 20 feet, a Smith rate-of-climb indicator, a Sperry artificial horizon and directional gyroscope and a Smith turn-and-bank indicator with a Standard two-way radio. The engines were conveniently started by portable batteries on trolleys that plugged into the belly of the fuselage. The short-range craft bought by Jersey Airways Ltd. could accommodate fourteen passengers and two crew members.

7th February 1935 D.H. 86 G-ACYF *The Giffard Bay* guarded by police on the beach.

The first D.H. 86 of the Jersey Airways fleet, G-ACYF, was named *The Giffard Bay*, continuing the naming convention established with the Dragons. The craft, piloted by Mr B.A. Blythe and co-piloted by Captain Broad of De Havilland was due to make its maiden flight to Jersey on Wednesday 6th February with the Director-General of Jersey, Lt.-Col. Sir Francis C. Shelmerdine, but the departure was cancelled at the last minute due to a north-easterly gale. The following day, Thursday 7th February, *The Giffard Bay* took off from Heston at 10.34 hours with nine passengers on board. Sir Francis Shelmerdine was unable to fly, but the passengers included Jersey Airways Ltd. Directors Thurgood and Greig, and Fountain Barber, the airline's publicity manager, along with Maurice Jackaman of Airports Ltd., Mortimer Sharpe from *Aeroplane* magazine, Taylor from *Flight* magazine and Jones of the *Daily Herald*. Two dignitaries were also on board; the aviator, Kathleen Pelham Moore, the Countess of Drogheda, C.B.E., and for some unexplained reason, His Excellency Cxatia Saraci, First Secretary of the Albanian Legation and Chamberlain to King Zog, the only crowned Muslim in Europe and previously Dictator President of Albania.

Boosted by a tail wind, the flight to Jersey, at 3,000 feet, took 1 hr. 11 min. at an average speed of 156 mph while the return flight against the wind was 1 hr. 35 min. giving an overall average speed of 137 mph. The D.H. 86 showed that it could cope with a north crosswind landing and take-off from the beach just as easily as the Dragons. She was guarded by the police on the beach and after lunch, *The Giffard Bay* took local dignitaries on a round-Island flight before she returned with her original passengers to Heston.

A safety feature of the D.H. 86 Express, pertinent to Jersey Airways Ltd. flights across the Channel, was that the craft would remain in the air following the failure of any two engines, even on the same wing. The Dragon could maintain flight on only one of its two engines and Jersey Airways had been grateful for this feature, but had managed to keep the incidents unreported. However, luck ran out on 18th February 1935 when The *Portelet Bay* was observed on the beach undergoing repairs to an engine and the *Jersey Evening Post*

The Giffard Bay on the sands.

reported that while she was Jersey bound with five passengers and a full luggage load, the craft suffered an engine failure near Alderney and the pilot, Mr Jenkins, managed to continue to Jersey on one engine with the passengers unaware of any problem as the affected propeller continued to spin freely in the rush of air. The airline suffered more bad luck three days later when Jersey suffered a 75 mph hurricane. *St. Ouen's Bay* was pegged down on Quennevais Racecourse overnight ready for the Rennes service next day, but she was torn from her moorings and tossed about before she could be lashed to the refuelling lorry. She was out of service for some days due to a damaged port wing.

Much to the chagrin of Portsmouth City Council and Portsmouth Aerodrome, Jersey Airways abandoned Portsmouth in February 1935 in favour of Eastleigh Airport when it gained status as a Customs airport. There were many advantages. Southampton had better transport facilities with a railway station only 50 yards from the aerodrome, the landing fees were lower and the hangars were bigger and cheaper to rent. Southampton was a major seaport and had excellent rail connections to the Midlands and the West with regular express trains to London, while Eastleigh Airport had good domestic airline connections with the rest of the country. The introduction of the D.H. 86 Express had reduced the crossing time from Portsmouth from 75 minutes to 60 minutes, but the 75 minutes had to be reinstated with this move to Eastleigh. Jersey Airways Ltd. now carried out all their own maintenance and installed an engine overhaul workshop at Eastleigh where they could also carry out their own Certificates of Airworthiness.

The next two D.H. 86's were delivered in March 1935. D.H. 86 Express, G-ACYG, named *The Grouville Bay* received its Certificate of Airworthiness on 8th March 1935 and her sister G-ACZN named *The St. Catherine's Bay* received her C. of A. on 22nd March 1935. Both were in service for the busy Easter holiday when Easter Sunday was on 21st April 1935.

Above left: Jersey Airways Ltd.'s second D.H. 86 Express, G-ACYG, named *The Grouville Bay* on the sands of West Park in March 1935. A Jersey Airways Ltd. tanker is refuelling the aircraft and a member of staff is loading luggage into the nose of the aircraft.

Above right: An 'air to air' inflight publicity photograph of *The St. Catherine's Bay*, Jersey Airways Ltd.'s third D.H. 86 Express, G-ACZN.

Right: Numerous snapshot photographs were taken of passengers with 'their aircraft' on the sands of West Park. This is a real photographic postcard by "HAPPY SNAPS" of a passenger being greeted from *The St. Catherine's Bay*.

In the week following Easter the fourth D.H. 86 was delivered to Jersey Airways Ltd.; G-ACZO was named *The Quaine Bay*. The craft had received her C. of A. on 9th April 1935.

Above left: The month of May saw delivery of the final two D.H. 86's with G-ACZP, named *The Belcroute Bay* receiving its C. of A. on 11th May 1935.

Above right: The sixth and final Jersey Airways Ltd. D.H. 86 Express, G-ACZR, named *La Saline Bay* receiving its C. of A. on 29th May 1935.

A Jersey Airways Ltd. ground engineer about to spin one of the props of *La Saline Bay*.

With a fleet of six D.H. 86 Expresses, Jersey Airways no longer required its Dragons. All were sold save G-ACNJ, *Rozel Bay* that was retained on Quennevais Racecourse for charters, emergencies, and possible flights to Alderney when the new airport was built.

May 1935 was a month of developments. Two new pilots, K.T. Murray and O.C.A. Hankey joined the company from Air Service Training. The Jersey Airport site, although not yet operative, had direction-finding apparatus installed that could be utilised by the D.H. 86's, and on 25th May 1935 Sir Herbert Walker opened offices at Victoria Station for the parent company, Channel Islands Airway.

The free Jersey Airways Ltd. coach service now departed for Heston Airport from Victoria Coach Station. This photographic postcard taken at Heston advertises both Thurgood's airline and coach building businesses.

On 24th May, a dramatic incident occurred on Quennevais Racecourse with the first night landing in the islands when Douglas Brecknell landed at 21.30 hours aided by the headlights of every car that could be mustered. He was returning from London on an emergency mission with Harley Street Specialist, Mr T. Izod Bennett. The aircraft used for this first night landing is unrecorded, but it was probably the Dragon G-ACNJ, *Rozel Bay* that had been retained specifically for such incidents.

The Guernsey and Alderney Connection

Thurgood wanted to expand to Guernsey and Alderney, but there was no land available for an airport on Guernsey and the only connection possible was by an unreliable seaplane service. He was luckier on Alderney where he was building his own airport. Connecting Alderney to Guernsey would still have to be by an amphibian until Guernsey built its own airport, but once the Alderney Airport was completed, he could make direct flights between Jersey and Alderney, and Alderney and Southampton. Such a service would seldom require a big D.H. 86, but his diminutive low powered D.H. 84 Dragon, *Rozel Bay* was inadequate for the job.

On 17th April 1934, De Havilland had flown a prototype bi-wing aircraft called the De Havilland D.H. 89 Dragon Six, but soon renamed the Dragon Rapide universally known as the 'Rapide'. The D.H. 89 Rapide was a development of the D.H. 84 Dragon. It resembled the Dragon in layout and size but had the tapered wings and streamlined undercarriage housing of a D.H. 86 Express as well as two of the powerful 200 hp Gipsy Six engines found on the D.H. 86. The Rapide was heavier than the Dragon and could carry eight passengers at a higher cruising speed; the first production aircraft averaged 158 mph in the 1934 King's Cup Air Race.

This more powerful small aircraft was ideal for Thurgood's Alderney service. He ordered two in anticipation of the opening of the airport and until then the Rapides would be used to supplement the mainline services or replace a D.H. 86 if fewer passengers were flying.

The two D.H. 89 Rapides were delivered in June 1935; the first Rapide, G-ADBV being named *The St. Ouen's Bay II*.

The second D.H. Rapide carried the consecutive registration G-ADBW, but never received a name, and all subsequent Jersey Airways Ltd. aircraft went unnamed.

Construction of the D.H. 89 Rapide was similar to the D.H. 86 with the same wing shape and boxy fuselage, but with the fabric covered plywood skin on the outside of the framing and sound proofing. The specifications of the Rapide included a wingspan of 48 ft, a length of 34 ft 6 in. and a height of 10 ft 3 in.. The power plant of two 200 hp De Havilland Gipsy Six air-cooled in-line engines produced a cruising speed of 132 mph over a range of 578 miles from a fuel capacity of 76 gallons. The Rapide required a longer and faster landing than the Dragon, but in 1937 all new craft would be fitted with trailing–edge flaps under the lower wing to assist with landing. This adapted craft became the D.H. 89A and most of the earlier craft were modified to conform to its specification. 731 civil and military Rapide production models were built, but few photographs exist of the Rapides on the beach at West Park.

During July the entire Jersey Airways Ltd. fleet was in operation breaking all records for the number of passengers carried, but in the island there was growing disquiet about the safety of the operation particularly for people on the beach when planes could appear ahead of schedule. The local press reported the concern felt by the Islanders. At the end of the month two machines arrived particularly early before the police constables had arrived to clear the beach and although the Jersey Airways ground staff tried to clear them there were still a number of people on the beach in the path of the planes when they landed and it "seemed to be a miracle" that the planes managed to avoid them. In future Jersey Airways Ltd. would fire a Verey light to stop planes landing if the beach was not clear.

With incredible cynicism Jersey Airways Ltd. announced in their Summer 1935 timetable:

> "Nearly 650,000 miles were completed in 1934 by Jersey Airways without injury to any passenger."

They failed to mention that in that year one of their planes had run into two young boys, killing one and seriously injuring the other; obviously the safety of fare paying passengers was more important than local children!

The Jersey Airway's fleet on the beach at West Park.

Two Calamities on the Same Day

Jersey Airways Ltd. was having a relatively trouble-free season until Saturday 17th August when calamity struck twice in the same day. At Heston, Mr Israel was taking off at 10.45 hours in G-ACZP, *The Belcroute Bay*, when a tyre burst. As he tried to control the aeroplane the other tyre burst and the craft swerved round, but Israel managed to keep her on an even keel and none of the passengers was injured. The passengers disembarked and *The Belcroute Bay* was taken out of service. A film company happened to be working at the airport at the time and the cameraman fortuitously recorded the whole incident, although I doubt if Thurgood thought it fortuitous.

Avro 642, G-ACFV, the "Big Avro".

As there were no other Jersey Airways' craft available, the company hired Commercial Air Hire's sixteen-seater, "Big Avro", G-ACFV to take over the service and deliver the thirteen shaken passengers to Jersey.

When the Avro 642, G-ACFV landed on the sands at West Park the huge machine naturally attracted a great deal of attention on the sunny summer afternoon which was also unfortunate for Thurgood as it meant there was a large crowd of holiday makers on the beach to witness the second calamity. Mr Orchard was landing G-ACZO, *The Quaine Bay* at 17.00 hours when his port wheel brake seized. This threw a sudden strain on the starboard undercarriage leg that collapsed smashing the starboard wing into the ground and shearing the tip off the starboard propeller that flew through the air narrowly missing the Jersey Airways staff who were waiting nearby.

The Quaine Bay was completely immobile with her starboard wing stuck in the sand under threat of being engulfed by a 38 ft spring high tide due in four and half hours. Jersey Airways scrambled all their staff

The Quaine Bay after the landing gear collapse.

The "Big Avro" on the sands at West Park.

and with both wings supported by and lashed to two lorries, they managed to remove the collapsed starboard undercarriage and very slowly drive the whole structure along the beach to the First Tower slipway. There was not enough room for two lorries and *The Quaine Bay* on the slipway so the damaged wing was ignominiously supported on a horse cart and the craft was slowly towed tail first up the slipway in a race against the rising tide, much to the entertainment of the crowds lining the promenade. A week later *The Quaine Bay* was shipped back to Southampton aboard the SR cargo steamer *Haslemere* for repair at Eastleigh.

There were now two D.H. 86's out of action leaving a gaping hole in the fleet during the airline's busiest time of year and so the Avro 642 was retained to maintain the service from Heston. For two weeks the exciting sight of the "Big Avro" could be seen landing on the sands at West Park, but then she too had to be taken out of service on 31st August and hauled up the First Tower slipway for repair. Once repaired the Avro returned to her normal duties as the holiday season was over and the damaged D.H. 86's were back in service.

The "Big Avro"

The "Big Avro" was the largest and latest in a line of Fokker derivatives, designed by A.V. Roe & Company Ltd. in February 1933 as the Avro 642 Eighteen. It was a high wing, cabin monoplane airliner for 16 passengers, baggage area and lavatory in a fuselage covered in fabric over a welded steel structure. There were numerous large windows along the side of the passenger cabin that made the interior very light and airy. The wooden wings were developed from those of the Avro 10 that in turn were a derivative of the Fokker single sheet plywood wing. These wooden wings were designed to house two integral, Armstrong-Siddeley Jaguar VID, 460 hp engines with four-blade propellers that produced a maximum speed of 160 mph and a cruising speed of 135 mph over a range of 600 miles for a duration of between 4 to 6 hours. The craft was dual control for a crew of two, had a length of 54 ft 6 in., a wingspan of 71 ft 3 in. and a height of 11 ft 6 in.

The first Avro 642, G-ACFV, was completed in December 1933 but required modifications before its handover to Midland and Scottish Air Ferries at Renfrew in Scotland on 6th April 1934. She flew to Speke Aerodrome for the official opening of the new air service between Glasgow, London and Belfast and was named *The Marchioness of Londonderry* by the Lord of Londonderry during the airport opening ceremony. G-ACFV was sold in May 1935 to Brian Allen Aviation, the associate company of Commercial Air Hire Ltd. and Air Dispatch Ltd.. Jersey Airways only used her for a few weeks. In September 1936 she was sold to Australia and used for mail transport. On 21st January 1942 she was destroyed in a strafing attack by the Japanese air force during the first attack by Japan on Papua New Guinea.

1935 progressed without further mishap to the fleet, but as they entered winter the main problem was gale force winds. In mid-September the gales were so severe that both the radio masts at Heston were blown down. A Jersey Airways Ltd. D.H. 86 created a record by flying the 184 miles from Jersey to Heston in 60 minutes aided by a 45 mph tail wind and in October another D.H. 86 made the Jersey to Southampton crossing in 35 minutes.

On 7th November Israel was the only pilot who managed to take-off from and land at Heston. He left on schedule in his D.H. 86 in the morning in fog of almost zero visibility and returned in the afternoon in similar zero visibility caused by a blinding rainstorm. The year ended with another beach incident on 30th December when a Rapide made four unsuccessful attempts to land in a 35 mph crosswind. A heavier and bigger D.H. 86 coped with the crosswind without problem, but the lighter D.H. 89 had considerable difficulty as each time she came in to land a gust of wind forced her up again and after the fourth failed attempt the pilot returned to Southampton.

By the end of 1935, 8,569 passengers had been carried on the Jersey-Heston route and 15,957 on the Southampton route. Many of the passengers on the Southampton route were from London, but found the service from Southampton more convenient and cheaper travelling by train from Waterloo, than making the journey to Heston and often having to change aircraft at Southampton if they were routed that way.

SPECTACULAR RAF LANDINGS IN ST PETER PORT HARBOUR

The *Guernsey Weekly Press* recorded with great excitement that just after 11.30 hours on Tuesday 19th March 1935 two RAF flying boats approached the harbour of St. Peter Port from a northerly direction about five minutes apart from each other. Amphibian Saro Clouds from RAF Calshot on the Solent on a training navigational flight to the Channel Islands, their registrations were K 3726 and K 2898. The first craft circled the harbour at about 500 feet and then dived steeply from the west to the east making a perfect and somewhat spectacular landing between the old harbour entrance and the New Jetty. She taxied in and out of the harbour and circled inside the old harbour where a mechanic could be observed attending to the engines and making adjustments. The second craft appeared from the north but made a direct landing inside the harbour without circling at all. The two machines only remained in St. Peter Port Harbour for a short while and once the mechanic was satisfied with his adjustments, they both left as promptly as they had arrived.

This was the first recorded visit of a military Saro Cloud to the Channel Islands and their visit was so fleeting that there is only one known photographic reference of their visit.

A military Saro Cloud K2898 in St. Peter Port Harbour.

GUERNSEY AIRWAYS LTD

The Arrival of Guernsey Airways Ltd with the Saro Windhover

Guernsey Airways Ltd. was a wholly owned subsidiary of Jersey Airways Ltd., set up on 1st December 1934 by Jersey Airways Ltd. Director, Walter Thurgood. At the same time, the newly formed Channel Islands Airways Ltd. was established as a holding company for both the Jersey and Guernsey airlines. Thurgood could not operate from Guernsey as the island did not have an airport and the beaches were unsuitable for landing, but Thurgood wanted to copyright the names "Guernsey Airways" and "Channel Islands Airways" before any competitor acquired them. "Guernsey Airways Ltd." was named to gain the approval of Guernsey residents, but it was in reality Jersey Airways Ltd. as the craft and structure were Jersey Airways Ltd.'s and the pilots and staff were all employees of Jersey Airways Ltd.. Although the three companies were one, each kept their own accounts to be able to claim government grants.

Jersey Airways had a monopoly on landing rights on the beach at St. Helier while on Alderney, Thurgood was building his own airport with the cooperation of the local residents. In Guernsey it was much more complicated. Three locations, at L'Erée, La Villiaze and L'Ancresse were proposed for the States' Airport, but no decision had been made and, in the meantime, a private company, Cobham Air Routes, was developing its own airport and service from L'Erée.

A seaplane service from Guernsey to the mainland was historically impractical. The only option available for Thurgood was to establish a seaplane link between Guernsey and Jersey for passengers to connect with Jersey Airways Ltd. flights to the mainland. He also required a craft that could run between Guernsey and his new Alderney Airport, and could come ashore at the St. Aubin's Bay Beach landing zone. A seaplane is confined to water, but Thurgood required an amphibian craft that could land on the sea, on a beach, that could drive up a beach from the sea, or land on a normal airfield; the Saro Windhover was the only craft of viable size available that met all these requirements.

The Saro A21 Windhover

The Saro A21 Windhover was designed and built by Saunders-Roe at Cowes on the Isle of Wight. It was an enlarged version of the Saro Cutty Sark with an additional third de Havilland Gipsy II engine. Construction followed the standard Saro design of a single wooden wing mounted directly on top of an "Alclad" hull with two floats under the wings. The three 120 hp, 4 cylinder, air cooled in-line Gipsy II engines were mounted on pylons above the wing clear of sea spray, and the craft had the unique design feature of a small auxiliary aerofoil above all three engines designed to improve airflow and lift. The Windhover had a length of 41 ft 4 in., a wingspan of 54 ft 4 in. and a height of 12 ft 7 in., her maximum speed was 108 mph and cruising speed 87 mph with a 400-mile range. She could accommodate two crew with six passengers. Although the Windhover was ideal for Thurgood's requirements, the craft had a very limited market and only two were ever built.

The only Windhover production model, Saro A21/2, G-ABJP, was completed in March 1931, and received its Certificate of Airworthiness on 8th July when it was sold to Francis Francia at Heston Airport. Francia was a Gibraltar merchant who bought the Windhover for the newly created Gibraltar Airways Ltd. for a twice-daily Gibraltar-Tangier service. G-ABJP was christened *General Godley* after the acting Governor of Gibraltar and on 21st September 1931 inaugurated the world's shortest intercontinental scheduled air service, between Europe and Africa; a 46 mile trip that took twenty minutes.

The 'Passenger Arrivals' in Tangier was novel, but the service was terminated in January 1932 after 117 flights.

The Hon. Mrs Victor Bruce, chartered G-ABJP in May 1932 for an attempt on the World Flight Endurance Record but when she collected G-ABJP from Gibraltar the craft was in such a dilapidated state that it crashed

The prototype Windhover Saro A21/1 first flew at Cowes on 16th October 1930 and went to Australia as VH-UPB, but was destroyed when blown ashore following a sea landing in strong winds in Tasmania on 13th May 1936.

and had to be shipped by steamer back to the UK for repair.

Mrs Bruce renamed G-ABJP *City of Portsmouth* but her bid for the World Flight Endurance Record failed after three attempts and nothing more significant happened to the Windhover until it was bought by Guernsey Airways Ltd. in early 1935.

As with all Jersey Airways Ltd. endeavours, Eckersley-Maslin inaugurate any new service and although the Windhover was a Guernsey Airways Ltd. craft, it was Eckersley-Maslin who flew her during the first month. On 22nd May 1935 the Saro Windhover flew from the Solent to Jersey on a proving flight and from there to St. Peter Port Harbour and finally on to Alderney although the airport on Alderney was not yet functioning. Thurgood determined to introduce a regular service between Guernsey and Jersey while the extension to Alderney would wait until the airport was finished as a beach landing was not practical due to the steep camber of the shingle.

The arrival of the Guernsey Airways Ltd. amphibian was well received in Guernsey, but Thurgood's publicity exercise calling it a "Guernsey Airways Ltd. service" was lost on the *Guernsey Evening Post* that in a poorly researched article welcoming the Windhover, headlined it with the title:

AIR SERVICES.
JERSEY AIRWAYS INTRODUCE
FAST AMPHIBIAN.
PLANE BUILT FOR ENDURANCE
RECORD.

On 1st June the twice-daily summer service of Jersey Airways Ltd. returned, and adverts appeared in Guernsey announcing a forthcoming Guernsey Airways Ltd. amphibian service from St. Peter Port to St. Aubin's Bay that would connect with these mainland services.

Unorthodox arrival proceedures in Tangier.

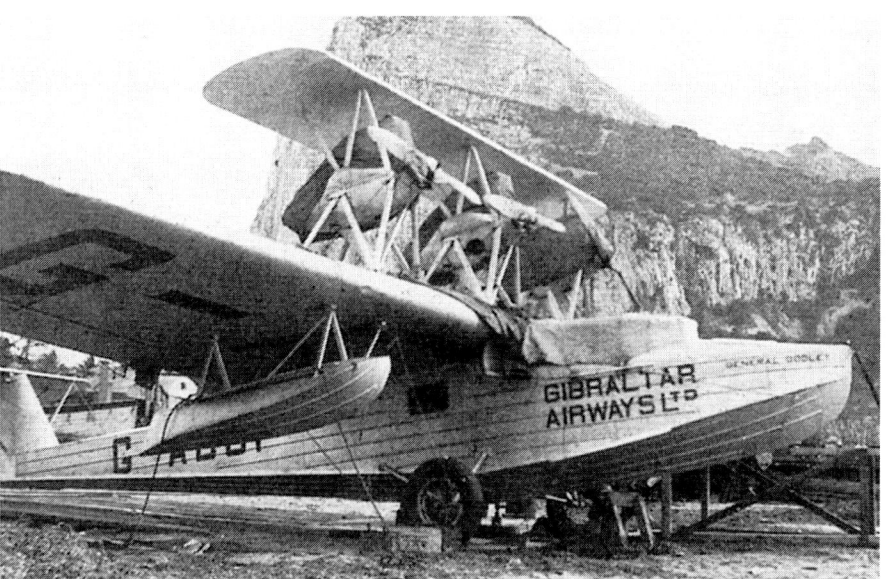
G-ABJP in storage at Gibraltar.

Now renamed *City of Portsmouth* on one of the failed round the world endurance record attempts.

Guernsey Airways Ltd. issued a simple timetable to commence on Sunday 9th June 1935.

In association with.
THE SOUTHERN & GT. WESTERN RAILWAYS.
RAILWAY AIR SERVICES LTD.
AND.
JERSEY AIRWAYS, LTD".

The timetable changed each month because it was determined by the high tides on the beach in St. Aubin's Bay.

Piloted by Eckersley-Maslin, the amphibian service started on Sunday 9th June and was planned to run daily except for Wednesdays when the Windhover required servicing. When the seaplane moored in St. Peter Port Harbour the passengers were landed and embarked by the SR and GWR mail boat tender. The service got off to an auspicious start with three return flights on the first day, On each of these six flights, five of the six available seats were taken except on the early morning positioning flight from Jersey to Guernsey when two passengers were transported.

Seaplanes are more susceptible to landing problems than land craft, especially sea fog, rough seas and high rollers and it was not long before the Windhover suffered the same service interruptions as previous Channel Islands' seaplanes. On Sunday 16th June a notice was posted outside the SR and GWR booking office on the New Jetty in St. Peter Port Harbour stating that all seaplane services were suspended until Tuesday 18th June; no reason was given. There was no service on Wednesday 19th as it was the aircraft's overhaul day and on Friday 21th June Guernsey had thick fog. Glimpses were caught of Pilot Eckersley-Maslin flying the Windhover very low looking for gaps in the fog off Moulin Huet and around the Pea Stacks and then passing low over the rooftops at Jerbourg, but Eckersley-Maslin failed to find a gap large enough to permit a landing and was forced to return to Jersey. The following week the Windhover left Jersey for Guernsey, but when she arrived over Guernsey the fog was again thick, and Eckersley-Maslin could only locate Sark. He circled Guernsey twice, but could not identify St. Peter Port Harbour and with petrol left for only 10 more minutes of flying, he put down on the water and taxied until he could find a boat to follow into the harbour.

On Friday 28th, Eckersley-Maslin was taking off at 19.10 hours on the last trip of the day, but when he had just brought the Windhover up to flying speed and was at a height of about ten feet, she dropped back down. This was not unusual, but instead of just skimming the crests of a few waves, the craft was confronted with an exceptionally large wave and her nose dug into it with such force that the impact damaged the bow of the plane and the nose of a lady passenger when she hit the back of the seat in front of her. More seriously, the hull of the Windhover had been strained out of alignment and she was withdrawn from service and sent to Southampton for repair; luckily she was still sufficiently airworthy to be able to fly there unaided.

Greig, the Jersey Airways Ltd. Director who two years previously had never even flown as a passenger in an aeroplane, had recently acquired a pilot's "A" licence and with his new font of flying knowledge, remonstrated with Flight-Lieutenant Eckersley-Maslin concerning his handling of the Windhover whereupon Eckersley-Maslin promptly resigned. Guernsey Airways Ltd. no longer had a seaplane pilot or a serviceable craft and in under a month the new inter-island service was at a standstill although between 9th and 28th of June the amphibian had managed to operate on thirteen days carrying 288 passengers.

The Return of the Saro Cloud

Following the accident to the Windhover the airline was now without an aircraft at a time when Alderney Airport was nearing completion. *The Star* of Guernsey optimistically reported that the Windhover would "… require a few days for repairs and adjustments", but repairs to the Windhover would take longer than expected as parts and spares were being commandeered by the RAF, consequently Guernsey Airways failed to run any inter-island service during July.

As a temporary solution, Guernsey Airways Ltd. decided to hire, at some considerable expense, the amphibian Saro Cloud, registration G-ABCJ; this was the prototype craft that had first visited Jersey in 1930.

The Saro Cloud restarted the service on 5th August, Bank Holiday Monday, and as before, three services a day were reinstated except for the Wednesday overhaul day. The times of the regular service had to change on 8th August because of the high tide and in the four flying days of that week, 118 passengers were flown in the Cloud, but on Saturday 10th August all services were cancelled because of carburettor problems discovered on Friday. Two specialist engineers arrived from Saunders-Roe to deal with the problem, but the services were not reinstated until Thursday 15th August when the Saro Cloud left Jersey at noon for Guernsey intending to fly on to the new Alderney Aerodrome later in the afternoon.

The First Plane to Land on the new Alderney Aerodrome

On Thursday 15th August at 14.00 hours, the Guernsey Airways Ltd. Saro Cloud, G-ABCJ made the second flight of the day piloted by Mr Brent to Guernsey, and at 14.45 hours continued on to Alderney with eight passengers to make the first landing of an aircraft on

The Saro Cloud now sported two 340 hp Napier Rapier IV power plants. These more powerful engines increased her cruising speed from 95 mph to 102 mph. She could carry seven passengers and a crew of two, and the new pilot was Mr Frank Brent, a competent seaplane pilot who had just completed five years of RAF service.

the newly completed Alderney Aerodrome. The Alderney Aerodrome did not yet have a licence and this inaugural flight was unannounced and carried no fare paying passengers, but passengers included Mr Greig the General Manager of both Guernsey and Jersey Airways Ltd., an Air Ministry official who was inspecting the new aerodrome, and a Guernsey *Star* correspondent who reported that "half of Alderney" turned out to greet the aircraft. After a flight of only seven minutes, the retractable undercarriage was lowered, and the Cloud required only half the length of the runway to make a perfect landing on the new aerodrome. She was met by Captain Hopton who had been responsible for constructing the aerodrome on behalf of Thurgood.

Crowds gathered to see the craft and await her departure while the Air Ministry inspector carried out his examination. He was occupied for over an hour but shortly after 16.30 hours the passengers re-boarded the Cloud and the plane taxied to the far end of the aerodrome, turned, and with the throttles wide open, headed back to Guernsey. The plane was taxiing into St. Peter Port Harbour long before most of the Alderney spectators had returned home.

It was business as normal on the 16th August, when G-ABCJ flew three return trips to Guernsey carrying a total of 33 passengers, but then disaster struck again when the following day's flights were cancelled, and all future flights postponed indefinitely because a crack was found in one of the craft's propellers. Guernsey Airways Ltd. expressed their regrets to passengers but admitted that the Saro Cloud was unsuitable for the Channel Islands and that they would have to suspend the inter-island service until the return of the Windhover. The Saro Cloud had flown the inter-island service for less than two weeks and in that time 77 passengers travelled from Jersey to Guernsey and 86 from Guernsey to Jersey.

The Windhover returned in October. In order to run a regular timetable, on the days when winds or tides prevented the craft from using the beach in St. Aubin's Bay, the Windhover would enter the harbour at St. Helier and moor to a buoy to disembark or load passengers as she did in the harbour at St. Peter Port. On 5th October the Windhover flew from Southampton to check her moorings in St. Helier Harbour and rehearse the embarkation drill; she did not visit Guernsey but returned to Southampton soon after completing her trials. A new Guernsey Airways Ltd. winter timetable was issued that consisted of only one return flight a day that was no longer dependent on the times of the tides in St. Aubins Bay.

On 12th October Alderney Aerodrome was granted its licence by the Royal Court. The Windhover returned to Jersey on 14th October to reopen the Jersey-Guernsey winter service of one return trip a day, excepting on her routine Wednesday service day, but she still could not fly to Alderney as Customs were not yet in place. Pilot Frank Brent initiated the inter-island amphibian service leaving St. Aubin's Bay at 10.45 hours and arriving in St. Peter Port Harbour at 11.15 hours with a return flight scheduled for 13.45 hours, but there were no passengers for the service. It was unrealistic to think that the Windhover service could be maintained throughout the winter even with only one return flight a day considering the airline had failed during the summer months, and inevitability, the amphibian service was cancelled on 1st November because of rough water off St. Peter Port. The service became completely erratic as the next day the Windhover was unable to land outside St. Peter Port and had to return to Jersey, and the bad weather thwarted any further attempts at landing except on November 5th and 9th. On Monday 18th November, one passenger flew to Guernsey and three were brought back to Jersey, but on 19th November the service was again suspended indefinitely when the Windhover had to return to Southampton for extensive repairs.

Flying from Jersey to London in a D.H. 86 was a comfortable experience with a certain amount of luxury but flying between Guernsey and Jersey in the Windhover was the opposite extreme. The air correspondent for the Guernsey *Star* wrote of his experiences,

> The Windhover is a veritable hen-coop with wings. You can't move a limb and you sit in an atmosphere of petrol fumes with the mechanic continually climbing over your knees… Taking off the sea, you spend most of your time ineffectively trying to keep dry. Water literally pours in from the supposedly closed windows.

The truth was, no amphibian aircraft had been built that was strong enough to cope with the extreme conditions found in the Channel Islands and a reliable inter-island service could never be established until an aerodrome was built on Guernsey. Without any prospect of a suitable seaplane becoming available in the near future, Pilot Frank Brent left Guernsey Airways Ltd., and the company ended 1935 without a serviceable amphibian and with no seaplane pilot.

The audited accounts for the year ending 31st December 1935 show that Guernsey Airways Ltd. made a loss of £2,911 in its first year of operation.

COBHAM AIR ROUTES LTD

Sir Alan J Cobham, KBE, AFC

Sir Alan J. Cobham, K.B.E., A.F.C. (6th May 1894 – 21st October 1973), was perhaps one of the most famous aviators in the United Kingdom between the two world wars. He joined the Royal Flying Corps in the First World War and after the war flew thousands of miles as a taxi-pilot. He was a competitor in the King's Cup Air Race and made long distance flights to Australia and around Africa. In 1927 he flew over Guernsey en route to Africa and commented, "we could scent the faint aroma of flowers in the air". He was notorious for landing a De Havilland D.H. 50 seaplane, G-EBFO, on the River Thames in front of the Houses of Parliament in 1926, in order to deliver a petition to Parliament promoting the benefits to the Nation of a civil aviation industry. Cobham was perhaps best known for his National Aviation Day Displays, or "Cobham's Air Circus" with which he toured the country. In 1929 his air display had one aircraft, the De Havilland D. H. 61 Giant Moth, G-AAEV, but by 1932 he had a large collection of aircraft carrying out aerobatics, wing-walking, comic turns, racing and of course joyriding.

Cobham Air Routes Ltd

Sir Alan's aim was to establish an airline between L'Erée Airfield in Guernsey and Christchurch

Sir Alan J Cobham

Christchurch Aerodrome

Westland Wessex, G-EBXK,

G-ADBA was a low wing Series 1 model with twin radial Cheetah IX engines of 350 hp, capable of carrying eight passengers. It, and the Monospar ST-10, were the only aircraft at the time with the aerodynamic benefit of a retractable undercarriage. The Airspeed Envoy had a wingspan of 52 ft 4 in., a length of 34 ft 6 in. and a cruising speed of 170 mph. It was considerably faster and more comfortable than the six-year-old Westland Wessex, but it could not fly to Guernsey because it was unable to land on the short L'Erée runways.

Aerodrome near Bournemouth with a London connection using Croydon Airport.

Christchurch Aerodrome was to be the Cobham Air Routes Ltd. mainland base with a new hangar built to house the Cobham fleet of Wessex Westland aircraft.

Cobham reasoned that if he could establish a commercial route between L'Erée and the mainland, the States of Guernsey might reconsider their intention to build Guernsey's new airport at La Villiaze. As the owner of L'Erée he would in effect have a monopoly.

Cobham's Air Display had already acquired a Westland Wessex, G-EBXK, which was the prototype Westland IV. The Wessex was a high-winged monoplane with three 105 hp Genet-Major engines. It had the distinct advantage that it could land in small fields and was credited with the ability to fly on only two engines, but it was not a fast aircraft; its cruising speed was 95 mph with a top speed of 105 mph and a landing speed of 65 mph.

In March 1935 Cobham bought three more Wessex models from the Belgian national airline, SABENA, at a cost of £4,500 each. These craft were the fleet for the cross-Channel sector of the route while for the overland route between Christchurch, Portsmouth and Croydon, Cobham had a more modern and much faster aircraft, an Airspeed Envoy, G-ADBA.

The Royal Court of Guernsey permitted Cobham to bring a Westland Wessex to L'Erée to perform trial flights in front of an Air Ministry expert whose report would guide the Court in issuing a licence for commercial flying. On the appointed day, Thursday 25th April 1935, crowds gathered at L'Erée to witness the arrival of the six-seater aeroplane.

The chosen Wessex was G-ABAJ and the pilot was Cobham's most experienced flyer, an ex RAF Flying Officer, Instructor and test pilot, Captain Cecil W. H. Bebb. G-ABAJ left Portsmouth at 12.55 hours, but flying over the Isle of Wight, Bebb immediately encountered a strong north-north-east wind that slowed the passage of the aircraft and they did not pass Alderney until 13.50 hours.

Cecil Noel and Clifton Smith of the Guernsey Aero Club, set out at 13.30 hours to greet the Wessex, but returned at 14.00 hours having failed to sight her. Five minutes later and 70 minutes after take-off from Portsmouth an engine purr was heard, and the dazzling white aircraft was sighted 2,000 feet up in the sky. On board the Wessex, Cobham was in despair because the wind was in the wrong direction for a safe landing at L'Erée. He ordered Bebb to land on a nearby beach, but Bebb said he would make a couple of dummy runs and if he felt confident enough not to hit the sea wall, he would land on the third pass.

In the event, Bebb only made one pass and two minutes later he made a perfect landing.

From the monoplane emerged: Sir Alan Cobham, Mr W. A. Campbell the Air Ministry expert, Pilot Captain C. W. Bebb, a second Pilot R. W. Ogden, Mr M. J. Meacock the Chief Engineer, and an unidentified wireless operator. The party were met on the airfield by Guernsey State's Deputy, B. Bartlett, who was also a Director of the Guernsey Aero Club, Advocate H.H. Randell, Cecil Noel, Customs Officers and the Guernsey State's Engineer.

Although Bebb had managed to make a safe landing, the wind was in the wrong direction to execute the test flights. Cobham was frustrated, but Cecil Noel advised there could be a wind change in the afternoon when the tide changed, and sure enough the wind swung round to the south-west. Bebb immediately commenced the trial flights carrying sandbags to replicate the weight of passengers. With each flight they increased the number of sandbags and Pilot Bebb always got away cleanly making a circuit of the White Tower and landing safely five minutes later

Captain Cecil W. H. Bebb.

on the field at L'Erée. At 16.40 hours they stopped the trials after Bebb had carried sandbags equivalent to the weight of a full load of six passengers. Bebb's only suggestion was that wires that ran along the roadsides bordering the airfield should be relocated underground as they would be invisible to pilots in poor visibility. The Air Ministry expert, Campbell, required no other improvements and immediately

Bebb's one and only pass over L'Erée Aerodrome.

licensed the airfield for a Wessex with six passengers. At 17.00 hours the whole party retired to the L'Erée Hotel for a snack and then G-ABAJ and her passengers returned to Portsmouth before sunset.

On 29th April 1935 the Guernsey Royal Court granted a temporary licence to the Guernsey Aero Club for the use of L'Erée Aerodrome for commercial flights by aircraft of the Wessex type carrying a maximum of six passengers. When State's Advocate V. G. Carey asked if Jersey Airways would be able to use the airfield, he received a resounding "No" from Advocate Randell acting for the Aero Club.

Cobham Air Routes Ltd. was registered on Friday 3rd May 1935 and Captain Bebb flew to L'Erée in G-ADEW with staff members of the new airline for meetings with the Directors of the Guernsey Aero Club Ltd. to discuss the planning of "L'Erée Airport". Cobham was unable to attend because he had influenza. Bebb arrived at L'Erée at about 12.30 hours and despite a stiff breeze from the most difficult quarter, he made a perfect landing using less than half of the available runway. The intention was to start services the following Monday. Captain Rodney Beresford arrived later in the afternoon piloting G-ABAJ with engineers Meacock and Sutherland on board, but a tyre burst on landing and part of the under-carriage collapsed forcing the machine to swing round and damage a propeller. Nobody was injured, but when Bebb returned to England at the end of the day in G-ADEW he left behind G-ABAJ in the care of Meacock and Sutherland to oversee its repair in Guernsey.

Mr. F. H. Mortimore, the London manager of the new airline had arrived on the island in the first Wessex flown by Captain Bebb. He explained to the local press the structure of the new air service that would operate via Southampton and Christchurch to London. There would be three routes to London:

Guernsey – Southampton – London,
Guernsey – Portsmouth – London,
Guernsey – Christchurch – Southampton – London

There was little difference in the lengths of the routes, but Christchrch and Southampton had been chosen for easy links to towns on the South Coast and the west of England. Three planes would be in operation and the proposed service would leave Croydon twice daily.

The times and fares were experimental for the first 28 days and it was anticipated that if the service proved a success it could operate hourly during the summer season if necessary.

The Guernsey newspapers advertised the new 'EXPRESS AIR SERVICE' that would run between Guernsey and London via Christchurch, Southampton and Portsmouth with road transport provided between the airports and towns at all

A newspaper cutting form the *Guernsey Weekly Press* of Saturday 4th May 1935 entitled "AT L'ERÉE AERODROME". The photographs show Cobham's Wessex on the airfield and part of the party including: (l. to r.) Pilot C. W. Bebb, Deputy B. Bartlett (and his daughter Rosemary), Mr E.F. Laine, Mr W.A. Cambell, Adv. H.H. Randell and Sir Alan Cobham.

points. The sole agent in Guernsey was Bougourd Brothers of the Esplanade and Pollett and the new service would commence on 'Jubilee Day', Monday 6th May 1935, the Silver Jubilee of the reigning King George V.

The United Kingdom including the Channel Islands was celebrating 6th May Jubilee Day, but there was no celebration of the first flight by Cobham Air Routes Ltd. from Croydon by the Airspeed Envoy. If anything, it was a rather sombre flight for although the aircraft carried five passengers including Sir Alan Cobham, the other passengers were insurance assessors flown at Cobham's expense to inspect the damaged Wessex G-ABAJ. Captain C. H. Colman was to be the regular Airspeed Envoy pilot and he got the party away from Croydon at 09.00 hours flying at an average speed of 153 mph via Portsmouth to Christchurch where they changed planes for the Wessex, G-ADEW. Captain Ogden, the third of the Cobham Air Routes Ltd. Wessex pilots, brought G-ADEW to L'Erée where she arrived at 11.30 hours to be greeted by hundreds of spectators for the inauguration of the service to England. Captain Ogden then piloted the return flight that left

L'Erée at 12.30 hours, but with only two passengers and neither of them fare-paying, as Mr Outram was one of the Insurance assessors and the other passenger Mr. V. A. Lewis, was a correspondent for *The Star* who was on a free flight to Croydon and back to report on the new service. Lewis' account appeared in a 'Special Silver Jubilee Edition' of *The Star* printed in red, (white) and blue and published the next day; it was by turns effusive and romantic. Lewis was credited as "'The Star's Air Correspondent" and his report starts:

> In years to come Guernsey will have another reason to recall Jubilee Day 1935. For it was on that day that the first Guernsey to London aeroplane service commenced.

Despite Lewis' enthusiasm for the event, the service would not last long nor attain the historical significance that he attributed to it. He returned to L'Erée in the afternoon in G-ADEW, this time piloted by Captain Bebb. The aircraft was then held at L'Erée and its return to Christchurch delayed to await the first fare-paying passenger. Mr Simpson Smith was a surgeon who had earlier in the day operated on the Bailiff of Guernsey, Mr A. Bell. He had an appointment in London the following morning and Cobham's new airline was the only means by which he could make the appointment. Sir Alan Cobham accompanied Simpson Smith while the third passenger was Mr Blunden, the new Manager to be of L'Erée Airport. Simpson Smith became one of the few 'regular' passengers of the airline as he was required to visit the Bailiff on several occasions. At 18.30 hours the Wessex left with its three passengers, completing the first day's timetable, and Guernsey's terrestrial air service had at long last come into being.

Cobham Air Routes Ltd. completed its first week with pilots Ogden and Bebb alternately flying the cross-Channel leg of the route in the Wessex aircraft and Colman flying the overland leg in the Airspeed Envoy. The new enterprise was hardly a success as the planes were seldom fully booked and often flew empty. Even when they did carry passengers, these were frequently non fare-paying staff, travel agents, journalists or Aero Club members. Within three days of the start of the service the fares were reduced when the magazine *The Aeroplane* unfavourably compared them to the costs of flying by Jersey Airways Ltd.

In the following weeks, Bebb took over the Airspeed Envoy route and Rodney Beresford re-joined the cross-Channel route alternating with Ogden, but bad weather cancelled some flights while others failed because of technical problems such as faults with the radio. The scheduling policy changed so that if there were no passengers booked for a flight, the plane did not fly empty unless of course it was required to collect passengers at the other end.

The visit of a Wessex was still a newsworthy event in Guernsey and the local press gave a daily account of the arrival times of the aircraft, the pilot's name and even the names of every passenger; a gross invasion of privacy by today's standards of data protection. *The Star* inaugurated a new section of its paper with the boxed title 'AIRPORT' which gave details of the daily flights including the 'flying weather', and when Guernsey Airways started its inter-island Windhover amphibian service in June, the 'AIRPORT' column required two titles;

'Cobham Air Routes' and 'Guernsey Airways'.

Obviously, *The Star's* Air Correspondent was justifying his title!

The demand for the service improved gradually and at the end of May, Cobham Air Routes Ltd., having suffered delays due to adverse winds, issued a new timetable allowing themselves more time to complete the journeys. On 30th May 1935 the third Wessex, G-ADFZ made its maiden flight to L'Erée piloted by Captain Beresford and the service settled into a routine with one return flight to Guernsey piloted by Beresford in G-ADFZ and the second piloted by Ogden in G-ADEW with Cecil Bebb flying the two daily return trips between Croydon and

G-ADEW, the first Cobham Air Routes aircraft to carry fare paying passengers. This is one of the very few images of an ex-SABENA Westland Wessex in Cobham colours.

Christchurch in the Airspeed Envoy. This made it easy to slot in an extra Wessex service from the mainland if the demand warranted it. On the Friday before Whit Sunday, Ogden managed to fly an extra Wessex service and the Air Correspondent of *The Star* proudly reported on Saturday 8th June that 30 passengers had flown between Guernsey and England in the preceding 24 hours. The service made steady progress throughout June with an occasional boost as when the entire band of the Dagenham Girl Pipers flew to Guernsey on the 14th June, but usually flying was at half capacity.

On 25th June Sir Alan Cobham inspected L'Erée Airport with Captain G. P. Olley and J. W. S. Comber of Olley Air Service Ltd. with a view to a possible merger and expansion of the service from Guernsey. With passenger numbers improving Bebb flew an extra service to the island on 29th June, but then tragedy struck.

Tragedy – The Loss of Captain Ogden and the Wessex, G-ADEW

On 3rd July 1935 Captain Ogden took off from L'Erée in G-ADEW at about 17.30 hours on the last flight of the day to Christchurch on a clear summer evening. His one passenger was Mr C. F. Granger, a Spitalfields merchant from Sanderstead, Surrey. Granger, a frequent business visitor to the Channel Islands, was returning to Portsmouth to meet with his wife and family who were staying in their summer cottage on the Isle of Wight. His appointment made him miss the Weymouth steamer and he took the plane instead. Fifty minutes into the flight at 18.20 hours, Ogden sent a radio message that he was experiencing trouble with the starboard engine and at 18.30 hours that the plane was losing height. The Wessex had a radio aerial that trailed behind, underneath it when in flight. A third message was sent at 18.40 hours, but the transmission was incomprehensible indicating that the plane was so low that the trailing aerial was dragging through the sea. Nothing more was heard from G-ADEW.

The sea was calm, visibility 40 miles, and the last estimated position of the craft prior to ditching was three to four miles off the Needles at the western end of the Isle of Wight en route to Christchurch. It was a bright clear early evening, and nothing should hinder a rescue. Two search aircraft left from Portsmouth and an RAF flying boat scrambled from RAF Calshot which was even closer to the search area. The Yarmouth and Swanage lifeboats were launched, and a steamer and several smaller craft joined the search. Bebb initiated his own search from Christchurch at 19.20 hours and did not return to base until 21.00 hours. The Royal Naval destroyer

The visit of an unidentified Cobham Air Routes Wessex to L'Erée Aerodrome. The visit of a Wessex always caused great interest with spectators wanting to be photographed by the machine but notice the distinct lack of 'airport security'!

Rowena set sail from Portland and continued the search into the night with her powerful searchlights, but nothing was found.

It was believed the Wessex should be capable of flying on any two of its three engines with a load much greater than one passenger. Ogden was a very experienced pilot with 3,000 flying hours to his credit and he would be perfectly capable of setting the craft down on the water where it should have floated for some time, allowing the pilot and passenger plenty of time to escape. Although the area was a busy shipping lane no boat reported seeing the Wessex in trouble and nothing was found of her, the pilot or passenger.

The search resumed next morning at daybreak, but when no wreckage was found all hope of a rescue was abandoned until at 09.00 hours a small steamer, the *Stanmore* of London, signalled a message to Prawle Point in Devon that they had Mr Granger on board, but that the pilot was lost. The radio wireless was not a common piece of equipment on some ships, especially smaller ones, and Granger had been rescued by a ship without a wireless so no details of the crash or rescue could be forthcoming until she put into port at Fowey in Cornwall later that evening. When he was brought ashore, Granger was shielded from the waiting spectators and journalists and taken to the offices of shipbrokers Hannan, Samuel & Co. where he and Captain Herbert of the *Stanmore* told their stories.

Granger said that before attempting to leave Guernsey the pilot had difficulty in starting the starboard engine which delayed their departure by about ten minutes to 17.40 hours. They had been flying for a little over half an hour when the engine again gave trouble and stopped. Ogden said that he was going to try and reach the English coast on the two remaining engines, but they might be forced to land on the water, so they put on lifebelts. The two engines were unable to bring the craft to land and the pilot had to make a forced landing on the water about ten miles from the coast. The impact threw Granger into the gangway of the cabin, but he was able to recover and open the emergency exit in the roof and escape. Captain Ogden was not so lucky; he had been incapacitated in the crash and remained strapped in his seat in the cockpit unable to escape. The plane floated for about 15 minuets until it sank with the pilot still on board. Granger was in the water for nearly an hour and a half, freezing and almost unconscious but with his head held up by his lifebelt, when the crew of the *Stanmore* sighted something floundering in the water. It was 20.05 hours and the ship was ten miles off Anvil Point and 22 miles from the Needles. They realised they had sighted a man in the last stages of exhaustion and within ten minutes got him on board and started artificial respiration. For 2½ hours the crew took it in turns to work on Granger and eventually he was sufficiently recovered for them to give him a warm change of clothes and put him to bed.

After Granger recounted his story, he caught the night sleeper train for London and was met the next morning by his parents at Paddington and taken to their home in Tulse Hill. He then set off by train for Portsmouth to meet up with his wife and family in the Isle of Wight. He took a motor launch from Portsmouth to Cowes and when he stepped ashore battered and bruised with his face swollen and a discoloured eye, he was greeted by his wife exclaiming "Oh! you naughty thing".

The Air Ministry report into the loss of G-ADEW concluded that 25 minutes into the flight and possibly due to a broken induction fan, the starboard engine completely failed. The plane was then flying for 30 minutes on two engines, the strain of which caused overheating and the loss of power to one or both engines. The failure of Ogden to make a successful landing on the water was attributed to the passenger moving to the rear of the cabin causing a loss of stability at a crucial point in the landing. As it was generally perceived that the Wessex could fly on two engines, Ogden was not unjustified in trying to reach the English coast, but a safer course of action would have been to turn downwind and head for the French coast.

The Demise of Cobham Air Routes

G-ABAJ, the Westland Wessex that had crashed on its first landing on L'Erée, had previously been sold by Cobham to the Portsmouth, Southsea and I.O.W. Aviation Ltd. when he considered that two craft were sufficient to run the Guernsey service. Now that they only had G-ADFZ, Beresford found it difficult to maintain the service and there were serious doubts about the viability of the six-year old machine. It was acknowledged that the Wessex was a slow aircraft, but its big advantage was the safety factor of three engines and the ability to fly on any two of them. Now that advantage had evaporated, replacement machines would be required, but L'Erée was only licenced for the Wessex. On Sunday 7th July 1935, Rodney Beresford took off from L'Erée at 11.45 hours in G-ADFZ with three passengers for the last time; although it was unannounced, this was the last scheduled flight of Cobham Air Routes Ltd. from Guernsey.

Following the loss of the Wessex and the death of Captain Ogden, Sir Alan Cobham lost enthusiasm for establishing an airline and spent the rest of his life developing improved safety features for aircraft including in-flight refuelling.

The remaining Wessex, G-ADFZ, joined Cobham's air display and was in collision over Blackpool with an Avro 504N on 7th September 1935. The Avro was written off and all the occupants were killed, but the Wessex survived, and the following year was bought by Trafalgar Advertising Co. Ltd. to carry illuminated advertising signs over London at night. The craft survived the Second World War but was withdrawn from the register in December 1946.

Cobham Air Routes' other remaining aircraft, the Airspeed Envoy, G-ADBA, and all Cobham's interests in L'Erée Aerodrome and the Guernsey Aero Club were taken over by Captain Olley of Olley Air Service Ltd. Cecil Bebb transferred to Olley Air Service Ltd. at the same time and returned to the company again in 1946 after his RAF war service.

THE FIRST PLYMOUTH TO JERSEY "AIRMAIL SERVICE" FLIGHT

The First Attempt to Establish a Viable Plymouth to Jersey Commercial Air Service

Mr C.W.R. Cann was a Plymouth businessman, farmer and managing director of Whoopee Sports Ltd.; a company that manufactured floats and inflatable balls for seaside bathing resorts. Cann saw the advantages of connecting the south-west of England to the Channel Islands and attempted to establish a bi-weekly air service between Plymouth and Jersey on Mondays and Fridays reducing the travel time of fifteen hours by boat down to one hour by air. He also hoped to obtain the lucrative General Post Office mail contract to the islands.

The Inaugural Flight to Jersey

As Jersey Airways Ltd. had the sole land landing rights in Jersey, Cann was forced to charter an aircraft from them for his service.

The only craft that was available for charter was the sole remaining D.H. Dragon G-ACNJ, *Rozel Bay* that was stationed on the island and hangared at Quennevais Racecourse in readiness for emergencies and charters.

On the morning of Friday 28th June 1935, chief pilot W. B. Caldwell flew *Rozel Bay* on a positioning flight from Jersey to the Plymouth Municipal Airport at Roborough. The flight went well and he collected five passengers at Roborough Aerodrome, including a reporter from the *Western Independent*, for the inaugural flight to Jersey at midday, following a civic send-off by the Lady Mayoress, Mrs Pillar, and a large party of local dignitaries. The man from the *Western Independent* wrote of the calm flight,

> ...after rising from Roborough and watching Plymouth slip away from under us we make out the Yealm, Bigbury, and Mothercombe before proceeding still seawise, aslant of Start Point, and creeping out over what looks like a remarkably empty Channel of gently rippling water....

Rozel Bay crossed the Channel in 75 minutes and Caldwell landed her safely on the beach at West Park at 13.15 hours.

The First Airmail Flown from England to Jersey

As well as establishing a passenger service from Plymouth to Jersey, Cann also hoped to obtain the contract for transporting mail. To demonstrate to the G.P.O. the efficacy of his new service, Cann had arranged for a number of envelopes (less than 100) to be posted in Plymouth, late in the evening of 27th June 1935, addressed to "Mr. R. F. E. Cock, c/o Major Dean, Municipal Aerodrome, Roborough". These envelopes each received the 1 am postmark of 28th June 1935 and were delivered to the airport that same morning and handed over to "Bill" Caldwell for him to carry on the inaugural flight to Jersey. On arrival in Jersey the envelopes were re-stamped and re-addressed to "Mr. R. F. E. Cock, Royal Yacht Hotel, Jersey." with a grey label covering the previous Roborough address. The envelopes were then re-posted in St. Helier and received the 4.15 pm machine cancellation of the main post office to be delivered later that evening to the Hotel, having

Rozel Bay, kept in readiness by Jersey Airways for emergencies and charters was used by Mr C.W.R. Cann for the first airmail flight to Jersey

travelled from Plymouth to St. Helier in under a day.

Although the flight was a success and the mail delivered in under a day the Post Office remained unconvinced about its viability as Cann had failed to take into account that there was no aerodrome on Jersey and the timetable was governed by the tide in St. Aubins Bay.

A bi-weekly service had been intended, but no further flights took place and although an Immigration and Customs Office was established at Roborough Aerodrome in early July it was redundant as the air service had already been suspended. Thurgood and Greig, had their own plans for opening a route between Jersey and the south-west of England and so it seems unlikely that they would facilitate the attempts of a rival operator. Having seen the success of the flight, the Jersey Airways Ltd. directors may have decided that they had other uses for *Rozel Bay* and no longer had a craft available for permanent charter to a rival concern.

Nothing more was heard of Cann or his plans for an aviation link to the islands.

The 'Whoopee Sports Flight'

This 1935 flight has always rather bizarrely been referred to as the "Whoopee Sports Flight", with no mention of Cann or even Mr Cock (the name on the address labels of the flown letters), but quite what the involvement was has never been explained as the company name does not appear on any of the documents associated with the flight nor on the envelopes flown. Nevertheless, the two flights on 28th June 1935 were significant to Channel Islands aviation history as one was the first flight from Jersey to Plymouth to position the craft for the return flight that was the first passenger flight from Plymouth to Jersey also carrying the first airmails from England to the Channel Islands.

A 'Whoopee Sports' experimental first flight cover flown from Roborough Aerodrome, Plymouth to Jersey on 28th June 1935. The cover was stamped by the post offices in Plymouth and St. Helier and signed in pencil by the pilot, 'WB Caldwell'.

THE VISIT OF HRH EDWARD PRINCE OF WALES TO GUERNSEY

6th May 1935 was the Silver Jubilee of the accession to the throne of HRH King George V. There were celebrations throughout Great Britain and the Empire to honour the King and HRH Queen Mary, especially wherever the King and Queen made Royal Visits. The Channel Islands were proud of their loyalty to the monarchy and each island organised massive celebrations for the Silver Jubilee. The Royal couple did not include the islands in their tours, but in their stead HRH Edward Prince of Wales, the future King Edward VIII, visited Jersey and Guernsey on Tuesday 23rd and Wednesday 24th July 1935.

Prince Edward was to fly by RAF seaplane to Jersey on 23rd July 1935 and after a day of official duties he would spend the night aboard the newly commissioned destroyer, *HMS Faulknor* before flying next morning to Guernsey from where, at the end of the Guernsey celebrations, he would return home by seaplane.

Squadron Leader A. F. Long, the Commanding Officer of 210 Squadron, was tasked with the safe transportation of the future King, and his Squadron had recently been equipped with the newest and largest RAF seaplane in service, the Short S19 Singapore III. Three Short Singapores lead by Squadron Leader Long made reconnaissance flights to Jersey and Guernsey during the week prior to the Royal Visit to check the passage into the harbours and the mooring facilities for the Royal plane and its escort.

A photograph in the *Guernsey Weekly Press* of Saturday 27th July 1935 shows a visiting aircraft in St. Peter Port Harbour with the recognition serial number K4582, but it does not record the identification numbers of the other two Singapores. These were probably K4580 and K4579, the two craft actually involved in the visit a week later.

Prince Edward was due to embark the seaplane at RAF Calshot on the Solent, but on the morning of Tuesday 23rd July 1935 there was thick fog, and the seaplanes could not fly. The Prince was transferred to Portsmouth where he embarked *HMS Faulknor* and made the journey to Jersey in the destroyer, depriving the people of Jersey the more dramatic spectacle of his arrival by air. As visibility in the Channel remained poor all day and the seaplanes still could not take-off, the Prince re-embarked *HMS Faulknor* in the evening and was taken overnight on the short journey to St. Peter Port in Guernsey.

On arrival HRH Prince Edward inspected a welcoming guard of honour on the harbour key.

The RAF Short S19 Singapore III's K4580 and K4579 moored in St. Peter Port Harbour on 24th July 1935 to await the embarkation of HRH Prince Edward prior to his flight to RAF Calshot. A flotilla of small boats waited to see the departure. Prince Edward had a full day of celebrations, but at 16.20 hours, escorted by His Excellency the Lieutenant Governor, the Bailiff of Guernsey and guests, he drove to Berth No. 5 at White Rock and from there embarked in a pinnace to be ferried to K4580 in the harbour. Squadron Leader Long fired up the four engines and with a great roar the huge machine taxied out of the harbour with K4579 following in its wake. The two seaplanes were quickly in the air travelling to St. Martin's Point before turning and then lifting away into the sky towards England. The Prince landed safely at RAF Calshot at 17.50 hours and later left for London in his own private plane, a Dragon Rapide, G-ADDD, piloted by Flight Lieutenant B.H. Fielden.

Visibility was much improved on Wednesday 24th July and Squadron Leader Long piloting the Prince's RAF Singapore K4580 and escorted by K4579 was finally able to make the crossing to Guernsey to collect his charge.

Within six months of Prince Edward's visit, his father, King George V, died on 20th January 1936 and the Prince succeeded him as King Edward VIII. Prince Edward was a qualified pilot having learnt to fly during the First World War. He was the first British monarch to fly in a plane and when he became King, he established the 'King's Flight' of Royal Aircraft on 21st July 1936; his Dragon Rapide being the first aircraft of the King's Flight. This was to be the only visit of Prince Edward to the Channel Islands as he abdicated the throne less than a year later in December 1936 to become Duke of Windsor and live out his life in exile, mainly in France.

The Short S19 Singapore Mk III

The Short Singapore III was the latest incarnation of Short's Singapore seaplane biplane design for the RAF. Prototype Short Singapore I was a biplane with single fin and rudder, powered by two engines. Only one was produced as it did not satisfy RAF requirements, and it was bought by Sir Alan Cobham for a 23,000 miles survey flight of Africa.

The Short Singapore II was a much more powerful machine with triple rudder fins on its tail and four engines in two pairs of back-to-back 'push pull' configuration. Again, only one was produced, but from this was developed the very successful Short Singapore III. The prototype Singapore III was a biplane, seaplane, designed and built in August 1933, and first flown on 15th June 1934. After testing four prototypes, the RAF accepted the design and production craft were built, the first entering service with 210 Squadron of the RAF in January 1935.

The new Singapore III was the largest craft in RAF service and was powered by four Rolls Royce 675 hp Kestral IX engines in two pairs of 'push pull' configuration producing a maximum speed of 145 mph. It had a wingspan of 90 ft and a length of 76 ft. Its wings were fabric covered, but the hull and wing floats were built of duralumin. The seaplane carried a crew of six and had a cabin and galley, three open observation or gun ports, fore, aft and amidships and a closed glazed cockpit where the pilot and co-pilot sat side by side. The craft had a deep keel and narrow beam giving it good water handling properties, and a distinctive upward curving high tail with triple rudders that facilitated a short steep take-off.

Following his Royal duties, Squadron Leader Long and 210 Squadron were relocated with their Singapore III's to Malta and eventually Singapore. The Singapore III was still in RAF service at the outbreak of the Second World War and saw action in the Pacific against Japan while in the service of the New Zealand RAF.

Short Singapore III.

THE GUERNSEY *POU DU CIEL*

The Flying Flea was the English translation for the French *Pou du Ciel* (literally translated Louse of the Sky); the correct title for the craft being the Mignet HM 14. This miniature single-seat, light aircraft with tandem wings could have various wingspans of between 16 to 20 feet with a length of only 13 feet and was designed by the Frenchman, Henri Mignet.

Mignet's intention was to design a 'motorcycle of the air'; a craft that anyone could build at home in their garage with only wood, fabric and a small amount of metal tube. He wanted to simplify the controls of the aircraft with one control only to make his machine turn and another to make it go up and down, and these controls would be on one central column that was pushed in the direction that the pilot wanted to go. Mignet designed several prototypes, but the Mignet HM 14 first flew in 1934 with a small 17 hp, 3 cylinder, two stroke motorcycle engine. He believed that the craft could be built for £25, or £75 with an engine. In November 1934 he published his plans for the aeroplane in his book *Le Sport de l'Air* and it was so successful that by 1935 'Pou Fever' had spread through Europe.

Henri Mignet with his *Pou du Ciel*.

Stephen Appleby

Twenty-three-year-old Stephen Appleby was the first pilot to build a Flying Flea in England. The craft cost him £90, was only 12 feet long and was powered by a modified car engine developing 32 hp.

His first flight was on 14th July 1935 and a week later on 25th July 1935, Appleby posed for the Press at Heston Airport with his Mignet HM 14 beside a Jersey Airways Ltd. D.H. 86 that lent scale to his diminutive machine.

Thirty minutes later while on a demonstration flight, Appleby crashed and overturned in a field next to the airport in front of the Press and newsreel cameras. (Stunning footage of Appleby walking unhurt from the spectacular crash of his HM 14 can be found on You Tube on the Internet.).

On 5th December 1935 he piloted an improved version of his HM 14, registration G-ADMH from Lympne Airport across the Channel to Saint Inglevert Airfield in France.

Mignet did not specify the size of engine that should be used with his craft. He had only ever used a small engine, but other pilots were eager to fly faster with more powerful engines.

Stephen Appleby with his Flying Flea G-ADMH at Heston Airport. Passing the nose of Jersey Airways *The Belcroute Bay*.

Unfortunately these altered the aerodynamics between the front and rear wing and there followed a series of fatal accidents in 1936. Aviation authorities in England and France identified the aerodynamic problem after carrying out wind tunnel tests on the HM 14 and promptly banned the craft from flying until modifications were made. A popular comment of the time was that "Mignet wanted to bring flying to the man in the street; he succeeded by dropping a 'Flea' on his head".

The Guernsey Pou

In Guernsey, Edward W. Laker and John E. Beasley had started building their 'Guernsey Pou' in August 1935 with the funds remaining after the closure of the Guernsey Gliding Club. *The Star* was very interested in the project and intended to issue 'bulletins' on the progress of the build in their weekly air transport column: 'Sky Writing'. On Wednesday 11th September 1935 *The Star* published 'Sky Writing No.16', which contained an interview with the two enthusiasts describing 'Why We Decided to Build the Flying Flea'. The two men praised the expertise of Cecil Noel as an instructor and talked about the Guernsey Gliding Club and attempts to fly its glider.

Appleby's Flea after its crash on its demonstration flight at Heston Airport. It would be restored to flying condition and later flew from Lympne Airport (near Hythe, Kent) across the Channel to Saint Inglevert Airfield (near Calais).

> ...all members received a certain amount of tuition in the handling of the machine, some proving more efficient than others but the results were usually the same. Sooner or later everybody (except the very able instructor) crashed the 'bus' just when they thought they were getting the better of it. As a consequence the machine was in the repair shop for nine tenths of its time ... (we) having virtually rebuilt the entire glider felt capable of building a 'Pou'....

In October *The Star* discussed the dilemma faced by the builders of the Pou. New light aircraft engines were now being produced and two were suitable for the Pou, but these would demand alterations in construction of the fuselage and lengthening of the wings by two feet for safe flying. Fortuitously for the builders of the Guernsey Pou, they decided to 'go with the smaller engine' and not alter the construction; had they chosen to rebuild and use more powerful engines, the outcome might have been fatal. Another problem that concerned *The Star* in October was a suitable name for the Guernsey Flying Flea; the editor decided to run a competition to name the miniature aircraft. Harking back to Noel's famous miniature aircraft *Wee Mite*, the most popular name was *Wee-Mite-Too*, but the newspaper failed to record how well this name was received by Laker and Beasley.

In November *The Star* recorded that Laker and Beasley were in frequent communication with Appleby discussing the improvements possible and that he had sent them his own drawings of the necessary alterations to improve Mignet's original design. In the same edition of the newspaper the constructors appealed to visitors to stay away because the workshops were small and their time was valuable.

The Star's interest in the project waned in the winter of 1935 -36 as no mention was made of the Pou. The build may have entered the doldrums with the various safety alterations that were required, or Laker and Beasley may have run out of funds. Nothing more was heard from the pair until the July 1936 edition of *Flight* magazine when Laker advertised: "Light aero engines wanted, suitable for 'Flying Flea', must be cheap." Beasley is no longer mentioned, but Laker did obtain his engine and the Guernsey Pou made a few 'hops' in 1936. The Guernsey Pou was never officially registered with the Civil Aviation Authority and unfortunately no photographs of her on the ground or in the air are recorded. When the German invasion was imminent in 1940, the Guernsey Pou was hidden from the Germans and they never found her; she was only rediscovered 30 years later in 1970.

GUERNSEY'S L'ERÉE AERODROME

Guernsey's L'Erée Aerodrome – More Comings and Goings

Following the failure of Sir Alan Cobham to establish a viable air service between L'Erée and London with Cobham Air Routes Ltd., the challenge was then taken up by Captain G. P. Olley and his airline Olley Air Service Ltd. Captain Olley heavily financed the Guernsey Aero Club Ltd. and together they expanded and developed L'Erée as an airport, but ultimately they were to have no greater success than Cobham. The developments meant that bigger and faster machines could use the airfield and this attracted some interesting aircraft and famous pilots and passengers over the next few years, until the States opened Guernsey's official airport in 1939 and there was no more use for L'Erée.

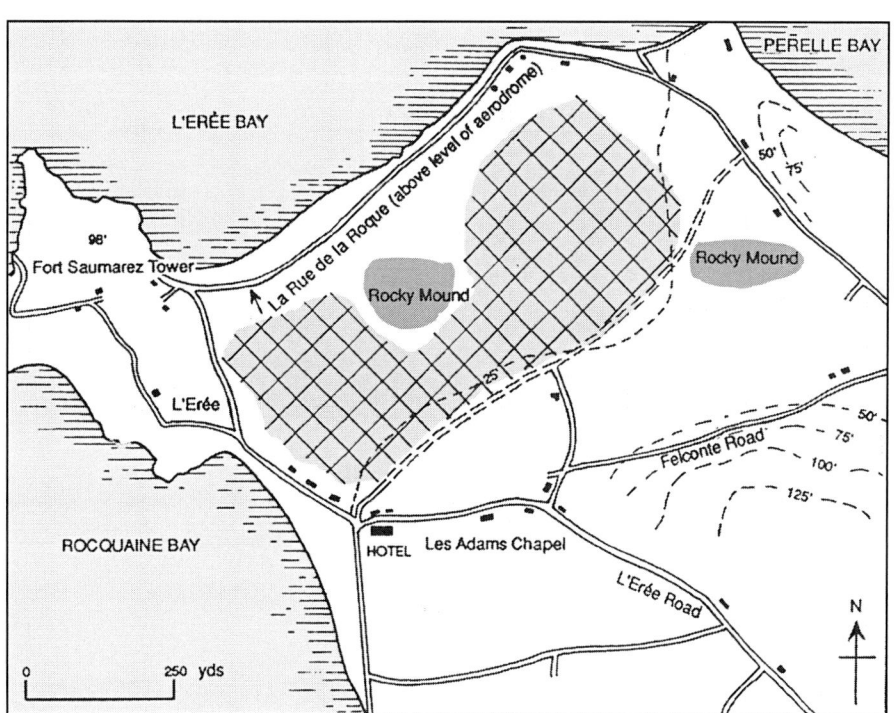

This sketch map of L'Erée Aerodrome shows the airfield surrounded by the sea. The safe landing area (crosshatched) is compromised by two rocky outcrop mounds. These granite mounds would always thwart attempts to extend the runways to comply with the Air Ministry minimum length requirements.

Amy Johnson's Puss Moth *The Desert Cloud*

As part of the celebrations for the Silver Jubilee of King George V, his son HRH Edward the Prince of Wales, made his only visit to the Channel Islands in July 1935. He visited Jersey on 23rd July 1935 and then sailed to Guernsey on 24th July on board *HMS Faulknor* before returning the same day by RAF seaplane to the mainland. (*see* THE VISIT OF HRH EDWARD PRINCE OF WALES TO GUERNSEY *page 166*) The *Daily Mirror* newspaper in England printed many photographs of the Prince's visit to Guernsey, but none of his visit to Jersey. Why? The *Daily Mirror* had chartered a Birkett Air Services Ltd. aeroplane to fly to Jersey with a staff photographer to take photographs of the visit by the Prince and then rush them back to London for publication, but they had not accounted for the bureaucracy of the island's officials. Jersey Airways Ltd. had a monopoly of the foreshore landing ground at West Park and they refused the Birkett plane permission to land there. As there was no airfield on the island, the pilot brought his craft down on the racecourse, but the racecourse was not a licensed aerodrome, nor did it have Customs facilities. The actions of the pilot and his passenger antagonised the island authorities who arrested them and impounded the aircraft, so they were unable to take any photographs of the Prince's visit.

The plane was released the following day and once they had cleared Customs the photographer, anxious to remedy his failure to take any photographs in Jersey, inveigled the pilot to fly to Guernsey and land at L'Erée. As they were arriving from Jersey, there were no immigration problems this time and the pilot, Mr G. Megaw, put his Puss Moth down on the airfield at 10.30 hours. The photographer was able to take his photographs and they left L'Erée with the pictures at 13.00 hours and landed at Heston at 15.05 hours, in time for the *Daily Mirror* to develop and publish the Guernsey photographs in the first editions of the paper the next morning.

The plane owned by Birkett Air Services Ltd. was a D.H.80A Puss Moth with the registration G-ACAB. This aeroplane had a famous history as it had been owned by the world-renowned aviator, Amy Johnson. In October 1932 the new D.H.80A Puss Moth, G-ACAB, was registered to Mrs. Amy Mollison (nee Johnson); she named it *The Desert Cloud*, fitted it with a powerful Gipsy Major engine and set about trying to break her husband's record flight to Cape Town, South Africa. She arrived in Cape Town on 18th November 1932 after a flight of 4 days, 6 hours and 54 minutes, breaking Mollison's record and becoming the first woman to fly solo to the Cape. Amy sold *The Desert Cloud* in 1933 and it was first bought by Henley's Ltd. of Heston and then registered on 11th May 1933 to Birkett Air Services Ltd., also of Heston. On 6th February 1939 Utility Airways Ltd. of Hooter Park purchased the aircraft, but it was destroyed by fire at Hooter Park the following year on 8th July 1940.

G-ACAB was displayed inside Lewis's Department Store in Sheffield, Yorkshire when Amy made a visit to the store during a publicity tour.

A Gipsy Moth on Sark?

The Wednesday 31st July 1935 edition of *The Star* reported with obvious glee the visit of the *Daily Mirror* photographer earlier in the week and his failure to obtain photographs of HRH Prince Edward's visit to Jersey. The same edition of the newspaper also published an intriguing report of another aircraft that visited L'Erée on Saturday 27th July. The report began: "L'Erée is apparently becoming known in flying circles – at least as a Club aerodrome if not as an airport." The report then went on to describe the visit of a De Havilland D.H.60 G Gipsy Moth, registration G-AAHP, owned by a Mr Tollemache who was accompanied by Mr R. Montague. Both these gentlemen were Cambridge University undergraduates and great flying enthusiasts who were returning to England via Guernsey at the end of a flying holiday that had taken them through Europe to North Africa.

A search of the Civil Aircraft Register reveals that although G-AAHP had been owned by a variety of pilots and companies, neither of these two undergraduates is recorded as an owner, which implies that the craft was either on loan, or hired by them.

The two pilots landed at L'Erée at 15.10 hours on the Saturday afternoon on the last leg of their journey. The pilots did not linger in Guernsey as the aircraft was serviced and refuelled at L'Erée and then took off again for Heston at 16.20 hours. The newspaper report ends with an intriguingly frustrating throwaway comment: "It is understood that they landed in Sark and called on La Dame." No more information is given and there seems to be no other evidence to corroborate the statement. Did G-AAHP actually land on Sark? Was this the second landing of an aeroplane on Sark? We will probably never know the answers unless the Dame of Sark recorded the visit in her diary.

Gipsy Moth, G-AAHP, which may have been the second aircraft to land on Sark.

A Dragon Arrives at L'Erée

Captain Olley first visited L'Erée with G-ACYR on Friday 25th October 1935. Flying from London and landing at 10.30 hours, Olley carried two passengers, Sir Hugo and Lady Cunliffe-Owen. Sir Hugo was the Chairman of the British American Tobacco Company with a large financial interest in Olley Air Service Ltd. and he was contemplating investing in L'Erée Aerodrome. The party were met on the airfield by Advocate H. H. Randell, Chairman of the Guernsey Aero Club Ltd., Deputy B. Bartlett and Cecil Noel, Directors of the club, and Mr H. G. Wheadon who drove the party into St. Peters for negotiations. A flight engineer, Mr G. Bryers, on board the Rapide remained with the craft on the airfield. After their meeting, Captain Olley flew the party back to London on the Friday afternoon, but was back at L'Erée two days later with G-ACYR.

Debates raged in the Guernsey newspapers about the relative merits of the three possible sites for the Guernsey airport. Olley took a whole page advert in *The Star* extolling the advantages of L'Erée, foremost amongst which was that L'Erée was the safest aerodrome because there was no fog at sea level; in a seven-month period La Villiaze had experienced 47 days of fog compared to only 30 minutes at L'Erée. Captain Olley and Sir Hugo flew to Guernsey for the debate in the States' Chambers on 30th October 1935, but they lost by a single vote when it was decided that the States would acquire the site at La Villiaze. Captain Olley was undeterred and still determined to develop L'Erée, so that its status as an airport might become a fait accompli. Olley's next visit with G-ACYR was at noon on Saturday 16th November when the craft remained overnight before returning to London at 11.00 hours on the Sunday morning.

Visitors and Expansion

Captain Olley's D.H. Dragon Rapide, G-ACYR, became a regular visitor to L'Erée, either piloted by Olley himself, if he was on a business trip associated with the expansion of the airport, or piloted by Cecil Bebb, if it was hired for a taxi flight.

On 3rd March 1936 Olley set off in his Dragon Rapide from Croydon at about 11.00 hours for L'Erée accompanied by two passengers, Mr R. L. Carter, the Manager of Olley Air Service Ltd. and Mr Gordon Hill, the Company Solicitor. They were attending an ordinary general meeting of the Guernsey Aero Club but encountered considerable fog en route and did not land at L'Erée until after 13.00 hours and the meeting was delayed to await

The famous ex-Imperial Airways pilot, Captain G. P. Olley, was the founder and principal of Olley Air Service Ltd. When he acquired all of Sir Alan Cobham's interests in L'Erée Aerodrome and Cobham Air Routes Ltd., including the Airspeed Envoy that had flown the mainland part of the route to Guernsey, he made frequent visits to L'Erée in a campaign to develop the airfield and have it recognised as Guernsey's main airport.

He invariably flew his own aircraft, a De Havilland D.H.89 Dragon Rapide, registration G-ACYR, acquired new on 15th October 1934. Jersey Airways Ltd. flew D.H. Dragons and they watched with annoyance Olley's landings at L'Erée with a similar craft.

their arrival. Financed by Olley, the Guernsey Aero Club Ltd. steadily bought up more land at L'Erée in order to increase the length of the runways. The 30th April 1936 edition of *The Star* in Guernsey reported that the aerodrome area was now nearly 120 Vergees. (Land measurement in the Channel Islands is by Vergee: a Guernsey Vergee is 17,640 square feet while a Jersey Vergee is 19,360 square feet. An acre is 43,560 square feet.) Two cottages, some greenhouses and various stone walls were to be demolished and part of a hill removed with dynamite!

Advocate H. H. Randell, the Chairman of the Company, stated that a service to London could run from the present aerodrome as Captain Olley was making regular visits in the Dragon Rapide, but 100 per cent efficiency was wanted for a regular service. It was hoped that the extensions to the airfield, which included the provision of runways in every direction of about 600 yards, would be completed in two to three months. This would make it possible for the Club to apply to the States for an 'unlimited' licence for the airfield and then initiate a regular service in August. The August service never materialised, but on Friday 11th September 1936 Olley returned to L'Erée in his Dragon Rapide in the evening, landing at 18.30 hours with five passengers; all were officials of Olley Air Service Ltd. They had come to attend a hearing of their plea in the Royal Court on Saturday morning for an unlimited licence for L'Erée. They failed yet again because a granite outcrop in the middle of the airfield had defeated attempts to fully extend the runways and two of the runways were still less than the minimum length required by the Air Ministry. After failing to obtain their unlimited licence, the Guernsey Aero Club set out with a vengeance on the Monday afternoon determined to blast the granite outcrop, known as 'Cuckoo Rock', into submission. A large gallery of sightseers turned up to watch the explosion of 160 lbs of dynamite set into three large holes under the outcrop. The explosion was a relative success, but many of the over-enthusiastic onlookers were covered in debris and at least one camera was smashed.

Two Puss Moth Weekend Visitors

Olley and his party returned to Croydon on Saturday afternoon, but it was a busy weekend for L'Erée as it received two new visitors.

G-AAXY, a Puss Moth piloted by Mr List with one passenger and flown from Heston, landed on Friday evening shortly after Olley had taken off. The pilot and passenger spent the weekend in Guernsey and returned to England on Monday morning. This was not the first visit by G-AAXY to the Channel Islands as she had visited Jersey on 15th May 1933 when owned by the British Petroleum Company, in order to execute aerial reconnoitres of the proposed St. Peter's site for the Jersey Airport.

The second Puss Moth, G-ABTD belonged to Brooklands Flying Club and was flown from that aerodrome, landing at L'Erée at 19.30 hours on Saturday 12th September. Piloted by Brooklands Club member Mr Harris and with Mr Beaumont as passenger, this craft also returned to England on Monday morning.

A Miles Falcon Visitor

On the first weekend of October, L'Erée again had two visitors.

The first a Miles Falcon, piloted by Mr Haigh with brothers Dennis and Dudley Beaumont as passengers, arrived on Friday evening, 2nd October and left for Croydon on Sunday. Unfortunately, there is no record of the registration of this new visitor to the islands or a photograph of her at L'Erée. The Miles M3 Falcon was a three-seater, single engine, low wing monoplane with the unusual feature of a "trousered" main undercarriage giving a very sporty look. The wingspan was 35 ft and the length 25 ft and she was powered by a 130 hp De Havilland Gipsy Major piston engine giving a maximum speed of 145 hp The prototype first flew in 1934 and production models started in 1935. The M3 was a three-seater craft, but a larger M3B Falcon Six was also built in 1935 that had seating for four with dual controls and a larger 200 hp De

A Miles Falcon G-AEEG – similar to the L'Erée visitor.

Havilland Gipsy Six engine. Without the registration number we cannot ascertain if the L'Erée visitor was a Miles Falcon M3 or an M3B Falcon Six.

Shortly after, at 16.00 hours in the afternoon, Captain Olley was back with G-ACYR. His two passengers were the Company's Solicitor Mr Gordon Hill and Mrs Hill and they had flown to Guernsey to attend yet another hearing of the Chief Pleas on Monday morning. The States convened to discuss the La Villiaze Airport scheme and the Chief Pleas convened to consider the renewal of the L'Erée licence. The L'Erée licence was renewed, but Olley was still not granted his unlimited licence and returned to England on the Monday afternoon.

Visit of the Littlewoods Football Pools aeroplane

An exciting visit was reported in the *Guernsey Weekly Press* of 3rd December 1936 under the title: "ISLANDER'S £6,482 CHEQUE ARRIVES BY AIR". The newspaper reported that Mr Hedley Garey, 38, a farmer residing at Les Pages, St. Martin's was the fortunate winner of £6,482 for a coupon in the Littlewoods football pools competition that had cost him three pence. At 17.00 hours the previous Wednesday he had received a telegram from Littlewoods that stated: "Congratulations. Our representative Mr Geo. E Carpenter coming by air Thurs. morning. He will arrive about 11.00 am…." The newspaper went on to report that just after 11.00 hours on Thursday, the Littlewoods plane arrived at L'Erée to be met by Customs officers. After the formal 'clearance' through Customs, the visiting party went by car to Mr Garey's residence. The paper described the flight of the Littlewoods plane, a D.H. Dragon that had left Heston Aerodrome at 9.25 hours and although it was misty flying overland, visibility had improved as it crossed the Channel. The Dragon landed at 11.20 hours and returned to Heston at 14.00 hours. It is very unlikely that Littlewoods had their own plane and it is almost certain that the D.H. Dragon belonged to Olley Air Service Ltd. as no other commercial craft would be given permission to land at L'Erée. It seems more than probable that the craft was Olley's own G-ACYR and that the pilot was Cecil Bebb.

More Olley Air Service Ltd's Flights

On 3rd April 1937 Captain Bebb was back at L'Erée with a De Havilland Dragon Rapide belonging to Olley Air Service Ltd.; the registration was not recorded but it was almost certainly G-ACYR. She arrived at 14.16 hours to pick up two passengers, Sir Hugo Cunliffe-Owen and Mr Hayes who were both investors in Olley Air Service Ltd.. The Dragon Rapide left almost immediately for Biarritz which it was anticipated they would reach at about 18.00 hours.

Coronation Day

Wednesday 12th May 1937 was the Coronation Day of King George VI and Queen Elizabeth. The whole nation was celebrating the event including Guernsey, and L'Erée Aerodrome was not to be left out. The island newspapers of Tuesday 11th May 1937 carried the following advert:

> YOUR CHANCE OF AN.
> AEROPLANE FLIGHT!
> Joy-Rides from L'Erée Aerodrome.
> TO-DAY from 3 pm.
> THURSDAY from 10 am to 1 pm
> and from 4.30 pm.
> FARE 5/- upwards.

There was no mention of the type of aircraft or who was offering the flights, but again we have to assume that it could only be a Dragon Rapide of Olley Air Service Ltd.

More High Drama for Cecil Bebb

Captain Cecil Bebb was involved in a 'drama' on Sunday 22nd August 1937 when he was party to an event that was more like a silent film melodrama. The newspapers headlined it: MOTHER'S PLANE DASH TO C.I. FOR HER CHILD. The mother's 3,000 mile dash across the Atlantic ended in the Channel Islands when Mrs Luvie Pearson, wife of Mr Drew Pearson an American journalist working in Washington, was reunited with her five year old son Tyler who had been illegally smuggled out of the United States via Canada to Europe and then Sark by her former husband, Mr George Abell. Conditions of their divorce stated the child should be with his father for six weeks of the year, but that neither parent should take Tyler out of the U.S.A.. When Mr and Mrs Pearson heard that the boy had been taken to Europe, they caught the first transatlantic steamer from New York, reported their mission to Scotland Yard and contacted a London solicitor who managed to trace the child to the Channel Islands.

They chartered a De Havilland D.H. Dragon Rapide from Olley Air Service Ltd. and the couple with their solicitor flew from Croydon to L'Erée Aerodrome. Cecil Noel had already arranged all the formalities for the landing in Guernsey. A Guernsey Police officer then accompanied Mr and Mrs Pearson and the solicitor to Sark. They hired a fast motorboat from St. Peter Port and shortly after landing on Sark, they miraculously found the boy walking along the road with his nurse. They returned with the child to Guernsey, but as soon

A three seater Farman F402.

Paul Grieu with his Farman F402.

Wreckage of F-AMTL at Le Bourget (near Paris).

as the party stepped ashore, they were detained by the Guernsey Police who had received a communication from the father accusing them of abduction. The solicitor produced papers that showed they were acting legally, and they were soon free to return to L'Erée Aerodrome from where Cecil Bebb set off for Croydon at 21.40 hours that evening.

L'Erée – a French Connection

Normally planes landing at L'Erée were English planes from a U.K. airport or occasionally English planes from a foreign airfield en route to England, but on Sunday 3rd October 1937 L'Erée saw its first French arrival.

At 13.00 hours a French monoplane, a three-seater Farman Lorraine F402, landed at L'Erée having commenced its flight from Le Havre. The pilot was Monsieur Paul Grieu and the two passengers were MM. Pichard, father and son. The trio had an eventful crossing as the plane initially cleared Customs at Deauville, but then proceeded first to Jersey as the pilot was under the misapprehension that there were no Customs facilities at L'Erée Airport.

The party were visiting Guernsey to view the recent wreck of the 3,330 ton French vessel *Briseis* from both the air and at sea with a view to salvage. Having viewed the wreck, they interviewed the master of the stricken vessel, Captain Le Hellida, but decided that salvage was not worthwhile. (The cargo of over three hundred barrels of Algerian wine and spirits had already been 'salvaged' by the local fishermen!) Following their fruitless visit, F-AMTL left L'Erée for home at 14.45 hours.

Farman F402, F-AMTL, was owned by Monsier Paul Grieu of Le Havre who piloted her to L'Erée. She was a high wing aircraft with rigid landing gear and unusual in that she had a joystick hanging from the ceiling of the cockpit as well as a vertical steering wheel for the rudder. F-AMTL was powered by a 9 cylinder 110 hp Lorraine 5 Pb engine.

Paul Grieu was killed fifteen months after his visit to L'Erée when he wrote off F-AMTL in a fatal crash on 15th February 1939 near Le Bourget. He had been unable to find safe landing in a thick mist and lost a wing when he hit a tall tree.

The visit of the Farman F402 may have been the only genuine international flight to and from L'Erée Aerodrome.

THE *HINDENBURG* OVER ALDERNEY

The massive bulk of the Zeppelin D-LZ 129 – *Hindenburg* is apparent when compared to people on the ground.

From 17.00 hours until 17.30 hours on the afternoon of Tuesday 31st March 1936 many hundreds of Channel Islanders witnessed the world's largest aircraft, the 804 foot long German dirigible airship *Hindenburg*, pass close to Alderney on her first transatlantic flight to South America. *The Star* newspaper in Guernsey proclaimed on Wednesday 1st April with the exaggerated headlines:

GUERNSEY SEES THE "HINDENBURG".
GIANT GERMAN ZEPPELIN CRUISES AROUND CHANNEL ISLANDS.
CLEAR VIEW OF WORLD'S LARGEST DIRIGIBLE.

Although many people on Guernsey caught a glimpse of the Zeppelin airship in the far distance, the view from Guernsey was obscured by haze, and the purr of the engines could not be heard, although strangely they were faintly heard on Sark. A perfect view of the vast craft was afforded from Alderney, but the giant German Zeppelin, on her first trip to Rio de Janeiro, did not spend time "cruising around the Channel Islands" as her British counterpart, the R100, had done for 45 minutes in July 1930. The report that followed these dramatic headlines in *The Star* was thankfully a little more accurate.

The *Hindenburg* left her base in the Zeppelin dockyards at Friedrichshafen, Germany at 06.00 hours (G.M.T.) on 31st March 1936, piloted by Captain Ernst Lehman and with Dr Hugo Echener, the Zeppelin Company Chairman, on board. She carried 35 fare-paying passengers including people from Great Britain, the United States, Brazil and Spain. Her earning power came from her vast freight carrying capabilities and included large quantities of mail and even an 'Opel' motorcar, the 500,000th car built by Opel, carried as a propaganda exercise.

France would not grant the airship permission to fly over French territory, so she flew to Holland and then down the English Channel, flying 4 miles off Dover at a height of 1,000 feet and passing Eastbourne at 15.15 hours at an increased height of 1,500 feet. The *Hindenburg* continued down the Channel and then turned south-west for the Atlantic passing very close to Alderney. Superb views of the airship were obtained from many parts of the island, especially Les Butes. The purring of the four Daimler Benz, 16 cylinder diesel engines could be heard, and the 6 foot high letters 'HINDENBURGH' and the two Nazi swastika emblems on her tail were clearly visible. The airship made good progress flying steadily in a south-westerly direction at an estimated speed of about 60 knots; she was capable of a top speed of 82 mph. On Guernsey, Mr Ingrouville, the lighthouse keeper on watch at his station on the Platte Fougère reported;

> The airship passed 15 miles to the north of the island. Through my glasses I could see the front carriage and the swastika on her tail. I think that she was travelling at 60 knots. I first spotted her when she was 2 miles off Alderney and she covered the 19 miles to a point off Fort Le Marchant in about 15 minuets. She was not very high.

For some local air passengers an exciting event occurred at 17.10 hours when two Jersey Airways Ltd., planes en route to England, encountered the *Hindenburg* about a mile and a half off Alderney and one of the aircraft passed immediately over the airship.

Later, in September 1936, the encounter was repeated 10 miles north of Alderney when the Hindenburg was en-route to North America and the pilot of the Jersey Airways plane managed to obtain a superb photograph of the airship off the starboard wing of his aircraft.

The *Hindenburg* had a range in excess of 8,000 miles and completed the transatlantic journey to Rio de Janeiro in four days. The total return flight covered 12,756 miles in a flight time of 203 hours and 32 minutes in a nine-day period. However, the flight was not without mishap. On the flight out to Rio de Janeiro one of the Daimler engines developed a fault that required the engine to be shut down. A repair was executed at Recife, Brazil but on the return flight the problem recurred.

The *Hindenburg* photographed form a Jersey Airways plane.

Although the airship managed to get back across the Atlantic, it was off Morocco when a second engine failed. With only two engines working, Captain Lehman no longer had the power to battle north-eastwards against the prevailing winds and the craft was in serious danger of drifting into the Sarah Desert. Without the facilities of a ground crew and mooring mast the only option available would be a crash landing in the desert with doubtless disastrous consequences. Captain Lehman decided to gain height in an attempt to reach the trade winds blowing into Europe even though these winds were normally at 6,000 feet, beyond the altitude threshold of the airship. With incredible luck the *Hindenburg* encountered a trade wind at 3,000 feet and was able to head north. France, on humanitarian grounds, permitted Lehman to fly over her territory so that he could safely return the *Hindenburg* to its home base at Friedrichshafen.

The *Hindenburg* was originally only known as D-LZ 129. Construction had started five years before her maiden test flight on 4th March 1936. She had a rib structure of duralumin (also known as duraluminum) housing 16 cotton gas bags of hydrogen, and her outer skin was silver reflective doped cotton protecting the gas bags from ultra-violet and infra-red radiation. In 1931 the Zeppelin Company had purchased 11,000 lbs of duralumin scrap salvaged from the wreckage of the British R101 airship and it is believed that the metal was re-cast for use in the construction of D-LZ 129.

Horrifically, on 6th May 1937 after completing her first North American transatlantic voyage of the new season she was struck by lightning as she was nearing her mooring mast at Lakehurst Naval Station, New Jersey, U.S.A. and engulfed in a ball of fire that reduced her to a charred skeleton within a matter of minutes. Amazingly there were survivors from the *Hindenburg* wreck, but 36 passengers and crew, including one member of the ground crew, were killed in the disaster.

When the problem with the engines had been resolved the *Hindenburg* made 17 round trips across the Atlantic in the 1936 season to both North and South America without any further mishap.

JERSEY AIRWAYS LTD OPENS ALDERNEY AIRPORT

Despite the weather, Jersey Airways Ltd. maintained a regular service in 1936. Even in January dense London fog, a D.H. Rapide achieved a regular weekday Heston to Eastleigh run to connect with the larger D.H. 86 Express for the cross-Channel flight, while at the weekends when demand could double, a D.H. 86 Express flew direct from Heston.

On 11th February 1936 Pilot Israel was approaching Eastleigh in a D.H. 86 Express when he experienced an alarming phenomenon; 'icing' of the aircraft when rain freezers on the leading edges of the wings, struts, and propellers and the craft loses height. Fortunately, Israel's load was light, and he landed before his instruments froze. 'Icing' was known in America but rare in the UK and formed when craft were ascending or descending near cloud, but not at very low temperatures. Unfortunately for Jersey Airways Ltd., the D.H. 86 Express was prone to icing and the only British defence against it was a disgusting brown paste named "Kilfrost" that had to be smeared on the leading edges of the wings. European and American aircraft were fitted with 'Goodrich de-icers'; a rubber tube fixed along the leading edges of the wings, that was expanded by compressed air and broke up the ice.

Alderney Airport opens for business

Alderney Airport had been viable since October 1935 but required additional drainage and re-seeding and was uneconomical to open purely for request stops on the mainland service. On 13th February the D.H. Dragon, G-ACNJ, *Rozel Bay* landed on Alderney, with Mr and Mrs Greig on board, to collect Miss Wilma Le Cocq and take her to Jersey for training to become the new Alderney representative of the airline. Wilma would manage Alderney Aerodrome and run the Guernsey Airways Ltd. office in St. Anne until the outbreak of war. Facilities at the airport were extremely primitive; the only airport building was a tin hut housing the airfield tractor. Wilma's duties comprised, driving the Customs Officer to the airport, completing her paperwork in the hut using the tractor bonnet as a table, and processing passengers. Bookings had to be made well in advance by telegram as there were no telephones on the island and Wilma's weather reports were sent by telegram to Jersey and the mainland. Sam Allen was the ground staff support; an old man who was porter, loader, groundsman, aircraft refueller and operator of the starter batteries for the aircraft engines.

The first day excursion to Alderney was planned for 10th March 1936 from Jersey using veteran, *Rozel Bay* and in the afternoon, she would fly the first passengers from Alderney to Southampton. A crowd were at Alderney Aerodrome to witness the event, but the agent received a wire postponing the trip as recent heavy rains would make landing difficult.

On 27th March the first Alderney request stop was made by a Jersey to Heston D.H. 86 Express that landed two passengers, Mr Gordon Rice and Mrs Faul on Alderney. The same two passengers became the first to travel in the opposite direction on 28th March when Bill Caldwell, flying from Eastleigh was requested to stop and collect them.

A week later on 6th April, Guernsey Airways Ltd. amphibian Saro Windhover G-ABJP, entered service and arrived at Alderney Airport piloted by Mr Bill Halmshaw, an ex RAF pilot, on the inaugural flight of the Southampton – Alderney – Guernsey – Jersey service.

Over the following weekend with Easter Sunday on 12th April, a special twice-daily flight from Jersey to Alderney was flown using the Jersey Airways Ltd. D.H. 86 Express G-ACZN, *St. Catherine's Bay*.

The summer twice daily timetable was reintroduced at the end of May and an extra D.H. Dragon was chartered to supplement the fleet when as many as six aircraft were in the air together, but the inter-island service found it hard to keep pace. On 29th June, after only three months of service, Alderney's first air crash occurred when G-ACNJ, *Rozel Bay* overshot the aerodrome and crashed into a bank. A new pilot, Mr Martin, was coming into land with six passengers, made a perfect landing, but then ran out of airfield. He claimed that the brakes failed and he was faced with the choice of hitting six

Saro Windhover G-ABJP.

cows or the perimeter bank. He chose the bank and damaged the starboard propeller and undercarriage of *Rozel Bay* and it was 2nd July before she could be fully repaired and flown back to Eastleigh. The inter-island service with the Saro Windhover only limped along intermittently for four months and when its replacement, the Saro Cloud, *Cloud of Iona*, was lost on 31st July, all services to Alderney were suspended.

The Inauguration of the Service to Plymouth

Jersey Airways Ltd. wanted to extend its range. A new continental route was experimented with on 30th March when a D.H. 86 Express made a day trip to Dinan but nothing came of it. A more successful service was due to start on Friday 3rd April to Plymouth, flying on Tuesdays and Fridays. The inaugural flight was scheduled to leave Jersey at 10.30 hours and reach Plymouth at 11.45 hours, but visibility was so bad in Jersey that the craft could not take-off. A civic reception with the Lord Mayor was planned at Roborough, Plymouth's municipal aerodrome. Eventually the D.H. Dragon, G-ACNJ, *Rozel Bay*, was sent from Eastleigh, but she had to remain on the ground at Plymouth as the visibility in Jersey remained very poor. At 16.30 hours the Lord Mayor gave up and left the airfield and *Rozel Bay* did not manage to take-off until 11.15 hours the following morning with only two lady passengers. The manager of Roborough Aerodrome, Flight-Lieut. Knowlden, and his assistant, K.T. Murray, were both ex-employees of Jersey Airways Ltd.. The scheduled time for the flight between Plymouth and Jersey was 75 minutes, but it was not until 10th April that the first paying passenger made the crossing from Jersey. When the summer service ended on 30th September the Plymouth service was discontinued. This was intended to only be for the winter months but was permanent as the next year Exeter became the Devon terminus.

The Jersey Airport

Construction of Jersey Airport continued with more money requested from the States for additional equipment such as night flying facilities. The airport would not open until the following year, but the radio and direction-finding equipment was already being used.

There was an unexpected emergency landing at the airport on 7th November 1936 when Douglas Brecknell flying D.H. 86 Express G-ACYG *The Grouville Bay*, with twelve passengers was seriously delayed by 70 mph head winds and arrived at the beach to find that the tide was too far in for him to make a safe landing in the strong southerly cross wind. He was permitted to make an unofficial first landing at the St. Peter's Airport site at 10.15 hours and after a quick thirty-minute turn around, he was pushed along by the 70 mph wind to reach Eastleigh by 11.30 hours. There were still strong winds the following day and although the D.H. Dragon, *Rozel Bay* managed to land on the beach at about 11.00 hours, the D.H. 86 Express that arrived at the same time from Southampton failed several attempts and had to return to Eastleigh; it is not known why she was not given permission to land at the St. Peter's Airport site as had happened only the previous day. On 11th November the Eastleigh machine had to turn back because of high winds and 1936 ended with a series of cancelled services due to the rough weather, fog and on one occasion, the presence of ice on the wings of the aircraft.

The accounts for December 1936 show that Jersey Airways Ltd. made a profit of £4,288, but Guernsey Airways Ltd. made a loss of £2,735 while Channel Islands Airways Ltd. somehow managed to achieve a profit of £9. The combined total for the three airlines gave a profit of £1,562.

Emergency landing a by D.H. 86 Express G-ACYG *The Grouville Bay*, at St. Peter's Airport.

DEMISE OF GUERNSEY AIRWAYS LTD

Guernsey Airways Ltd.'s sole responsibility was to provide the inter-island seaplane service, but as the airline entered 1936 the Saro Windhover G-ABJP, was under repair at Eastleigh and they had no seaplane pilot. There was no Guernsey Airport and although Alderney services appeared in *Bradshaw's International Air Guide*, there were no landings at Alderney as it was uneconomical to employ staff and Customs Officers to deal with an occasional stop.

The Windhover was eventually re-commissioned in March 1936 and the company employed a new seaplane pilot, Bill Halmshaw. He was an experienced, RAF trained, flying boat pilot with five years service with 201 and 210 Flying boat Squadrons. His RAF training taught Halmshaw to be adept at landing a seaplane in very confined spaces. These skills would be required to land the Windhover inside either St. Peter Port or St. Helier Harbours at times of rough seas and dangerous winds. Previous company pilots had not attempted this manoeuvre and although Halmshaw accomplished it with finesse, the action created added strain on an already fragile craft.

On 18th March 1936 Halmshaw flew Greig and Thurgood on an inspection flight in the Windhover from Eastleigh to Alderney and the craft was later stationed in Jersey. On the Monday 6th April 1936 of Easter Week, the long-awaited Guernsey Airways Ltd. Southampton-Alderney-Guernsey-Jersey service was finally inaugurated with Bill Halmshaw flying the inter-island links in the Windhover and the Alderney to Eastleigh leap being accomplished with a Jersey Airways Ltd. D.H. 89A Rapide. There were no paying passengers on the first Windhover flight from Jersey to Guernsey, but the continuing inaugural flight from Guernsey to Alderney took 33 minutes against a 40 mph head-wind with four passengers including Mr Kane of *The Star*, Mr Pritchard, and two young boys, Peter and John Newton, aged five and six. The reporter and the two boys continued to Eastleigh in the Rapide to become the first passengers to fly the Alderney – Eastleigh route. The pilot was Douglas Brecknell, brother of Adrian Brecknell, the Guernsey Airways Ltd. manager in St. Peter Port. Because of low cloud cover, Douglas crossed the Channel at 6,000 feet, but when they reached the Solent he took the craft down low on a sightseeing tour over Southampton Docks where the three passengers saw the new *Queen Mary* liner in the King George V graving dock prior to her maiden voyage. Douglas had three passengers on the return flight from Eastleigh to Alderney and these three people along with the returning Guernsey passenger, Mr Pritchard, boarded the amphibian Windhover for its first return flight to Guernsey. It was intended that the Southampton-Alderney-Guernsey-Jersey service would run one flight daily except Wednesday when the Windhover was serviced. In the week running up to Easter business was good especially on the inter-island routes and the *Guernsey Evening Press* eulogized about the "daily arrival of the fine triple-engined Saro Windhover in flight from Jersey"; six months previously, *The Star* reporter had described the Windhover as a "veritable hen-coop"!

Success was short-lived however as during the next two months the Windhover was intermittently out of service because of rough seas or repairs. The reintroduction of the summer service started for Jersey Airways Ltd. at the end of May with a doubling of the mainland services; the Guernsey-Alderney service was also doubled which put even greater stress on the seaplane and pilot. On Tuesday 2nd June, Mr Greig, along with Major and Mrs Giffard and a friend, made a special flight in the Windhover to Dinard on the Brittany coast. After disembarking his passengers, Halmshaw was taking off when the port engine seized up solidly with a broken crankshaft and he was forced to abort and be towed back into the harbour. The following day, a new engine was sent to Dinard, but tides in the harbour restricted work to three hour periods so that it was Saturday 6th June before the Windhover could fly to Jersey and then on to Eastleigh for the work to be completed. The amphibian was back in service two days later, but the service in June was constantly interrupted by fog, continuously for eight days at one point. Disaster finally struck on Thursday 9th July when as the Windhover touched

Saro Windhover G-ABJP.

down on the sands at St. Aubin on its last flight of the day, a passenger opened one of the cabin windows and as the plane turned into the wind the window and frame were forced out by the sudden strain and as the window flew away it fouled the cable of the undercarriage that had just been lowered. The blow on the cable unlocked the wheel and when it took the weight of the plane, it collapsed. The machine went down on its hull and violently lurched along the beach throwing the passengers out of their seats. Initially there appeared to be no structural damage to the hull, but she could not take-off from the beach and Halmshaw had to wait for the tide to float her. He was able to take-off, but with such an unpredictable undercarriage he chose to taxi into the harbour for the night rather than attempt a landing on the racecourse.

The next morning Halmshaw took to the air to test the landing gear but found the undercarriage completely unserviceable; plates in the hull were also buckled and the keelson twisted. The Windhover would have to return to Saunders-Roe for repairs, but the workers were on strike and a repair that should take up to a month would be considerably delayed. Guernsey Airways Ltd. was again an airline without an aircraft, but they had a considerable number of advanced bookings and Thurgood determined to secure another plane for the service. The Windhover would never return to the islands, but this was the least of Guernsey Airways Ltd.'s woes for a serious disaster loomed only weeks away.

The Windhover undergoing inspection.

The Tragic Loss of the *Cloud of Iona*

On 15th July 1932 the Duchess of Hamilton had christened Saro Cloud, G-ABXW, *Cloud of Iona*, at Saunders-Roe factory following her purchase by British Flying Boats Ltd. of Edinburgh. The managing director of the airline was Lord Malcolm Douglas-Hamilton, one of the Duchess's four pilot sons. *Cloud of Iona* was used for joyriding and charters in Scotland and the Isle of Man, and for one week in August 1932 she briefly trialled a service between Glasgow and Belfast. She returned to Saunders-Roe in December 1933 when British Flying Boats Ltd. ceased operations and she was then sold to Spartan Airways Ltd. of London on 14th September 1934 in a move to thwart Thurgood from obtaining her. The *Cloud of Iona* was based at Cowes with Saunders-Roe and seldom left there as the Spartan Airways Ltd.'s attempts to establish a Channel Islands service came to nothing and they had no other use for her. To maintain an inter-island service, Guernsey Airways Ltd. required an amphibian aircraft that could carry at least eight passengers plus crew, but few such craft existed. Thurgood already owned the unique Saro Windhover, and the only similar craft was the Saro Cloud that he had never been able to acquire. *Cloud of Iona*, was sitting in the Saunders-Roe sheds having just completed an extensive repair and overhaul following a mishap while on service in Scotland. Thurgood immediately acquired her from Saunders-Roe and Halmshaw flew her to Jersey.

Cloud of Iona was moored in St. Helier Harbour and on 12th July 1936 the inter-island service was restored with this new amphibian flying from Jersey to Guernsey with a full complement of passengers, but heavy seas made landing difficult and as the weather failed to moderate she had to shelter in St. Peter Port Harbour and could not continue to Alderney.

Saro Cloud, G-ABXW, *Cloud of Iona* being christened.

Cloud of Iona in St. Helier Harbour.

Cloud of Iona had seats for eight passengers and a crew of two, but her two 300 hp Wright Whirlwind J-6 radial engines had nearly twice the power of the Windhover's three engines and she was capable of carrying a much heavier load, so Thurgood was eager to add more seats. On 28th July, *Cloud of Iona* was flown to Eastleigh to have four extra seats and a radio fitted. The Air Ministry required that an aircraft carrying ten or more passengers should be equipped with a radio receiver and transmitter, but some operators obtained dispensation from this ruling by showing that their craft would only carry passengers over short distances. In the event, only three additional seats were fitted and the radio "could not be found!", but this sounds like a delaying tactic as three days earlier, Guernsey Airways Ltd. had sought dispensation from the Air Ministry to fly without a radio on its short inter-island routes. On Thursday 30th July *Cloud of Iona* returned to Jersey with seats for eleven passengers in readiness for the August Bank Holiday weekend – which until 1965 was at the beginning of August – but she carried no radio even though the Air Ministry had not yet granted a dispensation.

Typically for an August Bank Holiday, the weathermen were predicting a gloomy forecast worsening into the evening of Friday 31st July. *Cloud of Iona* was making two trips between the islands each day and the last scheduled flight for Alderney on the Friday left St. Peter Port on time at 16.15 hours and landed thirty minutes later on Alderney. At 17.25 hours, *Cloud of Iona* left Alderney, but her flight back to Guernsey was against an increasing gusty south-westerly wind and it took her 40 minutes before she landed outside the entrance to St. Peter Port Harbour just as the GWR mail boat *St. Helier* was leaving for Jersey. As soon as the mail boat cleared the harbour mouth, Halmshaw entered and moored *Cloud of Iona* to her buoy. The seas were rough with blinding rain, and an exceedingly low cloud base, and a heavy sea fret made visibility poor so Halmshaw ran ashore to telephone Jersey to ascertain the weather there. At 18.35 hours he was given the official weather report for Jersey: "wind, west-by-

Guernsey Airways Ltd. amphibian Saro Cloud G-ABXW, *Cloud of Iona* eventually made it to Alderney Airport on the reintroduction of the Southampton-Alderney-Guernsey-Jersey service and the service progressed well with only a few delays. On 23rd July the Guernsey stop had to be abandoned following three failed attempts by Halmshaw to land on rough seas outside St. Peter Port Harbour, and on 27th July the craft was delayed until the evening on Alderney when water was found in the petrol.

north, 40-45 mph, visibility 1,000 yards with clouds on the hills, sea very rough, and the tide falling rapidly" but as this report was probably an hour old, Halmshaw spoke to the Jersey Airways Ltd. manager, Mr Wieland, in his first-floor office above Bellingham's Travel Agents on Mulcaster Street and asked his opinion. Wieland went to the office window and peered down the street towards St. Helier Harbour where he could see that the weather was poor, but he thought, flyable; had he looked the other way up the street he would have seen that the cloud was so low that Fort Regent was completely obscured.

Halmshaw, along with the flight mechanic, Francis Sotinel, a twenty-year-old Jerseyman, who had served in the French Air Force before joining Jersey Airways Ltd. three months earlier, were collecting eight passengers for the flight from Guernsey to Jersey. Three were from Guernsey, two from Jersey and three holidaymakers were from the mainland; included in these eight passengers were two newly engaged young couples. All the passengers had reasons to get to Jersey that evening and later reports said that some of them urged Halmshaw to make the flight against his better judgement, but Halmshaw was an experienced flying boat pilot with a cautious Yorkshire disposition who would never make a rash decision. He decided to attempt the flight as it was scheduled for 30 minutes, but usually took twenty minutes. If the sea was too rough to land, he could land on the beach as the tide was out, or on the racecourse. Failing these options, he had two hours of fuel, which was more than enough to return to Guernsey or fly to a sheltered harbour on the French coast. At precisely 19.00 hours *Cloud of Iona* slipped her buoy in St. Peter Port Harbour and headed out to the open sea. After taxiing for a mile, she turned towards the land to take-off into the wind and at 19.05 hours lifted off from the water and made a gentle, right-handed turn climbing through 270 degrees as she headed for Jersey. All the witnesses who saw her departure confirmed that it was a perfect take-off although she quickly disappeared into low cloud.

The staff waiting at West Park, on an unpleasant evening with heavy rain driving in off the sea, were looking forward to going home once this last service arrived. The inter-island amphibian service was noted for its irregularity, but by 20.00 hours impatience gave way to anxiety and the realisation that something serious had happened. Wieland telephoned Mr Brecknell in Guernsey, only to be informed that the craft left at 19.05 hours and had not returned; without radio contact they had no indication of the whereabouts of *Cloud of Iona*. Wieland immediately notified the Air Ministry and all shipping was alerted, he then contacted the French Consul in Jersey who informed the French Air and Naval authorities and all the ports between Brest and Cherbourg. Two maroons were fired to summon the lifeboat crew and at 20.30 hours the Guernsey lifeboat *Queen Victoria* was launched with Brecknell on board and she started tracing the supposed route of *Cloud of Iona* to Jersey. Visibility was deteriorating and a big sea was running, and it was estimated that the aeroplane, if she was still flying or trying to taxi on the sea, would run out of fuel within fifteen minutes and darkness would fall at 20.53 hours. Searches were made on foot of the coasts of Jethou and Herm and at 21.30 the private motor yacht *Dodo*, captained by F.W. Noyon and accompanied by T. Mc Cathie and J. Wheadon, set sail from St. Peter Port to search between Sark and Jersey.

The authorities in Jersey were slower to respond. The crew of the Jersey lifeboat was mustered, but their lifeboat only had oars and a sail; she was intended for inshore rescues and was not suitable for a search and rescue operation. The mail boat *St. Helier* had arrived in Jersey from Guernsey at 20.00 hours, but her assistance was not requested and eventually it was decided to send the States of Jersey tug *Duke of Normandy* out to search, but her boiler was cold, and it was 22.30 hours before she had enough steam to put to sea. The *Duke of Normandy* searched off Corbière, but the seas were too heavy for her and she returned to harbour at 23.20 hours, but at 01.00 hours in the morning the French Government tug *Pintade* set sail from Cherbourg to join the search. The lifeboat *Queen Victoria* was instructed to find shelter until dawn, but the private motor yacht *Dodo* continued her search until 02.30 hours. The GWR cargo vessel *Roebuck* was making her normal night crossing from Guernsey to Weymouth and she made a wide detour to search south of Guernsey. Nothing more could be done until dawn on Saturday 1st August when aircraft could join the search. Because of the strong south-westerly wind it was thought that the amphibian must be somewhere to the north-east of a line between Guernsey and Jersey and it was hoped that she might have reached the French coast. Sadly, the search was in totally the wrong area as unbeknown to anyone at the time, *Cloud of Iona* had reached St. Aubin's Bay almost on schedule the previous evening.

The only aircraft on Jersey was a chartered Dragon that had not left for the mainland on the Friday evening because her radio was not working. It was intended that she would start a search at first light, but the weather was bad, and she could not take-off. Bill Caldwell took off from Eastleigh in a Jersey Airways D.H. 86 to search the French coast and a Supermarine Southampton flying boat, N 9900 of 201 Squadron was scrambled from RAF Calshot with a crew of six under the command of Flight-Lieut. Dunn. Jersey Airways had six aircraft booked for the morning Bank Holiday leaving Heston at 08.30 hours and Eastleigh at 08.45 hours, and each of these craft flew a different course in an attempt to cover as wide an area as possible. French Navy flying boats joined the search at dawn and the

Queen Victoria left the shelter of Brecqhou Island to resume her search, but after three hours a dejected Bill Caldwell returned to Eastleigh having made a fruitless search of the entire French coast. At 10.20 hours the *Queen Victoria* returned to St. Peter Port to refuel and replace a transformer in her radio, while in Jersey the Singapore N 9900 alighted in St. Aubin's Bay to refuel and for the crew to have lunch. The *Queen Victoria* resumed her search at 12.25 hours and the N 9900 joined her soon afterwards and the crews were relieved to see that the weather was clearing.

At about 14.00 hours a telegram was received in Jersey from the Préfet Maritime in Cherbourg stating that a French aircraft had sighted an aluminium aircraft float nine miles south-east of Corbière lighthouse and the tug *Pintade* had been sent to try and pick it up. This was ten miles south of the perimeter of the official search area and N 9900 immediately diverted to the area and at 15.50 hours reported finding a quantity of plywood and aircraft fabric floating in the vicinity of the Minquiers. The N 9900 wound in her trailing radio aerial in order to make some low-level passes over the area and messaged back to Jersey shortly afterwards:

> Have searched in the vicinity of the Minquier reef and located a considerable amount of fabric and plywood easily recognisable as aircraft material. Continuing search to the west.

They had found aircraft debris but had no way of identifying if it belonged to *Cloud of Iona*. The N 9900 found nothing more and as she could not search the Minquiers rocks, she returned to her base. The Guernsey lifeboat *Queen Victoria*, which was off the French coast, was also ordered to return to harbour as she could do no more and when she docked at 19.15 hours she had been on duty continuously for 23 hours. Daylight and a pilot with local knowledge were required to search the Minquiers so a search party was organised to set out at 04.00 hours the following morning.

The Plateau des Minquiers, known as the "Minkies" to Channel Islanders is, at low tide, a plateau of rocks and shoals covering an area of 130 square miles, larger than the island of Jersey. The rocks are part of the Bailiwick of Jersey, situated 12 miles south of the island, with the highest rock in the middle, Maîtresse Île, the only one visible at extreme high tides.

Derelict cottages once occupied by stone masons working on Maîtresse Île, were used by visiting fishermen as shelters. The area is extremely dangerous and can only be approached in calm weather by sailors with expert local knowledge.

At dawn on Sunday 2nd August under a grey sky with choppy sea and showers of blinding rain, three boats left St. Aubin's Harbour for the Minkies, but very soon one had to return to harbour with Captain Benest who had fallen into the sea attempting to transfer between boats. The remaining boats were *Diana* captained by F. Lawrence, a local pilot and second coxswain of the lifeboat, who had with him Greig and Peter Lee of Jersey Airways and two Jersey seamen, while the *Lady Annabelle*, was manned by her owner Mr Le Marquand, with four friends and a reporter and photographer from the *Jersey Evening Post*. When they were three miles north of Maîtresse Île, the *Diana* picked up a square piece of wood with a hole in the centre, and Peter Lee, the ground engineer of Jersey Airways, identified it as part of *Cloud of Iona's* emergency exit, one of the few wooden items in an otherwise metal hull. This terrible discovery confirmed that *Cloud of Iona* had broken up and the only hope was that survivors had managed to make it to the Maîtresse Île. The search party headed for the rock and their hopes were raised when they saw a flag flying from the mast on the island, but they were met by fishermen from Jersey who had been on the rock since Friday and who had neither seen nor heard anything of *Cloud of Iona*. Under the guidance of Mr Lawrence, the party searched the channels and rocks of the Minkies and eventually discovered more wreckage from *Cloud of*

Wreckage of the *Cloud of Iona* found on the Minkies.

A delicate salvage operation of *Cloud of Iona* ensued at low tide on Sunday 16th August when both engines, the compass, instrument panel, control wheel, rudder bar and a Verey light pistol and several cartridges as well as some personal effects were all recovered into a yawl and floated off on the next high tide.

Iona near Les Pipettes, a group of small islets on the north-western edge of the Minkies. Without a doubt the craft had been destroyed and there was no hope of finding survivors.

Wreckage of the *Cloud of Iona* found on the Minkies was brought ashore by the crews of the *Lady Annabelle* and the *Diana*, and Channel Island Airways Ltd., issued a statement that the wreckage indicated that a disaster had taken place between that position and Jersey. During the next week nine bodies were discovered either in the water off the French coast or washed ashore there. The body of 28 year-old Ernest Appleby from Guernsey who was a fiancé of one of the engaged couples, was picked up by a Jersey boat near St. Malo and brought to St. Helier which necessitated an inquest being held in Jersey, but the body of Claude Willis, the fiancé of the other engaged couple from Birmingham, was never found. A fortnight after the disaster, on Friday 14th August, two fishermen from La Rocque reported that they had found the smashed hull and engines of *Cloud of Iona* wedged into the rocks of Les Pipettes.

Exactly what happened to *Cloud of Iona* will never be known, but the evidence leads experts to one conclusion. Although visibility was very poor on the evening of Friday 31st July 1936, Bill Halmshaw did manage to reach St. Aubin's Bay in *Cloud of Iona* at about 19.30 hours as witnesses reported hearing her and seeing her fleetingly thorough the clouds at about that time. The sea was rough and Halmshaw intended to make a landing on the beach as the tide was out. The undercarriage of the amphibian was found to be locked in the down position on the wreck; if Halmshaw was going to return to Guernsey or fly on to France the undercarriage would have been in the up position. A catastrophic and immediate loss of power must have taken place in both engines as all switches were in the 'on' position and the settings for both engines were identical. If only one engine had failed, Halmshaw would have made adjustments to the other to keep flying for as long as possible. As the electrics for each engine were on different circuits a simultaneous loss of electrical power to both engines was not possible and this left only a loss of fuel. The craft left Alderney with enough fuel for two hours of flying so she did not run out of fuel, but as the fuel in the tanks was low it could "slosh" about with the extreme buffeting of the winds. If the craft experienced a sudden turbulence this could lift the fuel off the fuel

The engines of *Cloud of Iona* were landed on the dockside in St. Helier Harbour. Great care was taken not to disturb the positions of the throttle controls as these would indicate the settings of both engines at the time of the crash. When the engines were later stripped down, they were both found to be in full working order.

inlet pipe long enough for an air lock to develop and this would produce the immediate loss of power. Halmshaw managed to fly on after the loss of power and made a successful landing on the water, but he may not have known in which direction he was going as the visibility was so poor and it is likely that he was heading away from the St. Aubin Beach, south towards the Minkies. There was much evidence to prove that Halmshaw managed to get Cloud of Iona down safely on the water. The hull of the aircraft with both engines attached had floated on to the Minkies reef in the inverted position before being further buffeted by the seas. The bow and keel of the hull of the wreck and the propellers on the engines showed no impact signs of damage, only scratches from the rocks. All the passengers and crew had died from drowning and their bodies had no injuries from a crash; everyone had time to put on their life jackets and some were still inflated when the bodies were found. The passengers and crew had safely exited a sinking craft that was subsequently overturned and broken up by the sea and trapped by the rocks of Les Pipettes.

No blame could be apportioned for the loss of Cloud of Iona, but there was much conjecture about the lack of a radio and whether a rescue could have been effected if the location of the aircraft had been known. Six months later, Guernsey Airways Ltd. was convicted in the local Guernsey police courts for having flown Cloud of Iona on three days without a wireless and fined £300 which at the time was the biggest fine ever levied in the Guernsey court. Following the tragic loss of Cloud of Iona the inter-island service was suspended indefinitely and although the Windhover was repaired in September, she never flew to the islands again. The Guernsey Airways Ltd. service between Southampton and Alderney, flown by Jersey Airways Ltd. D.H. Rapides, was also suspended and the only service available on Alderney was the "request" stop of the mainland services.

Guernsey Airways Ltd – the Phantom Airline

Guernsey Airways Ltd. was once again without a service to fly and ended 1936 with a loss of £2,735. In 1937 the airline still failed to carry out any operations and made a loss of £2,069; much of this was accounted for by claims and expenses connected with the loss of the Cloud of Iona, as well as depreciation, insurance and expenses associated with the redundant Windhover. The company managed to accrue a further loss of £527 in 1938 without flying any services and this included a loss of £152 after selling the Windhover to Percival Aircraft Co. of Luton for only £200.

THE OPENING OF THE STATES OF JERSEY AIRPORT

Opened on 10th March 1937, the Sates' of Jersey Airport at St. Peter was the largest provincial airport in the U.K. (excluding the London International Airport at Croydon) and its facilities were the most advanced of any airport in Europe. This photograph was taken from a Jersey Airways Ltd. D.H.86 express while a second craft sits on the apron in front of the terminal. On the morning of 10th March, two Jersey Airways Ltd. aircraft made their final departures, officially for all time, from the beach at West Park. The licensed engineer, two fitters and the refueller as well as porters, the police, Customs and the office staff manning the mobile office and waiting room, all packed their equipment and left the sands for the last time allowing it to peacefully return for the use of holidaymakers, local residents and the seagulls. Never again would the dramatic sight of eight commercial aircraft flying in formation on a scheduled air service and landing in succession on a beach be seen anywhere in the world.

States of Jersey Airport.

Terminal buildings of St. Peter Airport before opening.

The construction of St. Peter Airport aroused much comment and criticism from local residents and the Jersey press who were highly sceptical of the vast investment made by the States using "their" money for such an extravagant venture. The States Airport officials created even more controversy when the opening ceremony at 15.15 hours on Wednesday 10th March 1937 was restricted to a mere 200 invited guests with many of them from the mainland and Guernsey, while none were Jersey school children.

The first aircraft to land at Jersey Airport were two Jersey Airways D.H. 86 Express machines from Heston led by Captain Bill Caldwell in G-ACZO, *The Quaine Bay* closely followed by G-ACZR, *La Saline Bay* with Caldwell taking the title of being the first pilot to officially land at the airport. The passengers in the two craft included mainland guests and visiting pressmen. The Piers and Harbours Committee entertained the principal guests with lunch at the St. Brelade's Bay Hotel while the Press were given lunch at The Grand.

The ceremony to declare the States of Jersey Airport open was very simple with only 30 minutes of speeches before the Bailiff's wife, Mrs Coutanche, unveiled a plaque and received a bouquet of flowers. There was no celebratory air display to welcome the event.

Unveiling the plaque during the opening of St Peter Airport.

The guests were taken on a tour of inspection of the airport and permitted to go onto the apron to view *The Quaine Bay* and *La Saline Bay* at close quarters until 16.00 hours when the two aircraft returned to England with Bill Caldwell in *The Quaine Bay* again having the honour of being officially the first pilot to take-off from the airport.

Although the general public were excluded from the opening ceremonies, they were invited to apply for tickets to tour the airport buildings at a later date. On the first Saturday following the opening, the airport was besieged with Islanders eager to go joyriding, experience the delights of the airport restaurant or crowd the balcony rails to watch the aircraft land and take-off. Most were curious to see what £128,000 of their tax money had bought, while the airport authorities very sensibly accommodated the non-flying public by supplying them with deckchairs and their own snack counter on the promenade. £128,000 bought the people of Jersey one of the most advanced airports in Europe, but flying was still a rich person's prerogative and few Jersey residents would be able to take advantage of their airport. Visitors to the airport were universally impressed by its huge size of 83 acres surrounded by two miles of chain link fencing with the four-storey terminal building being the largest single building on Jersey. There were two grass runways; the longer east/west runway was 980 yards with a white centre concrete line designed to assist aircraft to take-off in fog, while the shorter north/south runway was only 528 yards long. In front of the terminal and the two hangars that flanked it was a paved standing apron, while at each end of the building there were refuelling gantries with arms that swung out over the aircraft. Jersey Airways Ltd. refuelled their own aircraft and leased the larger of the two hangars, a building 220 feet by 100 feet that was large enough to house their entire fleet of six D.H. 86 Expresses, two D.H. 89A Dragon Rapides and one D.H. 84 Dragon, while the other refuelling gantry and hangar was managed by the States for servicing visiting private aircraft.

Guests touring the apron during the opening of the airport.

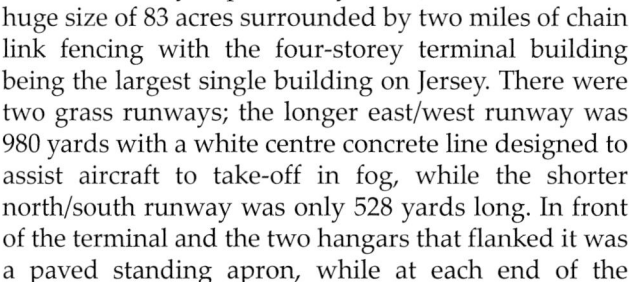

A *Jersey Evening Post* photographic aerial view of the airport clearly shows the airport terminal building (top right) and in front of it the concrete landing circle with the bold letters JERSEY, and the concrete fog take-off line running down the length of the airfield.

One of four huge G.E.C. floodlights could be switched on behind a landing aircraft at night to assist landing. There were even two wireless rooms, one to control the local Jersey Airport traffic and the other to direct craft passing through the Channel Islands Control Zone, such as Imperial Airways aircraft en route to Africa. A controversy that is still voiced today was that the airport was built in the wrong location as the high ground of St. Peter is very susceptible to low cloud and fog. This was put to the test only twelve days after the opening when on 22nd March the visibility at the airport was down to 50 yards. Captain Bill Caldwell added another first to his many achievements by being the first pilot to use the white concrete strip on the main runway in fog to enable him to get airborne in his D.H. 86, closely followed by a second Jersey Airways Ltd. craft. Jersey Airways Ltd. transferred their entire fleet and infrastructure from Eastleigh to their new headquarters at St. Peter and on 11th March, implemented a fixed timetable that was no longer reliant on the tides. With the aircraft now based at St. Peter the rhythm of the timetable was reversed with the Heston and Eastleigh mainland machines leaving Jersey at 10.30 hours and returning at 15.15 hours. An added attraction was joyriding on Sundays.

The first private aircraft to land at Jersey Airport and also become the first resident Jersey craft was a De Havilland D.H. 87 Hornet Moth, GADSK owned by Baron V. Richardson.

Jersey Airways Ltd Develops New Routes

1st May 1937 saw the introduction of a new timetable and the inauguration of a twice a week return service to Alderney but the departure of the first flight on 1st May was delayed until 15.00 hours because of fog on Alderney. On 31st May, new services were inaugurated to the mainland, one to Brighton, the other to Exeter. The first flight to Brighton on 31st May, was made by D.H. 86 *The St. Catherine's Bay*, piloted by J. Israel with chief radio-operator J. Lyons, Director Greig, and four fare-paying passengers including two children. Brighton Airport was opened in 1935 at Shoreham as a joint venture by the three adjacent towns of Brighton, Hove and Worthing and this accounted for the large number of civic dignitaries led by Lord Amherst, the manager of Shoreham Airport, who gathered to greet the arrival of *The St. Catherine's Bay*. Before the celebratory lunch in the airport lounge, various notables were taken on a flight along the coast to Newhaven accompanied by a Jersey Airways Ltd. D.H. Rapide carrying the Press and photographers. The new service flew once daily on Fridays, Mondays and Tuesdays, and twice daily on Saturdays and Sundays. It proved so popular that from 2nd July the service was increased to twice daily on all five days.

The first flight to Exeter on 31st May was flown by Bill Caldwell in D.H. 86 *The Quaine Bay* accompanied by First Officer Martin with only two fare-paying passengers both of whom happened to be from Guernsey. The arrival of the Jersey Airways first flight at Clyst Honiton at 10.30 hours coincided with the 'formal' opening of this new Exeter Airport. (The 'official' opening would take place when the airport buildings were completed.) A huge body of dignitaries including the Mayor of Exeter, the Sheriff of Devon and the Chief Constable were at the airport to greet *The Quaine Bay*. The Jersey-Exeter service ran on Friday, Saturday, Monday and Tuesday and like the service to Brighton, there were two services a day in the high season.

The First Airmail between Jersey and the UK

With the establishment of a regular summer timetable on 1st June 1937 the postal authorities were finally willing to grant Thurgood a contract to transport mail by air between Southampton and Jersey. On the morning of Tuesday 1st June, without pomp or ceremony, Jersey Airways Ltd. D.H. Rapide, G-ADBW, piloted by Captain B. Walker, left St. Peter Airport at 06.25 hours carrying 335 lb of mail and landed at Eastleigh at 07.37 hours where the mail sacks were handed over to the waiting postal authorities.

The flight in the opposite direction, although later and thus not truly the 'first flight', was to be the recognised 'inaugural flight' with an official reception awaiting it when it landed in Jersey. Caldwell was again responsible, and accompanied by First Officer J.

Dignitaries and a Jersey Post Office van receive the first airmail flown by G-ACYF, *The Giffard Bay* from the UK to Jersey.

Marten, they left Eastleigh bound for Jersey at 07.50 hours in G-ACYF, *The Giffard Bay*, with 229 lb of mail on board. They reached Jersey at 08.50 hours and the local press described their arrival in the usual romantically poetic terms that they reserved for arriving aircraft. More interesting was the description of the new décor of the craft: "Flying just above the cockpit was the blue Royal Mail Air pennant and on the bow stood boldly the words 'Royal Mail' surrounding the crown." Caldwell arrived ten minutes too early for the reception timed for 09.00 hours and had to skulk in a far corner of the airfield until the reception party including the Lieut. Governor and the Bailiff of Jersey arrived and were in position to welcome him, whereupon he taxied up to the apron in front of the main building to be greeted by the officials and the Jersey G.P.O. postmen with their van, waiting to collect the incoming mail.

Commemorative Flown Covers

To facilitate philatelists and airmail collectors, Jersey Airways Ltd. produced a number of commemorative flight covers in collaboration with airmail dealer, A. Phillips, from Newport, Monmouthshire. Collectors could send privately addressed envelopes for servicing by either the Jersey or Southampton airport offices while Phillips' official commemorative envelopes were addressed to one of the three Jersey Airways Ltd. offices, at Jersey Airport, Southampton Airport or the London head office. The London office used for the delivery was the office at Victoria Station, not Heston Airport.

Summer into Winter

Jersey Airways Ltd. maintained their charter and air ambulance availability and on 6th May D. Brecknell flew their longest charter air ambulance flight to date when he took a lady patient, Miss A. Mees, 700 miles to Rotterdam in a D.H. Rapide. On 7th July the company flew their largest charter when thirteen passengers off the mail boat from Southampton missed their connection to St. Malo on the *S.S. Brittany* and wanted to be taken by air to Dinard. Although it was summer, the month of July was very misty, delaying flights, and on 12th July five machines had to return to the mainland without landing because the mist was too dense. On 25th July the Heston D.H. 86 taxied onto the runway for take-off but collided with a Miles Whitney Straight that put it out of service at the busiest time of the year, but August Bank Holiday still broke all records with Jersey Airways Ltd. carrying 631 passengers on one day.

As the evenings got darker the last scheduled arrivals at St. Peter were on Fridays and Saturdays at 21.35 hours and these would often require the floodlights to be switched on. As early as 13th September, the 08.30 hours craft from St. Peter to Eastleigh reported icing and no other planes could take-off until 16.30 hours in the afternoon when all the day's services had to be compressed into a few hours. The Jersey Airways Ltd. craft had all been fitted with a thermometer below the cockpit window to measure the outside air temperature as a warning against this possible icing. Life got easier when the simpler winter timetable came into effect on 27th September.

Throughout the holiday season a specially chartered newspaper aircraft left London in the early morning hours to bring the latest editions of the national newspapers to Jersey, primarily for the tourists as the locals were accustomed to getting their news a day late. The service started as early as 12th April with the *Daily Sketch* being the first to arrive by air, soon followed by the *Daily Mirror*, and continued until the end of the season on Saturday 25th September. The service proved uneconomical for both the newspaper companies and Jersey Airways Ltd. as the flight added ½ penny to the cost of each newspaper while the preferential rates given to the newspaper companies by the airline failed to cover the increased landing costs and night flying expenses of an early morning flight. On 28th September there was a new excursion from Jersey to Paris leaving St. Peter at 16.45 hours and arriving at Le Bourget at 18.15 hours, returning the next day from Le Bourget at 16.00 hours. Twenty-two passengers travelling in two machines used the service and the exercise was repeated a fortnight later with the excursion leaving Jersey on 13th October, but there were no attempts to establish a permanent service to Paris. From 1st November the Heston service was operated entirely by four-engined D.H. 86's and this negated the need for the unpopular changeover of aircraft at Eastleigh. Jersey Airways Ltd. now only possessed one twin-engine machine as D.H. Rapide G-ADBV and the old D.H. Dragon, the *Rozel Bay*, had both been sold.

The improved facilities provided by the airport enabled Jersey Airways Ltd. to maintain a service throughout December, and on four days in the month flights to Dinard were reinstated. Special Christmas return day trips to London were organised in conjunction with the Southern & Great Western Railways from December to the end of January 1938, and the timetable was increased for Christmas week. On Christmas Eve the scheduled departure from St. Peter at 16.30 hours became the first U.K. night flight on a regular domestic air service.

Although the new airport had been a welcome boon to Jersey Airways Ltd. with increased custom it had also greatly increased their costs compared to the cheap beach landings and it came as an unpleasant shock to learn that they had actually made a loss of £9,963 during the year.

The opening of the superior airport at St. Peter equipped with all the latest features and facilities brought to an end the pioneer period of aviation for Jersey. Even Alderney with its limited facilities, but supported by Jersey Airways Ltd. could claim to be over the pioneer period, but poor Guernsey ended the year still with no inter-island service nor a viable link to the mainland although there was hope, as the Bailiff of Guernsey had cut the first sod of a new airport site at La Villiaze on 21st September.

Evaluating the Short S22 Scion Senior

Short Brothers were famous for seaplanes and flying boats, but in 1935 they designed a land-based aircraft. Named the Short S22 Scion Senior it was developed from the Short S16 Scion and was a cantilever monoplane with four Pobjoy Niagara III engines that was capable of carrying a crew of two and nine passengers. Unfortunately for Short Brothers, it arrived on the scene too late as the provincial airlines already had either the De Havilland D.H. Dragon or Rapide that fitted their requirements and had gained well-earned reputations.

The Scion Senior proved more attractive as a floatplane and of the six built, only one was built as a landplane demonstrator. This Scion Senior was registered G-AECU on 19th February 1936 and had a length of 42 ft, a wingspan of 55 ft and could attain a maximum speed of 140 mph for a range of 420 miles from a power plant of four Pobjoy Niagara III 90 hp engines. Within a week of the Airport opening, Jersey Airways Ltd. acquired G-AECU for evaluation and this unusual visitor created much interest. It is unclear why Jersey Airways Ltd. wanted to evaluate the craft as the floatplane version was of no use on the inter-island service, but perhaps they were considering replacing their D.H. Rapides or the D.H. Dragon with it. On 18th March 1937 the Short Scion Senior was flying joyrides from the airport and at least three pilots evaluated it, but nothing came of the trials and the craft was returned to Shorts.

Short S22 Scion Senior G-AECU.

JERSEY AIRWAYS LTD – CONSOLIDATION NOT INNOVATION

Three early morning newspaper D.H. 86 aircraft arrived at St. Peter Airport on 1st June 1938 when a new contract to deliver three tons of national newspapers daily from Eastleigh was implemented, and Jersey Airways Ltd. augmented their airmail Post Office contract with an additional departure from St. Peter at 15.30 hours on weekdays and 10.30 on Sundays.

Jersey Airways Ltd. had no new projects for 1938 and a service to Guernsey would have to wait until the airport was built, but by consolidating their established routes to Eastleigh, Heston, Brighton and Exeter, the airline hoped to be in profit by the end of the year. 1938 commenced with the accustomed winter delays, but joyriding was increasingly popular and available from St. Peter Airport on Thursday and Saturday afternoons for a price of 6s. 6d.

The threat of war increased military aviation exercises by French and British service flying boats in the vicinity of the Channel Islands. In January a French plane was reported in the sea 12 miles off Corbière. A Jersey Airways search mission failed to locate her but thankfully the aircraft returned safely to its Cherbourg base. In February a French seaplane was reported in distress 4 miles south-west of Guernsey. Two incoming Jersey Airways machines received the S.O.S. when passing Cap La Hague and diverted to the location, but again could find nothing. The French crew were later reported safe, but their aircraft was lost.

Jersey Airways Ltd. enjoyed the usual Easter rush from 14th to 19th April with all machines in service and a doubling of the timetable. Air traffic was so heavy on Bank Holiday Monday, 18th April, that it was dark before flying finished, and the last two machines from the mainland landed with the aid of the airport landing lights.

The airline's long-distance record was broken in May when Mr R.G. Maltwood chartered D.H. 86 G-ACZP, *The Belcroute Bay*, to make a 1,250 miles excursion to Cannes to collect his father. Mr Maltwood specifically requested Pilot J. Israel for the flight, and First Officer Challis and Flight-Engineer M. Lovell accompanied him.

Portsmouth reappeared in the 1938 timetable when aircraft would make a request stop, but the service closed as passenger traffic failed to increase, and costs increased with additional landing fees. On 28th May the summer timetable reintroduced the Brighton and Exeter routes.

The white concrete fog line could not help arrivals. On 22nd June G. Rayner was landing G-ACZP, *The Belcroute Bay*, at about 18.00 hours when he failed to find the airport in fog and diverted to the beach and parked his D.H. 86 on the First Tower slipway overnight. J. Israel was landing half an hour later but found a gap in the fog and got down safely. The following morning, 23rd June, the fog was still dense, and the three newspaper planes failed to land and had to return to Eastleigh while the mail plane could not get through until 10.40 hours.

On 28th June G-ACYF, *The Giffard Bay* was acquired by Wearnes Air Services Ltd. for their Singapore to Penang run and renamed *General Murchison*. She was repainted by Jersey Airways Ltd. ground staff with her Australian civil registration, VR-SDD, prior to her transfer to Singapore. The pilot, Captain Rodney Beresford, had only recently joined Jersey Airways Ltd. from Cobham Air Routes, and now took employment with Wearnes Air Services Ltd. to fly the craft out to Singapore.

June saw the sale of two aircraft. The twin engine D.H. Rapide, G-ADBW, went to Airwork, making Jersey Airways the only British airline to have an entire fleet of four engine craft.

August was the peak period especially the Bank Holiday when planes were still arriving at 23.00 hours and hundreds of cars a night parked near the aerodrome to witness the spectacle of night landings with the searchlights coming on as an aircraft approached.

On 18th August, Nigel Norman, a consultant working on Guernsey Airport, took off from St. Peter Airport in his private De Havilland D.H.85 Leopard Moth, G-ACNN, to make the first flight between the Jersey and Guernsey airports, culminating in the first landing on the unfinished Guernsey airport site at La Villiaze. August also saw another 'new airport' visit combined with an extravagant ambulance service by Jersey Airways Ltd.. A lady visitor to Alderney fractured her kneecap and chartered a Jersey Airways Ltd. D.H. 86 to fly her to Southampton, but as she found the four-engine airliner so comfortable she decided to extend the charter and have it fly her home to Birmingham. This was a first flight and landing for a Jersey Airways Ltd. craft at Birmingham Municipal Airport at Elmdon that would not officially open until July 1939.

The winter service was reintroduced in October, the Brighton and Exeter services closed for the winter and

Nigel Norman and Leopard Moth G-ACNN.

the Alderney service was reduced to one day a week with two flights on Fridays. The summer newspaper contract came to an end on 2nd October, but Jersey residents were now so accustomed to having their London papers delivered on the day of publication that a new contract was signed from 24th October when two Jersey Airways Ltd. D.H. 86's newspaper planes would leave Eastleigh every morning at 06.00 hours while the airmail service would continue as before.

Air France arrives in Jersey

Thurgood and Greig always wanted a service to France, but their previous forays to Rennes, Dinard and Paris were little more than excursions. Now based at Jersey Airport, they felt able to enter into negotiations with Air France to establish a joint Paris service, reasoning that working with the French airline would be more acceptable to the French authorities. The national French airline, Air France, was formed in 1933 by the amalgamation of Air Union, Air Orient and other small French companies that resulted in a combined fleet of eight Wibault-Penhouët 282 T12 passenger monoplanes. During 1934 ten more machines of an improved version were built for Air France; these were the Wibault-Penhouët 283 T12. They flew the Paris London route emblazoned with the logos 'Voile d'Or' and 'The Golden Clipper', competing with Imperial Airways.

The first intimation of collaboration between Air France and Jersey Airways Ltd. came on Monday 13th June when at 11.00 hours an Air France Wibault landed at St. Peter Airport with a party of Air France executives from Paris and Dinard. At 16.14 hours they returned to Paris with Greig and Mr Joualt of Boutin's Agency. A weekend service was inaugurated by Air France between Paris and Dinard on Saturday 9th July, but it was not extended to Jersey until Monday 8th August when the first Wibault to officially fly to Jersey, piloted by Durman, landed at 07.56 hours. All the passengers were guests and included the Mayor of Dinard, the President and Vice-President of the Dinard Aero Club, Frontin of *l'Ouest Éclair* (a French regional newspaper that closed in 1944) and Joualt of Boutin's Agency. The intended schedule was for the Wibault to leave Le Bourget for Dinard every Saturday at 13.15 and return from Dinard on the Monday morning. Over the weekend it would make one return flight from Dinard to Jersey on Saturday, two on Sunday and one early return flight on Monday morning before returning to Le Bourget, leaving Dinard at 09.00 hours.

On Tuesday 9th August, Jersey Airways Ltd. opened their service to Dinard to run on Tuesdays and Thursdays. The craft intended for the flight was the scheduled one that left Eastleigh at 12.15 hours so it was possible to leave Manchester at 09.00 hours on a Railway Air Services Ltd. aircraft, connect with the Jersey Airways Ltd. craft at Eastleigh and be in Dinard at 14.00 hours. A.G.M. Cary was the pilot for the first part of the inaugural flight on 9th August from Eastleigh in G-ACZO, *The Quaine Bay*, but when the craft reached Jersey, Bill Caldwell took over to fly *The Quaine Bay* to Dinard with official guests including Greig, to be greeted at a flag bedecked Dinard Aerodrome-cum-racecourse by the Deputy Mayor of Dinard and a grand champagne reception.

Wibault-Penhouët 283 T12, F-AMHN was originally built for Air-Union but is seen here with her early Air France colours and legend 'The Golden Clipper' (in English!). When she visited Jersey in 1938 and 1939, she was rebranded with a new Air France décor of silver and blue and the name *Le Vaillant*. The Wibault-Penhouët 282 T12 was a low-winged monoplane with three 350 hp Gnome-Rhône 7kd seven-cylinder radial engines giving a cruising speed of 125 mph. The wing-mounted engines were fitted with cowls, but not the nose engine. It had a wingspan of 74 ft 2 ins. and a length of 55 ft 9 ins. and could carry twelve passengers and two crew. The improved Wibault-Penhouët 283 T12 had the same dimension and seating capacity, but all three engines were cowled, and the undercarriage legs were fitted with huge fairings, like baggy tin trousers. The improvements increased the cruising speed to 140 mph with a heavier load.

The first scheduled Air France machine, Wibault F-AMHM, *L'Intrepide,* piloted by Chouard with radio-operator Fabre, landed at Jersey Airport on 13th August with one fare-paying passenger and a host of guests including the Mayor and Mayoress of Dinard and Air France officials. The plane flew from Dinard to Jersey in 18

Wibault-Penhouët 282 T12 F-AMHM, *L'Intrepide*.

minutes arriving at St. Peter Airport at 16.45 hours to be met by a large welcoming party and a reception that attempted to better Dinard's champagne reception for *The Quaine Bay* four days previously. *L'Intrepide* then left five minutes behind schedule at 17.05 hours for her return journey with ten passengers. Air France's busiest weekend started on Saturday 3rd September when its Wibault landed at St. Peter with ten passengers and left for Dinard with five. On the following day all four flights were almost full to capacity and on Monday even the early morning flight arrived at 07.54 with five passengers. The service was suspended for the winter after the flight to Dinard and Paris on Monday 12th September, but it would return for a longer summer service in 1939.

In 1938 three Wibault-Penhouët 282 T12s were recorded visiting Jersey, they were: F-AMHM, *L'Intrepide*, F-AMHN, *Le Vaillant* and F-AKEL, *La Rapide*, while in 1939 the Wibault-Penhouët 283 T12, F-AMYE, *L'Intigant*, is also known to have visited the island.

Wibault-Penhouët 282 T12 F-AMEL, *La Rapide*.

Wibault-Penhouët 282 T12 F-AMHN, *Le Vaillant*

Wibault 283 T12 F-AMYE, *L' Integant*. This improved 283 T12 with cowls to all engines and huge fairings to the undercarriage legs only visited Jersey in 1939.

The Tragic Disaster of the Crash of the *St. Catherines Bay* at Jersey Airport

The forecast for the Jersey Guy Fawkes weekend in 1938 was typical November weather of damp grey skies, mist and fog. On Friday 4th November the early morning mail plane leaving Jersey for Eastleigh was G-ACZN, *St. Catherines Bay*, and although it was dark and foggy, she got away safely at 06.28 hours using the concrete fog line. The pilot was A.G.M. (Geoff) Cary, an ex RAF officer living with his wife in St. Brelade, and with him was senior radio-operator Jack Lyons who had just obtained his pilot's "A" licence. They arrived safely at Eastleigh and returned to Jersey at 10.23 hours. Cary's next departure was scheduled for 10.30 hours and when he consulted the 10.00 hours Jersey Airport weather report, he read: "Visibility, three to four miles; Wind, W.S.W. 15 mph; Cloud, 10/10 at 120 ft" Ten-tenths cloud at 120 ft meant that the sky was completely obscured by low cloud. Three planes were scheduled to leave, but because of the weather they were delayed and ordered to take-off at four-minute intervals with *St. Catherines Bay* the last to leave at 10.52 hours.

Cary had eight passengers on board *St. Catherines Bay*; six Jersey residents, including a 14-month old baby girl, and two regular visitors. Two further prospective passengers were on the mail boat from Guernsey, but it was running late and Louis Morris, a wealthy film magnate wirelessed the airport requesting that they "hold" the aircraft until his arrival. The two men arrived at the airport about five minutes before *St. Catherines Bay* was due to take-off, but she was already warming up her engines and the load sheet had been completed and despite their vigorous protests, the men were not allowed to board. Having received permission to take-off, Cary taxied to the end of the fog line to take-off in a westerly direction. He followed the fog line and opened the throttles of his four engines increasing his speed and lifting the tail. *St. Catherines Bay* was soon airborne and

D.H. Dragon Rapide *St. Catherines Bay* G-ACzN.

lost to sight in the low cloud, but her progress could still be plotted as she was heard turning left into the wind to gain height and continuing on a left-hand circuit towards the south of the aerodrome and then round towards St. Peter's Church from where she would set a course north for Eastleigh.

Cary radioed Jersey control: "QBF 300 ft ASC", meaning he was still in cloud at 300 ft and climbing, but suddenly *St. Catherines Bay* burst through the low cloud base over St. Peter's with her engines roaring and in a steep left-hand side slip, dived towards the high banked lane separating St. Peter's Farm from Seadua Farm and a field called 'La Bataille'. She hit the ground in the field and skidded through the bank and hedge bordering the lane, bounced over the lane and ploughed into the opposite bank bordering St. Peter's Farm. For a while all was still except for the roar of the engines, but then there was an enormous explosion that shot a sheet of flame 50 feet into the air and engulfed the entire plane.

Several people witnessed the crash. Foreman Edmund Le Cornu and French labourer, Pierre Le Saux were mowing La Bataille field with scythes and were so accustomed to hearing aircraft at close quarters that they did not take any notice until *St. Catherines Bay* was almost upon them. They threw themselves to the ground and the plane grazed Pierre as it passed over him, but Mr Le Cornu was killed instantly and his body carried to the edge of the field by the plane where he was found with all his clothing torn from him. William Le Page was driving a Tyler's delivery van along the lane between the fields when he heard the plane very low overhead. Suddenly it loomed out of the mist with its engines running "all out" and crashed across the road 100 yards in front of him before exploding and bursting into flames.

Mr Huelin and his son, the owners of Seadua Farm, were working only 80 yards from the crash site and were the first on the scene, but the plane was already burning fiercely and the heat was too intense for them to approach. Bodies were strewn over the ground by the explosion; the first they found had its clothing alight, they found four bodies in their mangold field and one in the grass while the body of the baby, although dead, appeared unharmed.

Mr Louis Morris who had failed to board the plane was talking to his driver in the airport car park when they saw *St. Catherines Bay* crash. The two men raced to the plane and as they ran the petrol tanks exploded and they saw bodies flung from the wreck. They heard the airport siren sound and reached the site ahead of the fire engine and ambulance, but there was nothing that they could do. At the airport, Sydney Gallichan was on look-out duty on the balcony outside the

Rescuers attend the crash site of *St. Catherines Bay*.

Investigators examining the crash site.

This annotated view of the crash scene appeared in many newspapers in the days following the crash. *St. Catherine's Bay* travelled from left to right across the lane after landing in La Bataille field on the left and ended up on the bank at the edge of St. Peter's Farm on the right.

control tower when he saw the plane dive into the ground. He shouted through the open window of the control tower to Flight-Lieut. Phillips, the duty control officer, who immediately sounded the alarm siren and in less than two minutes the airport fire engine reached the burning craft. This was closely followed by the ambulance and later fire engines from St. Helier arrived, but it was impossible to extinguish the burning wreck and there were no survivors to save.

Debris, bodies, luggage and effects, were scattered over a radius of 50 feet around the wreck of the plane. The grim symbol of Mr Le Cornu's scythe lay across a pile of burnt items, but the *Last Will and Testament* of Mrs Wall, a visitor passenger, was found untouched by the flames. The *St. Catherines Bay* had not been carrying any mail or cargo.

A post-mortem on the body of pilot Geoff Cary could find no evidence of a condition that might cause the accident. All paperwork was in order and the craft had been fit for service. The Air Ministry investigation in April the following year concluded that the crash was caused by an error of airmanship on the part of the pilot who when making a climbing turn in cloud, inadvertently permitted the machine to fall into a sideslip at a height that did not permit recovery of control. Guernsey Airways Ltd. had lost *Cloud of Iona* with all souls and now Jersey Airways Ltd. had suffered an even more appalling accident with the loss of *St. Catherines Bay*; the real causes of both accidents would forever remain uncertain.

A Surprising End to the Year

With the loss of *St. Catherines Bay* and the sale of two of their older machines, Jersey Airway Ltd. now had a reduced fleet that could not meet their requirements and were looking for new aircraft to replace them. War rearmament pressures meant new civil aircraft were not being built as materials were all directed towards the production of military aircraft.

The latest version of the D.H. 86 was the De Havilland D.H. 86B that was introduced in 1936 following concerns about the handling of the D.H. 86A in turbulent weather following a series of accidents. Initially in 1936 any D.H. 86A's that gave cause for concern were recalled and modified to the new specifications of the D.H. 86B, while from 1937 all new builds were D.H. 86B's. The basic dimensions, cruising speed and top speed of the new D.H. 86B remained the same, but a dramatic improvement in lateral handling was achieved with the addition of two conspicuous vertical 'Zulu Shield' fins to the ends of the tail plane wings. With no new planes available Jersey Airways Ltd. had to search the second-hand market to buy two of these improved D.H. 86B's. On 8th December Jersey Airways Ltd. acquired G-ADVK that had received its first Certificate of Airworthiness on 21st April 1936 when, as a D.H. 86A, it had been supplied new to Blackpool and West Coast Air Services Ltd. It was recalled and converted to a D.H. 86B and sold to the Isle of Man Air Services Ltd. in 1937 before its sale to Jersey Airways Ltd. on 8th December 1938.

In February 1939, Jersey Airways Ltd. would acquire their second D.H. 86B, G-AENR. This was a new-build craft that had received its Certificate of Airworthiness on 8th February 1937 prior to being supplied to Blackpool and West Coast Air Services Ltd. She also went to the Isle of Man Air Services Ltd. in 1937.

Problematic winter weather could occasionally bring unexpected benefits. On 20th November pilot

Jersey Airways second D.H. 86B G-AENR.

George Rayner and radio-operator B. Worsley were taking off from Jersey and got G-ACYG, *The Grouville Bay,* away in a strong southerly gale. The tail wind was so strong that although Rayner had four passengers on board, he notched up the fastest Channel crossing to date of only 39 minutes from St. Peter to Eastleigh.

The weather could also produce dangerous conditions on the ground. Because of its height above sea level, St. Peter Airport was susceptible to heavy morning dews on the grass, or sodden grass when it rained. In such conditions aircraft had a tendency to skid, their wheels could lock and they needed a longer landing run, sometimes failing to pull up before running out of runway. Portsmouth Airport and Heston were both susceptible to this problem, but Eastleigh was built on a stratum of gravel with superb drainage and consequently never suffered in the same way. On 17th December 1938, the early morning newspaper plane from Eastleigh was G-ACYG, *The Grouville Bay*, flown by a new pilot, Captain Vernon Gorry Wilson who had just joined Jersey Airways Ltd. and was making his first landing at Jersey Airport. He came in to land at about 07.30 hours, but it was still dark and he couldn't see the windsock to see the strength or direction of the wind. A radio message from Jersey Control stated that it was calm and that he should land from the north-east corner where the landing floodlight was already switched on. Unfortunately for Wilson there was actually a wind of about seven mph coming from this north-east corner so he would be landing downwind in completely the wrong direction. He landed along the fog line, but there was a heavy dew, and the grass was so wet that the craft would not stop and with the momentum of a full load of newspapers, the wheels locked, and *The Grouville Bay* skidded several hundred yards before coming to rest against the perimeter fence.

It was a minor incident with little physical damage, but Wilson was landing according to instructions and felt that it was an accident that should not have happened. In future smoke would be used to ascertain wind direction when it was light as this was more reliable than a windsock.

1938 ended with the longest closure to services in the history of Jersey Airways Ltd. when all planes were cancelled from 19th December to 28th December due to snow. The only respite was on Christmas Eve when one service managed to fly to and from Heston. December was not a good month for the airline as on 31st December, they ended the year with a wet grass accident to the newly acquired D.H. 86B, G-ADVK. Pilot J. Israel with radio-operator P. Moss and five passengers were landing in G-ADVK at Jersey Airport at about 15.30 hours in misty weather on very sodden grass. They came in from the west heading towards the north fence, but when Israel applied the brakes, the wheels locked, and the machine continued in a skid hitting the northern floodlight installation with such force that the plane was spun round finishing fifteen yards off the landing area with its nose projecting over the boundary road. Nobody was hurt, but one wing was completely torn off and the other damaged. Jersey Airways Ltd. ended the year with their new three-week-old aircraft out of service indefinitely.

The biggest surprise at the end of the year came when Greig announced that he was severing his connection with Jersey Airways Ltd.. He would not give his reasons, but shortly afterwards his brother, H. Greig, also resigned from his post as maintenance manager and six months later Thurgood sold all his shares in the company. Jersey Airways, Guernsey Airways and Channel Islands Airways although supposedly the Channel Islands' own airlines, would in the future be owned solely by the mainland companies of Whitehall Securities and the Great Western Railway and Southern Railway airlines. There was no substantial increase in passengers or freight during 1938, but Jersey Airways Ltd. did achieve its objective of ending the year in profit. The accounts showed a profit to Jersey Airways Ltd. of £4,773, a loss to Guernsey Airways Ltd. of £527 and a small profit to Channel Islands Airways Ltd. of £178 making a combined profit of £4,425.

A poor snapshot of G-ACYG, *The Grouville Bay* after its collision with the perimeter fence of St. Peter Airport caused by skidding on the grass runway soaked by the morning dew.

BIRTH OF THE DE HAVILLAND D.H.95 FLAMINGO

Despite the appalling weather at the end of 1938 a new prototype aircraft taxied in the snow at Hatfield Aerodrome on 22nd December and did 'hops and bumps' the next day. It was the prototype De Havilland D.H.95 Flamingo, registration G-AFUE that made its maiden flight piloted by Geoffrey de Havilland jnr. from the snow on 28th December 1938.

Because of the impending war limitations, De Havilland were unable to design any new civil aircraft. A replacement for the D.H.86 biplane was desired by many airlines including Jersey Airways, but there was no possibility of an aircraft appearing in the near future. The D.H. Flamingo was already on the De Havilland drawing board and was a larger craft to rival the American Lockheed. It was an all-metal stressed-skin, high-wing monoplane with two 890 hp Bristol Perseus XIIc sleeve-valved radial engines and retractable undercarriage.

The prototype Flamingo trialled an experimental third central tailfin when in-flight publicity photographs were taken. The Flamingo's span was 68 ft with a length of 50 ft 7 ins.. It had a cruising speed of 184 mph and a maximum speed of 243 mph.

The production model would carry a crew of two pilots and one radio operator with eighteen passengers, but publicity photographs of the luxurious passenger cabin interior show the D.H.95 prototype only had space for twelve passengers.

On 12th December 1938 a White Paper on the Civil Air Transport Services announced that £100,000 was set aside by the government to subsidise internal airlines over a period of five years. The top rate of subsidy would apply to any airline operating new British aeroplanes; the first company to place an order for the new D.H. Flamingo was Jersey Airways Ltd. who promptly ordered three! War would foil Jersey Airways Ltd.'s intention to acquire three D.H. Flamingos, but the prototype G-AFUE did join their fleet in 1939 and 1940.

Prototype De Havilland D.H.95 Flamingo G-AFUE, in the snow at Hatfield Aerodrome.

Testing flight of the prototype, which was now fitted with a third tailfin.

Publicity photograph of the twelve seat interior of the Flamingo.

THE OPENING OF THE STATES OF GUERNSEY AIRPORT

1939 would see the Thurgood and Greig dream of Jersey Airways Ltd. and Guernsey Airways Ltd. jointly flying between the three major Channel Islands finally come to fruition with the opening of the States of Guernsey Airport in May, but sadly they were no longer at the helm of their airlines. On 2nd January 1939, Mr G.O. ('Jo') Walters arrived in Jersey to take over as General Manager of Jersey Airways Ltd., Guernsey Airways Ltd. and Channel Islands Airways Ltd. after his service with Railway Air Services and Imperial Airways while the new Chief Engineer replacing Greig's brother was Mr A. Lowe, also from Imperial Airways.

After the shut-down over Christmas caused by snow, the 1938 winter timetable continued into 1939 with the same limited service from Jersey to Heston, Southampton and Alderney, but the winter weather would always cause problems for landings in Jersey. Spring brought no improvement in the weather, and pilots were increasingly using the beach at West Park as an 'emergency landing-ground' when they could not find St. Peter Airport in low cloud.

Search and Rescue

Jersey Airways Ltd. was still being called upon to provide search and rescue services; a request they willingly honoured and freely supplied. On 6th April a French seaplane came down on the sea some five miles to the south-east of Jersey. The Jersey lifeboat, a Jersey Airways Ltd. plane, a French aircraft and a submarine mounted an intensive search, but nothing was located until the following morning when the seaplane was found still afloat ten miles west of St. Malo off Cap Frehel with the crew unharmed.

A Harrow Down on Alderney

On 25th April, a large Handley Page H.P.54 Harrow Mark II bomber, K7026, with a crew of five, was on a long-distance night flight from Feltwell in Norfolk to western France, when both its engines iced up as it was high above cloud approaching the Channel Islands. It was 05.50 hours and Squadron-Leader Glencross who was in command tried to control the rapid descent of the craft as his radio officer put out an S.O.S.. Other RAF machines in the vicinity immediately started a search and the Guernsey lifeboat, Jersey Airways Ltd. machines and the cross-Channel steamers joined them, but despite the improving daylight, the plane could not be found. The Harrow had been close to Alderney when it emerged from the clouds and Squadron-Leader Glencross managed to bring her down in a field on the island on La Grande Blaye, but she bounced through the hedge into the next field that turned out to be Alderney Aerodrome! With a length of 82 ft 2 in., a height of 19 ft 5 in. and a wingspan of 88 ft 5 in., she was by far the largest aircraft to ever visit Alderney Aerodrome. The airport was unmanned at that hour and the crew were unable to send a radio message giving their location as the Harrow's radio aerials had been ripped off during landing. There was no telephone connection with Guernsey or the mainland from Alderney, and when the Alderney postmaster arrived at the post office to open up for the day, he found the Squadron-Leader sitting on the post office steps waiting to send a telegram to his base.

The Harrow was too badly damaged to take-off, and Rollason Aircraft Service based at Croydon Airport, were tasked with the repair, but it was August before the work was sufficiently complete for her to be able to be flown to Tollerton Aerodrome in Nottingham for final preparation for her return to RAF service.

She was eventually flown to No. 24 Maintenance Unit at RAF Ternhill in Shropshire on 22nd April 1940, almost exactly a year after she had crashed on Alderney.

Handley Page H.P.54 Harrow Mark II bomber, K7028.

5th May 1939 – The opening of the States of Guernsey Airport at La Villiaze with some of the 600 people who attended the opening ceremony.

The Opening of the States of Guernsey Airport

The chosen location for the States of Guernsey Airport was La Villiaze on high ground centrally near the south of the island. It was larger than Jersey's Airport, with grass runways of 800 yds. south-west to north-east, 900 yds. north-west to south-east, and 1,000 yds. west-north-west to east-south-east with a concrete fog line. La Villiaze had full night landing facilities with four direction floodlights, a rotating beacon and boundary and obstruction lights, and it had the latest Marconi direction-finding radio equipment. The Chief Air Traffic Control Officer of the airport was Flight-Lieut. Frank Swoffer who had been air traffic controller at the Empire Air Base on Southampton Water, but more interestingly, his second-in-command was Guernsey's aviator, Cecil Noel.

The opening of La Villiaze on Friday, 5th May 1939 was unlike Jersey's subdued private affair. A grand opening ceremony was planned with 600 seats available on written application, and a quality illustrated souvenir brochure given to each guest. The opening ceremony was performed by Britain's Air Minister, Sir Kingsley Wood, and there then followed a spectacular air display by RAF and private aircraft.

A huge Vickers Wellington bomber delivered Air Chief Marshal, Sir Cyril Newall, to the ceremony, but the craft's landing approach path was a shade too low and a downdraught near the airport boundary ignominiously dropped the heavy machine onto the boundary fence, destroying the new fence and damaging the Wellington. Private aircraft visitors included a hired D.H. Rapide flown by Captain and Mrs de Havilland, an Airspeed Oxford, and the only single-engined craft, a Hornet Moth belonging to Shell Petrol.

The first plane to take-off from La Villiaze was a Jersey Airways D.H. 86 bound for Southampton with Southampton's Jersey Airways Ltd. Manager, W.L.G. Butt, carrying a gift of "rare Island blooms", Guernsey's national flower the Arum Lily, to be presented to Queen Elizabeth on board the *RMS Empress of Australia* as she was leaving Portsmouth with King George VI for a Royal Tour of Canada and America.

A Squadron of visiting RAF Ansons at Guernsey Airport with the pilots in the foreground in dress uniform.

The Squadron of RAF Ansons flying in formation at the start of the air display.

The Short S30 empire 'C' class flying boat G-AFCZ, *Australia*, flown by RAF Pilot Officer D.C.T. Bennett (an ex-Jersey Airways Ltd. pilot), gave an exciting low level flying demonstration during the display.

Following the air display, the 600 guests were permitted on the terminal apron to view the aircraft. The two aircraft in this photograph are Jersey Airways Ltd. D.H.86 Express G-ACZO and the very 'camera shy' D.H. 86B, G-ADVK. (This is the only known photographic record of G-ADVK in the Channel Islands.).

The new Guernsey Airport; a fine study of the 'air-side' of the terminal building.

The New 'Guernsey and Jersey Airways' Logo

On 5th May 1939 the six D.H. 86 aircraft of the Jersey Airways Ltd. fleet sported a new logo on the nose of each machine. Despite no longer owning any aircraft in 1939, Guernsey Airways Ltd. had applied for and been awarded the routes from Guernsey on the assumption that it had aircraft to fly the new routes. In order for both companies to still be able to claim the government subsidies, and to overcome the dilemma of there being no Guernsey Airways Ltd. aircraft, the Jersey Airways Ltd. fleet was re-branded with a new 'Guernsey & Jersey Airways' logo, even though such a company did not exist. With this new branding, gone were the names on the aircraft (which had all been names of only Jersey coastal bays) and in their place was a new double winged logo with the crest shields of both Jersey and Guernsey co-joined in the centre.

The Reincarnation of Guernsey Airways

As soon as La Villiaze was opened, a new summer timetable commenced with the direct services to Heston and Eastleigh from La Villiaze flown by Guernsey Airways Ltd., while the direct flights from St. Peter Airport were flown by Jersey Airways Ltd.. By having their own routes, it was hoped that each airline would still be treated separately for the government subsidies even though the only aircraft flying were Jersey Airways Ltd. D.H. 86s rebranded. The one casualty from the allocation of routes to Guernsey

A rare study of D.H.86B, G-AENR, sporting the new logo of 'Guernsey & Jersey Airways'.

Airways Ltd. was that the Alderney service now ran to and from Guernsey, with no longer a direct Jersey-Alderney service. Jersey passengers for Alderney had to catch the 06.00 hours flight to Guernsey and change to the Guernsey plane for Alderney, for which they were charged an additional 18s. for the return fare! This naturally caused consternation among regular patrons and after numerous complaints the fares were reduced, and the flight times adjusted with a more convenient 07.40 hours departure from St. Peter Airport.

On Wednesday 10th May, Douglas Brecknell notched up over 4,000 flying hours in 25 different types of aircraft when he flew the Jersey Airways Ltd. service from Eastleigh to St. Peter. He arrived over the airport with eight passengers at the scheduled time of 18.05 hours, but because St. Peter was hidden by fog, he put down safely on the beach at West Park. This was becoming so common that a routine was established to quickly move passengers and equipment to the beach to service the plane when the situation arose. Brecknell's turnaround was so efficient that his departure was only 20 minutes later than his normal scheduled time from the airport.

On 23rd May, the Jersey Airways Ltd. joint summer operation with Air France on the Dinard route was reinstated with flights on Tuesdays with a flight time of 25 minutes. Four days later on 27th May, it was Guernsey Airways Ltd.'s turn to reinstate the summer services to Exeter and Brighton from La Villiaze. A Guernsey *Star* reporter caught the 11.30 hours inaugural departure to Exeter piloted by G.F. Hales with radio-operator A.H. Clapham and three other passengers. He recorded the welcome they received at Exeter Airport by Mr Parkhouse, the airport manager, and Mr. Brumham the station officer for Great Western and Southern Railways Air Lines, as the railway companies now had a 50 per cent interest in Guernsey Airways Ltd.. Flying back immediately on the return flight to La Villiaze, the journalist arrived just in time to catch the other inaugural flight to Shoreham Airport, this time piloted by Captain J. Israel.

Guernsey Airways Ltd Air Ambulance

The first and only Guernsey Airways Ltd. air ambulance flight received national media attention when in June they flew a young girl, Olive Gallez, from La Villiaze to Eastleigh in 39 minutes. The child had swallowed an open safety pin that lodged in her throat. In a 'compassionate publicity exercise', the *Daily Express* was waiting with a chartered plane to fly her to Heston from where she was taken to the Great Ormond St. Children's Hospital to have the safety pin removed by the eminent surgeon, Mr Simpson-Smith, previously a regular customer of Cobham Air Routes Ltd. when treating the Bailiff of Guernsey.

The Dinard to Jersey Service

Air France attempted to commence their weekend Dinard to Jersey service on Saturday 1st July when the inaugural Wibault arrived at Dinard from Le Bourget at 11.00 hours. Unfortunately, the aircraft, an improved Wibault 283, F-AMYE, *L-Intigant*, did not make it to Jersey as after landing, the pilot taxied onto an unfinished area of the aerodrome and the heavy craft got bogged down in the mud.

It took the weekend to dig the machine out so she did not commence the service to Jersey until the following Saturday, 8th July.

The Saturday afternoon departure on 22nd July was delayed by six hours when one of the engines on the Wibault failed to start and the Air France mechanic was injured attempting to swing the propeller. Because the Wibault had a low tail wheel the engine in the nose of the craft was out of reach high in the air requiring the mechanic to swing the propeller while precariously balancing on top of a stepladder. The States of Jersey authorities were still concerned about aircraft importing the Colorado beetle from France and every machine landing from Dinard was thoroughly vacuum-cleaned and the dust bags burnt. Incoming passengers and their baggage were also liable to be inspected.

F-AMYE, *L-Intigant* arrives a week late at Jersey on 8th July 1939.

G-ACZP delivering the first airmail from the mainland to Guernsey.

The Guernsey Airways Ltd Airmail Flights

Three days after the opening of La Villiaze, on Monday 8th May, a newspaper flight started from Eastleigh to Guernsey and for the first time ever the London dailies were on sale in Guernsey on the morning of publication. The flight was also the inauguration of the airmail service from the mainland, and Captain B. Walker left Eastleigh at 08.00 hours in G-ACZP, and landed at La Villiaze at 08.59 hours, a minute ahead of schedule.

G-ACZP flown by Captain B. Walker was met on the apron of La Villiaze Airport by a Post Office van and an official reception committee including the Lieutenant Governor of Guernsey Sir Edward Broadbent, Bailiff Victor Carey, and the Guernsey Postmaster Mr W.A. Payne. Guernsey & Jersey Airways despatched a few official letters from their Southampton Airport Office to Guernsey Airways Ltd. at La Villiaze that were signed by the pilot and a quantity of souvenir covers were flown for members of the public, the *Aero Field* magazine and the dealer Francis J. Field. After the mail intended for Guernsey was unloaded, G-ACZP continued to Jersey with the Jersey airmail.

The airmail service from Guernsey to the mainland did not start until Monday 22nd May when the first inter-island airmail from Jersey was also inaugurated. Captain John Pugh in the D.H. 86B, G-ADVK, with radio-operator T. Mc. Cave took off from St. Peter Airport at 06.00 hours and landed at La Villiaze at 06.15 hours. They unloaded the airmail from Jersey (which would have been very little) and loaded the Guernsey airmail for the mainland in a very quick turnaround of just over ten minutes that saw them taking off from La Villiaze for Eastleigh at 06.28 hours. They were also carrying nine passengers on board, including a journalist and a photographer from the *Guernsey Evening Post*. They made a good crossing of the Channel at 2,000 ft to land at Eastleigh at 07.25 hours where they were met by a G.P.O. mail van and the airport manager, Mr L.F. Payne, and W.L.G. Butt of Jersey Airways.

The final link in the airmail service, the despatch of inter-island airmail in the opposite direction from Guernsey to Jersey, would not take place until Monday 10th July 1939. The flight had no official prior announcement either by the Post Office or airline and there is no record of the aircraft or pilot who flew the service.

The Post Office contract was only for Mondays because there was not a regular early morning service by the mail boats on Mondays, whereas on other days of the week the early morning inter-island mail boat service sufficed.

Flamingo Flights

On Sunday 2nd July 1939, Geoffrey de Havilland, jnr., unexpectedly flew the prototype D.H. 95 Flamingo, G-AFUE, from the De Havilland factory at Hatfield on a test flight to St. Peter Airport, Jersey. He made two local flights from the island before flying to Heston and back to the De Havilland base at Hatfield. Jersey Airways Ltd. had been the first airline to show interest in the new aircraft, and De Havilland was about to loan the Flamingo to Jersey Airways Ltd. to carry out familiarisation test flights. On the following evening of Monday 3rd July, Geoffrey de Havilland flew the machine to Eastleigh and on Tuesday morning he carried out test landings on the Eastleigh Aerodrome before flying again to Jersey and then back to Eastleigh via Guernsey, making his first landing at La Villiaze Airport.

On Thursday 6th July, Geoffrey was joined by Mr J. Israel, as a co-pilot for another flight to Jersey and the Flamingo spent the day being test flown from the St. Peter by various Jersey Airways pilots. The Flamingo spent the night on Jersey, returning to Eastleigh on Friday in a flight of only 45 minutes. Chief Pilot, Bill Caldwell was the co-pilot on Saturday 8th July when the Flamingo was flown to Birmingham as the star attraction at the opening of the Elmdon Aerodrome, the city's airport; and cargo flights were made in the following days with airmails and newspapers flown out of Heston and Eastleigh. On 12th July a party of reporters and photographers from London were flown to Guernsey leaving Heston at 10.00 hours, circling Alderney at 10.50 hours and flying low over Sark, Herm and Jethou to arrive at La Villiaze at 11.05 hours, five minutes ahead of schedule in time for a very alcoholic lunch! The exercise was repeated on 14th July with a more critical group of aeronautical press journalists who reported every nuance of the flight; Bill Caldwell was the pilot. His final destination was Jersey and he passed Alderney on the way out in two minutes under the hour against a 20 mph head wind, while the entire return flight from Jersey to Heston was made in 52 minutes with the Flamingo flown at only 50 per cent of its full power.

The Flamingo was due to go into service the following day but was grounded by an oil system

Flamingo G-AFUE pictured in flight over St Helier Harbour, with the Guernsey and Jersey Airways emblem on its nose.

problem, and the first fare-paying passenger was flown on Thursday 20th July. Geoffrey flew a positioning flight on the evening of 19th July to Eastleigh and on 20th July had a hectic day flying Eastleigh to Guernsey, Guernsey to Jersey, Jersey to Guernsey, Guernsey to Heston, Heston to Guernsey, Guernsey to Jersey, and Jersey back to Eastleigh. After three more days of familiarisation Geoffrey handed the Flamingo over to Jersey Airways Ltd. on 24th July. Jersey Airways Ltd. was so impressed with the Flamingo that they ordered three of the machines at £25,000 each, but they would never receive them because war was looming.

Jersey Airways Ltd. commissioned aviation photographer, Charles E. Brown to take stunning air to air publicity studies of the Flamingo over famous Jersey landmarks such as La Corbière Lighthouse. Unfortunately, the photos were never used as the Flamingo left Jersey Airways Ltd. when war was declared. Many of his images are rare because Brown lost most of the glass negatives when his premises on Shoe Lane, Fleet Street were bombed.

A Limited 'War Time Service' from Shoreham Airport.

Despite the threat of war, the 1939 summer season was even busier than previous years with the islands promoted as a calm holiday away from the mainland tensions of war. With the assurance of non-intervention from Russia following the signing of a Russo-German Non-Aggression Pact on 21st August, the German armies were free to move towards the Polish border prompting an urgent recall of the British Parliament from its Summer Recess. On Friday 25th August, British journalists left Berlin and the British Embassy began packing up. The French Government advised all non-essential workers and families with children to evacuate Paris and over the weekend Jersey Airways Ltd. experienced a massive increase in customers, but only on flights out of the islands. On 26th August Britain signed a mutual assistance pact with Poland that would bring Britain into conflict with Germany should Germany invade Poland. On 28th August, Air France announced the suspension of many services from Paris

The Flamingo at St Peter Airport.

Charles E. Brown's photograph of the Flamingo in flight over La Corbière Lighthouse.

including its summer seasonal service to Dinard and Jersey. Jersey Airways Ltd. maintained its service to Dinard but found that the demand was mainly from people fleeing France.

Airports on the mainland were increasingly coming under military control and Jersey Airways Ltd. was forced to limit its services solely to Eastleigh with passengers who would normally travel on the Heston, Brighton or Exeter services being obliged to make their own way on from Southampton. On 1st September, Germany attacked Poland, resulting on Sunday 3rd September with Britain declaring war on Germany; civil flying ceased and the summer season of the first full Channel Islands network came to an abrupt and premature end. Jersey and Guernsey Airways Ltd. aircraft and personnel were immediately placed at the disposal of the British Government with all the D.H. 86's being transferred to the National Air Communications scheme that was transporting men and materials around the country or to France. The Flamingo was returned to its De Havilland owners and would eventually go to RAF Squadron, No. 24, at Hendon for communications work.

It was soon realised that the Airways in the islands had become a necessity and the Government appreciated that the air link with the Channel Islands was vital for prosperity as well as morale, and so on 24th October Guernsey & Jersey Airways were asked to resume a passenger and freight service to the islands. Initially this could only be a very limited service; the airlines still had their pilots but having relinquished their D.H. 86's and the Flamingo, they had to hire suitable aircraft and could only obtain the smaller twin-engined D.H. Rapide.

The militarising of the nation's civil airports limited Guernsey and Jersey Airways' choice for a mainland terminal and the only airport available was the small Brighton Airport at Shoreham. A service between Shoreham and the islands was resumed on 8th November with services running to Jersey and Guernsey on Mondays, Wednesdays and Fridays and from the islands on Tuesdays, Thursdays and Saturdays. As the situation calmed down more aircraft became available with some of the airline's D.H. 86's returning, and from the 11th December a daily return service from Shoreham was established carrying freight, mail and passengers.

End of Year Account

Channel Islands Airways Ltd. was able to announce on 31st December, a combined profit of about £11,000, thanks to the subsidies of £15,000 to each of the two airlines. The airline also distributed its first shareholder's dividend of 3 per cent that in reality was public money.

Shorham Airport which after other airports were militarised in the build-up to the Second World War became Guernsey and Jersey Airways link with the rest of the UK. On the apron is Olley Air Service Short S.16 Scion 2 G-ADDO. They were mainly a charter airline and flew to the Channel Islands under the Channel Air Ferries name.

THE FLIGHT TOWARDS OCCUPATION

The "Phoney War" from September 1939 until May 1940, was a period when despite the declaration of war by Britain and France against Germany, no military engagement took place in Western Europe. Life returned to such normality that many of the early evacuees who had fled the big cities, both in England and France, returned home. The British Government was able to release all six D.H. 86's back into the control of Jersey Airways Ltd. to bolster the Shoreham service, while the total relaxation of travel regulations now encouraged the marketing of the islands as a safe and viable holiday destination. The 1940 Easter weekend came very early in the year with Good Friday on 22nd March. The Channel Islands experienced an Easter holiday rush that easily compared to previous peacetime Easter holidays. A bulletin issued by Jersey Airways Ltd. was cloaked in wartime terminology:

> Jersey Airways G.H.Q. report that the Easter 'raid' had been planned for some time and, as a result of a special propaganda campaign, had proved an unqualified success.
>
> The onslaught began in earnest on Thursday Last! Wave after wave of "Express" airliners were seen taking off fully loaded from Shoreham Airport throughout Thursday and Good Friday….

Summer Planning

A new Summer 1940 Timetable was planned entitled "Wartime Holiday Services" that would be effective from 1st June. The timetable was printed in stark red and black with a dramatic drawn image of the front of a D.H. 86 Express in flight sporting a Jersey Airways winged logo that never actually appeared on any aircraft. The service would once more run from Heston rather than Shoreham, and the timetable sported yet another new logo that intertwined the two names Jersey Airways and Guernsey Airways. This simple logo was painted on the aircraft fleet but would only be seen for a very short time.

German Invasion: Channel Islands Evacuation

The Easter weekend had been such a success that in the following month preparations were being made for an even great summer influx of visitors, but these plans were rudely shattered when on 10th May German panzer tank divisions burst into the Low Countries, overrunning Belgium, and the Nazi war machine smashed its way towards the Channel Ports. Following the evacuation of the British army from Dunkirk from 27th May until 4th June and the unhindered advance of the German army through northern France, Mr G. O. Waters, the general manager of the combined airlines of Jersey Airways, Guernsey Airways and Channel Islands Airways, began to devise a plan for the evacuation of all the airlines' equipment, documents, staff and families, as well as pilots and aircraft. There were 180 staff of which 100 were engaged on maintenance, and the flying staff consisted of twelve crews, each of a Pilot Captain and radio operator. Waters envisaged that it would take a week to execute a complete evacuation.

Jersey Airport experienced a constant flow of RAF and French Service aircraft calling upon the services of the Jersey Airways maintenance teams to carry out emergency repairs, and service and refuel craft that were either returning to England or on raids into France and Italy. On the night of 11th/12th June, the engineers were taken aback when unannounced, 36 RAF Armstrong Whitworth Whitley bombers put down at St. Peter and required refuelling before making their way to northern Italy to carry out a raid on the Fiat works at Turin. The Jersey Airways maintenance teams were still required to service their own aircraft at the same time! On 13th June, the Air Ministry instructed Jersey Airways to suspend all regular services to the islands and implement the evacuation plans. On Friday 14th June, Paris fell to the German invaders and once Cherbourg and St. Malo were taken, the Channel Islands would soon be overrun. The evacuation plan now had to be accomplished in two days with only five aircraft. The sixth member of the fleet, D.H. 86B, G-ADVK, was not airworthy as she was at the time undergoing a complete service. On that same Friday all the wives and families of staff were evacuated to their new base at Heston and on Saturday 15th June as much equipment and spares as possible was removed including five spare aircraft engines. Two RAF Ensigns arrived in Jersey with 50 ground staff from RAF No. 23 Wing Servicing Unit who were to take over from the Jersey Airways maintenance crews servicing incoming RAF aircraft. The Jersey Airways engineers were then evacuated except for a skeleton staff who remained to assist the RAF personnel. The RAF crews had been sent to destroy any equipment or vehicles that might be useful to the enemy as well as mine the airfields on Alderney and Guernsey. Rather than return empty, the Ensigns were loaded with as much useful equipment as possible. When it was realised that the D.H. 86B could not be made serviceable, all her equipment was removed, and she was left to the RAF demolition parties to make her completely unviable. A Scottish Airways D.H. Rapide was flown to Jersey to collect the last serviceable engine; this was strapped to her wing and flown back to Heston.

Escape from France and the islands

Aircraft in a constant flow were using Jersey Airport as a staging post in their escape from France. On 17th June a D.H. 89 Dragon Rapide arrived from Bordeaux evacuating the Général de Brigade, Charles de Gaulle. He was en route from France to London and stayed on the island for lunch whilst his plane was serviced and refuelled. From 19th to 21st June, RAF Hurricanes of No. 17 and No. 501 Squadrons retreated through Jersey from Dinard before flying on to the mainland. From dawn on 19th June to noon on 21st June the entire Jersey Airways fleet was recalled from Heston to help with the evacuation of civilians to the mainland. In a constant rota the craft evacuated 319 people to Bristol through Exeter, with one craft even touching down on the Guernsey Airfield as it was being mined. It was eventually decided that it was safer and more effective to evacuate the populations of both Islands by steam ships from the harbours and so the Jersey Airways fleet returned to Heston. The last flights of 'Jersey Airways Guernsey Airways' were for two of the craft to return one final time to Jersey to bring out the skeleton staff that had remained to assist the RAF.

Even though the airline was re-established at Heston there was no intention of a private civil airline running during wartime, and the remaining five D.H. 86 Expresses went to the Fleet Air Arm. Most of the pilots also offered themselves to the Fleet Air Arm although those on the RAF reserve list naturally re-joined the Royal Air Force.

This was the last publicity photograph of Jersey Airways and Guernsey Airways, at Heston in June 1940. The aircraft bear the legend 'Jersey Airways Limited' below the passenger windows and the fleeting intertwined Jersey Airways Guernsey Airways logo.

The days of pioneer flight in the Channel Islands had truly come to an end and for the next five years only German Luftwaffe aircraft would be seen in the islands. Civil aviation had not only ceased in the islands, but also on the mainland where Guernsey & Jersey Airways and Channel Islands Airways Ltd. continued in name only, but without an active participation in aviation and certainly without any pilots or aircraft to fly. Channel Islands Airways Ltd. would make a brief and very successful re-emergence after the war but would finally be killed off with nationalisation of the civil aviation industry on 1st April 1947.

SELECTED BIBLIOGRAPHY

Bao, Phil Lo and Hutchinson Iain: *BEAline to the islands*, Kea Publishing 2002.

Baldwin, N.C.: *Catalogue of Internal Air Mails, 1910-41*, Francis J. Field 1941.

Baldwin, N.C.: *Fifty Years of British Air Mails 1911-1960*, Francis J. Field 1961.

Batchelor, L.E.: *The Jersey Air Race – 1912*, Picton Publishing 1972.

Behrend, George: *Jersey Airlines*, Jersey Artists 1968.

Bluffield, Robert: *Imperial Airways – The Birth of the British Airline Industry 1914-1940*, Ian Allen 2009.

Chorlton, Martyn: *Golden Age of Flying Boats – Aeroplane Collectors' Archive*, Kelsey Publishing Group 2012.

Delve, Ken: *The Military Airfields of Britain – South-West England*, Crowood Press 2006.

Doyle, Neville: *From Sea-Eagle to Flamingo – Channel Island Airlines 1923-1939*, The Self Publishing Association 1991.

Eisendrath, Joseph L.: *Balloon Post of the Siege of Paris, 1870-71*, American Air Mail Society 1976.

Field, Francis J. and Baldwin, N.C.: *The Coronation Aerial Post 1911*, Francis J. Field 1934.

Finch, Robert: *The World's Airways*, University of London Press 1938.

Fuller, John G.: *The Airmen Who Would Not Die*, Souvenir Press 1979.

Harper, Harry: *The Romance of a Modern Airway*, Sampson Low, Marston & Co. (no date).

Hatchard, David: *Southampton/Eastleigh Airport*, Kingfisher 1990.

Higham, Robin: *Britain's Imperial Air Routes 1918-1939*, Foulis 1960.

Lake, Chris: *Jersey Airport, The First 50 Years*, Michael Stephen Publishers 1987.

Lake, Chris: *Flight in Jersey – The Story of Jersey Airport*, Jersey Airport 1997.

Layzell, Alastair: *Announcing The Arrival – Jersey Airport 1937-1987*, Channel Television 1987.

Layzell, Alistair and Haye, Michael de la: *Sixty Glorious Years that Have Flown Past* -.

The History of Aviation in Jersey 1912-1972, Private 1972 revised 1973.

Learmouth, Bob; Nash, Joanna; Cluett, Douglas: *The First Croydon Airport 1915-1928*, Sutton Libraries. and Arts Services 1977.

Mackay, James: *Airmails 1870-1970*, B.T. Batsford 1971.

McLeod, Murray: *Imperial Airways – Airline Pioneers and Trailblazers of the 1920' and 1930s*, Mcleodart 2015.

Moss, P.W.: *The de Havilland 84 Dragon*, Aircraft Illustrated 1969.

Munson, Kenneth G.: *Enemy Aircraft (German and Italian) of World War Two*, Ian Allen 1960.

New, Peter T.: *The Solent Sky – a local history of Aviation from 1908 to 1946*, 1976.

Newport, William: *The Airmails of the Channel Islands*, Channel Islands Specialists' Society 1957.

Nicolaou, Stéphane: *Flying Boats & Seaplanes – A History from 1905*, Bay View Books 1998.

Ord-Hume, Arthur W.J.G.: *Imperial Airways from Early Days to BOAC*, Stenlake Publishing 2010.

Rance, Adrian B.: *Sea Planes and Flying Boats of the Solent*, Southampton University & City Museums 1981.

Redgrove, H. Stanley: *The Air Mails of the British Isles*, Private, Aberdeen 1940.

Richardson, Joanna: *Paris under Siege*, The Folio Society 1982.

Romain, Michael: *Wings Over the Channel – The Romance of Channel Islands Airways*, Jersey Morning News (no date).

Sandford, Kendall C.: *Air Crash Mail of Imperial Airways and Predecessor Airlines*, Stuart Rossiter Trust Fund 2003.

Scott-Hill, Ian and Berhrend, George: Channel *Silver Wings – a record of Air Service 1947-1972*, Jersey Artists 1972.

Sinel, L.P.: *The German Occupation of Jersey – a Complete Diary of Events from June 1940 to June 1945*, The Evening Post, Jersey 1946.

Slade, J. Edouard: *The Pioneer Days of Aviation in Jersey – Volume I*, Slade, Germany 1965.

The Pioneer Days of Aviation in Jersey – Volume II, Slade, Germany 1966.

Triggs, Anthony: *Portsmouth Airport*, Halsgrove 2002

SOURCES

Institutions

British Library, St. Pancras.
British Newspaper Library, Colindale.
Brooklands Aviation Museum.
Imperial War Museum, London.
Jersey Library.
National Archives – Public Record Office, Kew.
National Portrait Gallery.
National War Museum, Papua New Guinea.
Musee de l'Air, Paris.
Museo del Aire, Madrid.
Priaulx Library, Guernsey.
Royal Air Force Museum.
Royal Aeronautical Society.

British Newspaper Library, Colindale – closed 2013 -.
The British Library Newsroom St. Pancras opened 2014:

Newspapers
Bournemouth Echo.
Guernsey Evening Press.
Guernsey Weekly Press.
Jersey Evening Post.
Jersey Morning News.
Nottingham Evening Post.
Southern Daily Echo.
The Evening Standard (London).
The News (Portsmouth).
The Star (Guernsey).
The Times (London).
Western Mail & Echo.

Magazines
Air.
Airways.
Aeroplane Monthly.
Flight.
Popular Flying.
The Aeroplane.
The London Gazette.
The Sailplane.
The Sphere.

Photographic Libraries
Guernsey Evening Press and Star.
Jersey Evening post.
Online Jersey Aviation Gallery; theislandwiki.org.

Photograph & Postcard Collections
Author's own collection.
Carl Toms, Retired Features Editor: *Guernsey evening Post.*
Moira and David Edwards.
Neville Doyle.   Author: *From Sea-Eagle to Flamingo.*
P. Law.
Terry Scott.
Warwick Jacobs.

Bulletins, Journals and Publications
Accident Investigation Branch Report No. C 282.
    Air Ministry 27th October 1934.
CISS Bulletins.
    Bi-monthly Bulletins of the Channel Islands Specialist Society, London 1950 – 1990.
De Havilland Gazette August 1939.
Flying News From Jersey Airways Ltd. 1939-40.
Gateway to Guernsey – Guernsey Airport Old & New
    The Guernsey Press 18th March 2004.
Instructions to Staff in Regard to Channel Islands Airways. (Jersey Airways Ltd.) Southern Railway June 1940.
Jersey Airways Limited letter- Air Ministry 28th January 1935.
Jersey Airways Limited letter- Air Ministry 10th April 1935.
Les Iles Normandes
    Quarterly Journal of the Channel Islands Specialist Society, London 1975 – to date.
Le Monde Illustré (The Illustrated World).
    The meeting of Hydro airplanes at St. Malo 1912.
Le Sport de l'Air.
Memorandum and Articles of Association Channel Islands Airways Limited 1st December 1934.
Memorandum and Articles of Association Guernsey Airways Limited 11th December 1942.
Memorandum and Articles of Association Jersey Airways Limited 9th December 1933.
The Aero Field Francis J. Field.
The Philatelic Magazine.
The Story of Guernsey Airport, 1939-1989, The Guernsey Society of Aviation Enthusiasts.

Unpublished Manuscript & Archive
Richard Mayne *Cuttings and Documents Archive.*
John Simpson *Seaplanes in the Channel Islands.*

Online Resources
49squadron.co.uk	RAF 49 Squadron.
aerobase.fr	Aerobase Zodiac Historique.
aerophilately.net	Aviation literature + links.
airhistory.org.uk	Civil Aircraft Register GB.
airshipsonline.com	Airship Heritage Trust.
aviationancestry.co.uk	British Aviation Advertisements.
bamuseum.com	British Airways Archives.
britishpathe.com	British Pathe News reels.
ciss1950.org.uk	Channel Islands Specialists' Society.
exeter-airport.co.uk	Exeter Airport History.
gracesguide.co.uk	Grace's Guide to British Industrial History.
theislandwiki.org	Guernsey Society Channel Islands archive/picture gallery.
timetableimages.com	Airline Timetable Images.
trove.nla.gov.au	National Library of Australia TROVE online archive.
ukairfieldguide.net	UK Airfield & Airports history.